U0331101

CLASSROOM ASSESSMENT

for Learning and Student Development

杨向东　崔允漷　主编

# 课堂评价

## 促进学生的学习和发展

华东师范大学出版社
·上海·

**图书在版编目(CIP)数据**

课堂评价:促进学生的学习和发展/杨向东,崔允漷主编.—上海:华东师范大学出版社,2012.8
ISBN 978-7-5617-9844-7

Ⅰ.①课… Ⅱ.①杨…②崔… Ⅲ.①课堂教学—教学评估—中小学 Ⅳ.①G632.421

中国版本图书馆 CIP 数据核字(2012)第 187950 号

**课堂评价:促进学生的学习和发展**

主　　编　杨向东　崔允漷
策划编辑　彭呈军
审读编辑　韩秀秀
责任校对　汤　定
版式设计　崔　楚
封面设计　高　山

出版发行　华东师范大学出版社
社　　址　上海市中山北路 3663 号　邮编 200062
网　　址　www.ecnupress.com.cn
电　　话　021-60821666　行政传真 021-62572105
客服电话　021-62865537　门市(邮购)电话 021-62869887
地　　址　上海市中山北路 3663 号华东师范大学校内先锋路口
网　　店　http://hdsdcbs.tmall.com

印 刷 者　常熟市文化印刷有限公司
开　　本　787 毫米 × 1092 毫米　1/16
印　　张　18.25
字　　数　361 千字
版　　次　2012 年 11 月第 1 版
印　　次　2025 年 2 月第 24 次
书　　号　ISBN 978-7-5617-9844-7/G·5825
定　　价　39.80 元

出 版 人　王　焰

# 前言

过去十年，我国基础教育课程改革取得了令人瞩目的成绩。无论是教育理念、课程设置，还是学校文化和课堂实践，都发生了翻天覆地的变化。但是，随着改革逐步深入，现有考试评价体系中存在的诸多问题逐渐浮出水面，成为制约改革进一步深化的瓶颈。这种制约作用突出体现在如下几个方面：首先，我国现有考试评价理念与基础课程教育改革的理念不一致。新课程改革提倡教育应该促进每个学生个性的发展，强调建构性的学习，通过主动的探究和思考来理解、建构和生成知识，强调学生创造性地运用在学校中学到的知识和技能解决现实生活中的实际问题。然而，现有考试评价体系仍然拘泥于学科本位，强调零散的知识点和孤立的技能的掌握。其次，受我国文化传统、政治经济状况等一系列社会因素的影响，现有考试评价制度仍然以选拔、排序和管理为主要功能，新课程所提倡的发展性和激励性评价功能并没有得到应有的体现和发展。因此，在我国现有考试评价体系中，以中高考为主体的各种总结性外部评价体系依然占据了绝对主导地位。这种以选拔为最终目的的总结性评价体系，再加上滞后的考试评价理念，严重阻碍我国基础教育课程改革进一步深化。它使得广大一线教育工作者虽然对新课程心向往之，但慑于现有考试评价理念和体制的现实压力，而心存顾忌，畏步不前，无法全身心地投入到课程改革的时代浪潮之中。最后，我国现有考试评价在科学化程度上还有待进一步提高。即便是在现有评价理念和功能诉求上，当前考试和评价在评价框架的制定、命题质量、测验编制、结果分析和运用等方面都存在缺乏研究或研究不够深入，仍然过分注重经验的问题。命题的随意性，评价质量的低下，对考试分数的错误理解和错误运用仍然是我国当前考试和评价领域面临的突出问题。因此，科学化水平的提高亦是我国当前考试评价领域的当务之急。

在这样一种现实背景下，我国当前的考试评价研究更多的集中在对中高考等大规模外部考试或评价模式的探索上，而与教学息息相关的课堂评价却长期以来无人问津，未能得到应有的重视和研究。受中高考指挥棒的影响，我国的课堂评价演化成变相的终结性评价。教师热衷于分析讲解各种终结性考试的试题，将考试题目直接作为课堂评价任务让学生进行练习，简单模仿考试题目设计课堂评价任务，忽略了课堂教学的系统性和学生学习的发展进程。此外，当前课堂评价研究主要是依赖一线教师自己的摸索，鲜有大学研究者从事相关的研究。研究以经验总结居多，缺少系统的实证研究，导致课堂评价的理论水平和研究质量都偏低。这与课堂评价在教育教学中的重要地位严重相悖。因而，研究和探讨与学校教学和学生学习紧密相关的课堂评价，对于推动当前基础教育改革具有重大的理论和现实意义。

正是出于这种思考，教育部人文社会科学重点研究基地华东师范大学课程与教学研究所于2011年11月4日至6日在华东师范大学召开"课堂评价国际研讨会"。本次研讨会以"促进学生的学习和发展的课堂评价"为主题，以圆桌会议、主题报告、分会场专题报告和现场对话等多种形式，就课堂评价、课程标准与外部考试的一致性，课堂评价设计和实施的理论与技术，学习进展、学生发展与课堂评价系统的设计，课堂评价与教师专业发展，促进学习的课堂评价：学校经验报告等五个专题进行了深入研讨。会议期间，来自美国、德国、法国、韩国和日本的多位国际知名专家与200多位国内教授、学者、教研员和其他教育工作者参加了会议。与会者既接触到国内外课堂评价设计和实施领域的最新研究成果，也聆听了来自我国教育一线的课堂评价实践的成功经验。多元化的理智传统和视角，理论与实践的立体碰撞，使众多的与会人员感触良多，受益匪浅。

本次国际研讨会中，尤为值得一提的是伦敦大学国王学院的 Paul Black 教授。作为国际上非常著名的教育评价专家，他欣然接受了本次大会组委会的邀请。但由于年事已高，再加身体原因，他未能前来与会。但是，Black 教授为了支持会议的召开，特意撰文发给本次大会组委会，其专业精神受到与会人员的大为赞赏。

历时三天的课堂评价国际研讨会虽然取得了圆满成功，但在课堂评价研究领域，我们才刚刚起步。为了让更多关心中国基础教育改革事业的教育研究和实践工作者分享本次国际会议的成果，我们特地从大会提交的学术论文中精选了25篇结集出版。我们衷心希望，这个论文集的出版能够引起大家对课堂评价研究的关注，促进和推动我国在课堂评价领域的研究和发展。华东师范大学课程与教学研究所也将继续举办课堂评价以及相关主题的国际或国内学术会议，让更多有质量、高水平的考试评价研究在我国广袤的大地上生根发芽，蓬勃壮大。

每一次成功的大型国际学术会议总是凝结着无数人的热情奉献和辛勤汗水。衷心感谢钟启泉、赵中建、张华、胡惠闵、孔企平、周勇、裴新宁、沈晓敏、周文胜、王小明、安桂清、柯政、黄小瑞等老师无偿担任本次大会的主持人。没有他们精彩的主持和精辟的点评，本次大会的交流和讨论不会如此热烈和深入。此外，特别感谢徐斌艳和沈晓敏两位教授在邀请和接待国外专家方面所做的努力，她们的大力协助使我们能够有机会聆听来自欧洲和美日韩的课堂评价专家的前沿报告。真诚感谢刘琪老师，他独到的视角和绝佳的摄影让我们每个与会人员都留下了美好而珍贵的瞬间。最值得感谢的是默默为大会付出艰苦劳动的大会工作人员，他们是付黎黎、何珊云、陈蓉、叶海龙、陈佳、程力、焦方瑞、曲琳、许瑜涵、朱倩、孔龙、施美、郑蕾、王巍。作为大会的核心组织者，付黎黎老师卓越的组织和协调能力令人钦佩不已。最后也是最重要的，感谢各位专家、教授、教研员和教育工作者积极参与本次大会和他们所作的精彩报告。因为，他们才是我国课堂评价乃至考试评价领域壮大和发展的燎原之火，带给我们对未来中国教育的无限希望和憧憬。

编者

2012年4月

# 目录

## 第三部分　学习进展、学生发展与课堂评价系统的设计



## 第四部分　课堂评价与教师专业发展

# 第一部分

## 课堂评价、课程标准与外部考试的一致性

# Formative and Summative Assessments by Teachers: Promises and Problems

Paul Black

King's College London

**Abstract**: Formative assessment was widely recognized as capable of improving student learning and was extensively studied in a diverse range of issues, namely, classroom questioning, comment-only marking, peer- and self-assessment, and formative use of tests. However, such issues were still presented as a set of diverse small changes, rather than as part of a unified approach, in which an underlying rationale that would link these changes together is lacking and clarity about the place of assessment in a comprehensive theory of teaching and learning is yet to be formulated. This current article presented basic principles for effective learning for which formative assessment to be followed and areas of practices to be studied for a successful formative assessment. Moreover, it is argued that a positive interaction between formative and summative assessment could serve as an opportunity to improve learning, but would require a national system in place in which teachers judgments are trusted, backed up by programmes of training and support to ensure that these judgments are dependable.

**Keyword**: formative assessment; summative assessment, principle of effective learning

## Introduction

The concept of formative assessment had featured in the literature for over thirty years before review articles (Black & Wiliam, 1998, a , b) drew attention to evidence of positive effects on learning and called for innovations in practice that this evidence suggested. Subsequent work on practical implementation showed that much could be achieved, but for many teachers it would call for radical change in their role (Black et al. 2002, 2003). Because they included a diverse range of practices, the research findings indicated a varied menu, namely classroom questioning, comment-only marking, peer- and self-assessment, and formative use of tests. This list could be read as a set of diverse set of small changes rather than part of a unified approach. This weakness arose in part from the absence of an underlying rationale that would link these changes with one another, and of clarity about the place of assessment in a comprehensive theory of teaching and learning.

In what follows I shall try first to describe and re-examine the menu under the headings of dialogic interaction and collaboration in learning. Then, in a final section. I shall discuss current problems in the light of a re-statement of the underlying principles and a further development of a theoretical scheme.

## Basic principles

A test as such may be either formative or summative or both - the distinction lies in the purpose for which information is interpreted and used, not in the means used to elicit that information (Wiliam & Black, P., 1996). The distinction is emphasized in the following definition:

> Assessment for learning is any assessment for which the first priority in its design and practice is to serve the purpose of promoting pupils' learning. It thus differs from assessment designed primarily to serve the purposes of accountability, or of ranking, or of certifying competence. An assessment activity can help learning if it provides information to be used as feedback, by teachers, and by their pupils, in assessing themselves and each other, to modify the teaching and learning activities in which they are engaged. Such assessment becomes 'formative assessment' when the evidence is actually used to adapt the teaching to meet learning needs.
>
> (Black, P. et al. 2002 – inside front cover)

Given that evidence is collected to promote learning, its use must be consistent with established principles for effective learning, which may be summarized as:

Start from a learner's existing understanding.

Involve the learner actively in the learning process.

Develop the learner's understanding of the aims and criteria for effective learning.

Promote social learning, i.e. learning through discussion.

These are concerned with the cognitive dimension of learning. The affective and motivational dimension is also important: feedback given as rewards or grades enhances ego rather than task involvement and task-involved students do better than the ego-involved (Butler, 1988). Furthermore those with ego-involvement have a mind-set focused on competitive performance, so that both high and low attainers are reluctant to take risks and react badly to new challenges, whilst failures simply damage self-esteem. With task-involvement, learners believe that they can improve by their own effort, thus they are willing to take on new challenges and to learn from failure (Dweck, 2000).

## Areas of practice

***Oral and written feedback***

A teacher who had learnt to use a formative approach summarized the changes she made in her use of questions in class as follows:

*Questioning*

- My whole teaching style has become more interactive. Instead of showing how to find solutions, a question is asked and students given time to explore answers together. My Year 8 target class is now well-used to this way of working. I find myself using this method more and more with other groups.

*No hands*

- Unless specifically asked students know not to put their hands up if they know the answer to a question. All students are expected to be able to answer at any time even if it is an 'I don't know'.

*Supportive climate*

- Students are comfortable with giving a wrong answer. They know that these can be as useful as correct ones. They are happy for other students to help explore their wrong answers further.

(Black P. et al. 2003, p.40)

Research results on 'wait time' (Rowe, 1974) impressed teachers with the need to give pupils time to think; many encouraged students to talk with one another before answers were called for, so that students as many as possible would feel confident about expressing their ideas. The corollary of this approach was that each question had to be sufficiently open, from the learners' perspective, that it called for thought, and had to be sufficiently central to the learning aims that it justified the time spent on discussing the ideas that ensued. It followed that closed questions, checking only on knowledge, would be seen to make little contribution to students' learning. If students had to think, their wrong or partly right answers would give information, about the students' understanding, which would help them choose the teacher to select the optimum way for the work to proceed.

The key issue was that the formative purpose of a question is achieved only if it elicits from students some significant indicator of their understanding and then enables the teacher or other students to respond by trying to correct or develop that understanding, and perhaps through several responses lead the whole class to share a discussion of the issue. This point highlights the delicate task of teachers, for on the one hand tight control over the discussion can inhibit involvement of the learners, but on the other hand loose control can lead to digression so that the purpose of the learning is lost. Given that student participation is often unpredictable, the task of steering such dialogue is a delicate one: this is an issue that requires further study. For example, a pupil's answer to a question can reveal how the pupil understands the issue, and the teacher can then respond to help develop that understanding. This is more difficult than it may seem. Consider this example, quoted by Fisher (2005) : a primary class had been drawing pictures of daffodils -

*Teacher*: "*What is this flower called?*"

*Child*: "*I think it's called Betty*"

The teacher might respond by asking other children the same question until someone produces the word daffodil. All could then be told that this was the 'right answer', but an alternative response could be to ask the class whether 'Betty' and 'daffodil' are the same sort of answer, which could start a discussion of the difference between individual names and generic names. The first response would have missed the learning opportunity which would be exploited by the second. What the pupil understood by the terms '*is .. called*' in the question was not the meaning that the teacher had in mind: it is commonplace that what is 'heard' in any discussion is not what the speaker intended. However, the teacher would have to pause and reflect on why the pupil might have given that answer before deciding how to respond.

In composing a useful response, the teacher has to interpret the thinking and the motivation that led the pupil to express the answer. It helps if the teacher first asks the pupil to explain how he or she arrived at that answer, then accepts any explanation without comment and asks others what they think. This gives value to the first answer, and draws the class into a shared exploration of the issue. In doing this the teacher changes role, from being an interviewer of pupils on a one-to-one basis to being a conductor of dialogue in which all may be involved. This is challenging, in that the diverse inputs from several pupils will create a more complex task of interpretation; a more detailed examination of this problem is given in Black and Wilam (2010). However, as pupil-pupil interactions are encouraged, the teacher will have time to reflect on how best to intervene. At the same time pupils can be helping one another to either resolve, or to express more clearly, their difficulties.

The fundamental reason for encouraging the mutual involvement of as many pupils as possible in class dialogue is explained by Alexander as follows:

> *Children, we now know, need to talk, and to experience a rich diet of spoken language, in order to think and to learn. Reading, writing and number may be acknowledged curriculum 'basics', but talk is arguably the true foundation of learning.*
>
> Alexander, 2006, p.9

Research in many classrooms shows that such dialogue is rarely achieved. The norm is the use of closed rather then open questions, very brief pupil responses, and a 'dialogue' which is a sequence of teacher-pupil-teacher-pupil-teacher interactions, with few examples of pupil-pupil interactions, so that the teacher dominates the 'discussion'. However, teachers find it difficult to change from this pattern, for some fear, that it will be difficult to deal with dealing with the unexpected in pupils' responses and that they may lose control of any free-ranging discussion.

Just as in questioning, in written work the purpose has to be to provide feedback that helps learning. The difficult change here was for teachers to stop giving marks or grades on written work. They were encouraged by research findings that comment-only marking led to improved learning (Butler, 1988), and came to justify the new practice as follows:

- students rarely read comments preferring to compare marks with peers as their first reaction on getting work back;
- teachers rarely give students time in class to read comments that are written on work and probably few, if any students, return to consider these at home;
- often the comments are brief and/or not specific, for example "*Details?*";
- the same written comments frequently recur in a student's book, implying that students do not take note of, or act on, the comments.

(Black P. et al. 2003, p.43)

In consequence, teachers' realized the need to spend more time on careful formulation of comments that would help students to understand their faults and to improve their work. Such comments as "Be more sensitive" and "You are mixing up the words 'solution' and 'mixture'" give the learner no useful guidance, but if the latter were expanded to read "Allan, this is generally fine but you are mixing up the words 'solution' and 'mixture'. Look up what we all wrote down about the difference and then check through this piece again" should help Allan to improve his understanding. The key point is that the written work is not to be treated as a terminal test, for which the marks produced are the end of the matter, but as an opportunity, through formative feedback, for improving learning.

One feature that distinguishes written from oral feedback is that there is time to frame comments that encourage further learning, with more opportunity for differentiation through separate interaction with individuals. The effects on motivation of the type of feedback is also important: as one teacher, involved in the work described by Black et al. (2003), discovered:

> The results were especially noticeable in lower attainers since grades can often have a de-motivating effect with such students which can be extremely destructive to their self-esteem.

***Peer- and self-assessment***

Self-assessment by students is essential to their development as independent and responsible learners. To meet this need, practice must involve them in assessing one another's work so that they might thereby develop the skills both of peer-assessment and, by seeing their work through the eyes of their peers, of self-assessment. To do this, students have to understand the aims of the work involved, and the criteria by which this work should be assessed. In some topics of some subjects the criteria might be well defined (e.g. calculating the value of a force in a physics problem), in others there might be many different ways in which work could achieve excellence (e.g. writing a critical appreciation of a poem). Overall the aim was to move students away from dependence on the teacher towards independence in the power to guide their own learning. As one teacher expressed it:

> The kids are not skilled in what I am trying to get them to do. I think the process is more effective long term. If you invest time in it, it will pay off big dividends, this process of getting the students to be more independent in the way that they learn and taking the responsibility themselves.
>
> (Black et al., 2003, p.52)

In helping students to develop their self-assessment, teachers must clearly specify aims that students can both steer their work towards attaining them and understand the criteria by which that work can be judged.

Peer-assessment is another powerful tool: helping pupils collaborate effectively in groups is essential to such work. However, whilst there is strong evidence that collaborative groups can improve attainment (Johnson *et al*. 2000), a survey of group work in a large sample of U. K. classrooms (Blatchford et al. 2006) shows that the type of collaboration that can engage pupils in reasoned arguments about their own and one another's contributions is not often found. Intervention programmes by Blatchford and colleagues and by Mercer et al. (2004) have demonstrated that students trained in such collaboration produce improved attainments, both in the quality of their arguments and in subsequent tests. The work of Dawes et al. (2004) is a good example of dissemination of the lessons learnt about effective group work.

## Formative assessment and summative assessment

Summative assessment by teachers can be considered from two perspectives, the first being the more or less frequent use of tests to check on pupils' progress, whilst the second involves the use of summative tests for high-takes testing, e. g. for awarding school-leaving certificates and/or for checking of the achievements of teachers and their schools.

For the first perspective, it is helpful to consider the formative use of summative tests. Students learn by marking one another's test responses, particularly if they have to develop the marking schemes in the light of their understanding of the criteria. As for the new way of looking at written work generally, the point is that a test, whilst serving the summative function, might also be used, through formative feedback, as an opportunity for improving learning . One addition in this area was that teachers would strengthen preparation by asking students to compose questions which might well be suitable for the coming tests, for in so doing they would have to identify for themselves the main aims of the work. They would also learn about the need to frame the text of a question with care, and to exercise similar care in responding to questions framed by others.

This possibility of a helpful link between formative and summative roles of assessment in pedagogy can be further explored by the following simple and restricted view of pedagogy using a model of the five steps or phases involved in designing a learning exercise.

***Clear aims*** Here there can be wide, and legitimate, differences. For example, priority may be given either to understanding the concepts and methods of a particular subject, or to developing pupils' reasoning skills: in the latter case the topic may only be used as a suitable context for such development.

***Planning activities*** One important criterion here is the potential of any activity to elicit responses which help clarify the pupil's understanding. A 'closed' question with a 'right answer' cannot do this. Other relevant features are the level of cognitive demand that a task makes, its relation to previous learning experiences, and its potential to generate interest and engagement.

***Interaction*** The way in which a plan is implemented in the classroom is crucial. If pupils are engaged, then the teacher can elicit responses and work with these to help advance pupils' learning. This aspect has been discussed above in relation to dialogue in oral and written work. Formative interaction is a necessary condition for successful learning, but it must be so implemented that it is supported by, works in harmony with, the aims and the planned activities.

***Review of the learning*** At the end of any learning episode, there should be review, to check before moving on. It is here that tests, with formative use of their outcomes, can play a useful part. Further work by pupils to deal with problems revealed by a summative tests can be a contribute to their learning. Thus work in this phase may lead back to work in the previous phase.

***Summing up*** This is a more formal version of the *Review*: here the results may be used to make decisions about a pupil's future work or career, to report progress to other teachers, school managements and parents, and to report the overall achievements more widely to satisfy the need for accountability. This may be done by assessments by teachers, by external testing, or by a combination of the two. For this final phase, tensions arise between formative and summative requirements.

The outstanding problem here is the dominance, in many national systems, of external summative testing with attendant high-stakes consequences. Whereas for their own in-school work, teachers can make tests serve both the purpose of learning through dialogue and of overall reviews, the perceived need to teach the superficial tactics which improve performance on imposed tests, limits teachers' freedom of manoeuvre in classroom work.

The resolution of this problem will depend on trusting teachers to play a more responsible part in the summative assessment of their pupils (Mansell & James, 2009). Then the problems of establishing synergy over the formative summative interface might be tackled. However, to achieve this trust teachers may have to improve their own practices in summative assessment, which will require many to develop a basic understanding of and skills in assessment, based on a broad understanding of the main principles and practices involved, including a thorough understanding of the criteria of validity and reliability. Gardner (2007) has argued that the lack of such expertise is a notable weakness because it means that the profession cannot take control of an essential component of its work, it is a 'partial profession'. Thus, developing understanding and skills in formative practices is only one component in building the assessment strengths of the profession-one that can only achieve limited success on its own.

This view is borne out in work that has sought to develop teachers' summative assessment practices (Black, P. et al., 2010, 2011). In this work, detailed attention had to be paid to developing teachers the skills, insights, and practical experiences that are needed, in each of the five phases. Such work was shown to produce several rewards. One was that the need to share understanding of standards and criteria between teachers, within their own school, and then between schools who collaborate in local groups, helped to meet these needs through close professional collaboration between teachers. As one teacher explained:

> .. everybody in this department seems to do it in a very different fashion at the moment and it would be nicer to do it in a way that meant that we are all singing from the same hymn sheet if you like. I think it made us think very carefully about how we construct our year and construct our year span in terms of what comes when and what's being assessed when.
>
> *English teacher*

A second was that parents and pupils could be assured that the judgments made about pupils' progress by schools were rigorous and are based on standards and criteria that are comparable across all schools. Several teachers commented on this advantage - for example:

> But I think if all the teachers had more, possibly more ownership of what we are

> actually doing in terms of summative assessment then you would have more confidence in saying to parents, which I think is one of the biggest things I find with lower school.
>
> *Mathematics teacher*

A third potential reward would be secured if teachers could be given more responsibility in high-stakes assessments, and develop the confidence in their ability to do this effectively, they were better able to work out ways of making creative alignments between the formative and the summative aspects of their work. The following quotation illustrates how the involvement of pupils in summative assessment tasks became a positive contribution to learning:

> I think it changed the dynamic of the lesson a little bit, in terms of well, in terms of there being much more an element of them getting on trying to find out ... they were trying to be more independent, I think, I think some of them struggled with that, and others .. some of them, some still find it quite difficult if they are not hand held all the way through. When others were happier to sort of, go their own way.
>
> *Mathematics teacher*

However, these findings were only achieved as a result of about 30 months of work in which teachers were given extra support, from the King's College research team with ideas and materials, and by support for their schools and district governments so that they could spend time on meetings both within schools and between the schools involved.

## Challenges for the future

The preceding section sets out one of the most formidable challenges. To achieve a positive interaction between the formative assessment for learning, and the summative assessment of learning, requires national systems in which teachers judgments are trusted, backed up by programmes of training and support to ensure that these judgments are dependable, i.e. so that they deserve this trust. Examples of such systems are described in the study by Stanley et al. (2009).

A second challenge is to escape from the superficial interpretations which have misled those attempting to develop formative practices (Black, P., 2007). For example, teachers may ask open questions, but then 'correct' the answers rather than use them to re-direct their work, or they may ask pupils to self-assess their work but then fail to use this information to formulate formative feedback. Many have interpreted the terms 'formative assessment' or 'assessment for learning' as incorporating all uses of assessment, and in this perspective focused on enhancing established practices of frequent testing, which may damage rather than enhance pupils' learning. For example, a recent text entitled *Learner-Centred Classroom Practices and Assessments* pays no attention to formative assessment (McCombs, B. L. & Miller, L, 2007).

A third challenge is that implementing new formative practices is a very demanding task for any teacher. Practical implementation will depend in part on exploring the differences in formative practices between different school subjects (Hodgen & Marshall, 2005). However, the difficulty, for many teachers, is that these practices call for a deep change in their beliefs about their role in the classroom, with practical implications which many find 'pretty scary'. As pointed out one of the earliest reviews:

> To incorporate formative assessment into their teaching would involve teachers in far more than acquisition of the necessary skills. ... The changes in their classroom practice might also involve profound changes of role, even for teachers regarded by themselves and others as already successful ... devotion to formative assessment is risky, taking a great deal of time and energy. (Black, P., 1993, p.79)

This initial disorientation was felt not only by teachers but also by students.

> The first time I asked a Year 10 top set to work in groups to examine the errors they had made in a test and to help each other to understand fully what was being asked of them, it was unsuccessful ... That lesson I heard several times 'Why don't you just tell us?' ... they have realised that they have more to do in my classroom than absorb the syllabus—they have to take responsibility for their learning.
>
> (Black, P. et al., 2003, p.87)

The changes needed cannot be produced by a short training session - they need the sustained support of collegial collaboration (Black & Wiliam, 2003). Studies of individual teachers shows that each changes in a different way and with different personal perceptions of the task (Black et al. 2003 - chapter 6; Harrison, 2005; Lee & Wiliam 2005).

**References**


Alexander, R. (2006) *Towards Dialogic teaching: rethinking classroom talk*. 3rd Edn. Cambridge UK: Dialogos

Black, P.J. (1993) Formative and Summative Assessment by Teachers. *Studies in Science Education*. 21, 49 - 97.

Black, P. (2007) Full marks for feedback *Making the Grade* (*Journal of the Institute of Educational Assessors*) Spring Issue pp. 18 - 21. ISSN 1750 - 0613.

Black, P.J. & Wiliam, D. (1998a) Assessment and Classroom Learning. *Assessment in Education*. 5(1) 7 - 74. ISSN 0969 - 594X

Black, P. J. & Wiliam, D. (1998b) *Inside the Black Box: Raising standards through classroom assessment*. GL Assessment: London. ISBN: 1 871984 68 8. (reprinted in PhiDelta Kappan 80(2)pp. 139 - 148 October 1998)

Black, P., Harrison, C., Lee, C., Marshall, B. & Wiliam, D. (2002) *Working inside the black box: assessment for learning in the classroom*. nferNelson: London ISBN 0 7087 1379 3. (Reprinted in Phi Delta Kappan 86(1),8 - 21.2004)

Black, P., Harrison, C., Lee, C., Marshall, B. & Wiliam, D, (2003) *Assessment for Learning-putting it into practice*. Buckingham: Open University Press. ISBN 0 - 335 - 21297 - 2 (pbk.) and ISBN 0 - 335 - 21298 - 0 (hbk.).

Black, P. & Wiliam, D. (2003) 'In Praise of Educational Research': formative assessment. *British Educational Research Journal*. 29(5),623 - 37.

Black, P. & Wiliam, D. (2009) Developing the theory of formative assessment. *Educational Assessment, Evaluation and Accountability*, 21(1),5 - 31.

Black, P., Harrison, C., Hodgen, J., Marshall, M. & Serret, N. (2010) Validity in teachers' summative assessments. *Assessment in Education* 17(2)215 - 232.

Black, P., Harrison, C., Hodgen, J., Marshall, M. & Serret, N. (2011) Can teachers' summative assessments produce dependable results and also enhance classroom learning? *Assessment in Education* in press.

www. spring-project. org. uk /spring-Publications. htm *accessed January* 2008

Blatchford, P., Baines, E., Rubie-Davies, C.,Bassett, P., & Chowne, A. (2006) The effect of a new approach to group-work on pupil-pupil and teacher-pupil interaction. *Journal of Educational Psychology*, 98,750 - 765. See also:

www. spring-project. org. uk /spring-Publications. htm *accessed January* 2008

Butler, R. (1988). Enhancing and undermining intrinsic motivation; the effects of task-involving and ego-involving evaluation on interest and performance. *British Journal of Educational Psychology*, 58, 1-14.

Dawes, L., Mercer, N. & Wegerif, R. (2004) *Thinking Together*. 2nd edn. York UK: Imaginative Minds

Dweck, C.S.(2000), *Self-Theories : Their role in motivation, personality and development*, London UK: Taylor & Francis

Fisher, R.(2005) *Teaching Children to Learn* (*2nd Ed.*) London: Nelson Thornes.

Gardner, J.(2007) Is teaching a 'partial' profession? *Making the Grade* (*Journal of the Institute of Educational Assessors*) Summer pp.18-21.

Harrison, C.(2005) Teachers developing assessment for learning: mappring teacher change. *Teacher Development*, 9(2), 255-263.

Hodgen, J., & Marshall, B. (2005). Assessment for learning in English and mathematics: a comparison. *The Curriculum Journal*, 16(2),153-176.

Johnson, D.W., Johnson, R.T. & Stanne, M.B. 2000 *Co-operative learning methods: a meta-analysis*. Down-loadable from: http://www.co-operation.org/pages/cl-methods.html

Lee, C. & Wiliam, D.(2005) Studying changes in the practice of two teachers developing assessment for learning, *Teacher Development*, 9(2),265-283.

Mansell, W. & James, M.(2009) *Assessment in Schools. Fir for purpose? A commentary on the Teaching and Learning Research Programme*. London: Economic and Social Research Council, Teaching and Learning Research Programme. Available for down-load on http://www.assessment-reform-group.org/publications.html

Mercer, N., Dawes, L., Wegerif, R. & Sams, C.(2004) Reasoning as a scientist: ways of helping children to use language to learn science. *British Educational Research Journal* 30(3),359-377.

McCombs, B.L. & Miller, L (2007) *Learner-Centred Classroom Practices and Assessments: maximising student motivation, learning and achievement*. Thousand Oaks, CA.: Corwin Press.

Rowe, M.B (1974) Wait time and rewards as instructional variables, their influence on language, logic and fate control. *Journal of Research in Science Teaching*, 11,81-94

Stanley, G., MacCann, R., Gardner, J., Reynolds, L. & Wild, I.(2009). *Review of teacher assessment: what works best and issues for development*. Oxford University Centre for Educational Development; Report commissioned by the QCA. Available for down-load on:
http://www.education.ox.ac.uk/assessment/publications.php

Wiliam, D. & Black, P.J. 1996 Meanings and consequences: a basis for distinguishing formative and summative functions of assessment. *British Educational Research Journal*, 22(5), 537-548.

# 教师的形成性和总结性评价：前景和问题

Paul Black

【摘要】形成性评价被广泛地认为能促进学生学习，其研究领域也多种多样，如课堂提问、评价等级、同伴互评、自我评价和形成性测验的应用。然而，这些研究主题仍然孤立分散，未能成为一个统一系统的有机构成，依然缺乏统整的基本原理将这些主题加以链接，形成性评价在教学和学习的复杂理论中的位置还尚未明确。本文呈现了形成性评价需要遵循的有效学习的基本原则，以及成功的形成性评价的实践研究领域。此外，文章认为形成性和总结性评价之间的良性互动能提供促进学习的机会，但需要能够充分相信教师判断的合理的国家管理制度，同时加强相应的教师培训和支持项目，从而确保教师判断是可靠的。

【关键词】形成性评价；总结性评价；有效学习的原则

【作者简介】Paul Black/伦敦国王学院教授，学习性评价研究专家

# “三维目标”论

钟启泉

【摘要】我国义务教育课程标准倡导的“三维目标”体现了教育思想的进步。“三维目标”是基础学力的一种具体表述，体现了崭新的学力观，体现了现代学科的内在价值以及学科教学的对话与修炼的本质。课堂教学改革必须从推进“三维目标链”的教学设计做起，这种变革的核心课题是从教案设计到学案设计的重心转移，从显性学力到隐性学力的重心转移，从个体认知到集体思维的重心转移。“三维目标链”教学设计的框架有助于将我国中小学的学科教学提升到“人的学习”的高度。

【关键词】三维目标；知识哲学；三维目标链；教学设计；教学反思能力

【作者简介】钟启泉/华东师范大学课程与教学研究所教授、博士生导师

我国义务教育课程标准倡导的“三维目标”体现了教育思想的进步。“新课程改革”十年来，围绕“三维目标”的界定，引发了持续的忽隐忽现的论争。这场论争恰恰表明，我国教育界倘若仍然迷醉于凯洛夫教育学，排斥教育科学的新启蒙运动，那么，我国中小学的学科教育研究和学科教学的实践是不可能有任何进展的。其实，认识“三维目标”是同现代学科教育学的重建联系在一起的。本文的任务旨在阐明“三维目标”的内涵及其背后的知识哲学，揭示“三维目标链”教学设计的框架及其核心课题。

## 一、“三维目标”的界定及其意义

### （一）“三维目标”的界定

1. “三维目标”的内涵。“三维目标”是基础学力的一种具体表述。第一维目标（知识与技能）意指人类生存所不可或缺的核心知识和基本技能；第二维目标（过程与方法）的“过程”意指应答性学习环境与交往体验，“方法”指基本学习方式和生活方式；第三维目标（情感态度与价值观）意指学习兴趣、学习态度、人生态度以及个人价值与社会价值的统一。在学校教学中，既不能离开了过程与方法、情感态度与价值观去求得知识与技能，也不能离开了知识与技能去空讲过程与方法、情感态度与价值观的发展。“三维目标”是一个整体，不可分割，三者是融为一体的。有人反对“三维目标”，说“‘三维目标’是‘虚化知识’，因此是‘轻视知识’的表现”。这是形而上思维方式的典型表述。“三维目标”恰恰是基于现代的“学科”概念的界定，因此恰恰是“重视知识”的表现。

2. “三维目标”的隐喻。借用日本学者梶田叡一的“扎实学力”(基础学力)的“四层冰山模型”来说明这个问题。[1]假定有一座冰山,浮在水面上的不过是“冰山”的一角。倘若露出水面的一层是显性学力——“知识与技能”、“理解与记忆”,那么,藏在水面下的三层则是支撑冰山上方显性学力的隐性学力——“思考力和问题解决力”、“兴趣与意欲”以及“体验与实感”。所谓“基础学力”即是由上述的显性学力和隐性学力组成的,它们是相辅相成、不可分割的一个整体。为了实现指向“基础学力”的“扎实的教学”,我们必须把握“基础学力”形成的两条运动路径,这就是:从下层向上层推进的学力形成路径——即从“体验与实感”、“兴趣与意欲”向“思考力和问题解决力”以及“知识与理解”的运动;从上层向下层延伸的学力形成路径——即从“知识、技能”与“理解与记忆”向“思考力和问题解决力”以及“兴趣与意欲”、“体验与实感”的运动。梶田叡一强调,这种表层与深层的循环往复的学力形成路径,正是培养扎实的基础学力所需要的。

**(二)“三维目标”界定的意义**

“三维目标”是对传统“双基论”的一种超越,体现了崭新的学力观。“双基论”原本是从苏联搬过来的。苏联《教师报》曾经自我批判“双基”是违背马克思主义的,因为它抽去了人的主观能动性的要素,是“唯技术主义”的标本。教育是一种有目的、有计划的活动,它是指向教育目标、制订教育计划并据以展开实践的,而作为教育实践的基本形态的教学当然也是瞄准教育目标的。教育的宗旨终究在于人格的陶冶。教学目标当然必须贯穿这种育人的目标、人格的陶冶。“育人”还是“育分”?教学实践不同于机器人的学习(渗透着情感与态度),也不同于动物的训练(渗透着社会性与价值观)。传统的“双基论”的流毒就在于把“训练”等同于“教育”。日本新的《学习指导要领》针对“应试教育”的弊端,重新界定“基础学力”的概念,突出了“扎实学力”的具体内涵:(1)一切学习之基础的“语言能力”的涵养;(2)称雄国际水准的“数理学力”的培育;(3)日本前人积累起来的“传统文化”的传承;(4)引进当代儿童所缺失的自然体验、福利体验和劳动体验之类的“多元体验”;(5)伴随教育国际化的进展,从小学开始的英语学习的实施。当然,这种“扎实学力”必然是由内省能力、规范意识之类的道德品性和艺术感之类的“丰富心灵”所支撑的。[2]人的学习当然不能没有记忆与训练,但不能随意放大“训练”,甚至混同了“训练”与“教育”的区别。有人片面强调“读书百遍,其义自见”,却有意无意抹杀了“学而不思则罔,思而不学则殆”的辩证法,不能不说是一种片面性和无知的偏见。

“三维目标”是对传统“学科观”的一种扬弃,体现了现代学科的内在价值。“学科”(subject)的设定是以教育目标为依归,以扩大和深化学习者的知识积累与变化为前提的。构成“学科”的元素,绝不是片断的内容和细分化的知识的堆积,学科结构必须具有逻辑。“学科”必须根据学生的身心发展阶段及其能力发展实际来组织体现知识体系和价值体系的教学内容。因此,任何学科的构成总是包含了知识、方法、价值这样三个层面的要素:其一,构成该学科的基础知识和基本概念的体系；其二，该学科的基础知识和基本概念体系背后的思考方式与行为方式；其三，该思考方式与行为方式背后的情感、态度和价值观。换言之，它囊括了理论概念的建构，牵涉知、情、意的操作方式和真善美之类的价值，以及探索未来和未知世界的方略。这种以逻辑的知识形态来表现知识体系和价值体系的，就是“学科”。因此，“三维目标”不是在学科之外强加于学科教学的价值追求，而是学科自身内在的隐含的价值：认知价值、社会价值、伦理价值。以日本的新课程改革为例。新《学习指导要领》重视“语言能力”的培养，把它视为培养“扎实学力”的最基础性的课题。这不仅表现为增加国语科的课时，而且在教学方法上，特别提出：“进一步重视语言教育的立场；提高对国语的兴趣，培育尊重国语的态度；掌握实际生活中须臾不可离的学习各科之基本的国语能力；培育享受、传承和发展日本的语言文化的态度。”[3]

“三维目标”是荡涤“应试教育”的一帖解毒剂，体现了学科教学的对话与修炼的本质。学科教学是一种“对话学习”和“修炼学习”的过程。这里的“对话学习”是指通过同他人的沟通，展开探究对象意义的行为；“修炼学习”则是指追求自我完善的行为。[4]哲学认识论把“知识”界定为“人类认识的成果”，它是前人经过系统的理性思维并以“符号”形式保存下来的“人类的文化遗产”。这种“本体论知识观”揭示人类总体知识的普遍性质，为我们提供了普适的世界观和方法论。不过，倘若教师仅仅满足于搬用这种“本体论知识观”，是无法把握作为“学习主体”的学生是如何建构知识、如何再生产知识的。换言之，哲学认识论的“知识”界定替代不了认知心理学、课程教学论的知识论研究。西尔伯曼说：“我们的社会不是静止的，我们需要的是教育，不是训练。”[5]因为“教育是人的灵魂的教育，而非理智知识和认识的堆集”[6]。“训练是一种心灵隔离的活动，教育则是人与人精神相契合，文化得以传承的活动。”[7]我国一些学者一味强调客观主义知识观，鼓吹“知识百宝箱”论，把知识视为普遍的、外在于人的、供人掌握的真理，学生的学习不过是从“知识百宝箱”里获取现成知识而已。“知识百宝箱”论宣扬“课程即知识”、“训练即教育”，追求单纯的以“知识点”为核心概念的教学目标，是一种“目中无人”的教育，是一种“反发展”、“反教育”的把戏，同素质教育格格不入。“三维目标”落实之时，就是“应试教育”崩溃之日。这就容易理解：为什么新课程改革实施以来一些人抵制“三维目标”的奥妙所在。

## 二、“三维目标”的知识哲学

### （一）“三维目标”体现了人类科学的诉求

教育是一种技术，更是一种艺术，教育工作兼具技术性和艺术性。教育研究不能没有人类科学的视野。何谓“人类科学”？人类科学的对象是人。作为人类科学的对象——人类现象，不仅有“确凿侧面”，也包含“混沌侧面”。因为，人类现象有其生物学构造的“确凿侧面”，也包括了人类的心理的、意义层面的“混沌侧面”。研究人类的“混沌侧面”的领域统称“软科学”，例如解释学的案例、研究文化人类学的野外研究等。这样，所谓"人类科学"是涵盖了人类现象的"确凿侧面"的"硬科学"和"混沌侧面"的"软科学"的一种集合领域。通常所谓"科学"被视为"客观性"的活动。因此，软科学根据其"主观性"的方法获得的见解，往往被认为具有同客观世界存在"不一致"的所谓"差距"问题。因为，主观解释介入的程度越大，越是会远离客观世界的描述。这样，基于解释学方法的案例研究往往会受到来自硬科学的"缺乏客观性"的批判。人类学是不能无条件地认可这种"客观性"批判的。"正如不能'见树不见林'一样，我们也不能'见科学不见人类'。"[8]同样，教育问题的研究不能满足于硬科学的线性研究，还需要软科学的非线性研究。事实上，"三维目标"是当今世界各国课程标准或教学大纲的共同元素。从泰勒、布卢姆倡导"行为目标"论，到艾斯纳主张"行为目标、问题解决目标、表现性目标"并列论[9]，清晰地体现了国际教育界统整地把握"软目标"与"硬目标"（或是"开放目标"与"封闭目标"）的诉求。[10]

**（二）"三维目标"立足于新的知识哲学**

知识不是纯粹客观的，而是主观建构的。客观主义知识观认为，世界是实在的、有结构的，这种结构是可以被认知的。因此，存在着关于客观世界的可靠知识。知识是独立于人之外而存在的。学生只能通过教师的传授被动地习得知识。不同于客观主义知识观，建构主义认为，世界是客观存在的，但对于世界的理解和赋予的意义不过是知者的心中之物，是知者构造了现实，至少是按照自己的经验解释了现实。建构主义认为，学习是建构内在心理表征的过程。教学并不是教师把知识从外界搬到学生的记忆之中，而是以学生既有的经验为基础通过与外界的交互作用来建构新知识的。这种建构不是外界刺激的直接反应，而是借助既有的认知结构对新的信息进行主动加工而建构的。就是说，知识是作为学习者的主体"能动地建构"的，而不是灌输的。两种知识观，形成了两种根本不同的教学：听命于教师的"灌输式教学"与尊重学生能动性的"建构式教学"。

建构主义知识观是由认知主义发展而来的知识哲学。不过，建构主义作为一个整体，正在从"个人建构主义"过渡到"社会建构主义"。就是说，其射程从个人扩展到社会与文化。个人建构主义的代表人物是皮亚杰。皮亚杰的认知发展论主张：人是能动地建构知识的。以往谓之"建构主义"者大多属于这个范畴。它把个人置于中心地位，所以谓之"个人建构主义"。在个人建构主义看来，"我思故我在"。作为认知结构的主体的个人，是借助同作为客体的环境的能动的交互作用，使得认知结构（知识结构）发生变化和建构的。而这种变化和建构，就是学习和发展。可以说，这是基于认知结构的建构主义。认知结构发生质的变化可分若干时期，这就是所谓的"发展阶段"。社会建构主义知识观认为，"我们思故我们在"。人的知识广泛地播散于社会文化的环境之中，借助于个人之间的交往而得以"社会地建构"。社会建构主义的第一个代表性理论是社会心理学家格根的交往理论。格根有一句格言："我们交往故我们存在。"在网络化社会的今日，仍然拘泥于个人的知识和孤立的个人主义，是无法应对的。因此，他主张“借助相互合作来社会地建构必要的知识”。第二个代表性理论是维果茨基的发展理论。维果茨基强调，人是通过学习和经验获得知识，并在认识和问题解决中发挥知识的作用的。

### （三）“三维目标”彰显了心智活动发展的法则

按照维果茨基的高级心智活动发展的法则，第一，儿童是借助同周边的成人展开集团性、社会性的活动，特别是在教师的帮助之下，来获得作为历史的、社会文化的知识的。第二，这种知识的获得过程是儿童自身的内在过程。作为文化遗产的知识，唯有在儿童自主地把它置于自身既有的知识体系之中加以结构化，并且能够适当地用来解决问题或是应用于新的情境，才能达到理解，加以掌握。当学习者在同既有知识息息相关之际，即在同所传递、所观察的一连串事实和概念之间发现了一贯性、整合性之际，才会感受到“理解”的境界，才能形成“科学概念”。“科学概念不是自发发生的，而是基于学校的教学过程中所确立起来的概念间的共通性关系之中而自觉产生的。”[11]容易掌握的新的知识，是充分结构化了的知识。知识越是丰富，借助同既有知识的关联，新的知识的获得与保存就越是容易。在问题解决中，来自既有知识的推理是有用的。当新的信息同既有知识的体系不具有整合性之际，就会产生好奇心。通过提示不同于儿童既有观念的信息和观点，可以唤起好奇心，激发学习的需求是必要的。我们需要重视兴趣、动机和态度，而知识和理解的实现，可以说，也是提高兴趣、动机和态度的一个必要条件。

在这里，我们需要谨防两个极端。其一，谨防片面的知识灌输。学习者是借助同外界的交往来积累知识的。倘若不是自主地同知识发生关系（联系）、重组先行知识，用来解决问题，那么，这种知识是不会有用的。无视学习者的既有知识体系和经验，片面地灌输知识的“灌输式教学”，是不可能达于“理解”的。其二，谨防轻视概念性知识的“体验式教学”。因为它不能实现知识的结构化。在学校教育活动中，关键的课题在于，如何调动学习者的实践经验，去习得从经验中不能自然掌握的科学概念。

## 三、“三维目标链”教学设计的框架与课题

### （一）作为假设的教学目标

教学目标是教师基于对教学实践过程的预设所设定的假设。所谓教师能够指导教学过程，就是指能够抽取实践过程内蕴的发展方向，并且沿着该发展方向推进实践的过程。不过，实践过程能够预设却不能预知。因此，教学目标无非是一种假设而已。教学目标要在实践过程中发挥其引领的作用，唯有在实践过程之中加以探讨与修正。教学目标的具体化就是借助这种探讨与修正得以实现的。离开了动态的实践过程之中的教学目标的具体化，儿童潜能的实现只能停留于空洞的口号。就教师自身而言，倘若满足于静止不动的教学目标，教师的专业

成长也就不可能了。这是因为，盲目的执行并不是实践。就是说，所谓“实践”是同时把假设与事实加以相对化，视为相互发展的一种契机，相互参照、相互修正而形成的。这样一种进展就是过程（流程）。因此，目标一旦确定，过程（流程）也就决定了。同时，也就获得了在过程（流程）之中重建目标的地盘。通过目标与过程（流程）的相互制约，一旦重建了目标，就能够发挥目标原本应当发挥的作用——指导过程（流程）朝着理想的方向进展。过程（流程）是由目标决定的，而目标的价值则是由过程（流程）决定的。教学目标的具体化是在具体的实践过程（流程）之中展开的。这样，所谓目标的具体化不能离开过程（流程），无非就是指目标一旦具体化了，同时，内容与方法也就具体化了。目标的具体化是没有终点的，目标的实现是无止境的。

**（二）“三维目标链”教学设计的框架**

“三维目标”的落实取决于教师的洞察力。教学目标不是单一的。当我们实现教学目标A之际，就得设定其若干下位目标以及相应的若干下下位目标。它们相互关联，形成一个复杂的体系，这就是“教学目标链”。当然，“教学目标链”的探讨离不开教材特质的研究和儿童身心发展的研究。我国新课程的“三维目标”类似于国际教育界“认知目标、行为目标、体验目标”的表述，体现了我国教学研究的进步。不过，尚须教师把“三维目标”作为一个整体来把握，并在“课程标准目标—学科教学目标—单元教学目标—课时教学目标”的链索中，加以落实。

日本教育学者早在20世纪70年代末就提出了“教学目标链”的教学设计思路，可供借鉴。他们区分“目标层级”与“目标领域”两个维度，建构了教学目标分析的框架（见表1），即在“Ⅰ学科・领域”、“Ⅱ单元・题材”、“Ⅲ课时・阶段”这样渐次细化的“层级”（称之为“列”）中，配以“A认知目标”（概念结构）、“B行为目标”（问题解决过程中的能力）、“C体验目标”（情感、意志与态度）这些“领域”（称之为“行”）。即便是同样的“认知目标”，在Ⅰ-A和Ⅲ-A中，层级也是完全不同的。或者正如Ⅱ-A、Ⅱ-B、Ⅱ-C所表明的，一个单元和题材（小单元）的目标，不仅要把握其概念和法则的掌握之类的认知性目标，也要把握其探究意欲、探究能力之类的诸多领域。这样，在教师的教学目标分析中必须兼顾这九个“细胞”（由于Ⅲ-A往往被融合在Ⅱ-C中的居多，而在低年级，Ⅱ-B和Ⅲ-B大体也是合并在一起的。因此，实际上并没有九个）。同时，必须兼顾三个层级、三个领域之间的内在关联，而不仅仅关注Ⅱ-B或Ⅲ-A的问题。

**表1　教学目标分析的层级与领域**

| 层级\领域 | A认知目标 | B行为目标 | C体验目标 |
| --- | --- | --- | --- |
| Ⅰ学科・领域 | | | |
| Ⅱ单元・题材 | | | |
| Ⅲ课时・阶段 | | | |

出处：水越敏行《教学改造的视点与方法》，明治图书1979年版，第35页。

在“三维目标链”教学设计的框架中，一个关键的问题是，不要把目标视为一个凝固的静态的东西，需要认识目标与流程之间的复杂关系。既然具体的实践过程是一个有机的动态地运动着的流程，那么，“三维目标”只能根据流程的态势加以相应地落实，绝不可能机械地以课时为单位进行平均分摊式的一一对应。这里所谓“流程”是指教学的过程性结构的描述，它是从师生的“行为范式”的互动之中产生的。

**（三）推进“三维目标链”教学设计的核心课题**

“三维目标链”教学设计的框架有助于打破单纯知识点的教学设计的束缚，因而有助于我国中小学的学科教学真正从“动物训练”的层次提升到“人的学习”的高度。这正是推进素质教育的本意所在。课堂教学改革必须从变革教学设计做起，从推进“三维目标链”的教学设计做起。这种变革的核心课题是：从“教师中心”向“学生中心”的重心转移，具体包括如下几点。

第一，从教案设计到学案设计①的重心转移，求得教师的教与学生的学的统一。教案设计往往容易陷入告知式、训练式的权威控制的教学，而不是对话式、修炼式、平等协商的教学。

第二，从显性学力到隐性学力的重心转移，求得显性目标与隐性目标的统一。从学力理论的角度分析，应试教育与素质教育的根本区别就在于，前者由于仅仅关注于显性学力而抹杀了隐性学力，这种没有根基的学力终究是没有活力的，不是真正的学力。

第三，从个体认知到集体思维的重心转移，求得个性发展与群性发展的统一。个体的认知能力的发展当然重要，但是，离开了集体思维，就不可能有个体认知的健全发展。

这里需要强调的是，不能把“重心转移”同“二元对立”的思想混为一谈。恰恰相反，它力图消弭教学设计中常见的种种关系的对立：(1)教学性质的艺术侧面与技术侧面的对立；(2)教学的教材与教学的课题中重视生活内容与重科学内容的对立；(3)教学目标中重知识点与重思考力的对立；(4)教学目标中重知识性与重体验性的对立；(5)教学中重教师控制性与重儿童自主性的对立；(6)教学中重同步教学（普遍性）与重个别教学（差异性）的对立；(7)教学中重个人内与重人际间的对立，等等。

---

① 日本教师着力于“学案”的设计与实施，把学生置于中心地位。“独立思考”、“小组思考”、“全班思考”贯穿全程。通过反复阅读、思考、讨论，引导学生达到教师所期望的思想境界。中国教师着力于“教案”的设计与实施，这是以教师为中心的“教学思路图”，旨在按照教师预设的逻辑顺序为学生铺就学习之路。最终的结论是，前者的课堂是由学生讨论的观点来结束的，后者则是由教师预设的。我的一位博士生曾经做了一个“中日课堂教学比较研究”，日本教师看了中国教师的教学录像后说：“课堂进度似乎太快了。这对10%—20%的学生是有利的，但很可能伤害其他的学生。”“中国的课堂似乎仍然受控于一种控制力。”“日本30年前的课堂也是这样的。但如今日本的课堂不是由教师的力量来推动课的进程，而是借助学生的力量来创造教学的。”毫无疑问，各国的课堂文化各有其优势和劣势，我国的中小学课堂同样如此。我并不认为日本教师的整体素质比中国教师高出一筹，但不能不承认的一点是，日本教师的教学观念中突出了作为教育对象的“儿童”。这位博士生发现，日本教师的角色定位是：为学生营造自由的学习氛围，揣测学生的需求，引导学生的思考，辅助学生的活动。他们把学生看做自主的，有足够认知能力和思维能力的人，有着与教师不同的情感体验、道德标准和人生准则。因此，在这些教师看来，学生应该得到最大限度的尊重。即便他们现在并不完美、并不成熟，但是，那是他们以自己的经验为基础的，是真正属于他们自己的学习和成长。

教学创造的过程分为三个阶段,即计划(或设计)、实施(或实践)和"评价"(或反思)。不过,在行为科学的教学研究中,教学的创造被视为"计划·达成·评价"三个阶段的线性过程。在这里受到重视的是"计划",是对照"教学目标"的"评价"。而行为科学之后的质性研究方法却不同,它转向重视教学的过程及其经验本身的研究。[12]这样,教学是由教师展开设计,在课堂活动中不断得以修正,借助反思复杂课堂事件的意义得以创造更有意义的经验的过程。在这里,教学的"设计"、"实践"、"反思"不是阶段性的过程,而是周而复始的循环往复过程。可以说,教师的教学反思能力构成了作为专家的教师能力的核心。

建构主义主张"我思故我在",社会建构主义进一步主张"我们思故我们在"。真正的学生的学习是如此,教师的教学设计也概莫能外。我们需要在"我的思考"和"我们的共同思考"之中,不断锤炼教师的教学反思能力——这就是作为革新的教育工作者应有的姿态。

参考文献

[1] 梶田叡一.学力观与评价观的转换[M].东京:金子书房,1994:86.

[2][3] 人类教育研究协议会编.新《学习指导要领》——课程改革的理念与课题[M].东京:金子书房,2008:10,11.

[4] 佐藤学.学习的快乐——走向对话[M].北京:教育科学出版社,2004:10—11.

[5] 西尔伯曼.课堂的危机[M].东京:萨依玛尔出版会,1973:225.

[6][7] 雅斯贝尔斯.什么是教育[M].北京:生活·读书·新知三联书店,1991:42.

[8] 西条刚央.何谓建构主义——新生代人类科学的原理[M].京都:北大路书房,2005:7.

[9] 艾斯纳.教育想象——学校课程设计与评价[M].北京:教育科学出版社,2008:113—130.

[10] 佐藤三郎,稻叶宏雄.学校与课程[M].东京:第一法规,1984:154—164.

[11] 中村和夫.维果茨基心理学[M].东京:新读书社,2004:31—32.

[12] 佐藤学.教育方法[M].东京:左右社,2010:16.

## On the Three-Dimension Objectives

Qiquan Zhong

**Abstract**: The three-dimension objectives advocated by our country's curriculum standard of compulsory education reflect the progress of educational thought. The three-dimension objectives are the specific illustration of fundamental academic achievement. It embodies the new academic achievement perspective, the intrinsic value of modern discipline and the essence of subject teaching characterized by dialogue and spiritual exercise. The reform of classroom instruction must start from promoting the instruction design characterized by three-dimension objective chain. The key research topics of this reform include the focus shift from teaching plan design to learning plan design, from explicit academic achievement to implicit academic achievement, from personal cognition to group thinking. The framework of instruction design characterized by three-dimension objective chain helps promote subject teaching of primary and secondary schools of our county to the high degree of "people learning".

**Keywords**: three-dimension objectives; knowledge philosophy; three-dimension objective chain; instruction design; teaching reflection ability

# 论促进教学的表现性评价：标准-教学-评价一致性的视角

周文叶　崔允漷

【摘要】表现性评价的内涵特征和构成要素决定着它在一定的条件下能统整标准、教学、学习与评价，并能促进教师的教学与学生的学习。首先，表现性任务与标准存在共生的关系，彼此互相依赖，并且表现性任务同时可以是教学活动；而评分规则则是标准的具体化。其次，评分规则提供了衡量学生表现水平的具体指标，可以根据这些语言来描述学生的表现状况，而不是用简单化的等级或分数来判定学生的表现。再次，依据表现标准开发的评分规则为学生提供了清晰的目标图景，他们可以利用评价的指标来了解自己的进步，评判自己的成绩，监控自己的发展，从而成为学习的主人。

【关键词】表现性评价；教学；学习

【作者简介】周文叶/华东师范大学教研员研修中心讲师
崔允漷/华东师范大学课程与教学研究所所长、教授

表现性评价在20世纪末的兴起是由于人们对标准化测验不满，看到了它给教学所带来的巨大的负面影响。人们试图在评价改革中强调运用表现性评价，来支持系统的改革目的，同时改善课程、教学与学生的学习。表现性评价自身的特征决定着它在以下这些方面存在着巨大的潜力：检测客观纸笔测验检测不了的学习结果；促使课程标准—教学—学习与评价的一体化；促进学生的学习。本文聚焦于后两个问题的探讨，企图揭示表现性评价与教学的关系以及促进教与学的发挥机制，为表现性评价在课堂教学中的应用提供借鉴。

## 一、促使标准、教学与评价的一体化

人们总是批判老师们“为测验而教”，学生们“为考试而学”。老师和学生这么做为什么不行呢？因为目前的测验、考试方式太单一，能测的和能考的只是我们期望学生要获得的学习结果的一小部分，并且所测的和所考的不能给教学带来积极的影响。反之，如果我们采用的评价方式能检测多种学习结果，并能为教学决策带来丰富的有用信息，那么考什么教什么，怎么考怎么教，又何尝不可呢？在很多教育者看来，相对于传统的纸笔测验而言，表现性评价更能对教师的教学目标构成积极的影响。“如果在高利害评价中合理使用表现性评价，教师教学活动的中心将会发生积极的转变。”[1]弗彻斯（Fuchs，L.）就认为，表现性评价的一个主要驱动是重

新连接大规模评价与课堂评价从而积极地影响学习，促进教学的需要。[2]卡特雷（Khattri, N.）等人也提出了相类似的观点：表现性评价作为一种评价方式并不是什么新鲜事，而引起人们关注的是在当前的评价改革中对表现性评价的强调，并以此来支持系统的改革目的，从而改变教学、课程与学生的学习。[3]总的来说，表现性评价促使课程标准、教学与评价的一体化主要体现在以下两个方面。

**（一）表现性评价是基于标准的教学的有效途径，即"评价即教学"意义上的一体化**

马扎诺（Marzano, R.）在《评价学生的学习成果：应用学习维度模式的表现性评价》[4]中详细分析了课程标准与表现性评价的共生关系，他指出，基于标准的教学需要对学生应该知道什么和做什么做出清晰的界定，而基于标准教学的运动就是出于这样的假设：唯一能确保学生获得具体的知识和技能的途径是界定并教给学生所期望的具体知识和技能的表现水平。教师要求学生通过完成表现性任务实现清晰界定的标准。事实上，标准和表现任务维系着一种共生的关系，他们彼此互相依赖，分别是综合评价体系的必要组成部分。标准和表现性评价的共生关系，使得表现性评价成为基于标准的教学的有效途径，两者存在许多相吻合的地方：（1）表现性准则（Performance Critera）是对标准的进一步清晰界定——是对标准的最终定义；（2）开发表现性准则的过程不仅仅是评价的过程，并且它能促进教学；（3）表现性准则将标准更清晰地展示给学生；（4）将表现性准则教给学生能促进评价与教学的统整。[5]艾特和麦克泰（Arter, J. & McTighe, J.）也指出，表现性评价的许多特征体现了基于标准的教学的实质：（1）帮助教师弄清楚复杂学习目标的实质，使他们在教学中感觉轻松；（2）评价学生的进步和现状，在不同学生、不同科目之间和不同时间里都使用统一的评价标准；（3）让学生了解合格表现的标准，以提高学生的成绩；（4）把评价和教学结合起来。[6]这些研究及其观点都旨在说明表现性评价与基于标准的教学所存在的共性：清晰界定学生应知和能做的；学生通过完成表现性任务实现这些标准；把评价与教学结合起来。

表现性评价不仅仅从内容标准出发，清晰地界定表现标准，而且将表现标准进一步细化、具体化，制定具体的评分规则。而评分规则则是教学评价与测验中可以直接应用的评分工具。它回答了以下问题：哪些要素将被用来判断或评价学生的表现？我们需要关注哪些方面来判断成功的表现？表现的质量范围是什么？如何决定给什么分数以及所给分数代表的意义？如何描述不同的质量水平？"不管课程标准、课程结构或教材是如何规定的，评分规则的内容规定了教师和学生借以决定要采取什么措施来获得成功的依据——他们所看到的就是他们需要去做的。"[7]也就是说，开发和实施表现性评价的过程，就是对课程标准不断分解细化，进一步清晰界定的过程。内容标准起着统领作用，它规定了学生学习的范围，表现标准解读了内容标准，化抽象为具体，它详细地描述了课程内容标准的深度（如难度和复杂性）。评分规则依据内容标准和表现标准，在教学实践、教学评价中，为广大教师提供了一种重要工具，它是对表现标准的描述，也是对内容标准的进一步细化。可以说，三者缺一不可，构成了一个统一的整体，它覆盖了从课程到教学实践的范围。同时，这也就促成了课程到教学的转换，从为什么教到教什么和教到什么程度，这些问题的一致性回答将课程、教学和评价统一起来。

**（二）表现性评价能很好地促进教学，即“评价助教学”意义上的一体化**

教学的过程包含了一连串互相关联的、以促进学生的学习为目的的教学决策，在很大程度上，教学的有效性取决于那些作为决策基础的信息的性质和质量。在教学中，几乎任何一个真正重要的学习目标领域都是相当丰富的，以至于在实践中教师很难通过评价这些领域的所有内容来确定学生的状况。一个可行的办法就是，教师从所有这些目标领域中抽样选取有代表性的学习目标，也即“大观念”，以此作为课堂评价真正应该实施的内容。学生在评价中的表现应该被看作是一种标志/证据，表明学生达到预期学习目标的程度与水平。教师可以利用这一结论来制定教学决策。这样的一个决策链如图 1 所示。正是基于评价的有关推论，影响着教师的教学决策。[8]

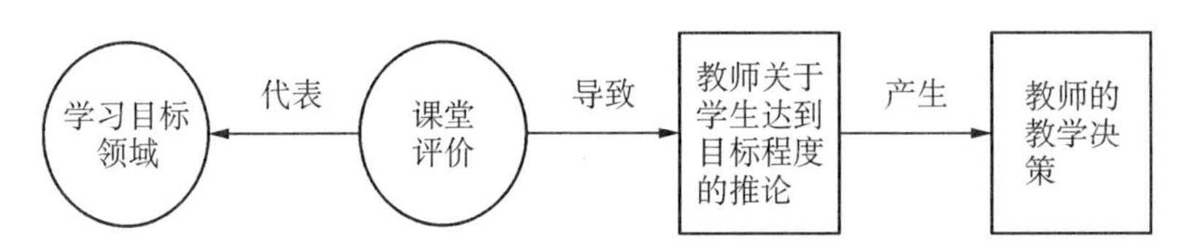


**图 1　教学决策链**

课堂中的表现性评价最主要的功能就是有助于教师做出更好的教学决策：学生在多大程度上达到了学习目标？学生的学习困难在哪里？该将哪些重要信息反馈给学生？下一步的教学该从哪里出发？……从“教学决策链”中我们可以看到，最关键的一环就是教师根据课堂评价的情况来推论学生达到目标的程度。而表现性评价根据学习结果所设计的表现任务和明确规定的评分规则，都使得教师的推论简单易行，并且可靠有效。教师利用这些推论的结果以重新审视自己的教学，从而调整教学。可见，课堂中的表现性评价融合了诊断、推论、反馈和评价等多个教学过程，从而为教师的教学决策提供了高质量的信息。

从上述的分析中，可以勾勒出表现性评价与课程标准和教学的关系图（图 2）；无论是作为教学的评价还是助教学的评价，与课程标准和教学统整的表现性评价都极大地促进了教与学。这一点也得到了很多研究者的认同。邦尼（Bonnie，A.）就认为，统整的表现性评价不仅能评价学生在不断靠近标准的进步过程，而且在天衣无缝的方式中将基于标准的课堂教学与评价实践连接起来，两者不断互相渗透，从而促进教与学。[9]奥尼尔（O'Neil）也指出，表现性评价给教和学带来较大的进步，给教师、学生和决策者带来许多收获：（1）对学生的能力将作一个更为完整的描述；（2）教师将有更多的机会参与到学业评定过程中去，并把它直接与教和学联系起来；（3）给学生带来取得更好成绩的动力；（4）将会得到家长的理解和欣赏。[10]

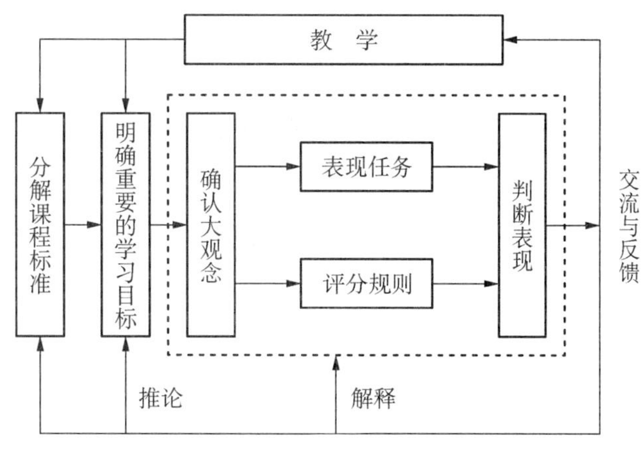

图 2　表现性评价与课程标准和教学的关系

## 二、促进学生学习的潜能

表现性评价不仅能统整标准和教学，从而服务于教学，更重要的是具有促进和改善学生学习的潜能。

### （一）能为学生阐明期望他们达到的学习结果

教学的目的在于促使学生有效、高效地学习。要使学生有卓越的学习表现，首先应当让他们知道学习结果，要求他们改进不理想或令人不满意的结果。但事实上，很多"不幸运的学生可能经常在课堂上感到困惑，不知道学业优秀意味着什么。他们的教师对成功的认识也许并不充分或者关注了错误的方面，或者他们想把成功的秘诀保留起来，以保证自己对课堂的权威性和控制力。当他们的学生试图猜测真正的目标而又猜错时，他们在评价中就会失败。在这种情况下，他们的失败不是因为缺乏学习动力，而是根本不知道努力的目标和方向。如果有明晰的目标，这些学生可能本来可以取得学业上的成功的"。[11]而表现性评价中的评分规则清晰详细地描述了预期的目标，强调可以判断学生表现的指标，从而给学生提供了努力的方向，有助于激发学生的学习动机。

### （二）能为学生提供促进学习的反馈信息

表现性评价非常注重在学习过程中向学生提供反馈，以便于学生获取和利用可了解自己表现的各种机会，从而能不断地根据评价目标对自我表现进行自我评价和自我调整，逐步完善自己的表现。反馈是每个完整学习中的一个核心部分，只有持续的单项练习和测验，而没有与此同时进行的反馈，意味着学生的答案与学生在校学习的实际结果、原因和意图是相互脱节的。一个人只有知道了自己是如何表现的，他才能改进或学着改进自己的表现。听起来这好像是基本常识，但在传统的课堂中却并非如此。在表现性评价中，反馈贯穿于评价的整个过程，而不仅是评价后的事情。同时，教师改变了提供反馈信息的传统形式，诸如评分、分等和简单的表扬等，而是为学生提供频繁的、持续的、经过证实的、有帮助的、关系到意图的证据，能使学生把当前表现与欲达到的结果（准则）进行比较。这些建设性的评价反馈明确地告知学生学习上的优缺点，用学生能理解的语言描述学生表现的质量。表现性评价中，教师通过评分规则所提供的有效反馈能极大地帮助学生的学习。

**（三）能培养学生自我监控并对学习负责任的能力**

"教是为了不教"，也即教学应当发展学生自我学习的能力与责任。传统的测验导致了以教师为中心的评价模式，而表现性评价却旨在培养学生的自我评价能力，希望学生成为教室的主人，成为评价的主体。在这样的评价中，教师的主要角色是辅助学生使其对他们的学习负责，辅助他们成为熟练的自我评价者。表现性评价中清晰界定的目标图景和能为学生提供的有效的反馈信息，为学生对自己的学习做出客观的评价提供了可能，它能使学生逐渐习惯把持续性的评价作为所完成任务的一个自然的、有意义的过程来对待。在这一个过程中，他们利用评价的指标来了解自己的进步，评判自己的成绩，监控自己的发展，也即清楚自己要到哪里，现在在哪里，还有多少距离要完成，接下来要做什么……他们逐渐内化评价的标准，明晰自己的弱点和长处，并充分利用所学的知识来改善自己的表现。因此，也就有利于学生对自己的学习负起更多的责任，真正成为学习的主人。

## 三、表现性评价促进学习的条件

表现性评价作为一种特定的评价方式，具有促进学习的巨大潜力。但这并不意味着，表现性评价必然能有效促进学生学习，要发挥表现性评价促进学习的功能，我们在设计和应用表现性评价时就必须关注以下几个方面。

**（一）在教学-学习-评价一体化关系中设计表现性评价**

在流行的课程实施理论中，评价是课程实施也即教学之后的一个环节，通常是凌驾于教学之上的一个孤立的环节，用以检测教学的效果，也即学生学习的效果。如果表现性评价也被作为这样一个孤立的环节，那么其形成性功能的发挥必然会受到极大的限制。

在当前正在发生的评价范式转换中，教学-学习-评价逐渐被看成三位一体的关系，评价与教学、学习紧密地交缠在一起，相互制约，相互影响。教学、学习应当是"数据驱动"（data-driven）的，而数据来自于评价；评价应当持续于教学、学习的过程之中，而不只在教学、学习终结之后实施；教学、学习的目标同样是评价的目标。换言之，评价应当是教学-学习过程的一个有机组成部分。

为了使表现性评价镶嵌于教学-学习过程之中，成为教-学过程的一个有机组成部分，教师首先必须将教学过程视作表现性评价的过程，将学习活动当作表现性任务来设计，随时收集学生在学习活动中的表现信息。在这一方面，表现性评价具有明显的优势，因为它能够关注到学习的过程而不只是学习的结果。其次，表现性评价必须以学习目标为焦点。所设计的表现性任务应当能够让学生充分地展示学习目标所要求的知识和技能，所运用的评分规则应当能够准确反映学生的表现水平。但表现性评价不能只关注孤立的知识或技能，尽管学习结果体现在学生学习之后所知和能做的事上，但更重要的是所知和所能背后的“大观念”。只关注孤立的知识、技能会导致评价“一英寸深，一英里宽”(inch deep, mile wide)——这种评价只需要以选择题为主体的纸笔测验就可以完成。表现性评价不能只引发学生的对错式思维，而要引发学生的批判性思考、问题解决等高层次的认知技能——这种高层次的认知技能就是特定的知识、技能背后的大观念。表现性任务就应当围绕着这样的大观念来设计，评分规则也必须能够反映学生在这一大观念上的表现水平。

### （二）充分利用评分规则提供及时的、持续的和有效的描述性信息

以往的形成性评价有一种假定，只要我们向学生提供反馈，告诉他们我们对其表现的判断，剩下的事学生自己会解决——学生会知道自己错在哪里，会知道自己当前的表现与目标状态之间的距离，也会主动有效地调节自己的行动，改善自己的表现。其实，只告诉学生对或错，好或不好的评价性反馈对于促进学习作用有限，甚至“学生得到的评价性反馈越多，对其学习产生的潜在的干扰也就越多”[12]。能够有效促进学习的反馈应当是描述性反馈，即向学生提供直接与学习相关的具体的描述性信息。学生在学习时得到的特定的描述性反馈越多，学习就可能越易发生。按照戴维斯(Davies, A.)的观点，描述性信息应当是关于学生的表现或作品的信息，而不应是关于学生本人的信息；这种信息依据学生的表现，但又要与良好的表现样例或描述性指标相比较而得出；这种信息是特定的、具体的、指向明确的，不是抽象的、空泛的符号或等级；这种信息与学习直接相关，且应当易于学生理解；这种信息不仅应当在学习之后，更应当在学习的过程中及时、持续地交流。[13]

因此，我们必须充分利用表现性评价中的评分规则，评分规则为衡量学生表现水平描述了具体的指标，评价就必须运用评分规则的语言来描述学生的表现状况，而不是用简单化的等级或分数来表示学生的表现。而且，在很多时候表现性评价只能进行描述性评价，因为表现性评价所要评价的并不是可以客观量化的事实性知识和技能，而是知识技能的综合应用、复杂的问题解决、对合作活动的参与等等，其中许多不能简单地量化，不能用分数或等级来表示。当我们用评分规则的语言来描述学生的表现时，学生不仅能够知道自己当前的表现水平，而且能够判断自己的现有水平与期望水平之间的差距。更重要的是，这种描述性反馈的持续提供会使学生形成用评分规则评价自己的表现的习惯，从而发展对于学习的改善十分重要的元认知技能。

### （三）让学生全面参与表现性评价

要使表现性评价真正发挥促进学习的作用，教师运用表现性评价的结果来调整教学自然

十分重要。但如果我们将教师当作教学-学习过程中唯一重要的决策者，那就完全错了。学生是学习的主体，任何教学策略最终都要通过学生自己才能发挥作用。从学习过程看，学生是比教师更为重要的决策者，因为所有直接影响他们学习过程及结果的决策都是由他们自己做出的。学生要成为“数据驱动”的学习者，做出关于自己学习的决策，当然需要来自于评价的“数据”。因此要通过各种途径使学生成为表现性评价信息的重要用户。

但学生仅仅成为表现性评价结果信息的用户，而不参与表现性评价的其他环节，那么表现性评价在促进学习上的效能会受到极大的局限。要使表现性评价对学习的促进作用最大化，学生就必须参与表现性评价的全过程，而不只是成为评价结果的消费者。

**与学生分享学习目标。**很多时候老师们往往非常详细地向学生解释了学习任务，却没有和学生分享自己期望他们从中学到什么，在完成任务时该学到什么程度。这样，学习也往往成为学生为完成老师的任务而做的事。只有当学生获知与自己学习有关的信息时，才能为自己的学习承担更多的责任。因此，教师在一开始就应当与学生分享学习目标。而易于学生接受和理解的目标，就要求目标必须是清晰的、简洁的，且以学生易于理解的语言叙写的。在必要的时候，也可以让学生参与具体目标的设定。

**让学生参与评分规则的制定。**从某一角度讲，制定评分规则也就是将设定的学习目标具体化。学生参与评分规则的制定，最大的好处就是能够让学生在头脑中形成良好的表现的清晰图景。这种图景对学生的表现会有强大的引导作用，促使学生朝着明确而清晰的具体目标而努力。同时，学生掌握了清晰的目标或表现标准就能让教师不再成为唯一的反馈提供者，能够让学生在学习过程中进行有效的自我监控，成为反馈的提供者，而不只是他人提供的反馈的消费者。让学生参与评分规则的制定通常有两种做法：一种是教师提供评分规则的框架，并向学生解释评分规则的内容，然后让学生联系实际的表现样例讨论评分规则，用自己的语言重新组织评分规则。这种做法更适合于处于起步阶段的学生；另一种方法是让学生合作从具体的表现样例中抽象出评分规则。这种做法对学生的能力要求较高，低年级的学生或者缺少制定评分规则经历的学生难以胜任。

**让学生参与记录自己的表现。**表现性评价给予学生展示自己最佳表现的机会，而不是像在标准化测验中那样只能展示典型的表现。为了展示自己的最佳表现水平，学生需要提供证明自己表现的证据。为此，他们必须学会有效记录自己的表现，以为表现性评价提供证据。当记录自己的表现时，他们就得运用事先确定的标准或评分规则作为记录的参照框架，并且运用这一参照框架进行自我评价。当整理自己的记录，如建立成长档案袋时，他们能够看到自己的变化，并对这些变化进行反思。如果他们能够看到自己的进步，就会获得对自己学习的控制感，[14]这是信心的重要来源。而当学生增强了学习的信心时，他们获得成功的可能性就会大大增加。

**让学生参与表现性评价结果的交流。**如果学生要与他人讨论评价的结果，他就得充分地考虑评价的正确性、准确性，因此就必须保证清晰地了解要达成的目标，保证全面地记录自己的表现，保证运用评分规则来对照自己的表现。在这一过程中，他会提高目标意识，会有更强的达标意识。更重要的是，“当学生有成功的故事可讲，且在令人信服地讲述故事时体验到自豪感，这会激励学生对进一步的学习的责任感”[15]。这种责任感会驱使他们更加努力地学习。


参考文献

[1][8] Popham, James. W. 促进教学的课堂评价[M]. 促进教师发展与学生成长的评价研究项目组，译. 北京：中国轻工业出版社，2003：137，204.

[2] Fuchs, Lynn S. *Connecting Performance Assessment to Instruction: A Comparison of Behavioral Assessment, Mastery Learning, Curriculum-Based Measurement, and Performance Assessment*. http://www.ericdigests.org/1996-1/based.htm.

[3] Khattri, Nidhi, & others. *Assessment of Student Performance*. http://www.eric.ed.gov/ERICWebPortal/custom/portlets/recordDetails/detailmini.jsp?_nfpb=true&_&ERICExtSearch_SearchValue_0=ED397532&ERICExtSearch_SearchType_0=no&accno=ED397532.

[4] Marzano, Robert J. Debra Pickering, & Jay McTighe. (1993). *Assessing Student Outcomes: Performance Assessment Using the Dimensions of Learning Model*.

[5] Arter, Judy. Performance Assessment about Teaching. *Educational Measurement: Issues and Practice*, 1998(4).

[6][7] Arter, Judith, & McTighe, Jay. 课堂教学评分规则[M]. 促进教师发展与学生成长的评价研究项目组，译. 北京：中国轻工业出版社，2005：16，50.

[9] Bonnie Adair-Hauck, ect. (2006). *The Integrated Performance Assessment (IPA): Connecting Assessment to Instruction and Learning*. *ERIC Digest*, No. EJ766749.

[10] Marsh, Colin. 初任教师手册[M]. 吴刚平，等，译. 北京：教育科学出版社，2005：276.

[11] Stiggins, Richard J. 促进学习的学生参与式课堂评价[M]. 促进教师发展和学生成长的评价研究项目组，译. 北京：中国轻工业出版社，2005：17.

[12] Winggins, Grant. 教育性评价[M]. 促进教师发展与学生成长的评价研究项目组，译. 北京：中国轻工业出版社，2003：42.

[13] Davies, A.. *Quality Classroom Assessment is Learning*. http://www.nzpf.ac.nz/resources/magazine/2004/nov/Assessment.htm.

[14][15] Stiggins, Richard J. & Chappuis, J. (2005). Using Student-Involved Classroom Assessment to Close Achievement Gaps. *Theory into Practice*.

# Performance Assessment Integrated with Teaching and Learning

Wenye Zhou Yunhuo Cui

**Abstract**: The main characteristics and core components of performance assessment determine that it can be integrated with the standards, teaching and learning under certain conditions and promote teachers' teaching and students' learning. First, there is a symbiosis between performance tasks and the standards, which means that they depend on each other. A performance task can also be a teaching activity at the same time, and the grading rules can be the specification of the standards. Second, the grading rules provide the specific indicators to evaluate students' performance levels and teachers can use them as a language to describe students' performance instead of using simplistic grades or points to judge. Also, by means of the grading rules developed on the basis of the performance standards, students acquire clear visions of targets. They can use the assessment indicators to know their own progress, assess their own achievements, monitor their own development and thereby become the master of their own learning.

**Key words**: performance assessment; teaching; learning

# 论综合素质评价的本质

李雁冰

【摘要】综合素质评价既是一种评价观,又是一种评价方式。作为一种评价观,它是素质教育评价体系的基本价值取向。作为一种评价方式,它与中考、高考等外部评价互动、结合,共同构成素质教育评价体系的基本内容。综合素质评价的本质是个性发展评价,也是真实性、过程性评价,还是内部评价。我国当前教育评价改革的误区是依然坚持具有"应试教育"性质的"工具主义素质观和评价观",致使综合素质评价蜕变为"强化的外部评价",进而使其成为"变相应试教育"。

【关键词】综合素质评价;个性发展;真实性评价;内部评价;工具主义素质观

【作者简介】李雁冰/华东师范大学课程与教学研究所副教授

## 一、问题的提出

2001年6月,国务院颁布的《基础教育课程改革纲要(试行)》指出:"改变课程评价过分强调甄别与选拔的功能,发挥评价促进学生发展、教师提高和改进教学实践的功能。""建立促进学生全面发展的评价体系。……发挥评价的教育功能,促进学生在原有水平上的发展。"[1]这里把评价改革视为基础教育课程改革的有机构成,并初步确立起"发展性评价"的理念,为随后提出的综合素质评价打下基础。

2002年12月,教育部颁发《关于积极推进中小学评价与考试制度改革的通知》,明确指出:"中小学评价与考试制度改革的根本目的是为了更好地提高学生的综合素质和教师的教学水平,为学校实施素质教育提供保障。充分发挥评价的促进发展的功能,使评价的过程成为促进教学发展与提高的过程。"并把学生的"综合素质"目标概括为"基础性发展目标"和"学科学习目标"两个方面。其中,"基础性发展目标"又被具体化为六个方面:道德品质、公民素养、学习能力、交流与合作能力、运动与健康、审美与表现。[2]我国综合素质评价体系在国家政策层面系统确立起来。

2003年3月,教育部颁布《普通高中课程方案(实验)》,明确提出"建立发展性评价制度",具体内容包括:"实行学生学业成绩与成长记录相结合的综合评价方式。学校应根据目标多元、方式多样、注重过程的评价原则,综合运用观察、交流、测验、实际操作、作品展示、自评与互评等多种方式,为学生建立综合、动态的成长记录手册,全面反映学生的成长历程。"[3]这不仅使“综合素质评价”的理念系统贯彻于高中课程改革之中，而且明确指出了评价原则与具体方法。

这就是我国基础教育领域综合素质评价政策确立的大致历程。自2004年以后，该政策首先在“中考”改革中被广泛倡导和执行，进而在“高考”改革中进行局部尝试。

由上可见，综合素质评价是我国新课程改革的有机构成和自然延伸，是新课程理念的内在要求。新课程改革及相应的综合素质评价是我国新时期全面推进素质教育的根本举措。实践充分证明，凡深刻理解其本质并真诚实施综合素质评价的学校或地区，都取得了积极的效果，学生及教师素质获得了明显提升。

然而，由于对综合素质评价本质的诸多误解，伴随其推广和实施，也产生了种种不容忽视的问题：

第一，把综合素质评价变成传统纸笔测验的简单延伸，不改变评价理念和方法，只是增加评价内容，即由评价学科知识和技能延伸到评价道德品质、公民素养等“综合素质”。这实际上是变相支持和捍卫传统“应试教育”，所采用的评价改革策略是“用考试指挥素质教育”。这种观点和做法非但丝毫不能解决“应试教育”的积弊，反而雪上加霜。

第二，把“综合素质”理解为道德品质、公民素养、学习能力等不同种类“素质”的组合，其中每一类素质又被细分为若干“分目标”。综合素质评价就是以每一类“素质”及其“分目标”为“观测点”，建立“常模”，给出分数或等级。这种观点的依据是“人的全面发展理论”，“素质教育”就是“人的全面发展教育”。这显然是一种机械论、原子论的素质观。当前，许多地区的中考、高考改革即循此思路而行。这种观点和做法违背了素质教育的本质，忽视了每一个学生个性发展的独特性，无法解决我国教育的根本问题。

第三，把“综合素质”理解为某些素质，如认为综合素质评价就是对教育部规定的六类“基础性发展目标”的评价，而中高考、学业水平考试或会考则是对“学科学习目标”的评价，二者平分秋色，变成“两张皮”。这种观点和做法显然是上述机械论、原子论素质观的变种。

第四，把综合素质评价主要作为外部评价，使之成为中考、高考体系的一部分。它由此被人为赋予“高利害”性质，成为对学生进行强制分层的依据。直接后果是，在综合素质评价实践中形式主义、弄虚作假之风猖獗，产生许多负面效应，引发强烈社会不满。

这些问题可总体概括为关于综合素质评价的“变相应试教育观”、“工具主义素质观”与“外部评价观”。解决这些问题的基本出路在于重新理解综合素质评价的本质，并据此制定切实可行的实践策略。

## 二、综合素质评价是个性发展评价

综合素质评价是建构素质教育评价观的内在要求。而理解综合素质评价的本质，首先需要思考的是：应试教育的根本问题在哪里？素质教育的本质是什么？

应试教育及其评价体系的根本问题不在于只采用了“考试”这一种评价手段，也不在于仅仅评价了学科知识及技能这一类“素质”，而在于其根深蒂固的工具主义教育价值观。它首先把教育视为社会控制的工具。教育的职能蜕变为根据社会既有的统治秩序、意识形态、阶层结构、职业构成等等将学生区分开来并分别加以培养，以符合社会控制和统治的需要。其次，它把人视为控制的对象。教育的工具化同时意味着教师和学生的工具化。在工具主义教育价值观看来，人的素质不过是教育和社会控制的工具。就学生而言，其素质不仅可以被分割为“身”与“心”两个方面，而且每一方面都可以层层分割。分割的目的是为了层层控制、有效控制。因此，从工具主义教育价值观必然派生出“工具主义素质观”。再次，它采用目标取向的评价。基于“工具主义素质观”把人的素质从整体肢解为部分的过程，就是确定具体教育目标的过程。根据预定教育目标装配、控制课程与教学，并最终检验教育结果，这是工具化教育、应试教育的内在逻辑。在这里，评价起的作用是检验教育培养的“工具”是否合格。课程思想史上的“泰勒原理”、“布卢姆教育目标分类学”均属于目标取向的评价，其价值基础即为“工具理性”或“技术理性”。[4]在西方，这种评价观主要受“唯科学主义”、“社会工程思维”、“行为主义心理学”之影响。而我国应试教育的评价体系除受“唯科学主义”等影响外，还受我国源远流长的“考试文化”（主要代表是“科举文化”）和当代集权管理体制的影响。

素质教育的意义不在于培养某种或某些“素质”，如“创新精神”、“实践能力”、“道德品质”等，它在本质上是尊重每一个人个性发展的独特性与整体性并促进其实现。素质教育即追求人的个性发展的独特性与整体性的教育。[5]首先，它把教育视为社会的能动力量，而非被动适应社会的工具。教育不只是受社会制约和影响，还通过“批判意识”揭示社会存在的不公正和不平等，并通过“反思性实践”而积极改造社会。其次，它尊重每一个人的个性自由以及人与人之间的合作精神。人不是被控制的对象或被使用的工具，而是拥有自由个性和内在价值的独特整体。任何“素质”，只有放到个性整体中去观照才有意义，“割下来的手就不再是手”（黑格尔语）。素质教育所崇尚的是“整体主义素质观”。再次，它采用主体取向或解放取向的评价。这既包括对每一自由个性的欣赏与珍视，又包括对一切摧残个性自由的制度、规范和价值体系的反思与批判。这种评价追求的是“解放理性”，本质上是一种“自由实践”。[6]

既然素质教育的实质是个性发展教育，那么综合素质评价本质上就是个性发展评价。这至少包括下列内涵：

第一，综合素质评价的对象是每一个学生的个性整体。“综合素质”不是各类素质的“组合”、“组装”，不是“整体等于部分之和”，而是发现不同素质间的内在联系，使之融合起来，变成个性整体。首先，要基于整体思维评价每一个学生。学生的素质可以在理论上进行分析，但却无法在实践上去分解和还原。如果基于某种普遍的外部标准，无论是参照“常模”还是课程标准或“考试大纲”中的目标要求，评价学生的某种素质而不及其余，这本身就是使学生的个性片段化并使之扭曲、摧残的过程。其次，要基于复杂性思维评价学生素质。任何一种素质，对不同学生的个性发展而言,其意义是迥然不同的。同一种素质在不同学生之间是不可比的。只有将某种或某些素质与每一个学生个性发展的整体联系起来的时候,才产生教育意义。这是综合素质评价的一个重要基点。再次,要基于情境思维或认知评价学生个性。每一个学生的个性发展既处于与其周围环境的持续互动中,又处于其独特的个人生活史中。只有将综合素质评价植根于每一个学生的生活情境和生活史,才能更好地促进学生的个性发展。最后,要基于教育思维评价学生素质。综合素质评价的过程就是促进学生个性发展的过程。这意味着评价者既要发挥教育智慧在各种素质之间建立关系,使被肢解、破坏了的个性得到修复,又要有勇气保护学生个性,使未被肢解的个性保持原样并获得发展。

第二,综合素质评价的方法论是"欣赏性评价"。个性发展是"内在价值"。杜威曾说"内在价值是无价之宝(invaluable)"[7]。既是"无价之宝",那就不能比较,只能欣赏。因此,符合个性发展要求的评价是"欣赏性评价"。这自然也是符合素质教育理念的评价。[8]所谓"欣赏性评价",即对每一个学生的独特个性发自内心地欣赏,实实在在体验到其价值,敏锐感受到其发展潜能和需求,并提供恰当的帮助。综合素质评价的过程即是创造情境和条件让学生展示自己的个性,在彼此欣赏和体验中保护个性,在相互研讨和帮助中促进个性发展。

第三,综合素质评价允许学生选择自己的表现形式,展示自己的学习特长与个性独特性。学生个性发展的独特性不是抽象的,而是具体而鲜活地表现在学习过程中、学校生活的日常经验中。面对任何学科知识或共同生活经验,每一个学生不仅有自己的独特见解或个人经验,而且有表现自己见解和经验的独特方式。综合素质评价恰恰为每一个学生选择自己喜好的表现方式提供了空间。正是在个性化表现及相互间欣赏、学习和研究中,每一个学生自己的观点不断完善、个性特长日渐彰显。从这个意义上说,综合素质评价是一种"表现性评价"(performance assessment)。西方国家自20世纪80年代以后,为了帮助学生在学习过程中不断发展自己的个性化表现,兴起了"表现性评价运动",创造了"表现性评价体系"[9]。美国著名教育评价专家艾斯纳(Elliot W. Eisner)也曾说过:"在评定的新方式中,学生将不仅有机会对所学的东西构建他们自己的反应方式,他们也将有机会选择公布他们所学知识的方式。"[10]这充分表明,倡导个性发展评价已成为世界范围内教育评价领域中的时代精神。我国的综合素质评价正体现了这种精神。

需要特别指出的是,教育部在《关于积极推进中小学评价与考试制度改革的通知》中所规定的六类"基础性发展目标"以及源自各科课程标准的"学科学习目标"所提供的是理解综合素质评价的理论框架和基本线索,而非倡导一种机械论、原子论和工具论的素质观,也非主张把素质教育的目标层层分解并让目标和内容一一对应。实践中有的地方或学校甚至把文件中每一项目标下面具有说明、列举性质的内容变成更下位的目标并规定相应等级的"达成度",这显然严重背离了文件的精神和要求。首先,这些目标并未穷尽"综合素质"的全部,而是大致内容和基本要点。其次,这些目标彼此间并非割裂和对立,而是相互渗透和交叉的,如"道德品质”显然会渗透到其他任何素质之中，“学习能力”、审美能力也同样如此。再次，素质目标和学习内容之间也非一一对应的线性关系，因为一个目标可以通过多个内容来达到，一项内容也可同时指向多个目标。

总之，我们需要基于每一个学生个性发展的整体性和独特性来理解素质教育目标，开发评价任务，创设评价情境，展开评价过程。

## 三、综合素质评价是真实性、过程性评价

以促进学生个性发展为宗旨的综合素质评价必然面向学生真实的生活世界和学习过程，必然尊重教育过程的开放性、生成性和不可预测性，因而是真实性、过程性评价。

在西方，尤其是美国，20 世纪 90 年代以来最引人瞩目的评价新理念大概就是“真实性评价”(authentic assessment)。[11]“真实性源于评价什么是最重要的，而非评价什么是最方便的。”[12]现实中的许多评价往往出于管理和控制的方便而进行，它们脱离了学生真实的生活和个性发展需要，不仅是人为的、虚假的，而且是扭曲学生个性的、反教育的。评价需要走向真实——回归学生真实的生活世界、真实的学科知识和个性发展的真实需要。诚如马什(Collin J. Marsh)所言：“真实性评定认为课程必须以尽可能广泛的学习为指导。因此，课程本身应该根据它在多大程度上有利于发展学生的深刻理解力来评价，不仅是对学科的理解力，而且包括对自己生活的理解。”[13]真实性评价既是广阔的——从学科拓展到生活、从学校开放到社会，又是深刻的——包括人的思想、情感、探究与创造。

超越目标取向，走向过程取向，让教育过程、学习过程从僵化的预定目标中获得解放、实现自身的价值，是真实性评价的必然要求。因此，过程性评价是真实性评价的题中应有之义。这首先意味着要走出“从课程到教学再到评价”的线性回路，使课程、教学、评价变成三位一体，评价由此成为丰富多彩的教育过程的一部分，本身就具有教育价值。其次，要走出把评价视为过程开始前的预定目标与过程结束后的最终结果两相对照的做法，关注教育过程、学习过程本身的独特之处、“不可预测之物”及其教育价值，并把“预定目标”、“最终结果”均视为持续发展过程的一部分，体现其“过程性”。

“综合素质评价即真实性评价、过程性评价”这一命题，包括下列内涵：

第一，综合素质评价的内容及任务设计不仅体现学生的校内生活，还要体现校外生活，以及二者的内在联系。艾斯纳教授曾说过：“学校教育的目的不是保证学校的优秀，而是提高学生解决校内和校外问题的能力，甚至更普遍地说，是深化和拓展学生在日常生活中所能理解的意义。”[14]生活是一个整体。学生的生活经验也是一个整体。学生的学校生活、家庭生活、社会生活存在内在联系。杜威曾说，你把学生的经验关在学校大门之外，它会从窗子爬进来。传统纸笔测验的问题不仅在其形式的单一性，还在于其内容因脱离活生生的现实生活而变得虚假化、人为化。综合素质评价之“综合”的内涵还包括学生校内外生活的整合。这意味着学

校中一切知识的学习要植根于生活问题情境并据此设计评价任务、做出评价，使知识学习变成解决生活问题、承担生活责任的过程。与此同时，把学生参与社会实践和社区服务，在从事反思性实践的过程中发展实践能力和关爱社会的情感作为学校教育的核心内容并对其过程和结果做出评价。

第二，综合素质评价的设计不仅要关注学生对特定学习内容或任务所获得的结论，还要关注学生解决问题的过程及策略。传统的纸笔测验或其他所谓的“客观性测验”往往只评价学生是否得出了正确结论，而不关注学生如何获得此结论、其学习或思维的过程如何、解决问题的认知策略是什么，这很可能排除了个性发展中、也即教育中最重要的东西。综合素质评价的设计一定致力于让学生展开其学习或思维过程，呈现其解决问题的假设和策略，欣赏每一个学生对学习同一项内容、解决同一个问题的不同学习方式、思维风格和独特理解。既然“学会学习”比学会某种或某些具体知识和技能更重要，那针对学习过程或解决问题过程的评价就一定比对学习结论或结果的评价更重要。[15]

第三，综合素质评价的设计应包含一个问题有一个以上的正确解决方法或答案这样的内容。一个问题只有一个正确答案，这往往是封闭的“标准化测验”的特征。然而，无论是真实的理智生活还是日常生活，人们所发现的问题或遇到的困难往往存在多个解决问题的方法或答案。解决问题的过程不只是获得答案，还包括在多种可能性中明智地选择更好的方法、策略和方案。综合素质评价的一个重要特点是追求“理智的真实性”和“实践的适切性”。因此，无论是评价学生的学科学习，还是评价其生活实践学习，它都应设计存在多种解决方法或答案的评价任务，以真正培养学生的问题解决能力。

第四，综合素质评价的基本方法和形式是档案袋评价。所谓“档案袋评价”（portfolios assessment），是把学生的真实学习经历及相应的典型的、富有代表性的各类作品或其他材料作为证据，以对学生的学习和个性发展状况做出判断并加以改进的过程。如果说“真实性评价”是当今教育评价领域的核心理念的话，那么“档案袋评价”则是体现这一理念的基本形式和主要载体。正如马什所观察的那样：“20 世纪 90 年代中期，在美国，档案袋评价由于认知心理学的观点为人们所接受而成为一种主要的学业评定形式。”“对学生使用档案袋是真实性评定运动的中心。”[16]档案袋评价的显著特点是：(1)学生是档案袋的主要创造者和维护者，这不仅极大地提高了学生学习的兴趣和积极性，而且发展了学生的学习责任感，学生的发展特长和个性独特性由此获得真实而充分的体现；(2)学生持续建设自己的档案袋的过程，就是不断反思自己的学习过程、发展探究能力并形成学习兴趣和价值观的过程，档案袋由此实现了知识与技能、过程与方法、情感态度价值观等学习目标的整体融合；(3)学生建设自己的档案袋的过程，就是不断建构自己的课程的过程，档案袋即“学生的课程”，评价与课程因而融合；(4)教师研究学生档案袋的过程，就是不断研究、理解学生的学习和个性发展并给予指导的过程，档案袋即教学，评价和教学因而融合。总之，档案袋评价最好地体现了学习的真实性和过程性，并充分体现了学生个性发展的需求，因而是综合素质评价的基本方法和形式。

就我国当前教育改革实践而言，综合素质评价已深陷目标取向与结果取向的泥沼中。这一方面背离了综合素质评价最可宝贵的品质：将评价植根于生活情境和学习过程之中，使评价本身富有教育性并成为教育过程；另一方面又因为过度追求结果的完美而导致评价的虚假化、异化与反教育化。走出这些误区的关键是始终体现综合素质评价的真实性与过程性。这意味着要到教育内部、到学校里和课堂上去实现综合素质评价的理想。

## 四、综合素质评价是内部评价

综合素质评价究竟是内部评价，还是外部评价？谁是评价的主体？对此问题的回答不仅关系到综合素质评价的命运，而且深深影响我国教育评价改革的方向。

素质教育是追寻教育内在价值的教育，综合素质评价是内部评价。由于我国深陷应试教育渊薮中，教育日益工具化。教育工具化的过程就是教育被动适应、依附社会既有的意识形态和制度安排、不断失去自身内在价值的过程。以中考、高考为核心的各类外部评价之所以日益膨胀并束缚教育发展，根源在于教育工具价值膨胀、内在价值泯灭。因此，我国教育评价改革的根本方向是走向内部评价，即珍视并发展教育的内在价值。中心任务是建立每一所学校的"校本评价体系"。

倡导综合素质评价是我国教育走向内部评价、找回久已失落的内在价值的重要举措。由于综合素质评价植根于真实教育情境、关注学生学习和问题解决的具体过程并以每一个学生的个性发展为目的，其评价主体必然包括教师和学生，评价发生的主要场所是一个个班级、一所所学校。综合素质评价是内部评价，是"校本评价体系"的有机构成。

放眼世界，无论是类似"真实性评价"、"过程性评价"、"为了学习的评价"等评价理念或思潮，还是类似"表现性评价"、"档案袋评价"、"研讨式评价"等方法或策略，均旨在体现教育的内在价值，倡导内部评价。再从教育评价制度设计来看，绝大多数国家的做法是既从制度上保证学校内部评价的独立性与合法性，又在科学上保证外部评价的专业性。有少数国家（如瑞士）甚至只有学校内部评价，大学招生主要依据学生的学习经历而进行，不再单独组织所谓"高考"。

"综合素质评价即内部评价"的内涵至少包括如下三个方面：

第一，教师和学生是综合素质评价的主体。教师不再是以中考、高考为核心的各类外部评价的准备者、复制者和依附者，而是评价主体。无论是综合素质评价的项目，还是其具体内容，教师均可根据学生的年龄特征、个性差异以及自己的专业特长创造性地开发与实施。尤为重要的是，教师还是学生自我评价和相互评价的指导者。学生不再只是各类外部评价的客体，不再被动等待别人给自己"下结论"，而开始学会基于证据对自己的学习过程、个性特长与不足、未来的职业生涯等做出判断与选择。学生还可以对同伴、教师、家长、学校生活、社会生活等方面做出评价。总之，教师和学生成为评价主体，这是综合素质评价所带来的最重要的评价理念变化之一。

为充分发挥教师和学生的主体性，综合素质评价需要植根于鲜活的教育过程，以及教师和学生的现实生活情境。用加拿大著名课程理论家奥凯（Ted T. Aoki）的术语来说，综合素质评价是“情境解释性评价”（situational interpretive evaluation），这种评价中的认知方式是“情境认知”（situational knowing）。“指向于情境解释性评价的评价者必须牢牢把握该评价的两个特征：（1）人们对所经历的每一个情境都产生个人意义；（2）人们以不同的方式解释同一个事件。”[17]学生对所经历的学习过程和生活情境的个人意义是综合素质评价的核心价值。这集中表现为学生创建和发展学习档案袋过程中的独特作品、独特表现和个人解释。

第二，在综合素质评价中，教师和学生合作建构教育意义。综合素质评价既尊重教师和学生各自的主体性，又植根于关系之中，植根于教师与学生的合作、互动之中。传统纸笔测验或“客观性测验”的根本问题不只是用单一手段、片面评价学生素质并扭曲学生个性，还在于它体现并不断复制着一种割裂目的与手段、设置评价主体与评价客体并使之对立起来的“工具主义评价观”。这种评价观的典型特征是“二元论”。综合素质评价所体现的是“交往评价观”。在这里评价者与被评价者之间不再是主客体关系，而是交互主体性的对话关系。评价即评价者与被评价者通过交往、对话、协商而合作建构意义的过程。美国著名评价专家古巴（E. G. Guba）和林肯（Y. S. Lincoln）将这种评价观称为“第四代评价”（fourth generation evaluation），其基本特征是“协商建构意义”。[18]奥凯说：“在情境解释性评价框架中，评价者最关心的活动是人与人之间的交往。”“评价者……必须进入评价情境，与人们展开交互主体性对话。”[19]

综合素质评价中的交互主体性对话过程即是不同教育内部人员视角的互动与融合过程。面对一个学生的学习与个性发展状况，教师的看法是什么？不同教师的观点之间有哪些差异和共同之处？家长的看法是什么？学生同伴的看法是什么？学生本人如何认识和评价自己？学生的自我评价、同伴互评、教师评价、家长评价等视角的互动、对话、协商、融合过程，是评价，更是学习与发展。这种评价、学习与发展的三位一体，是综合素质评价应达和能达的境界。

第三，综合素质评价与外部评价的互动、结合，构成素质教育评价体系。综合素质评价与中考、高考等外部评价是什么关系？综合素质评价能够纳入中考、高考吗？回答这些问题既关系到我国教育评价改革的方向，又影响我国素质教育体系的整体构建。

作为一种具体评价方式的综合素质评价与中考、高考等外部评价存在重要区别。前者所追求的是教育的内在价值，核心是关注每一个学生个性发展的独特性；后者则追求教育的工具价值，如满足大学学术发展的需要或适应某种社会职业岗位的需要，它自然以特定情境的需要为标准对所有学生进行比较，以选取最适合某种情境的学生，它强调的是学生的工具价值、比较价值，关注的是不同学生之间在某些方面的共同性。前者强调的是评价情境中不同评价主体的合作解释与共同建构，后者则主要基于源自测量学的量化评价手段，追求评价的客观性；前者主要是过程性、形成性评价，后者主要是结果性、终结性评价；前者以档案袋评价为基本形式，后者则主要是学业成绩测验。

综合素质评价与中考、高考等外部评价又存在内在联系。首先，教育的内在价值与工具价值之间相互依存。教育当然要适应社会选拔人才等工具性需要，但却不能把人当工具，不能以摧毁学生的个性发展和教师的专业成长为代价。教育内在价值的实现是其所有工具价值发挥的前提。皮之不存，毛将焉附？另一方面，让教育变成生活、不断促进学生个性发展和教师专业成长等教育内在价值的实现又依赖于现实社会条件。教育在保持自身独立性的同时要向社会开放，积极适应社会需求并发挥改变社会的功能。教育在与外部社会生活的积极互动中不断丰富自身的社会性，社会性由此成为自身内在价值的有机构成。其次，学生个性发展是综合素质评价与中考、高考等外部评价的共同目标。综合素质评价所体现和追求的个性发展观显然适用于各类外部评价。促进学生个性发展不仅是外部评价改革的永恒方向，而且是衡量一种外部评价是否具有教育性的基本标准。综合素质评价与各类外部评价的区别不在于是否促进个性发展，而在于促进学生个性发展的方式、方法和具体功能的区别。再次，综合素质评价与中考、高考等外部评价之间可以相互促进。综合素质评价中关注过程、关注情境的评价理念可以为外部评价的任务设计提供借鉴。而外部评价的科学化诉求，如关注评价的“信度”、“效度”等，亦可对综合素质评价的科学化产生重要启示。

我国构建素质教育评价体系的关键是：让综合素质评价与中考、高考等外部评价既发挥各自独特功能，又彼此互动、协同发展。综合素质评价是内部评价，评价主体是教师和学生，评价对象或内容为每一个学生素质的整体发展，评价过程渗透于教育全过程。因此，不能用“客观性测验”等学业成绩测验的方式来进行综合素质评价。要深刻意识到，素质教育优先重视的是那些不能用“客观性测验”来测量的“素质”，如人的道德品质、审美情趣、生活责任感等等。如果把“道德品质”、“公民素养”、“学习能力”、“交流与合作能力”、“运动与健康”、“审美与表现”这些相互联系并交织在一起的“素质”强行割裂开来并进一步细化为更下位的目标，然后分别进行“等级制”或“百分制”的评价，根据学生成绩决定是否上高中或大学以及上何种层次的高中或大学，这种做法不仅增加了学生的负担，而且进一步扭曲了学生的个性发展。当前我国许多地方的“评价改革”深陷这一误区。问题的根本不在于科学发展尚未达到能够测量人的某些“素质”的程度，而在于人的个性发展在本质上具有不可分割性、不可测量性。科学测量的手段无论如何进步，都对人的个性发展的整体评价鞭长莫及，这是综合素质评价的存在依据。

因此，将综合素质评价纳入中考、高考并不是改变综合素质评价的性质，将其变成外部评价，用学业成绩测验的方式评价人的“综合素质”，得出类似“用考试指挥素质教育”这类变相应试教育的言论和做法。相反，将综合素质评价纳入中考、高考意味着首先尊重其内部评价的性质，深入学校内部和教育过程做评价，通过学习档案袋的创建和延续而真实和整体地反映每一个学生的个性发展状况。当学生一个阶段的学习过程结束时，以学生的学习档案袋为依据，将学生的个性发展特长与即将进入的学校或大学的性质、特色做比较，以决定学生要进入什么学校或大学、选择何种专业领域来学习。这样看来，将综合素质评价纳入中考、高考意味着我国招生制度性质的改变：由单纯的外部评价转变为内部评价与外部评价相结合。学生自己的意愿与教师的判断开始在中考、高考中得到体现。高等学校和社会人才选拔不再以漠视或牺牲教育的内在价值为代价，反而以尊重教育的内在价值为前提。

另一方面，传统的中考、高考等外部评价的改革方向是走向专业化。这意味着要逐步与各级教育行政权力分离，由教育测量与评价的专业人员依据科学标准和专业程序从事外部评价，特别是"高利害"的中考与高考。同时，各类外部评价要以促进学生个性发展为改革方向和原则，更加具有开放性、选择性和探究性。

总之，构建以综合素质评价为核心的教育内部评价体系，走向外部评价的专业化、科学化，让每一个学生的个性发展获得充分保障，使学校教育的个人发展与社会发展两种功能得到统一与融合，是我国教育评价改革的基本方向。

## 五、结论

我国方兴未艾的综合素质评价既是一种评价观，又是一种具体评价方式。作为一种评价观，它欣赏教育的内在价值，追求学生的个性发展，倡导交往、对话和意义建构，强调评价的真实性与过程性。作为一种评价方式，它是以教师和学生为评价主体的教育内部评价或校本评价，其基本呈现形态是学生的学习档案袋，它伴随学生学习的全过程，并具有鲜明的个人生活史色彩。

作为一种评价观的综合素质评价，适用于所有教育评价方式，包括中考、高考、会考、学业水平考试等外部评价。作为一种具体评价方式，它主要适用于校本评价体系的建构。

我国当前综合素质评价改革实践存在的主要问题，一是未能实现评价观的转型，未把学生个性发展视为评价的根本目的，依然延续"工具主义评价观"，只是拓展了评价内容，补充了一些人为割裂的所谓"素质"，导致了"变相的应试教育"；二是未能实现评价方式的改变，未使综合素质评价成为学校内部评价，教师与学生未成为评价主体，综合素质评价成为外部评价的另一种形式，由此导致了"强化的外部评价"。走出"变相的应试教育"和"强化的外部评价"这两个误区，是我国当前教育评价改革迫在眉睫的任务。

参考文献

[1] 中共中央国务院.基础教育课程改革纲要(试行),2001.

[2] 中华人民共和国教育部.关于积极推进中小学评价与考试制度改革的通知,2002.

[3] 中华人民共和国教育部.普通高中课程方案(实验),2003.

[4] 李雁冰.课程评价论[M].上海:上海教育出版社,2002:59.

[5] 李雁冰.关于素质教育评价的理论问题[J].教育发展研究,2009(24).
[6] Pinar, W.F. & Irwin, R.L.(2005). *Curriculum in a New Key: The Collected Works of Ted T. Aoki*. New Jersey: Lawrence Erlbaum Associates, Inc:144-150.
[7] [美]约翰·杜威.民主主义与教育[M].王承绪,译.北京:人民教育出版社,2001:256.
[8] 李雁冰.关于素质教育评价的理论问题[J].教育发展研究,2009(24).
[9] [美]比尔·约翰逊.学生表现评定手册[M].李雁冰,主译.上海:华东师范大学出版社,2001.
[10][14][15] [美]埃利奥特·W.艾斯纳.教育想象——学校课程设计与评价[M].李雁冰,主译.北京:教育科学出版社,2008:216,210,211.
[11] See Wiggins, G. (1998). *Educative Assessment*. San Francisco, Jossey-Bass; Eisner, E. W. (1993). Reshaping Assessment in Education: Some Criteria in Search of Practice. *Journal of Curriculum Studies*, 25(3):219-233.
[12][13][16] [澳]科林·马什.理解课程的关键概念[M].徐佳,吴刚平,译.北京:教育科学出版社,2009:65,67.
[17][19] Pinar, W.F. & Irwin, R.L.(2005). *Curriculum in a New Key: The Collected Works of Ted T. Aoki*. New Jersey: Lawrence Erlbaum Associates, Inc:143.
[18] Guba, E.G. & Lincoln, Y.W.(1989). *Fourth Generation Evaluation*. Newbury Park, CA, Sage.

## On the Essence of Comprehensive Literacy Evaluation

Yanbing Li

**Abstract**: Comprehensive literacy evaluation (CLE) is both an evaluation orientation and an evaluation method. As an evaluation orientation, CLE is the basic orientation of evaluation system for quality education. As an evaluation method, CLE can positively interact with and be connected to the entrance examination for high schools and colleges. All of them form the basic content of evaluation system for quality education. The essence of CLE is evaluation for personal development, authentic and developmental assessment, and insider evaluation. The main mistake of evaluation reform in China's current education is "instrumentalist literacy and evaluation", which changes CLE into outsider and instrumentalist evaluation, resulting in another kind of education to tests.

**Keywords**: comprehensive literacy evaluation; personal development; authentic assessment; insider evaluation; instrumental literacy

# 布卢姆认知目标分类学（修订版）视野下的课堂评价

王小明

【摘要】布卢姆认知目标分类学(修订版)主张从知识与认知过程两个维度的结合来厘定认知领域的教学目标,这一思想不仅有助于我们从知识和认知过程两方面来明确课堂评价要评价什么,还可以通过对教学目标、教学活动、教学评价的分析,判断三者的一致性,从而对教学的有效性做出评价。

【关键词】课堂评价;知识;认知过程;目标、教学与评价的一致性

【作者简介】王小明/上海华东师范大学课程与教学研究所副教授

课堂评价是课堂教学的一项重要工作,有助于教育工作者了解教学质量、诊断学生的学习困难、促进学生的学习。为了做好这项工作,教育评价的研究人员一直致力于研发课堂评价的具体技术和工具,2001 年修订出版的布卢姆认知目标分类学也体现了教育评价研究人员在这方面所做的工作。这次修订的认知目标分类学融合了课程与教学、认知心理学、测量与评价三个领域专家的智慧,它从新的视角为我们阐释了课程(教学)目标、课堂教学过程及课堂评价,其中的基本思想对我们做好课堂评价不无启发。

## 一、布卢姆认知目标分类学(修订版)的基本思想

布卢姆认知目标分类学(修订版)深受当代认知心理学研究和发展的影响。认知心理学主要研究知识的习得、储存、提取和应用,因而在有关"知识"的研究方面积累了丰富的成果。修订者们充分利用认知心理学在这方面的积淀,对课程之父泰勒提出的从内容和行为两方面来界定课程教学目标的思想做了发展,即用认知心理学的"知识"取代"内容",用学习者头脑中执行的"认知过程"取代"行为",于是,在修订版的体系中,课程与教学的目标其实涉及知识和认知过程两种成分的结合:学习者对教材中的知识执行一定的认知过程,或者学习者对教材中的知识达到一定的掌握程度(用认知过程来表示)就是教育目标;仅有教材中的知识或仅有学习者认知过程都构不成完整意义上的课程与教学的目标。这一观点其实反映了认知心理学对知识与能力关系的认识,即用认知心理学家所言的"知识"来解释认知能力,或者认知领域中的习得的能力本质上是学习者对不同类型知识的掌握[1]。

在用知识与认知过程的结合来解释认知领域教学目标的基础上,修订者们综合认知心理学对知识类型的研究,同时又继承和发展了布卢姆 1956 年认知目标分类学的思想,区分出了

教材中的四种类型的知识和学习者可执行的六种认知过程，从而为我们提供了一个从知识与认知过程两个维度来厘定教学目标的框架（见表1）：

**表1　布卢姆认知目标分类学（修订版）的两个维度**

| 知识维度 | 认知过程维度 | | | | | |
|---|---|---|---|---|---|---|
| | 记忆 | 理解 | 运用 | 分析 | 评价 | 创造 |
| 事实性知识 | | | | | | |
| 概念性知识 | | | | | | |
| 程序性知识 | | | | | | |
| 元认知知识 | | | | | | |

根据修订者们的观点，这一两维的分类表不仅适用于分析教学目标，还可用来分析教学过程、测量与评价以及判断教学目标、教学活动与教学评价三者之间一致性的程度。这就是说，这一新的分类也可用来分析、研究课堂评价的有关问题。从这一认识出发，本文从学生学习结果的评价以及教师教学的评价两个方面来阐释布卢姆认知目标分类学（修订版）在课堂评价这一问题上带给我们的新认识。

## 二、运用布卢姆认知目标分类学（修订版）评价学生的学习结果

学习结果即教学目标，是经过教学后，教师期望学生能做什么。修订版对期望学生做什么给出了细致的描述，即学生针对教材中的知识采取何种认知过程。这样看来，对学习结果的评价要针对知识与认知过程的结合来进行。在具体的课堂评价中，评价的首要问题不是确定采用什么样的评价技术或程序，而是弄清楚要评价的究竟是什么。布卢姆认知目标分类学（修订版）对认知领域的能力从知识和认知过程两方面加以分析，这对于我们深入认识课堂评价要评什么这一问题并进而设计课堂评价很有启发。很多时候，课堂评价对象的含糊，主要原因在于评价者没有明晰知识与认知过程这两种成分。

一种情况是，要评价的学习结果中知识成分很清楚，但由于在认知过程成分上把握不准而导致评价的含糊或缺乏针对性，因而这时评价设计的重点就在于确定学生对知识的掌握程度或执行的认知过程。

在数学、科学（物理、化学）等学科中，教材中明确列出了需要学生学习的学科知识，这些知识按修订版的观点，涉及事实性知识、概念性知识、程序性知识、元认知知识四种类型。在对学生的学习结果进行评价时，教师常犯的错误是将学生针对这些知识而采取的认知过程限制为“记忆”，具体的体现是用填空、简答、选择、搭配等题型考察学生是否能正确回答或再认教材中的知识。对于学科中较为零碎、具体的事实性知识来说，这样的评价无可厚非。但对于较概括的概念性知识、程序性知识（如数学学科中的定理、计算步骤），如果评价还定位在记忆这种水平，这会给学生的学习造成不良的定向，学生可能会机械地记住了这些概括程度较高的规律

性知识，但不理解，也不会运用，这显然不是我们要追求的学习结果。因此，在知识成分明确的条件下，评价的设计的重点是确定与知识相对应的认知过程。

如数学教科书中有"点到直线的距离公式"的教学内容。学生学完这些部分内容后，我们应如何对他们进行评价？从知识类型的角度看，这里的教学内容属于概念性知识，要明确评价的学习结果是什么，就需要进一步确定与这类知识相应的认知过程是什么。首先，教学结束之后，我们想知道学生是否能记住这一公式，这里的认知过程便是"记忆"。其次，我们不期望学生仅仅记住这一公式，还要知道这一公式为什么是这样，即知道公式不是人为规定的，而是一步一步地有根据地推导出来的，这里涉及的是"理解"这一认知过程。此外，我们还期望学生能用这一公式去实际计算某一点到直线的距离，这里涉及的认知过程便是"运用"。于是，教学之后对学生的评价就基本明确了：我们要考察学生对概念性知识（点到直线的距离公式）的记忆、理解和运用，相应的检测形式分别是让学生默写出该公式、口述或实际演示该公式是如何得来的、实际计算某一点到某一直线的距离。

又如，数学教科书中有关"图形的平移、轴对称、旋转"的内容。这些内容涉及一些概念性知识（如"平移"的概念）和一些程序性知识（如如何做出一个图形的轴对称图形）。在评价学生的学习结果时，我们期望他们针对这些知识执行哪些认知过程呢？一种较简单的要求是让学生理解概念性知识和执行程序性知识。在测验时可以要求学生举出日常生活中平移、旋转、轴对称图形的例子；可以要求他们画出给定图形的轴对称图形或平移、旋转后的图形。另一种较复杂的要求是让学生执行"创造"这一认知过程，即以轴对称、平移、旋转的概念性知识和程序性知识为基础，学生设计出较为复杂的图案，这一图案是学生综合运用有关的概念性知识和程序性知识后创造出来的。在这种情况下，相应的测验可以要求学生去解决实际问题，如为窗帘设计图案。在这种测验形式中，知识与认知过程的结合方式不同于较简单的记忆、理解、运用等认知过程与知识结合的方式，后者的结合中认知过程要作用于所学习的知识，而这里的结合则是学生基于各种知识去分析、评价、创造另一个对象、事物或假设（如学生基于轴对称、平移、旋转的知识去创造窗帘的图案）。在这种评价形式中，通常要求学生针对一定的产品、对象执行相应的认知过程，而相关的知识则是认知过程执行的基础，评价的重点是学生能否按照各种知识去执行某一种或几种认知过程。

不同的认知过程往往需要特定的评价形式，修订者们对此做了总结和梳理（见表2）。在明确了课堂上评价学生学习结果所涉及的知识与认知过程成分之后，便可以参照修订者们提供的建议选择和设计评价的具体形式了[2]。

**表2　与六种认知过程相对应的评价形式**

| 认知过程 | 评 价 形 式 |
|---|---|
| 记忆 | 判断正误，匹配，选择，问答，填空 |

续 表

| 认知过程 | 评 价 形 式 |
| --- | --- |
| 理解 | 建构式题目(提供解释、例子),选择题,分类,类比,推理,重新设计,预测,检测故障 |
| 运用 | 针对熟悉或不熟悉的问题执行程序,程序和答案对评价而言都重要 |
| 分析 | 建构式题目和选择题 |
| 评价 | 给学生提供自己或他人的产品、创造、过程,学生依据标准来判断 |
| 创造 | 建构式题目,要求学生生成多种方案、计划 |

另一种情况是,要评价的学习结果中,认知过程成分较明确,而相应的知识成分却不是很清楚,因而评价的重点应放在明确知识成分上。

在语文、历史等学科的评价中,经常可以见到要求学生进行分析、评价的情况,如分析课文,评价历史人物和历史事件等。在这些评价题目中,要求学生执行的认知过程(如分析、评价)及认知过程作用的对象(如课文、历史人物)是清楚的,但执行认知过程的知识基础不是很清楚,如"评价李鸿章"这一题目中,涉及的认知过程是"评价",认知过程作用的对象是历史人物李鸿章,但从知识与认知过程结合的方式来看,评价这种较复杂的认知过程与知识相结合的方式应是基于某些类型的知识或标准(一种概念性知识)来评价某一对象,题目中要求学生基于什么样的知识或标准没有明确规定,在对学生做出的评价进行评判时,我们会遇到如何确定学生的何种评价为优,何种评价为劣这一问题。如果我们对测验题目中"评价"这种认知过程基于的知识有了较为明确的认识(如基于历史唯物主义的立场、基于有关李鸿章的历史事实等知识),那么,评判学生做出的评价这一问题也就有了明确的解决方向,而不会对学生随意的、漫无边际的评价也给予好的等级。

又如学生学习了一篇课文,我们要评价他们归纳或概括段落大意的能力,如何评价这种能力呢?这需要我们从"概括段落大意的能力"这一目标所涉及的知识与认知过程成分去寻找答案。这里的知识是什么?认知过程是什么?作为概括能力的知识成分,应当是归纳段落大意的程序,具体某篇课文的某段段意并不是这种知识。如语文特级教师潘凤湘提出了一种概括段落大意的方法:先找出这一段涉及的基本概念,而后再在基本概念上加上修饰或限制成分,便构成了段意。如"我们的课桌长 1.1 米,宽 0.6 米,高 0.8 米"。这一段的基本概念是"尺码",修饰成分是"我们的课桌",于是段意就是"我们课桌的尺码"[3]。与归纳段意相应的认知过程是"运用",于是,对归纳课文段意的能力这一目标,我们可以将其解释成"运用程序性知识",当然这里的程序性知识是归纳段意的程序,包括但不限于潘凤湘提出的程序。因而评价学生的这一能力时,我们要把评价的重点放在对程序性知识运用的评价上,不仅要看学生归纳的段意是否准确,还要看他们对归纳程序的执行情况,如是否先选定基本概念,而后再加上修饰成分。这一点正如修订者们所言的,答案和程序的执行对评价来说都很重要。正好像在数学学科评价学生解一元二次方程的能力,对测验题"$x^2+2x-3=0$,求 $x=?$",我们关注的不应只是学生最后求得的 $x$ 是否正确，还要看他是否运用了因式分解来求解的程序。在数学学科中，测题中涉及的知识成分很容易确定，但在语文等学科中，这类知识成分往往比较含糊，因而评价设计的重点是明确教学目标中涉及的知识成分。

### 三、运用布卢姆认知目标分类学(修订版)评价教师的教学

“有效教学”是当前对教学的一种追求。在修订者们看来，落实有效教学的理念，就需要做到教学目标、教学活动、教学评价三者的一致。当三者高度一致时，说明教学的效率高；反之，教学就是低效的。修订版还借助知识与认知过程的两维表格形式，为我们提供了一种相对直观的评价教学有效性的工具或技术。在两维表格中，分别就知识和认知过程两个维度将教学目标、教学活动与教学评价置于表中的方格内，一般来说，如果三者都落在一个格子内，则三者的一致性最高；如果三者散落在不同的格子里，说明三者之间的一致性程度较低，教学的效率也低。

如上《奇妙的桥》一课，教师制定的教学目标是，能仿照课文第二、三、四节的格式，介绍各种奇妙的桥。教学过程是让学生自读课文二、三、四节，师生讨论交流，得出课文在写玻璃桥、纸桥、盐桥时都是先用设问句，然后介绍造桥材料、桥的长宽、载重量等特点。在写桥的长宽、载重量时，或者用数字直接描写，或者通过人的感受来写。最后在对学生进行评价时，教师要求学生在纸上画出自己设计的桥。

如何用两维表的形式评价教师的教学呢？首先，要把教学目标归入到两维表的格子中。教学目标只有一个，涉及段落的组织格式，这是一种概念性知识，相应的认知过程是“运用”，因而目标可放入“运用概念性知识”的格子中。教学活动是结合课文二、三、四节的学习，引导学生认识到三节共同的组织方式，其中涉及的知识类型仍是段落组织的概念性知识，相应的认知过程则是“理解”，因而教学活动主要落在“理解概念性知识”的格子中。最后的评价要求学生设计桥梁，这里涉及的是“创造”这一认知过程。执行这一过程的知识基础除了有关桥的事实性知识、概念性知识外，还有绘画的程序性知识，因而最后的课堂评价属于基于事实性知识、概念性知识、程序性知识的创造。显然，评价中要求的知识与目标和教学活动中涉及的知识没有多大关联。教学目标、教学活动、教学评价的分类情况总结见表 3。

**表 3 《奇妙的桥》一课的教学情况分析**

| 知识维度 | 认知过程维度 | | | | | |
|---|---|---|---|---|---|---|
| | 记忆 | 理解 | 运用 | 分析 | 评价 | 创造 |
| 事实性知识 | | | | | | 课堂评价 |
| 概念性知识 | | 教学活动 | 教学目标 | | | 课堂评价 |
| 程序性知识 | | | | | | 课堂评价 |
| 元认知知识 | | | | | | |

从表中可以看出，这一教学的教学目标、教学活动、教学评价落在不同的格子里，三者的一致性较低。如何对教学进行修改才能提高三者的一致性呢？在教学活动中，可以增加让学生按段落格式描写桥的练习活动，在进行课堂评价时，可以要求学生按照段落格式写出或口头描述自己将来要建设的桥，这样，教学活动中便有了对概念性知识的运用，课堂评价也涉及到对概念性知识的运用，教学目标、教学活动与教学评价三者的一致性也因此而有所提高，进而改善教学效率。

但是，我们不能机械地认为，如果目标、教学活动、评价不在一个格子内，三者的一致性肯定就低。有时，教学活动并没有落在目标的分类格子中，但三者的一致性仍是很高的，这主要是由于教学活动通过较为复杂的认知过程（如分析、评价、创造）促进了较简单的认知过程（如记忆、理解、运用）的缘故，这种情况在实际的教学中是很常见的，在分析教学一致性的时候需要我们对此给予特别关注。如教学“一元二次方程的求根公式”，教学目标是“1.理解一元二次方程的求根公式”、“2.会用一元二次方程的求根公式解一元二次方程”，这两个目标前者涉及“理解概念性知识”，后者涉及“运用程序性知识”。教学的过程则是在学生复习用已学过的配方法解某一具体的一元二次方程基础上，学生用配方的方法来解一个一般的一元二次方程 $ax^2+bx+c=0(a\neq 0)$。具体步骤如下（教学活动 1）：

$$x^2+\frac{b}{a}x+\frac{c}{a}=0$$

$$x^2+\frac{b}{a}x=-\frac{c}{a}$$

$$x^2+\frac{b}{a}x+\left(\frac{b}{2a}\right)^2=-\frac{c}{a}+\left(\frac{b}{2a}\right)^2$$

$$\left(x+\frac{b}{2a}\right)^2=\frac{b^2-4ac}{4a^2}$$

当 $b^2-4ac\geqslant 0$ 时，$x+\dfrac{b}{2a}=\pm\dfrac{\sqrt{b^2-4ac}}{2a}$

$$x_{1,2}=\frac{-b\pm\sqrt{b^2-4ac}}{2a}$$

当 $b^2-4ac<0$ 时，方程无实数根。

接下来的教学活动（教学活动 2）是运用公式解一些方程，如 $(x+3)(x-4)=-6$，$2x^2+1$ 与 $4x^2-2x-5$ 互为相反数，则 $x=$ ________，并归纳用公式法解一元二次方程的步骤。最后则布置一些解一元二次方程的作业作为评价，如解方程 $x^2-14|x|+24=0$[4]。

从知识与认知过程结合的角度看，教学活动 1 涉及学生基于配方法解方程的程序性知识创造出一元二次方程的求根公式，但学生的这一创造活动，其目的是促进其对求根公式的理解，虽然对目标和教学活动分析没有落在同一个格子里，但这部分的教学活动仍与第一个目标有较高的一致性，都是致力于"理解概念性知识"。教学活动 2 涉及归纳并运用公式法解方程的步骤，从两维分类的角度看，属于"运用程序性知识"。最后的评价也针对的是"运用程序性知识"这一目标。目标、教学活动与评价的分类情况见表 4。

**表 4 "一元二次方程的求根公式"的教学情况分析**

| 知识维度 | 认知过程维度 | | | | | |
|---|---|---|---|---|---|---|
| | 记忆 | 理解 | 运用 | 分析 | 评价 | 创造 |
| 事实性知识 | | | | | | |
| 概念性知识 | | 教学目标 1 | | | | |
| 程序性知识 | | | 教学目标 2<br>教学活动 2<br>课堂评价 | | | 教学活动 1 |
| 元认知知识 | | | | | | |

从表中可看出，在第二个目标"运用程序性知识"上，目标、教学活动与评价高度一致，但在第一个目标上，虽然目标和教学活动分散在不同格子里，但二者还是有较高一致性的，都致力于"理解概念性知识"，不过是通过较复杂的认知过程来促进较简单的认知过程的。这种通过教学中运用较复杂的认知过程以促进学生对相关知识执行较简单的认知过程，在语文教学中更为常见。如教学过程中让学生经过对课文中具体词句的分析、比较、评价，以促进学生理解作者是如何根据写作目的、要表达的思想感情选用适当词语这一规律的(一种概念性知识)。因此，在用两维表评价教学时，既要利用两维表直观的特点来判断，又要细致分析目标、教学活动、教学评价三者之间在知识与认知过程上的关系，这样才能对教学作出客观的评价。

可见，布卢姆认知目标分类学(修订版)指导下的课堂评价，核心的思想是用知识和认知过程的结合来解释课堂评价题目的设计以及对教学有效性的评价。要想用好这一新的目标分类学指导课堂评价，就要牢牢把握知识与认知过程的结合这一主线，这是需要我们特别注意的。

参考文献

[1] 皮连生.智育心理学[M].北京:人民教育出版社,1996:41—42.

[2] 安德森,等.学习,教学与评估的分类学——布卢姆教育目标分类学修订版[M].皮连生,等,译.上海:华东师范大学出版社,2008:61—67.

[3] 潘凤湘.我的教读法[M].南昌:江西教育出版社,1993:108.

[4] 马维民,孟令奇.新课程理念下的创新教学设计(初中数学)[M].长春:东北师范大学出版社,2002:51—53.

# Classroom Assessment in the Perspective of Revised Taxonomy of Bloom's Cognitive Objective

Xiaoming Wang

**Abstract**: The revised taxonomy of Bloom's cognitive objective argues that instructional objectives in cognitive domain can be defined by links between knowledge types and cognitive processes. This idea contributes not only to clarify what we want to assess our students, but also to judge the alignment among objectives, activities and assessments.

**Keywords**: classroom assessment; knowledge; cognitive process; the alignment among objectives; activities and assessments

# 学业成就评价与课程标准一致性的理论、模型、方法

## ——基于多领域的实践研究与反思

张雨强　张志红　焦传玲　李　伟　周传昌

【摘要】评价与标准一致性研究源于对高质量教育的追求，主要有韦伯模式、实施课程调查模式、成就公司模式、基础教育协会模式。其中韦伯模式的分析维度有四个：知识类别一致性、知识深度一致性、知识广度一致性、知识分布平衡性。应用韦伯模式，课题组进行了初中化学、高中化学、高中英语的学业成就评价与课程标准的一致性分析，以及初中化学教材习题与课程标准的一致性分析。研究发现，我国基础教育的评价与课程标准的一致性在整体上有待提升。通过中考命题者评价素养调查，本文也探讨了学业成就评价与课程标准一致性的影响因素。

【关键词】学业成就评价；课程标准；一致性；评价与标准一致性；评价素养

【作者简介】张雨强/教育部基础教育课程研究曲阜师范大学中心兼职研究员
张志红/西藏大学理学院教师，焦传玲/山东枣庄四中教师
李伟/山东日照开发区中学教师、曲阜师范大学化学与化工学院教育硕士
周传昌/山东枣庄市教育局教研室教研员

评价与标准一致性研究源于对高质量教育的追求，目前比较成熟的有韦伯模式（Webb model）、实施课程调查模式（Surveys of Enacted Curriculum model）、成就公司模式（Achieve Inc. model）、基础教育协会模式（Council for Basic Education model）。评估基础教育课程改革的整体质量、为新课程推进与完善提供建议，是目前我国基础教育课程改革的工作重点。学业成就评价与课程标准的一致性分析，是保证基础教育课程政策与方案执行效果的重要工具。

### 一、学业成就评价与课程标准一致性研究的缘起与意义[1]

#### （一）"2061计划"与"基于标准的教育改革"是韦伯模式的研究背景

鉴于中小学生在TIMSS测验中表现的科学素养严重缺失，美国20世纪90年代初启动了以数学与科学教育为起点的"基于标准的教育改革"。90年代中后期，公众开始质疑教育改革的成效，同时亟需对美国基础教育改革整体质量进行系统评估。基于此，美国开始了"基于标准的评价"的探索，特别是2001年NCLB法颁布后，这一问题引起了越来越多的关注，相关研究成果大多成为基础教育质量监控与课程决策的重要依据。

### （二）基于课程标准的学业成就评价的依据与挑战

1979 年 Goodlad 曾提出 5 种不同层次的课程形式，从课程编制者眼中的理想课程与正式课程，到学生的习得课程。这与 Glatthorn1997 年提出的建议课程与书面课程、学习课程的基本涵义相似。[2]“从正式课程到习得课程”流程中，历经了课程编制/课程培训、教师对课程与教材的二次加工、学习者的学习等环节，涉及课程编制者、培训者、教师、学生等。因此，课程实施中的“课程执行”效果就会直接影响课程改革的初衷落实与最终效果。

课程改革始自课程标准制定，继而到教材编制与课程实施，再以课程评价作为下一个课程循环起点。因此，判断“评价与标准一致性”就成为评价课程改革整体效果的最重要手段。

判断“评价与标准一致性”从哪些维度入手？运用何种评价技术才能保证这一分析过程的“高匹配度”？这一判断过程与传统的“效度与信度评判”有何区别？多级课程管理体制下如何保证国家课程标准的“学术底限”与地方课程实施的“区域灵活”间的和谐统一？如何判断中高考新增的开放性试题与课程标准的一致性？等等，都是很有挑战性的话题。

### （三）基于课程标准的学业成就评价的意义

第一，课程标准规范了学业成就评价的设计理念，提供了维度框架，限定了内容范围和认知要求。[3]“基于课程标准”是进行学生学业成就评价的必然要求，也是唯一准绳。第二，基于课程标准的学业成就评价是进行国家层面教育质量监控的客观需要，是保障基础教育课程改革整体质量的重要技术手段，也是进行教育督导、应对社会公众质询的信息窗口；是提升教学有效性的重要工具，是保证“基于课程标准的课堂教学”的同行者，它能够引导教师把课程标准中规定的课程目标更好地贯彻在课堂教学中，保证优良的教学质量。第三，评价与标准一致性是教育评价的技术问题，但更是教育伦理学的重要课题。如果根据与课程标准不一致的评价结果而做出教育推论与决策，对学校、教师、学生都是极大的不公正。

## 二、学业成就评价与课程标准一致性的分析工具

### （一）评价与标准一致性的几种关系[4]

“如果说课程改革是整个基础教育改革的核心的话，那么，课程标准是整个基础教育课程改革的核心，是基础教育改革的核心中的核心。”[5]国家课程标准就是“国家对基础教育课程的基本规范和质量要求”。[6]“课程标准是学生学业成就评价达至公平、有效的基石，它承担着学业成就评价标准的功能和职责。”[7]新课程改革的成功不仅有赖于新课程标准的出台，还需要有体现标准精神的测试与评价。科学的评价是衡量学生的“标尺”，是“温度计和改革杠杆”。[8]

学业成就评价与课程标准的一致性就是学业成就评价以课程标准为基准，达到类别、深度、广度的一致性和分布平衡性。图 1－4 展示了评价与标准匹配程度的四种情况[9]：

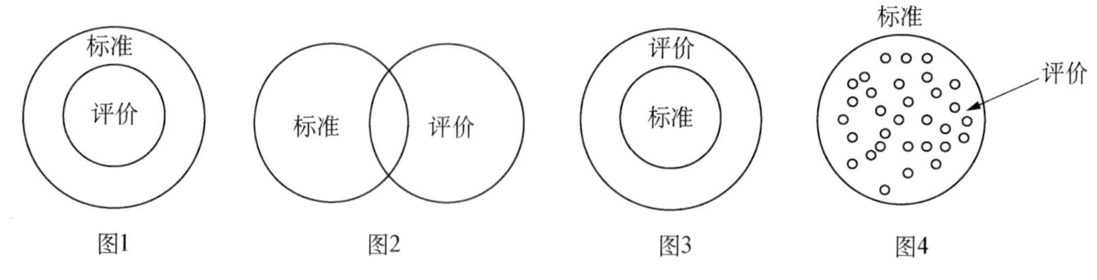


**图 1－4　评价与标准之间的几种匹配关系**

图 1 显示评价只涉及了标准的部分内容，产生了评价真空，图 3 则与之相反，评价超出了标准所要求的范围，即“超纲”。图 2 显示评价与标准只有部分交集。而图 4 则表示评价与标准基本一致，且评价项目在标准范围内分布均匀，能够达到标准所设定的预期目标。

### （二）评价与标准一致性的分析维度

下表总结了几种典型的评价与标准一致性研究，从中大致可以看出一致性分析维度，如测试内容、认知要求、知识范围、难度、试题分布、教学引导、价值取向等。

**表 1　评价与标准一致性的分析维度[10]**

| 维度 | 测试内容 | 认知要求 | 范围 | 区分度 | 题目分布 | 教学引导 | 价值取向 |
|---|---|---|---|---|---|---|---|
| Webb 模式 | 测试内容与课程标准内容是一样的 | 测试要求的认知深度与课程期望学生达到的要求一样 | 标准期望的知识范围与测试需要学生正确答题所需的一样 | | 测试题目均衡分布于各测试所考察的课程目标 | | |
| Achieve Inc. 模式 | 测试内容与课程标准内容是否一样或一致 | 测试要求的认知深度与课程期望学生达到要求的一致程度 | | 测试题目中是否含有具有挑战性的学科问题 | 课程标准内容有相应题目来测试；标准内容的不同认知要求都被评价 | | |
| SEC 模式 | 测试的内容与标准是否一致 | 记忆、执行程序、交流理解、解决非常规问题、猜想/概括/证明 | | | | | |
| Wixson 模式 | 标准的内容均衡分布于测试题目 | 测试的认知要求与标准要求一致 | 测试范围与标准范围一致 | | 测试题目均衡分布于所测试的标准内容 | | 测试题目隐藏的价值观与标准一致 |
| Buros Centre 模式 | 从评估一致性、核查者评价一致性、一致性题目的数量来判定，如果有五个以上的题目被 50% 的核查者评定为高、中程度一致，则标准被认为充分测量了 | | | | | | |

续 表

| 维度 | 测试内容 | 认知要求 | 范围 | 区分度 | 题目分布 | 教学引导 | 价值取向 |
| --- | --- | --- | --- | --- | --- | --- | --- |
| CRESST模式 | 明确测试内容与标准内容是否一致 | 运用评价量表判断测试题目的认知深度 | 运用评价量表评估测试范围与标准范围一致性 | | 判断题目是否含有与标准不相关的难度特征 | | |
| Project 2061 | 测试题目必须反映出相应的课程标准目标 | 测试题目还需充分反映出相应的课程标准具体目标 | | 应关注课程标准的“理解”等高级认知水平；测试包含学生熟悉、新奇任务 | | 理解学生反应；从测试材料获得具体建议，能决定下一步要解决问题 | |

### (三) 本研究所用到的评价与标准一致性分析工具

韦伯(Webb, N.L.)是“基于标准的评价”的代表人物，他开发的韦伯模式在美国17个州广泛应用，用于评估各州学业成就评价与国家标准及州标准的一致性。分析维度主要有四个：知识类别一致性、知识深度一致性、知识广度一致性、知识分布平衡性。[11]

1. 分析维度与可接受水平

(1) 知识类别一致性，即评价与标准内容主题间的匹配程度。通过审阅试题是否包含了每一条标准的相应内容，来判断类别等同性标准的达成与否。如果击中主题目标测验题目的平均数大于或等于6，则为达到一致，如果小于6，则为不一致。

(2) 知识深度一致性，即学业成就评价中相应内容对学生认知水平的要求，是否与课程标准中对学生学习目标的期望保持一致。判断标准是：测验试题的认知水平，至少有50%命中课程标准中的某个目标所要求的认知水平(或高于)。

(3) 知识广度共同性，即判断学业成就评价中要求学生正确回答某道试题或完成某项学习活动时所必需的知识，是否与课程标准中的“内容标准”规定的课程内容的知识范围保持一致。如果测验题目击中具体目标百分比的平均数大于或等于50%，就认为达到了一致性，如果小于50%，则认为未达到一致性。

(4) 知识分布平衡性是指考察各个测验题目在各项具体目标之间分布的均匀程度，用平衡性指数来描述知识分布平衡性。其计算公式如下：

$$\text{平衡性指数} = 1 - \frac{\left(\sum \left| \frac{1}{O} - \frac{I_k}{H} \right| \right)}{2}$$

其中，$O$=被命中的某内容标准所包括的目标总数，$I_k$=命中目标的试题数，$H$=命中该内容标准的试题总数。当某一内容标准对应的所有评价试题都平均分布在各个目标上时，平衡性指数达到最大值 1。知识分布平衡性指数大于或等于 0.70，则认为达到了知识分布平衡性，如果小于 0.7，则认为未达到知识分布平衡性。

2. 对知识深度的界定

知识深度是一致性检验中的核心概念，Webb 把它分为 4 种水平：[12]

水平 1：回忆(Recall)。包括回忆事实性知识、定义、术语或简单程序，进行简单运算或使用公式等，如识别、回忆、确认、使用、测量。水平 2：技能/概念(Skill/Concept)。包含智力运算，而不仅是习惯性反应，要求学生做出决策来处理问题或活动，如归类、组织、估计、观察、收集与展示数据、比较数据。水平 3：策略性思维(Strategic Thinking)。含推理、计划、使用证据，及通过观察得出结论，引用证据并提出有逻辑性的论点，运用概念与术语解释现象，以及运用概念来解决问题。水平 4：拓展性思维(Extended Thinking)。要求复杂推理、计划、设计与思维能力，如建立与证明联结，设计与进行实验，在已有发现与相关概念、现象间建立联结，合并、综合观点形成新概念，以及评价实验设计。

3. 分析方法

(1) 序列性开发，即评估框架的所有部分间必须保持一致性。从前期研究成果到评价蓝图制定，从预期学习目标(标准)到表现标准的确立，再到评价实践等等都要保持一致性。

(2) 专家审议。专家审议小组一般至少要 5 人以上，主要为评估专家、学科内容专家，且专家必须熟悉标准所涵盖的课程内容以及测验开发程序。[13] 专家审议的核心要素有 8 个：明确的学习目标、与这些目标相关联的教学、基于证据的论证、反馈、对学习目标的具体界定、明确的评价标准(评价量规)、对评价标准的具体界定、如何应用评价标准的案例。[14]

(3) 文件分析，是指使用某个系统来分析标准与评估文件，并对二者的内容与结构进行编码，通过定量、系统的比较来说明它们的一致性程度。例如，组织人员先对某学科课程标准进行编码，即用二维矩阵(类似命题双向细目表)确定课程内容(知识点)与其对应的认知水平，再对待分析的评价系统(试卷或单个试题)进行类似的编码，然后确定某一课程内容上标准与评价系统所要求的认知水平是否达到一致。

4. 分析程序

一致性会议需要 3—4 天，时间长短依照课程标准的长度、评价规模、涉及的标准数量等因素而定。为保证分析结果的效力，每个分析小组由 5—8 名人员组成，包括内容领域专家、地区督学、内容领域教师等。[15]

审议者首先要接受培训，来确认学习目标与评价试题中的知识深度。培训包括审议关于 4 级知识深度的定义及其对应的具体案例，然后分析程序分为两步：第一步，全体分析人员对州学习目标的知识深度 4 级水平进行理解与分析，达成一致；第二步，每个审议者单独分析每个试题的知识深度水平与课程标准或课程目标间的匹配度，然后，全体审议者深入讨论对于评价与州课程标准一致性的全面认识。

## 三、学业成就评价与课程标准一致性的个案实践研究

### （一）初中化学中考试题与课程标准的一致性[16]

随机抽取了一套山东某市 2009 年中考试题，从《全日制义务教育化学课程标准（实验稿）》中随机抽取了一个内容主题“物质构成的奥秘”，利用韦伯一致性分析标准进行分析。

1. 课程标准内容目标分析与编码

本文只分析认知性学习目标维度，目标要求包含以下三级水平，用 A、B、C 编码：

A. 知道、记住、说出、列举、找到（即明确“是什么”）

B. 认识、了解、看懂、识别、能表示（即懂得“为什么”）

C. 理解、解释、说明、区分、判断（即能够“应用”）

2. 一致性分析结果

（1）知识种类一致性。由表 2，击中“物质构成的奥秘”这一领域的题目总数为 12 个，因此知识种类的一致性可接受。

（2）知识深度一致性。由表 3，75%的题目符合课程标准的认知水平，因此知识深度一致性的可接受水平为“是”。

（3）知识广度一致性。由表 4，测验题目击中具体目标的百分比为 42%，小于 50%，因此知识范围一致性的可接受水平为“否”。

表 2 “物质构成的奥秘”之“水与常见的溶液”的具体内容标准及其编码

<table>
<tr><th>主题</th><th>标准</th><th>具体目标</th><th>具体目标水平</th><th>击中目标的题目数</th></tr>
<tr><td rowspan="10">物质构成的奥秘</td><td rowspan="4">1. 化学物质的多样性</td><td>1.1 认识物质的三态及其转化。</td><td>B</td><td rowspan="4">2</td></tr>
<tr><td>1.2 能从组成上识别氧化物。</td><td>B</td></tr>
<tr><td>1.3 区分纯净物和混合物、单质和化合物、有机物和无机物。</td><td>C</td></tr>
<tr><td>1.4 认识物质的多样性。</td><td>B</td></tr>
<tr><td rowspan="6">2. 微粒构成物质</td><td>2.1 认识物质的微粒性。</td><td>B</td><td rowspan="5">1</td></tr>
<tr><td>2.2 知道分子、原子、离子等都是构成物质的微粒。</td><td>A</td></tr>
<tr><td>2.3 能用微粒的观点解释某些常见的现象。</td><td>C</td></tr>
<tr><td>2.4 知道元素的简单分类。</td><td>A</td></tr>
<tr><td>2.5 知道原子可以结合成分子、同一元素的原子和离子可以互相转化。</td><td>A</td></tr>
<tr><td>2.6 初步认识核外电子在化学反应中的作用。</td><td>B</td><td>1</td></tr>
</table>

续 表

| 主题 | 标准 | 具体目标 | 具体目标水平 | 击中目标的题目数 |
|---|---|---|---|---|
| 物质构成的奥秘 | 3. 认识化学元素 | 3.1 认识氢、碳、氧、氮等与人类关系密切的常见元素。 | B | |
| | | 3.2 记住一些常见元素的名称和符号。 | A | |
| | | 3.3 知道元素的简单分类。 | A | |
| | | 3.4 能根据原子序数在元素周期表中找到指定的元素。 | A | |
| | | 3.5 形成“化学变化过程中元素不变”的观念。 | C | 1 |
| | 4. 物质组成的表示 | 4.1 说出几种常见元素的化合价。 | A | 1 |
| | | 4.2 能用化学式表示某些常见物质的组成。 | B | 2 |
| | | 4.3 利用相对原子质量、相对分子质量进行物质组成的简单计算。 | C | 2 |
| | | 4.4 能看懂某些商品标签上标示的物质成分及其含量。 | B | 2 |
| 合计 | | 19 个目标，被命中 8 个 | | 12 |

注：此表融合了多位一线教师和专家的建议。对于填空题，一个空确定为一个题，对于计算题，一个问题确定为一个题。限于篇幅仅截取“水与常见的溶液”一个二级主题。

**表 3 中考试题与课程标准的知识深度一致性**

| 与目标对照的深度水平(%) | | | 知识深度一致性的可接受水平 |
|---|---|---|---|
| 低于 | 符合 | 高于 | |
| 8(1 个) | 75(9 个) | 17(2 个) | 是 |

**表 4 中考试题与课程标准的知识范围一致性**

| 目标击中情况 | | 知识范围一致性的可接受水平 |
|---|---|---|
| 目标击中数 | 目标击中百分比(%) | |
| 10 | 42 | 否 |

(4) 知识分布平衡性。把 $O=8$, $H=12$，命中目标的题目数详见表 2，代入公式计算出平衡性指数为 0.83，大于 0.7，因此知识分布平衡性的一致性可接受水平为“是”。

### (二) 初中化学教材习题与课程标准的一致性[①]

1. 教材习题与内容标准的认知水平编码

(1) 内容标准的编码。以“水与常见的溶液”为例，对内容标准进行分析编码(表 5)。

① 本部分主要内容会后发表于《中学化学教学参考》2012 年 1—2 期，作者为李伟，张雨强，董玉芬，尹萍萍。

**表 5 “水与常见的溶液”内容标准的目标水平分析**

| | | 具体标准 | 目标水平 |
|---|---|---|---|
| 水与常见的溶液 | 1 | (1) 认识水的组成 | B |
| | | (2) 知道纯水与矿泉水、硬水与软水的区别 | A |
| | 2 | 了解吸附、沉淀、过滤和蒸馏等净化水的常用方法 | B |
| | 3 | (1) 认识溶解现象 | B |
| | | (2) 知道水是重要的溶剂 | A |
| | | (3) 知道酒精、汽油等也是常见的溶剂 | A |
| | 4 | (1) 了解饱和溶液涵义 | B |
| | | (2) 了解溶解度的涵义 | B |
| | 5 | 能进行溶质质量分数的简单计算 | C |
| | 6 | 了解结晶现象 | B |
| | 7 | 能说出一些常见的乳化现象 | A |
| | 8 | 了解溶液在生产、生活中的重要意义 | B |

(2) 习题的分类与编码

第一,习题的选取。本文选取“身边的化学物质”主题所涉及的课后习题。具体有,第一,“地球周围的空气”包括:第二单元(我们周围的空气)中课题 1、课题 2 中的习题,以及第六单元(碳和碳的氧化物)课题 3 中的课后习题。第二,“水与常见的溶液”包括:第三单元(自然界中的水)课题 1—4 中的习题、第九单元(溶液)课题 1—3 中课后习题。第三,“金属与金属矿物”包括:第八单元(金属材料)课题 1—3 中的习题。第四,“生活中常见的化合物”包括:第十单元(酸和碱)课题 1—2 中的课后习题、第十一单元(盐化肥)课题 1—2,以及第十二单元(化学与生活)课题 1 中的课后习题。

第二,习题的分类与编码(表 6)。本文只分析认知性学习目标。习题的认知性学习目标水平的界定方法为:第一种,直接根据题目中的行为动词,把该题的认知性学习目标水平定为相应的层次。第二种,如果题目中没有明显的行为动词,则分析该题是考察“是什么”、“为什么”还是“应用”,然后确定其水平。如:“怎样鉴别石灰水和氢氧化钠溶液?”本题为鉴别题,应属于“区分”水平,所以学习目标水平定为 C。“十(二)7(1)①—②”表示第十单元课题 2 第七题第一小题中的第一问和第二问。

(3) 习题与内容标准的认知水平一致性编码

**表 6 “身边的化学物质”习题与标准一致性数据**

| | | 具体标准 | 标准水平 | 对应习题 | 习题水平 |
|---|---|---|---|---|---|
| 水与常见的溶液 | 1 | (1) 认识水的组成 | B | 三(一)4(2) | A |
| | | | | 三(一)4(3) | B |
| | | (2) 知道纯水与矿泉水、硬水与软水的区别 | A | 三(三)1(2) | A |
| | | | | 三(三)3 | B |
| | | | | 三(三)5 | C |
| | 2 | 了解吸附、沉淀、过滤和蒸馏等净化水的常用方法 | B | 三(三)1(1)/(2),4 | 3 个 A |

续 表

| 具体标准 | | | 标准水平 | 对应习题 | 习题水平 |
|---|---|---|---|---|---|
| 水与常见的溶液 | 3 | (1) 认识溶解现象 | B | 九(一)1(1)<br>九(二)5(1) | 2个B |
| | | | | 九(一)2(1) | A |
| | | (2) 知道水是重要的溶剂 | A | 九(一)2(2) | A |
| | | (3) 知道酒精、汽油等也是常见的溶剂 | A | 九(一)2(2) | A |
| | 4 | (1) 了解饱和溶液涵义 | B | 九(二)1 | A |
| | | (2) 了解溶解度的涵义 | B | 九(二)4,9 | 2个A |
| | | | | 九(二)2,3,7(1)—(2),8,10 | 6个B |
| | 5 | 能进行溶质质量分数的简单计算 | C | 九(三)1—9 | 9个C |
| | 6 | 了解结晶现象 | B | 九(二)5(2) | B |
| | | | | 九(二)6 | C |
| | 7 | 能说出一些常见的乳化现象 | A | 九(一)5 | B |
| | 8 | 了解溶液在生产、生活中的重要意义 | B | 九(一)3(3) | C |
| | | 共12条标准,命中12条 | | 35 | |

2. 分析结果①

(1) 知识种类的一致性

由表6,“水与常见的溶液”、“金属与常见的矿物”、“生活中常见的化合物”、“地球周围的空气”各主题分别35、20、38、27个教材习题命中,习题与课程标准的知识种类的一致性都较高。

(2) 知识深度一致性

“水与常见的溶液”、“地球周围的空气”、“金属与金属矿物”习题的知识深度与课程标准保持了良好一致性,而“生活中常见的化合物”部分的知识深度一致性稍弱(表7)。

**表7 习题与课程标准的知识深度一致性数据**

| 身边的化学物质 | 符合的习题数(百分率) | 高于的习题数目(百分率) | 低于的习题数(百分率) |
|---|---|---|---|
| 水与常见的溶液 | 22(62.9%) | 5(14.3%) | 8(22.9%) |
| 金属与金属矿物 | 12(57.1%) | 4(19.0%) | 5(23.8%) |
| 生活中常见的化合物 | 17(44.7%) | 17(44.7%) | 4(10.5%) |
| 地球周围的空气 | 13(50%) | 11(42.3%) | 2(7.7%) |

(3) 知识广度一致性

目标的命中率远大于50%,因此习题和课程标准的知识广度一致性较高(表8)。

① 分析结果包含了所有二级主题。限于篇幅,本文只呈现了“水与常见的溶液”一个二级主题。

表 8　习题与课程标准的知识广度一致性数据

| 目标总数 | 击中目标总数 | 命中率 |
| --- | --- | --- |
| 38 | 32 | 84.2% |

（4）知识分布的平衡性

表 9　习题与课程标准的知识分布平衡性数据

| 内容主题 | 水与常见的溶液 | 金属与金属矿物 | 生活中常见的化合物 | 地球周围的空气 |
| --- | --- | --- | --- | --- |
| 平衡指数 | 0.67 | 0.79 | 0.69 | 0.39 |

“金属与金属矿物”的平衡性指数为 0.79，大于 0.7，知识分布的平衡性较高。“水与常见的溶液”、“生活中常见的化合物”的平衡性指数分别为 0.67、0.68，均在 0.6—0.69 之间，知识分布的平衡性稍弱，而“地球周围的空气”的平衡性指数为 0.39，小于 0.6，知识分布的平衡性较差。

### （三）化学高考试题与课程标准的一致性[17]

1. 内容标准的目标水平

《标准》中分为认知性学习目标、技能性学习目标、体验性学习目标等三个维度。本文只对认知性学习目标加以分析，目标要求包含四级水平，分别用 A、B、C、D 进行编码：

A. 知道、说出、识别、描述、举例、列举

B. 了解、认识、能表示、辨认、区分、比较

C. 理解、解释、说明、判断、预期、分类、归纳、概述

D. 应用、设计、评价、优选、使用、解决、检验、证明

随机抽取 2010 年某高考化学试题，利用韦伯一致性模式，分析该套试题与课程标准中“化学反应速率与化学平衡”主题之间的一致性。

2. 一致性分析结果

（1）知识种类一致性

击中该主题的题目为 8 个（表 10），因此化学试题与课程标准的知识种类一致性可接受。

表 10　“化学反应速率与化学平衡”的内容标准及对应的目标水平

| 主题 | 内 容 标 准 | 具体目标水平 | 击中目标的题目数 |
| --- | --- | --- | --- |
| 化学反应速率与化学平衡 | 1. 知道化学反应速率的定量表示方法 | A | |
| | 2. 通过实验测定某些化学反应的速率 | D | 2 |
| | 3. 知道活化能的涵义及其对化学反应速率的影响 | A | |
| | 4. 通过实验探究温度、浓度、压强和催化剂对化学反应速率的影响，认识其一般规律。 | B | 1 |

续 表

| 主题 | 内 容 标 准 | 具体目标水平 | 击中目标的题目数 |
|---|---|---|---|
| | 5. 通过催化剂实际应用的事例，认识其在生产、生活和科学研究领域中的重大作用。 | B | |
| | 6. 能用焓变和熵变说明化学反应的方向 | C | 2 |
| | 7. 描述化学平衡建立的过程 | A | |
| | 8. 知道化学平衡常数的涵义 | A | |
| | 9. 能利用化学平衡常数计算反应物的转化率。 | D | 2 |
| | 10. 通过实验探究温度、浓度和压强对化学平衡的影响，并能用相关理论加以解释。 | C | 1 |
| | 11. 认识化学反应速率和化学平衡的调控在生活、生产和科学研究领域中的重要作用。 | B | |
| 合计 | 11 个内容目标，被命中 5 个 | | 8 |

注：此表融合了多位专家和一线教师的建议。对于填空题，一个空标记为一道题目。

（2）知识深度一致性

据表 11，75% 的题目符合课程标准对知识深度目标水平的要求，因此试题与课程标准的知识深度一致性可接受。

**表 11　高考试题与课程标准知识深度一致性**

| 与目标对照的深度水平(%) | | |
|---|---|---|
| 低于 | 符合 | 高于 |
| 12.5(1 个) | 75(6 个) | 12.5(1 个) |

（3）知识广度一致性

据表 12，测试题击中课程标准具体目标的百分比为 45%，小于 50%，因此该试题与课程标准的知识广度一致性为“勉强接受”。

**表 12　高考题与课程标准知识广度一致性**

| 目标击中情况 | | |
|---|---|---|
| 目标击中数 | 目标总数 | 目标击中百分比(%) |
| 5 | 11 | 45 |

（4）知识分布平衡性

本研究中，$O=5$，$H=8$，命中目标的题目数详见表 10，代入平衡性指数公式：

$$平衡性指数 = 1 - \frac{\left(\left|\frac{1}{5}-\frac{2}{8}\right|+\left|\frac{1}{5}-\frac{1}{8}\right|+\left|\frac{1}{5}-\frac{2}{8}\right|+\left|\frac{1}{5}-\frac{2}{8}\right|+\left|\frac{1}{5}-\frac{1}{8}\right|\right)}{2} = 0.85$$

可判断该试题与课程标准在知识分布平衡性的一致性维度上可接受水平为“是”。

## 四、学业成就评价与课程标准一致性的区域实践研究①

### （一）化学学业水平考试试题与课程标准一致性水平的总体特征分析

符号C1、C2、C3、C4分别代表四个城市，其中C1和C2的经济发展水平处于中上层，C3和C4处于中下层，C1和C3为化学单科考试，C2和C4为理科综合考试。D1、D2、D3、D4、D5分别代表五个领域。得出四地市化学学业水平考试与课程标准的一致性情况(图5)。

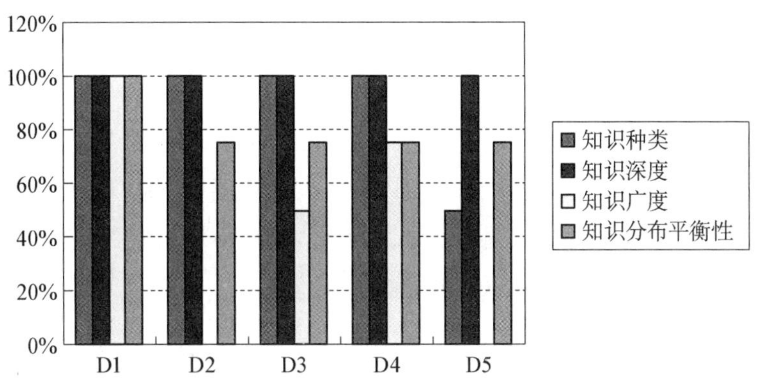


**图5 初中化学学业水平考试与课程标准的一致性总体水平统计表**

由图5知，五大学习领域的知识种类一致性率分别为100%、100%、100%、100%、50%，知识深度一致性率分别为100%、100%、100%、100%、100%，知识广度一致性率分别为100%、0、50%、75%、0，知识分布平衡性一致性率分别为100%、75%、75%、75%、75%。

1. 五大学习领域之间的一致性存在差异

研究发现，一致性最好的领域为“科学探究”，其他依次为物质的化学变化、物质构成的奥秘、身边的化学物质，最差的为化学与社会发展。科学探究的一致性率最高的原因可能是只考虑了“学习基本实验技能”一个二级主题，容易达到一致性。“物质的化学变化”一致性处于第二，是因为化学变化是学习化学的基础，是贯穿整个基础化学教育的主线，是衔接初中和高中化学的桥梁，因此物质的化学变化受关注度较高。身边的化学物质和物质构成的奥秘也是学习化学的基础，也是考察的重点。“化学与社会发展”的内容更适合于在真实情景中考察学生解决社会问题的能力和情感态度，但是这种评价技术在我国还处于探索阶段。访谈发现，五个领域在命题中占的比重基本为2:3:2:2:1，基本能说明以上统计结果。

2. 四个维度之间的一致性存在差异

五个内容领域的知识深度一致性都达到了100%，在四个维度中最好，实现了“初中毕业、

① 课程标准与习题的认知水平的编码、统计、结果处理同上几个案例。大部分内容见张志红.初中化学学业水平考试与课程标准的一致性研究[D].曲阜师范大学，2011.

升学考试命题必须依据国家课程标准，杜绝设置偏题、怪题”的要求。[19]其次是知识种类一致性，除了“化学与社会发展”领域的一致性为50%，其他领域的一致性都达到了100%。再次就是知识分布平衡性一致性较高，都大于或者等于75%。一致性最差的为知识广度一致性，身边的化学物质、化学与社会发展一致性为0，主要原因在于：在一定的知识种类范围内，评价并不总能覆盖标准中的知识范围。经常需要做出权衡，时间限制、评分时间的消耗、工具的获得以及其他对评价的限制都可能阻碍评价中的所有内容范围。

### （二）化学学业水平考试试题与课程标准一致性水平的市区特征分析

1. 地市间知识种类一致性存在的差异

由图6知，四个城市知识种类一致性在“科学探究”内容领域的差异性最小，说明S省通过纸笔测验评价学生实验能力具有普遍性，而且把实验作为纸笔测验的考查重难点。一致性差异最大的为身边的化学物质，说明各个城市对该领域的重视程度不同。其中C1和C2城市的测试击中化学与社会发展这一主题的试题数都小于6，知识种类一致性都为“否”，C3和C4两个城市的五个主题领域都达到了知识种类一致性。

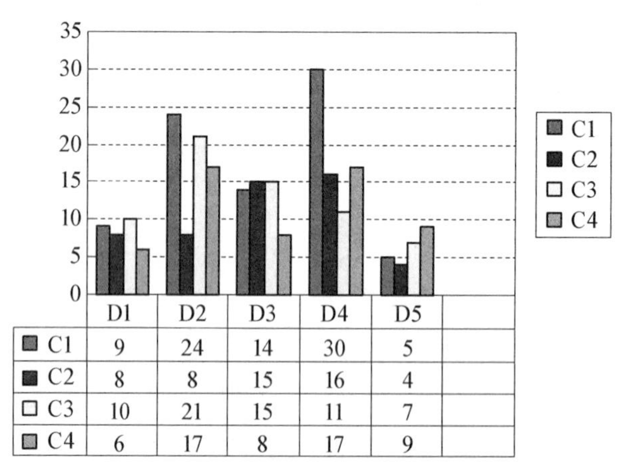


| | D1 | D2 | D3 | D4 | D5 |
|---|---|---|---|---|---|
| C1 | 9 | 24 | 14 | 30 | 5 |
| C2 | 8 | 8 | 15 | 16 | 4 |
| C3 | 10 | 21 | 15 | 11 | 7 |
| C4 | 6 | 17 | 8 | 17 | 9 |

**图6 知识种类一致性的差异性**

2. 地市间知识深度和广度一致性的差异

由图7知，四个城市中知识深度一致性差异最小的领域为“化学与社会发展”，虽然该领域受重视程度不够，但难易程度却与课程标准吻合得最好。相对于其它领域，知识深度一致性差异最大的为物质的化学变化，由于该领域是考察的重点和难点，在高利害考试中把握难易度时，命题者很容易脱离课程标准的要求而从主观上决定试题的难易程度。知识广度一致性差异性最小的领域为“物质的化学变化”，说明该领域受重视；知识广度一致性差异最大的领域为科学探究，因为实验更适合于表现性评价，而且初中学业水平考试包含实验操作评价，所以在纸笔测验中，各地区对其重视度存在着差异性。

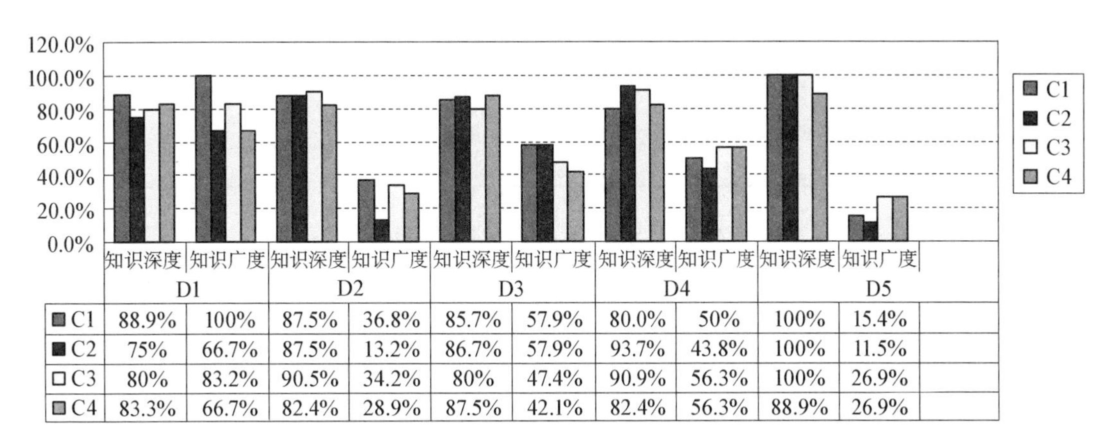


| | D1 知识深度 | D1 知识广度 | D2 知识深度 | D2 知识广度 | D3 知识深度 | D3 知识广度 | D4 知识深度 | D4 知识广度 | D5 知识深度 | D5 知识广度 |
|---|---|---|---|---|---|---|---|---|---|---|
| C1 | 88.9% | 100% | 87.5% | 36.8% | 85.7% | 57.9% | 80.0% | 50% | 100% | 15.4% |
| C2 | 75% | 66.7% | 87.5% | 13.2% | 86.7% | 57.9% | 93.7% | 43.8% | 100% | 11.5% |
| C3 | 80% | 83.2% | 90.5% | 34.2% | 80% | 47.4% | 90.9% | 56.3% | 100% | 26.9% |
| C4 | 83.3% | 66.7% | 82.4% | 28.9% | 87.5% | 42.1% | 82.4% | 56.3% | 88.9% | 26.9% |

**图 7　四个城市知识深度和广度一致性的差异**

### 3. 地市间知识分布平衡性存在的差异

由图 8 知，知识分布平衡性差异性最小的内容领域为“科学探究”，其中的每个被测目标，四个城市试卷都有大致均衡的试题与之相对应，且平衡性指数差异性较小。知识分布平衡性差异最大的内容领域为“物质的化学变化”，其中 C1 未达到分布平衡性；其他三个城市都达到了分布平衡性，但是平衡指数存在一定的差异。

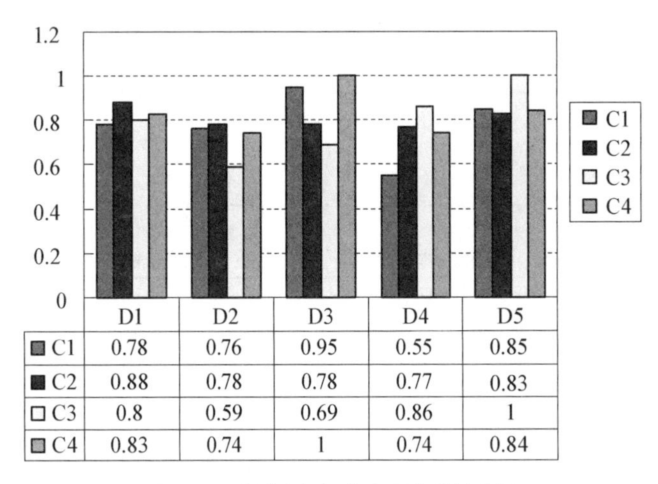


| | D1 | D2 | D3 | D4 | D5 |
|---|---|---|---|---|---|
| C1 | 0.78 | 0.76 | 0.95 | 0.55 | 0.85 |
| C2 | 0.88 | 0.78 | 0.78 | 0.77 | 0.83 |
| C3 | 0.8 | 0.59 | 0.69 | 0.86 | 1 |
| C4 | 0.83 | 0.74 | 1 | 0.74 | 0.84 |

**图 8　四个城市知识分布平衡性的差异**

### 4. 经济发展水平、分科与综合因素对一致性差异的影响

C1 和 C2 在 S 省中经济水平处于中上游，C3 和 C4 处于中下游，C1 和 C3 为单科考试，C2 和 C4 为综合考试。研究发现，经济发展水平对一致性的影响并不明显。那么，同为单科或综合考试，经济发展水平不同的情况下，一致性有无显著性差异呢？

表 13　C1 和 C3 城市知识种类一致性间的显著性水平

| | 平方和 | df | 均方 | F | 显著性 |
|---|---|---|---|---|---|
| 组间 | 32.400 | 1 | 32.400 | .471 | .512 |
| 组内 | 550.000 | 8 | 68.750 | | |
| 总数 | 582.400 | 9 | | | |

表 14　C2 和 C4 城市知识种类一致性间的显著性水平

| | 平方和 | df | 均方 | F | 显著性 |
|---|---|---|---|---|---|
| 组间 | 3.600 | 1 | 3.600 | .135 | .723 |
| 组内 | 214.000 | 8 | 26.750 | | |
| 总数 | 217.600 | 9 | | | |

C1 和 C3 城市知识种类一致性间的显著性水平为 0.512，数值大于 0.05，C2 和 C4 城市知识种类一致性间的显著性水平为 0.723，数值大于 0.05，因此经济发展水平不同的 C1 和 C3 城市、C2 和 C4 知识种类一致性不存在显著性差异。同理可得知识深度、知识广度和知识分布平衡性之间也不存在显著性差异。可见经济发展水平对一致性影响不明显。

在经济发展水平差异不大，考试方式不同的情况下，以 C1 和 C2、C3 和 C4 城市中的知识种类一致性差异为例说单科和综合对一致性的影响(表 15、表 16)。

表 15　C1 和 C2 城市知识种类一致性间的显著性水平

| | 平方和 | df | 均方 | F | 显著性 |
|---|---|---|---|---|---|
| 组间 | 96.100 | 1 | 96.100 | 1.429 | .266 |
| 组内 | 538.000 | 8 | 67.250 | | |
| 总数 | 634.100 | 9 | | | |

表 16　C3 和 C4 城市知识种类一致性间的显著性水平

| | 平方和 | df | 均方 | F | 显著性 |
|---|---|---|---|---|---|
| 组间 | 4.900 | 1 | 4.900 | .173 | .688 |
| 组内 | 226.000 | 8 | 28.250 | | |
| 总数 | 230.900 | 9 | | | |

可见，C1 和 C2 城市知识种类一致性间的显著性水平为 0.266，大于 0.05，C3 和 C4 城市知识种类一致性间的显著性水平为 0.688，数值大于 0.05，因此命题形式不同的 C1 和 C2 城市、C3 和 C4 知识种类一致性不存显著性差异。同理可得知识深度、知识广度和知识分布平衡性之间也不存在显著性差异。可见分科或综合对一致性影响不明显。

综合，经济发展水平、单科或综合考试对初中化学学业水平考试与课程标准的一致性差异的影响并不大。

## 五、学业成就评价与课程标准一致性的影响因素

影响学业水平考试与课程标准一致性的重要因素有三个：课程标准、命题者、命题工具与技术。第一，课程标准如果过于粗放，只有内容标准而未清晰表述学生的预期学习结果（表现标准），就不能准确界定学生学习结果所涉及的行为动词的确切含义，或不能提供具体教学与评价案例供教师与命题者参考，这不仅影响一线教师对课程标准的执行，更影响学业成就评价命题者的试题编制工作。[20]术语解释是课程标准的一个重要组成部分，因此需要“对标准中出现的一些重要术语进行解释与说明，使使用者能更好地理解与实施标准”。[21]

第二，命题者评价素养的高低会极大影响到命题质量，从而会影响到对评价结果的客观公正解释，更可能影响对某一段时期的课程与教学改革成果的整体评价。但命题者的评价素养培育除了依靠自发自为的自学以外，更应该依靠有规划的职前教育和持续的在职教育，而且要加强命题理论与工具在实践中的训练。台湾“评量人才养成工作坊”项目基于台湾学生学习成就评量资料库建设的需要，通过了解国内外的评价方式、亲自参与评价实践来提升评价理论和实践素养，分初、中、高三个阶段进行培训，旨在提升台湾地区教师使用、运用多元评量及纸笔测验命题技巧的能力，主要培训内容为“国内外评价经验、纸笔测验命题原则、修订版的布卢姆教育目标分类、命题实做、命题修订等内容”。[22]

第三，命题工具与技术是命题工作中的核心问题。命题工具的技术含量将很大程度上决定试题的效度与信度，应该大量吸收认知心理学、教育测量学等学科的先进成果，促进学业成就评价命题工作从“经验型命题”走向“专业化命题”。[23][24]

基于以上判断，课题组以初中化学命题者为研究对象，主要关注两个问题，其一为命题者的评价素养现状以及评价素养培育的途径，其二则重点关注命题者对评价与课程标准一致性的认识。本文只呈现评价与标准一致性的调查结果。①

调查问卷全为封闭的单项选择题：第一部分是命题者的背景信息；第二部分是命题者关于评价知识的学习经历，共 13 道问题；第三部分是命题者关于学业评价与课程标准一致性的认识，共 13 道问题。为保证问卷效度和信度，先在 S 省某市对参与初中化学学业水平考试的命题者进行了试测，经过专家、教师、研究生共同对试测结果分析，剔除和修订了部分问题，使问卷结构更加合理。然后以 S 省所有参与初中化学学业水平考试命题的教研员和教师为研究总体，调查样本为 S 省九地市的 18 位命题者。调查从 2010 年 6 月开始，11 月结束。还访谈了 2 位命题者，作为了解命题整体情况、问卷统计分析的参照。

### （一）命题者对课程标准的认识

对课程标准的把握是实现评价与课程标准一致性的前提和关键。问卷设计了四个有关

---

① 调查得到山东省教研室孔令鹏老师、枣庄市教研室周传昌老师、各地市教研员等支持，一并感谢！

问题，来调查命题者对课程标准的认识。统计结果如下：

表 17　命题者对课程标准的认识调查结果(%)

| | | | | | |
|---|---|---|---|---|---|
| 您对现行课程标准熟悉程度如何？ | 非常熟悉<br>37.5% | 比较熟悉<br>56.3% | 一般<br>6.3% | 不熟悉<br>0 | 非常不熟悉<br>0 |
| 您对现行课程标准满意吗？ | 非常满意<br>25% | 比较满意<br>50% | 一般<br>25% | 不满意<br>0 | 非常不满意<br>0 |
| 您对“国家课程标准是教材编写、教学、评估和考试命题的依据，是国家管理和评价课程的基础”这句话熟悉吗？ | 非常熟悉<br>56.3% | 比较熟悉<br>37.5% | 一般<br>6.3% | 不熟悉<br>0 | 非常不熟悉<br>0 |
| 您赞同“课程标准过于抽象、可操作性差，不便于教学与评价的参考”说法吗？ | 非常赞同<br>25% | 比较赞同<br>31.3% | 一般<br>37.5% | 不赞同<br>6.3% | 非常不赞同<br>0 |

可见，大部分的命题者对课程标准是熟悉和满意的，并且熟悉“课程标准是命题的依据”这一理念。新课程标准相对于以往的教学大纲从本质上做出了革新，但不否认新课程标准确实存在着某些问题。调查结果显示，命题者对于课程标准的看法出现了较大分歧，说明命题者对新课程标准已形成了不同的解读和思考。

### （二）命题者对学生学业成就评价与课程标准一致性的认识

为了解命题者对学生学业成就评价与课程标准一致性的认识，本调查设计了四个相关问题，统计结果如下表：

表 18　命题者对学生学业成就评价与课程标准一致性的认识

| | | | | | |
|---|---|---|---|---|---|
| 您熟悉学业成就与评价与课程标准的一致性问题吗？ | 非常熟悉<br>18.8% | 比较熟悉<br>31.3% | 一般<br>37.5% | 不熟悉<br>12.5% | 非常不熟悉<br>0 |
| 您接受过学业成就评价与课程标准的一致性培训吗？ | 是<br>12.5% | 否<br>87.5% | | | |
| 您认为学业评价与课程标准之间保持一致性的必要性大吗？ | 非常大<br>50% | 比较大<br>31.3% | 一般<br>12.5% | 不大<br>6.3% | 非常小<br>0 |
| 您是否需要充实评价与课程标准的一致性相关知识？ | 非常需要<br>31.3% | 比较需要<br>56.3% | 一般<br>12.5% | 不需要<br>0 | 非常不需要<br>0 |

具备学业成就评价与课程标准一致性的理念，是实施评价与课程标准一致的重要保证。表 18 显示，18.8%的命题者对此已非常熟悉，31.3%的命题者达到了比较熟悉的程度，但仍有 37.5%的命题者不够了解，甚至有 12.5%的命题者仍不熟悉。

87.5%的命题者未接受过相关培训，这也是导致很大一部分命题者对学业成就评价与课程标准一致性不够了解的主要原因。已有 50%以上的命题者认识到一致性的重要性，但是在新课程要求评价以课程标准为依据的背景下，提高命题者的学业成就评价与课程标准一致性的认识仍然亟待加强。由于评价知识的缺乏，80%以上的命题者表达了充实一致性知识的愿望，因此在实践中，应增加对命题者关于学业成就评价与课程标准一致性的培训。

### （三）命题者对评价与课程标准一致性的实践认识

研究发现，50%以上的命题者对学业成就评价与课程标准一致性已经熟悉，那么在实践中，命题者是否也遵循了一致性的理念呢？我们设计了5个问题，统计结果如下：

表19 对命题者一致性实践活动的调查

| | | | | | |
|---|---|---|---|---|---|
| 您及您周围的教师上课依据课程标准吗？ | 一直<br>18.75% | 经常<br>18.75% | 有时<br>62.5% | 很少<br>0 | 从不<br>0 |
| 您在编制化学试题时是以什么为基准？ | 教材/课程标准<br>50% | 课程标准<br>43.75% | 其他/课程标准<br>6.25% | | |
| 如果您命题是依据课程标准，依据的频率如何？ | 一直<br>50% | 经常<br>37.5% | 有时<br>12.5% | 很少<br>0 | 从不<br>0 |
| 您编制试题的方式是？ | 使用现成试题<br>0 | 自己设计<br>37.5% | 改编/自己设计<br>62.5% | | |
| 您采用技术手段分析过命题与课程标准间的一致性了吗？ | 是<br>31.25% | 否<br>68.75% | | | |

仅有18.75%的命题者一直依据课程标准教学，18.75%会经常依据课程标准，但是剩下的62.5%却是偶尔依据课程标准，未能把课程标准作为上课的主要依据。关于命题的依据，同时选择教材和课程标准的命题者有50%（但并不说明每次命题会同时参考二者，即有时只会参考教材而脱离课程标准），只选择课程标准的命题者为43.75%，同时选择课程标准和其他的为6.25%。命题者命题时都会选择课程标准为依据，但是依据的频率如何？我们发现有50%的命题者会一直以课程标准为命题依据，有37.5%的命题者会经常以课程标准为命题依据（偶尔会以其他为主要依据），剩下的12.5%的命题者命题的主要依据是其他。

37.5%的命题者能够自己设计试题，62.5%的命题者采取对已有试题改编或者自己设计试题，说明绝大多数命题者能做到以课程标准为命题依据，命题者已经实现了从评价理念到评价实践的巨大突破。值得注意的是，虽然大部分命题者能够以课程标准为依据命题，但68.75%的命题者并未分析试题与课程标准的一致性，这也是导致命题虽以课程标准为基准但是结果却有时并不一致的原因。

## 六、学业成就评价与课程标准一致性的几个问题①

### （一）一致性的涵义究竟是什么？

尽管Webb重点讨论了评价与标准的一致性，但他也认为，作为复杂系统的整体课程改革，一致性研究绝不应该仅仅关注“评价”与“标准”，这也是他给出水平与垂直一致性模型的原

① 主要内容见Webb，张雨强编译.判断评价与课程标准一致性的若干问题[J].比较教育研究，2011，(12).

因。课程、教学、评价、教师专业发展、学校组织与变革等诸多要素之间的整体良性一致性才是真正决定课程改革成效的要因。

“知识深度”在一致性检验中是核心概念，它与“认知水平”有着千丝万缕的联系，但不能简单地认定其就是心理学领域内的认知水平。因为知识深度没有经过心理学的实证研究。但作为对内容复杂性的描述手段，它在比较试题的评价目标与课程标准的课程目标的一致性上显示了强大功能。

需要指出的是，一致性不是绝对意义上的，这从 Webb 的一致性判断技术指标可以看出。这就提醒我们，尽管“课程执行”应该是“自上而下”的贯彻与实施，但更不能忽略一线实践者“自下而上”的反馈与修正；“课程实施”不应该是“刚性的一一映射”，而是一项充满着教师主动创生的“弹性的二次开发”。但这种“弹性的二次开发”更多应该是课堂层面的课程与教学的实践创造，而不应是对充满国家意志的课程政策与文本的“曲解与随意篡改”。

**（二）什么程度的一致性才是足够的好？**

第一，每个内容标准所对应试题的合理数目。Webb 模式对于每一个内容标准至少使用 6 道试题来分析评价与标准的一致性，这一数量来自于 Subkoviak1988 年进行的关于判断学生对试题掌握情况的信度研究。但在具体应用时，这一数字会或多或少地发生变化。关于某州的内容集中性分析就暴露出了问题：美国三年级科学课程共有 6 条标准，结果显示该州对其中的两个标准（探究、学科事实与概念）更为重视，而对其他的 4 条标准重视不够。特别是对设计与应用、个人与社会两条标准，由于其很难评价，则只有少数试题与此相关。[27]

第二，不同认知水平的试题之间的数量分配。对于某一知识深度水平的内容标准而言，有 50% 的试题（与相应目标的知识深度水平相当或高于）与之对应是否是最低可接受水平？根据不同的评估目的，应该有不同的方法来确定不同水平试题的比例。如果评估是为了区分哪些学生是熟练掌握而哪些不是，试题的认知水平应该与相应标准的认知水平一致；但如果评估是为了对学生的熟练水平做出准确判断（基准以下、基准、熟练、高级等），试题的认知水平则可以涵盖一系列的认知水平，而不是仅仅与相应标准保持绝对一致。

鉴于很多目标其实涵盖了宽泛的内容领域，因此对于同一个目标而言，应该有不同知识深度水平的试题与之对应，这样才合理。可以让试题尽可能在更大范围内代表相应标准与内容的认知水平，如水平 1、2、3 分别占 20%、60%、20%。

第三，不同年级间的认知水平试题的比例如何确定？学习者心理发展水平与认知发展水平会随着年龄增长而不断提高，因而推理、分析技能在学业评价中的比例应该越来越高。但迄今没有相应的评估指南来确定不同认知水平试题的比例到底应该是什么样的。因此，只能依据测验惯例与经验来确定，如五年级数学测验中水平 1、2、3 试题的比例分别是 30%、50%、20%，而十年级数学测验中水平 1、2、3、4 试题的比例分别是 5%、45%、47%、3%。

### （三）一致性检验面临的主要问题

第一，审议专家对试题所能测验的学习目标的认同度不高。[28] 在美国迈阿密州学生评估中，三分之二的专家表示只有 35%的试题（43 道中的 15 道）评价了具体的课程目标，加州这一比例则有 71%（43 道试题中的 30 道）。原因可能是对课程目标的表述不清晰，也可能是标准开发的不完善、对标准与评估的认同度不高、标准陈述模糊、评估试题指向不明、专家意见不一致等。但需要进一步确定不一致的根本原因，从而找到正确的解决方法。

第二，知识深度的确定涉及 8 个主要因素：不同年级间的变化、复杂性与难度、试题类型、课程目标中的核心学业成就表现、培训中分析专家之间的意见趋同过程、知识深度代码的整合、稳定性。不同年级间的不同知识深度的试题分量应该如何确定？某一具体课程目标中的核心学业成就表现在哪些方面？不同背景的分析专家如何能就知识深度的理解达成一致等问题都是评价与标准一致性检验中的重点问题。

第三，知识深度与认知水平到底是什么样的关系？作为评价与标准一致性的核心概念，目前缺乏对"知识深度"这一概念的心理学实证研究。研究者大多参照泰勒的目标行为学、布卢姆认知目标分类学等研究成果对知识深度的不同水平进行限定，但这种限定的科学性引起了另一些研究者的质疑。[29]

### （四）韦伯模式在中国应用的可能性与现状

第一，中美均有基础教育质量监测的教育诉求，均需应对基础教育课程改革教育问责的社会期待。国内也亟须收集相关研究证据，以对近年来的课程改革的实效进行专业判断。基于课程标准进行学业成就评价无疑是一条可行之路。

第二，基于（课程）标准，是中美基础教育课程（评价）改革的共同特征。但不同的是，美国"国家课程标准"并非我国的"学科课程标准"，基本类似于我国"课程改革纲要与学科课程标准的中间体形态"，而且在同一学科内存在若干"州课程标准"。美国的州课程标准一般包括内容标准与表现标准，我国的学科课程标准只包含内容标准，未体现学生学业成就的表现标准。但国内学业成就评价标准研究在进行中，而且可以借鉴高考大纲的开发技术。

第三，评价与标准一致性研究在国内已经起步，且正显示出越来越强的生命力与适应性。自 2005 年 7 月"中美教学与评价一致性会议"（China-US Conference on Alignment of Assessments and Instruction）起，国内已发表相关论文 20 余篇，大部分被 CSSCI 收录，引起了不少关注。① 研究范围为评价与标准一致性的一般技术与策略、评价与标准一致性的典型范式、基于标准的教学理念与策略、评价与标准一致性在学科学业成就评价中的应用等。

---

① 除本课题组外，国内研究者主要有崔允漷、夏雪梅、王少非、刘学智、马云鹏、朱行建、朱伟强、邵朝友、汪贤泽、王磊、刘恩山等人（大致按成果发表时间排序，如有遗漏，敬请谅解）。

需要说明的是，评价与标准一致性是专业性很强的系统工程，其技术开发除了课程与教学领域专家外，还需要教育测量与评价专家、教育技术专业人员的加盟，更需要众多有学科背景的课程专家与研究型教师的协作。

参考文献

[1] 张雨强.基于课程标准的学业成就评价：韦伯模式之研究[J].全球教育展望，2011(10).

[2] Glatthorn, A.A.(1997). *The Principal as Curriculum Leader*. Thousand Oaks, CA: Corwin:83-89.

[3][7] 崔允漷，夏雪梅.试论基于课程标准的学生学业成就评价[J].课程·教材·教法，2007(1).

[4] 刘建海，康淑敏，张雨强.英语开放性学业成就评价与课程标准的匹配策略初探[J].教育科学研究，2010(4).

[5] 朱伟强."基于课程标准"：内涵和意义[J].当代教育科学，2006(8).

[6] 钟启泉，崔允漷.新课程的理念与创新-师范生读本[M].北京：高等教育出版社，2003:38.

[8] Robert L. Lin & Norman E. Gronlund.教学中的测验与评价[M].国家基础教育课程改革"促进教师发展与学生成长的评价研究"项目组，译.北京：中国轻工业出版社，2003:2.

[9] H. Gary Cook (2005). *Aligning English Language Proficiency Tests to English Language Learning Students*. http://www.ccsso.org/content/pdfs/ELPAlignmentFinalReport.pdf, 2008-12-08.

[10] 崔允漷，等.基于标准的学生学业成就评价[M].上海：华东师范大学出版社，2008:113—114.

[11][13][14] *Criteria for Alignment of Expectations and Assessments in Mathematics and Science Education* (CCSSO and NISE Research Monograph No. 6). Madison: University of Wisconsin, Wisconsin Center for Education Research. 14-21,9,10,13.

[12] Webb, N. L. (2002). *Alignment Study in Language Arts, Mathematics, Science, and Social Studies of State Standards and Assessments for Four States*. Washington, DC: CCSSO. 5-6.

[15][27] Webb, N. L. (2007). Issues Related to Judging the Alignment of Curriculum Standards and Assessments. *Applied Measurement in Education*, 20(1):7-25.

[16][20] 张志红，张雨强，周传昌.化学中考试题与课程标准的一致性初探[J].化学教育，2010(9).

[17] 焦传玲，张雨强.化学高考试题与课程标准的一致性初探[J].化学教育，2011(8).

[18] 张志红.初中化学学业水平考试与课程标准的一致性研究[D].曲阜：曲阜师范大学，2011.

[19] 中华人民共和国教育部.教育部关于积极推进中小学评价与考试制度改革的通知，2002.

[21] 崔允漷.国家课程标准与框架解读[J].全球教育展望，2001(8).

[22] 张雨强，张志红.我国台湾地区"评量人才养成工作坊"及其启示[J].课程·教材·教法，2010(9).

[23] 张雨强，秦凤.认知目标分类研究新进展及对学业成就评价的启示[J].当代教育科学，2011(2).

[24] 张雨强.试论我国命题专业化的现状与发展途径[J].全球教育展望，2006(6).

[25] 张雨强,张志红.初中化学学业成就评价命题者的评价素养调查[C].长沙:第八届化学课程与教学论专业委员会年会论文,2011.11.

[26] 岳喜腾,张雨强.基于课程标准的学业成就评价:韦伯模式之研究[J].全球教育展望,2011(10).

[28] Webb, N., et al. (2006). Alignment of Mathematics State-level Standards and Assessments: The Role of Reviewer Agreement. CSE Report 685:22.

[29] Webb, N. L. (2005). Alignment, Depth of Knowledge, & Change. Florida educational research association 50th annual meeting. Miami, Florida. November 17. http://facstaff.wcer.wisc.edu/normw/. 2007-11-18.

# 第二部分

# 课堂评价设计和实施的理论与技术

# Development of Formative Assessment in Japan

Koji Tanaka
Kyoto University

**Abstract**: This paper examines how the understanding of formative assessment in Japan has developed as well as how it has been implemented in the past and at present, and explores future challenges that may arise. The most distinctive feature of this theory was the "reversal idea." In the past, teachers and students, alike, had an aversion to missteps made during lessons. As a response to reversal ideology, teachers tenaciously pursued children's "missteps" and identified the cause, giving insight into the abundant "logic" behind them. Moreover, the teachers that discovered this did not consider these "missteps" as negative, but learned from them, creating lessons that capitalized on these "missteps." Formative assessment, which emanated from educational assessment research, gained importance as a compass for improving "teaching" and "learning" by supporting the ideology of utilizing "missteps."

**Keywords**: Formative Assessment; missteps ;Constructivism

## 1. Introduction to formative assessments in Japan

Today, I would like to consider the current situation of lesson assessments by examining how formative assessment is understood and put into practice in Japan.

The formative assessment approach, advocated by Bloom (B. S. 1913 - 1999), was introduced in Japan in the mid - 1970s. Contemporary thought in Japan recognized that "relative assessment" was problematic and the alternative educational assessment approach was explored as its replacement. Mastery learning, as advocated by Bloom, in addition to criticizing relative assessment, guaranteed academic achievement for all children and became largely influential in Japan. Specifically, many people were drawn to formative assessment, which was crucial to mastery learning[1].

According to Bloom, educational assessment could be classified into three categories: "diagnostic assessment," "formative assessment," and "summative assessment." Within the context of relative assessment, educational assessment would be beneficial only as "general assessments" or "summative assessment" at the end of classroom teaching to rank and sort children. However, if educational assessment was to be implemented to ensure children's academic achievement, then diagnostic assessment would also be necessary to grasp the students' levels before administering lessons.

Furthermore, the evaluations performed during a class period are formative assessment. The information extracted from formative assessment is received as feedback. If the class is not in synchronism with the educational objectives, corrective activities would be set in place to correct children and revise the syllabus. On the other hand, if most of the children in the class understood the material, then enrichment activities would be organized. Thus, formative assessment adapted and conducted during class would further secure children's right to learn.

Bloom's proposed "the mastery learning theory" had a great impact on Japan's educational world in the 1970s as an instruction theory that surpassed relative assessment. In particular, the formative assessment approach showed Japan's teachers the importance of using educational assessment during class. At the same time, Japan's teachers observed that formative assessment was not just conducting quizzes, but also "oral questioning" and "circulating among students' desks and checking on their work." For example, "oral questioning" was a medium through which teachers ask students a "question" that encourages them to think and also ascertains their level of understanding through formative assessment.

## 2. "Idea of utilizing missteps (tsumazuki)" to support formative assessment

However, there was a certain opposition to the rise of formative assessment. This critique argued that formative assessment might be nothing more than an efficient check of children's goals for academic achievement through repetitive correction of missteps. In other words, views on formative assessment remain to be framed by the indication of Behaviorism, typical of programmed instruction. Behaviorism, as mentioned here, is defined as "a process of forming connections between stimuli and responses" and there in the learning agent is considered to be a black box.

The basis for these complaints was founded in "Lesson study (Jugyo kenkyu)" that Japanese teachers worked hard to establish. It featured the "idea that missteps (tsumazuki) can be utilized," the origins of which were apparent in the practices of Yoshio Toui, 1912-1991, and Kihaku Saito, 1911-1981. Yoshio Toui and Kihaku Saito developed "lesson study" in Japan, most notably after World War II. In essence, Japan's teachers tackled the notions within lesson study: "cooperation instead of individual action," "repeating incidents instead of isolated incidents," and "conducting investigations by one's self instead of subcontracting a researcher" [2] The most distinctive feature of this theory was the "reversal idea." In the past, teachers and students, alike, had an aversion to missteps made during lessons. As a response to the reversal idea, teachers tenaciously pursued children's "missteps" and identified the cause, giving insight into the abundant "logic" behind them. Moreover, the teachers that discovered this did not consider these "missteps" as negative, but learned from them, creating lessons that capitalized on these "missteps." Formative assessment, which originated from educational assessment research, gained importance as a compass for improving "teaching" and "learning" by supporting the idea of utilizing "missteps."

In 1957, Yoshio Toui left behind the following famous words: "Children are stumbling geniuses" [3] Teachers viewed children's missteps as detrimental to the lesson and wanted to avoid them as much as possible. In contrast, Toui thought that children were not randomly making mistakes, but that they were geniuses making missteps based on given "rules." He identified these rules as "the Logic of Everyday Life," derived from the thought process characteristic of children (hereafter, the "naive concept" indicated by the "miss concept" of children) and "the Logic of Subject Matter" from problems in teaching (i.e., problems with text books and teaching skills). He claimed that analysis of missteps reveals teaching gems. Quite precisely, "children are stumbling geniuses."

Of course, Toui was not aware of formative assessment. However, analysis of these missteps highlights the Logic of Everyday Life and the Logic of Subject Matter. Given this, it would not be an exaggeration to say that his approaches attempting to improve the current state of teaching and learning are themselves the essence of formative assessment. Accordingly, Toui earlier indicated that formative assessment is not merely skills of examining children's success or failure, but a means to improve classroom practices by utilizing children's missteps.

On the other hand, in 1958, Kihaku Saito also proposed "the sharing system of error in an attempt to share each misstep" [4] This was an attempt to dismiss blame for the child who made the misstep during class. By formulating and classifying it instead as "the sharing system of error in an attempt to share each misstep", the misstep would then be shared by the class and transformed into an object of corrective learning. "Reversal idea" for missteps, which shared common ground with Toui, and the concept of expanding formative assessment to learning groups was extremely novel from a contemporary perspective.

Thus, formative assessment originated in Japan over the course of the 1980s as support for the idea that missteps can be utilized.

## 3. Constructivism and formative assessment

However, in the mid - 1990s, there was a further shift in the main subject of this "utilization," which was influenced by constructivist learning theories. This new way of thinking emphasized the idea that children's cognitive abilities were not merely structured by what they had been taught, instead, were actively and independently gaining new knowledge from the relationship to their existing knowledge. In doing so, the role of self-assessment became even more critical in demonstrating how well the students themselves grasped this active and independent cognitive activity. It was deemed essential that formative assessment must merge with self-assessment.

Life-experience writing or the life-experience composition ( seikatsu tsuzurikata ) approach emphasized the importance of self-assessment in Japan's educational practices before World War II [5] This life-experience writing approach was unique to Japan. It encouraged students to self-assess by writing down facts about situations they confront in their daily lives or their actual thoughts at the time. This process of teaching shifted from life-experience writing to reading these writings in front of the class and finally discussing them with the class. Through this process, children are able to clearly evaluate themselves based on their own lives.

Kazuaki-Shougi, who practiced the Hypothesis-Verification-Through Experimentation Learning System (Kasetsu Jikken-Jugyo), affirmed the importance of self-assessment from 1965. According to Shougi, since "education is the work of constantly driving children to realize that they are improving," teachers "construct avenues for children to easily evaluate themselves" for this purpose. Then, they suggest various methods for self-assessment. Shougi does not claim that self-assessment is linked with specific method of assessment , but essentially, he does indicate the necessity of always creating innate opportunities for self-assessment to establish true educational assessment. On the contrary, he indicates that assessment methods that lack the opportunities for self-assessment are little more than simple skills of judgment.

These life experience writing and Shougi's approach were the seeds for constructivist learning theories in Japan and the educational legacy that needed to be learned to bring formative assessment to a new stage of development.

## 4. Practice of formative assessment that integrate self-assessment

Now, I will introduce two formative assessment practices that integrate self-assessment. One is "Learning System based by Learning Task" advocated by Yasutaro Tamada, 1927 - 2002, who is known in Japan as a "master of lesson planning". The other is the practice of "One Page Portfolio Assessment: OPPA" devised by Tetsuo Hori, who introduced Japan to "naive concept" research.

(a) Practice of Learning System based on Learning Task

Steps for Tamada's Learning System based on Learning Task are as follows[7]

① The teacher presents the learning task.

② The children write their own thoughts in a section titled "What I think" in a notebook.

③ The teacher offers different ideas and asks for a show of hands to determine the distribution of that idea among the students.

④ The children express and debate their own opinions.

⑤ The students write down the opinions of others under "Other People's Opinion" in their notebooks.

⑥ After debate, the teacher checks the distribution of ideas and how it has changed by a show of hands.

⑦ The teacher (or in some cases, a student) confirms the hypothesis with an experiment.

⑧ The children write down what they think under "Experiment results and what I learned" in their notebooks.

⑨ The children read what they wrote in step 8 starting with those children who are done writing first.

For their learning task, while considering the foundation of cooperative learning, the children consciously "write in their notebooks" as in steps ②, ⑤, and ⑧. According to Tamada, writing in their notebooks is a "formative assessment." The role of evaluation for the teachers is to "try to understand what is going on in the minds of the children" who have addressed the learning task, participated in the debate, and learned the results of the experiment. On the other hand, this is a "confirmation for children of their independent learning" and a self-assessment of what they are learning as part of the learning group and how their awareness has changed. Formative assessment like these provides important clues for the "teacher's evaluation of the class."

As an example, I would like to introduce the lesson development with the attainment target of "for plants, flowers are the organs of reproduction." First, a rapeseed plant is used as instruction material; the students observe the structure of the plant and the mechanism of pollination. Then, as a developmental learning task, children are asked "can you identify the fruit and seeds on this blooming tulip"? (①) and a discussion begins. Of course, from their life and learning experience thus far, many children think "tulips are raised from bulbs and so do not produce fruit or seeds" (②, ③). On the other hand, some children think that "tulips can also produce fruit and seeds" and "the children's expression and debate of their own opinions" begins (④).

Afterwards, a child wrote the following under "Other People's Opinion" in their notebook: "First, there was the opinion that the tulip was a plant so of course it produces seeds. I disagreed with that opinion. The reason was that I had never heard of a tulip seed, and tulips are planted as bulbs, so I disagreed. Next, someone strongly proposed that tulips grew from bulbs. I agreed with that. Then, someone asked "if that is true, then why do they have stamens and pistils"? This provides a glimpse of the children's debate.

Then the students observe the pistil ovaries and ovules and by confirming the fruit and seeds harvested (⑤), they are surprised by the realization that tulips do in fact have fruit and seeds. A student wrote the following in his notebook under "Experiment results and what I learned" (⑧, ⑨): "There was an ovule. I saw what was raised afterwards. The ripened seed was a reddish purple, thin, and triangular. Based on this, it is certain that it can produce seeds. I learned that bulbous plants have flowers that bloom ,and produce fruit and seeds. Uchida, my classmate, asked how is that they do not spread seeds but instead grow from a bulb, and I thought that it takes too long before the flower blossoms if seeds are planted, which is probably why they plant bulbs." The children actively debate this learning task, and it can be understood through formative assessment in this notebook that the children listening to the arguments are also steadily participating in cooperative learning.

(b) Practice of "One Page Portfolio Assessment: OPPA"

OPPA is a practice that many teachers follow. (See, Figure1, 2). It was devised by Tetsuo Hori, who introduced the "naive concept" to Japan (⑧). OPPA is a method where students record their class achievements before, during, and after class on one sheet (OPP sheet: One Page Portfolio Paper) as a learning record, causing students to evaluate themselves. As opposed to a normal portfolio assessment, the point is to maximize the least amount of information necessary for assessment, because it uses one sheet of paper,

It allows teachers to review the learning progress before, during, and after the lesson, as well as organize and prepare what students record on the sheet of paper to utilize the results in their teaching. Students can visibly track their growth following this specific information. It is thought to foster the ability to learn and think independently in students.

Usually for OPPA, one OPP sheet is created to grade each unit's lesson plan. Next, students are made to fill in their learning record after each class. Teachers review these sheets by making appropriate comments and attempt to improve their learning. Through this repetition, students evaluate their learning progress as a whole after each unit is completed. It is a method that makes students evaluate themselves.

I will explain the essential structure on which this is based.

An OPP sheet is organized into four parts: "I. Unit Title ," "II. Essential Questions Before and After the Learning," "III. Learning History," and "IV. Self-Evaluation after the Learning."

The teacher may write down "I. Unit Title," although some teachers have the students write it down after the unit is complete. This is to improve their ability to reflect on the whole unit and summarize it accurately.

"II. Essential Questions Before and After the Learning " establishes exactly the same questions before and after learning so that students can compare and recognize differences. This questions include points such as what the teacher wants to confirm and transmit through the unit. Questions that simply ask whether they remember are unsuitable. "II. Essential Questions Before the Learning " is a diagnostic assessment, and "II. Essential Questions After the Learning" is equivalent to a summative assessment.

"III. Learning History" is a column where students write "the most important point in today's lesson" for each class. Since the OPP sheet uses a single sheet of paper, when there are many periods in a unit, it is necessary to divide and group it into smaller units so that the learning record is on one page. The students are made to write the most important point in today's lesson so as to allow the students to improve their ability to choose the essentials from the topics and information dealt with in class, consider it, and summarize and express it in their own way. Some teachers have the students write the title in the learning history column. This causes them to improve their ability to appropriately express the information from a given class period. This learning history is equivalent to a formative assessment.

"IV. Self-Evaluation after the Learning" is a column where students reflect on their learning as a whole and question how they feel about what, why, and how something changed. This self-evaluation is a final, all-encompassing assessment and it is especially important. This is reported to have the ability to reach students, and instill within them a sense of their own personal growth and self-efficacy.

## 5. Summary

This is an introduction on the development of formative assessments in Japan. In summary, I would like to correlate the history of this development to the different stances on missteps.

"Missteps are the children's fault"— This relative assessment stance considers the cause of missteps to be the children's insufficient ability or effort.

"Lessons without missteps"— This is the belief that a misstep in a lesson should not occur. So that missteps can be promptly corrected, the objective is to eliminate them and emphasis is placed on efficient teaching alone. This stance grasps formative assessment from a behaviorist perspective.

"Lessons where teachers utilize missteps" — Missteps are treated as important teaching opportunities and lessons arrange missteps in an attempt to shape academic achievement, but this utilization is limited by teachers and the reality of children's learning is not nearly sufficient. This is a formative assessment stance derived from educational research by Japan's teachers.

"Lessons where both students and teachers utilize missteps" — Students and teachers cooperate to subjectively overcome missteps. Then, they review their progress and missteps, along with creating settings where they can proactively voice what they did not understand in the classroom, working to transform missteps that are confronted and differentiated within the learning group into learning tasks. This stance grasps formative assessment from a constructivist perspective.

This self-assessment is dependent on the trust in children's competency and ability to develop. Integrating this self-assessment into formative assessment in this way makes it possible for children to become confident learning agents. Furthermore, in the 2000s, amidst globalization, a large scale Academic Achievement Survey is being implemented in Japan and academic competition has become more intense in educational institutions. Given this situation, there is a concern that scholarship will become meaningless. In this situation, there is indeed a strong demand for the practice of formative assessment that incorporates self-assessment.


**References**

[1] Bloom, B.S and et al, Handbook on Formative and Summative Evaluation of Student Learning, McGraw-Hill Book Co, 1971.

[2] National Association for the Study of Educational Methods(ed), Lesson Study in Japan. Keisuisha Co, 2011.

[3] Toui, Yoshio, Mura wo Sodateru Gakuryoku , Meijitosho Shuppan Corporation, 1957.

[4] Saito, Kihaku, Mirai Tsunagaru Gakuryoku , Mugi Shoubo, 1958.

[5] Nakauchi Toshio, Seikatsu Tsukurikata Seiritsushi Kenkyuu , Meijitosho Shuppan Corporation, 1970

[6] Shouji, Kazuaki, Kasetsu Jikken Jugyou , Kokudosha, Co., 1965.

[7] Tamada, Yasutaro, Rika no Toutatsu Mokuhyou to Kyouzai Kousei, Azumi Shoubo, 1990.

[8] Hori, Tetsuo, Manabi no Imi wo Sodateru Rika no Kyouiku Hyouka , Toyokan Publishing, 2003.


Figure1: Components and Overview of the OPP sheet
Please paste PDF(Fig1) here.

Figure2: Example OPP Sheet Entries for Mechanism and Function of Roots and Stems.
Please paste PDF(Fig2) here.

## 日本形成性评价的历史回顾与展望


田中耕治

东京大学



【摘要】文章研究日本的形成性评价的理解如何发展,它过去和现在是如何实施的,未来将面临什么挑战。这个理论最显著的特征是“逆向思维”。在过去,教师和学生一样对课堂中的失误行为感到厌恶。作为逆向思想的回应,教师坚持找出孩子的“失误”,还要确认发生的原因,并深入研究它们背后大量的逻辑问题。此外,发现原因的教师不认为这些“失误”是消极的,而是从中吸取教训,利用这些“失误”的资源来设计教学。形成性评价,源自教育评估研究,作为利用“失误”促进教与学的思想,显得极为重要。



【关键词】形成性评价;失误;建构主义

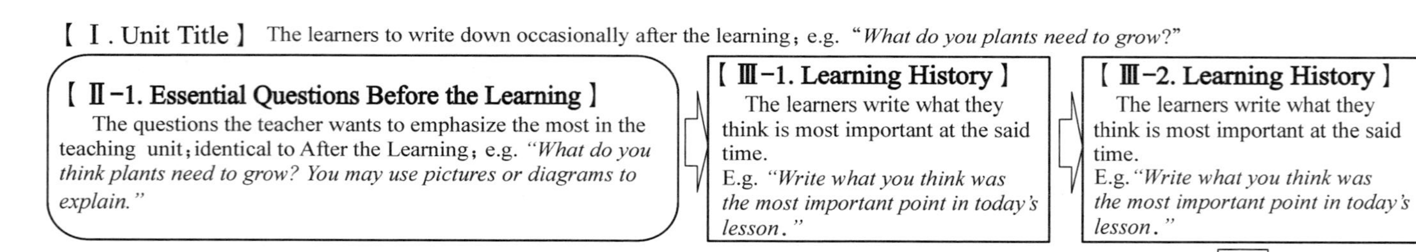


**【 Ⅳ. Self-Evaluation after the Learning 】**

Thoughts on one's own opinion and expression such as the significance of the learner's own learning(metacognition); e.g. *"Looking at the responses to essential questions before and after the learning and the learning history, what has changed and how?"*

Components and Overview of the OPP Sheet

**Figure 1: Components and Overview of the OPP sheet**

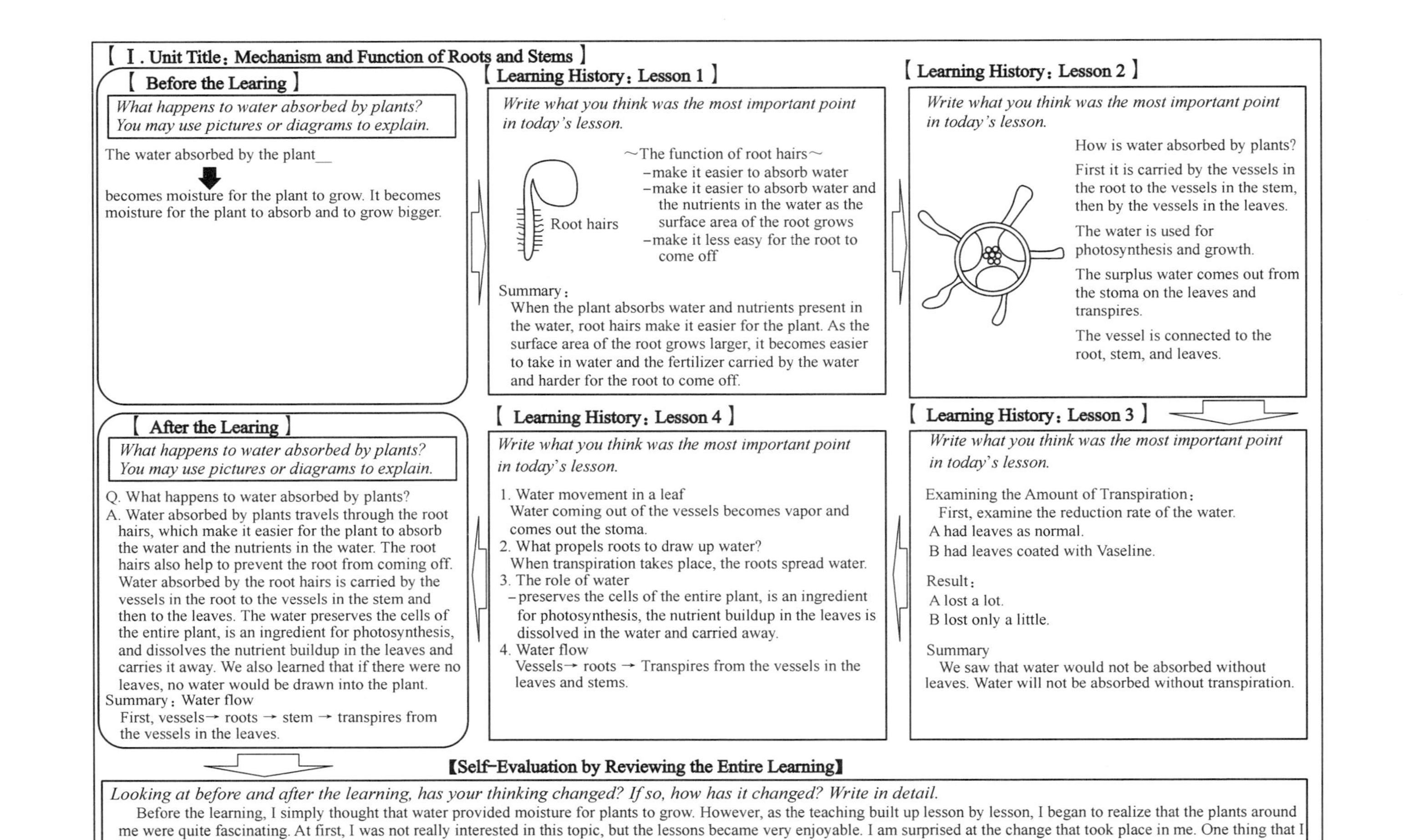

【Ⅰ. Unit Title: Mechanism and Function of Roots and Stems】

【Before the Learing】

*What happens to water absorbed by plants?*
*You may use pictures or diagrams to explain.*

The water absorbed by the plant__

becomes moisture for the plant to grow. It becomes moisture for the plant to absorb and to grow bigger.

【Learning History: Lesson 1】

*Write what you think was the most important point in today's lesson.*

Root hairs

~The function of root hairs~
- make it easier to absorb water
- make it easier to absorb water and the nutrients in the water as the surface area of the root grows
- make it less easy for the root to come off

Summary:
When the plant absorbs water and nutrients present in the water, root hairs make it easier for the plant. As the surface area of the root grows larger, it becomes easier to take in water and the fertilizer carried by the water and harder for the root to come off.

【Learning History: Lesson 2】

*Write what you think was the most important point in today's lesson.*

How is water absorbed by plants?

First it is carried by the vessels in the root to the vessels in the stem, then by the vessels in the leaves.

The water is used for photosynthesis and growth.

The surplus water comes out from the stoma on the leaves and transpires.

The vessel is connected to the root, stem, and leaves.

【Learning History: Lesson 3】

*Write what you think was the most important point in today's lesson.*

Examining the Amount of Transpiration:
First, examine the reduction rate of the water.
A had leaves as normal.
B had leaves coated with Vaseline.

Result:
A lost a lot.
B lost only a little.

Summary
We saw that water would not be absorbed without leaves. Water will not be absorbed without transpiration.

【Learning History: Lesson 4】

*Write what you think was the most important point in today's lesson.*

1. Water movement in a leaf
   Water coming out of the vessels becomes vapor and comes out the stoma.
2. What propels roots to draw up water?
   When transpiration takes place, the roots spread water.
3. The role of water
   - preserves the cells of the entire plant, is an ingredient for photosynthesis, the nutrient buildup in the leaves is dissolved in the water and carried away.
4. Water flow
   Vessels→ roots → Transpires from the vessels in the leaves and stems.

【After the Learing】

*What happens to water absorbed by plants?*
*You may use pictures or diagrams to explain.*

Q. What happens to water absorbed by plants?
A. Water absorbed by plants travels through the root hairs, which make it easier for the plant to absorb the water and the nutrients in the water. The root hairs also help to prevent the root from coming off. Water absorbed by the root hairs is carried by the vessels in the root to the vessels in the stem and then to the leaves. The water preserves the cells of the entire plant, is an ingredient for photosynthesis, and dissolves the nutrient buildup in the leaves and carries it away. We also learned that if there were no leaves, no water would be drawn into the plant.
Summary: Water flow
First, vessels→ roots → stem → transpires from the vessels in the leaves.

【Self-Evaluation by Reviewing the Entire Learning】

*Looking at before and after the learning, has your thinking changed? If so, how has it changed? Write in detail.*

Before the learning, I simply thought that water provided moisture for plants to grow. However, as the teaching built up lesson by lesson, I began to realize that the plants around me were quite fascinating. At first, I was not really interested in this topic, but the lessons became very enjoyable. I am surprised at the change that took place in me. One thing that I learned was to hope that I can become someone who does not start out with thinking something as boring but makes an effort to enjoy the learning process.

Example OPP Sheet Entries for "Mechanism and Function of Roots and Stems." (Filled by First-grade Junior High School Girl)

**Figure 2: Example OPP Sheet Entries for Mechanism and Function of Roots and Stems.**

# Understanding Formative Assessment in the Classroom

Ellen Osmundson

National Center for Research on Evaluation, Standards and Student Testing (CRESST)
UCLA Graduate School of Education and Information Science

**Abstract**: This paper focuses on understanding formative assessment in the classroom, one effective strategy for improving student learning. I begin by explaining a basic problem facing the educational system in the United States, and suggest a potential solution-formative assessment. I follow with a brief overview of the background and research on formative assessment, and then present our current working model of the formative assessment process. In the next section, I discuss emerging findings from our research work with teachers and formative assessment. The paper concludes by proposing next steps in understanding formative assessment.

**Keywords**: Formative Assessment; working model; Embedded Assessment System

## 1. Current Problem

The news is filled with dismal reports on the depressing state of education in the United States; fifty percent of students at our lowest performing schools drop out before completing high school, undergraduate educators bemoan the necessity of remedial mathematics and writing classes for entering freshman, while businesses complain that college graduates are woefully underprepared to join the work force, lacking problem solving and critical thinking skills. Teachers too are suffering; schools, districts and states are facing massive budget cuts to all programs, while teacher professional development to continue learning and growing conceptual, pedagogical and assessment knowledge is nearly absent from the teaching landscape. We are clearly in the midst of an on-going teaching and learning crisis.

Amidst this educational doom and gloom is a glimmer of encouraging news. *The No Child Left Behind Act of 2001* and more recent *Race to the Top* (2009) legislation has produced an explosion of interest in the use of assessment to measure and improve student learning. Evidence from classroom-level assessment is compelling: teachers' on-going use of assessment to guide and inform instruction-formative assessment can lead to statistically significant gains in student learning (Black & Wiliam, 1998, 2001, 2004). This ongoing assessment process, one designed to close the gap between the learner's current state of knowing and the desired goal, is particularly effective in helping low-performing students make progress in their learning. Recent studies, however, have revealed challenges in implementing quality formative practices that lead to strong effects on student learning.

A companion paper by my colleague CRESST Dr. Joan Herman, outlines the critical importance of a coherent, comprehensive and continuous assessment system (NRC, 2001), with assessment of, for and as learning. While this paper focuses exclusively on formation assessment, it must be viewed as part of a comprehensive assessment system, one designed to support student learning and achievement.

## 2. Background and Research on Formative Assessment

In their comprehensive review of more than 250 studies on teaching and learning, Paul Black and Dylan William, in 1998, concluded that gains in student learning in classrooms with formative assessment strategies in use were among the largest reported for educational interventions. These effect sizes, in the range of .4 to .7, were particularly strong for low-performing students.

The National Research Council, in their seminal book, "Knowing what Students Know" (2001), highlighted the importance of the relationship between instruction and formative assessment, noting: "Students will learn more if instruction and assessment are integrally related. *In the classroom, providing students with information about particular qualities of their work and about what they can do to improve is crucial for maximizing learning.*" (p.8).

A broad research base supportive of the significance of formative practices in improving learning now exists (Bell & Cowie, 2000; Black, Harrison et al.; 2004; Black & Wiliam, 1998; Hattie & Timperley, 2007; Meisels, Atkins-Burnett, Xue, & Bickel, 2003; NRC, 2001; OECD, 2005; Ruiz-Primo & Furtak, 2006; Shepard, 2000; Shepard, Hammerness, Darling-Hammond, & Rust, 2005). This research is based on different theoretical perspectives including motivation, metacognition, self-regulation, classroom assessment, teachers' discourse practices, and feedback. In practice, formative assessment is a dynamic, interactive process that involves:

—learning goals and success criteria that are shared and understood by teachers and students;

—continuous monitoring of how learning is evolving through teacher, self- and peer-assessment;

—feedback and subsequent adjustments to teaching and learning to meet the needs of learners.

Yet, recent research indicates that teachers face significant challenges in learning and integrating formative assessment practices into instruction to help learning move forward (Gearhart & Osmundson, 2008; Gearhart et al., 2006; Heritage et al., 2009; Herman, Osmundson & Silver, 2010; Osmundson, Dai & Herman 2011).

## 3. Working Model of Formative Assessment

Figure 1 below displays our current working model for the formative assessment process. We credit and thank our CRESST colleague Margaret Heritage for this version of the formative assessment cycle (Heritage, 2010). There are ten components integral to formative assessment; the relationship between these components is dynamic and interactive, that is, changes to one component in the cycle are likely to result in shifts in other aspects of the formative assessment process. A brief description of each component follows. Specifically:

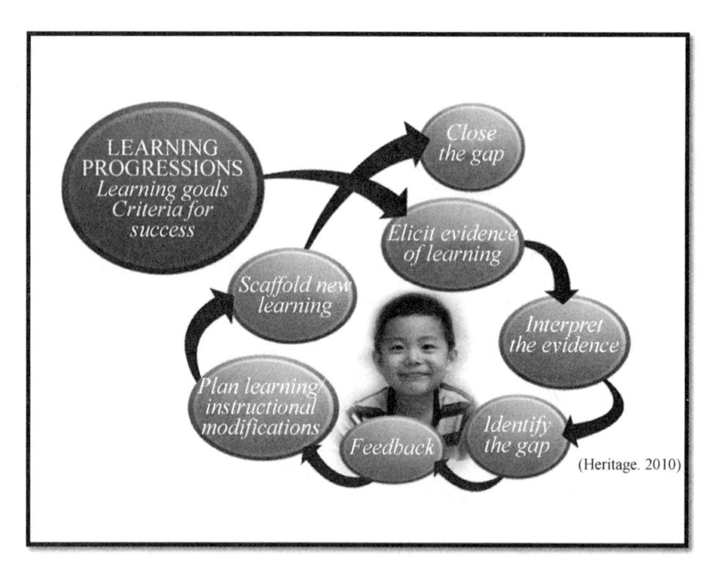


**Figure 1: The Process of Formative Assessment**

—*learning progressions* are empirically based descriptions of how learning develops/progresses in a particular content area or domain over an extended period of time. Learning progressions inform and guide more immediate learning goals and success criteria.

—*learning goals* describe what students will learn during the course of instruction, not the activity for the day. Learning goals should be clear, manageable, fit the students' learning needs, be aligned with the success criteria, and be communicated and understood by students and teachers alike.

—*criteria for success* are the ways in which students express their understanding of the learning goals. Students provide evidence of where they are in relationship to the goal through their explanations, demonstrations, presentations, problem solving, etc. To be effective, success criteria should be clear, aligned with learning goals, fair and unbiased, communicated with and understood by the learner, and made explicit through examples.

—*eliciting evidence of learning* involves specific strategies and approaches for systematically gathering evidence of student learning as it is occurring. These strategies and approaches should be aligned with the learning goals and success criteria, and be appropriate to their purpose. Further, the evidence elicited should reflect important concepts and skills.

—*interpreting the evidence* involves teachers analyzing the information elicited during the course of instruction, to establish where students are in their learning, and where additional teaching and learning is needed. Coding guides support teachers with analysis and interpretation of.

—*identifying the gap* refers to the teachers understanding where students are in their learning with relationship to the learning goals and success criteria.

—*feedback* to students regarding their learning is essential to keep students moving forward. Feedback supports student learning when it is detailed and specific to the learning, and outlines areas of success and areas where improvement is needed, rather than total solutions.

—*instructional modifications* are the next steps to support student learning. Teachers may decide to provide additional learning experiences, engage students in discussions or ask probing questions to help students improve their learning.

—*scaffolding new learning* involves providing the appropriate level of support to students so that new learnings are progressively internalized, and become part of a student's independent achievement and performance.

—*closing the gap* refers to moving students along in their learning to close the gap between what they currently know, say and do, and the learning goal. Closing the gap is the ultimate goal in teaching and learning.

Classroom culture, the context in which learning takes place, is the final component to our model. Classrooms that are collaborative, where learning goals and success criteria are clearly understood, and detailed, specific feedback is provided, and where there is adequate time and opportunity for students to strengthen their learning through self- and peer-reflection support student achievement. The quality of the classroom climate plays an essential role in supporting learning. Students need to believe the classroom is a place where they belong and that their teacher and their peers are there to help them learn. The teacher must establish, explicitly teach, and model classroom expectations that reflect positive social behavior, non-threatening interactions, and collaborative routines.

Lorrie Sheppard, in her 2000 AERA presidential address, raised several questions about classroom culture, formative assessment and learning:

> "How might the culture of classrooms be shifted so that students no longer feign competence or work to perform well on a test as an end separate from real learning? ... How should what we do in classrooms be changed so that students and teachers look to assessment as a source of insight and help...? To accomplish this transformation, we have to make assessment more useful, more helpful in learning... (pp. 12 - 15).

## 4. Recent Research

At CRESST, we've been researching and conducting professional development on formative assessment for the past seven years. In this section, I summarize findings from these on-going efforts to build teachers' formative assessment capacity, and to understand how teachers' formative assessment practices develop.

***State-wide Initiative***

The first project was a multi-year effort that involved various levels of participation and collaboration between state department educators, leadership teams, pre-service education providers, administrators and teachers. Participants attended a series of face-to-face meetings, which focused on building knowledge and understanding of different components of the formative assessment process. These sessions were followed-up by Webinars, Professional Learning Communities (PLCs), and opportunities for participants to try out new formative assessment strategies in the context of the classroom, school or district. Each successive year of the project involved a larger and more varied audience, with formative assessment being integrated into other statewide initiatives, (e.g., state-standards adoption).

Several findings from this project are worth noting. Buy-in and a long-term commitment to change are essential to building formative assessment capacity at the statewide level. On-going multiple agency collaborations, while challenging, are valuable, due in large part to leveling the learning/playing field, as participants engaged in the learning about formative assessment together. Finally, planning, feedback and revision are critical to any large-scale initiative, as it takes time and hard work to develop quality formative assessment practices.

### Professional Development Project

The second project was a professional development effort to build K - 12 teachers' formative assessment knowledge through institutes, rich in content (science) and assessment learning opportunities. Formative assessment portfolios, used to document teacher learning, were a resource for data and information on the development of teachers' formative assessment knowledge and practices. Teachers used existing science curriculum and assessments in formative ways to deepen their assessment knowledge and practices. At the district level, Professional Learning Communities, provided teachers with opportunities to collaborate, and build leadership. Additionally, each district had access to formative assessment experts, to provide participants support and scaffolding as participants worked to implement new strategies and approaches to understanding student learning.

From this project, we came to understand the importance of building on teacher knowledge and expertise, and that rich learning opportunities could be both advantages and disadvantages. The institutes provided teachers with multiple opportunities to build their knowledge of content and formative assessment, but the challenge of trying out complex ideas and strategies, in addition to regular classroom activities, was often burdensome. The use of existing materials, including assessments, became something of a treasure hunt, with "nuggets of gold" regularly discovered by teachers as they reviewed their curriculum. Teachers came to better understand how classroom activities, such as small group discussions, investigations and problem-solving, could provide rich information about student learning, if aligned with articulated learning goals and success criteria. Finally, collaboration between teachers at the K - 12 level was beneficial to all participants. Elementary teachers deepened their science content knowledge through conversations with more highly knowledgeable high school teachers. High school teachers in turn enriched their teaching and pedagogical knowledge through interactions with elementary teachers.

### Embedded Assessment System

The final project was a randomized, controlled study with 3rd and 4th grade elementary teachers who learned to use a curriculum-embedded formative assessment system in science. Treatment teachers used an inquiry-based curriculum in concert with pre/post assessments, science notebooks, end-of-investigation checks, and coding guides for analyzing student work. Additionally, teachers met with colleagues in study groups to support student learning. Control teachers engaged in "business as usual" science teaching and assessment. We used research tools that were conceptually aligned with quality formative assessment practices to gather data on teachers' formative assessment practices. The data sources included a pre/post content survey of teachers' content and pedagogical content knowledge, electronic logs to capture weekly teaching and learning, and classroom observations and interviews.

Results from this study are preliminary at this point - data analyses are currently in progress. Dr. Yunyun Dai will present some of the emerging findings in her presentation. It appears that teachers in the treatment group, through the use of the embedded assessment system, deepened their own content and pedagogical content knowledge, which in turn *may* have increased student science learning, as measured on a curriculum-specific pre/post test.

Lessons learned from the last study reveal the importance of practice; after the second year of using the embedded assessment system, treatment teachers reported more clearly understanding the tools and protocols for examining student work, more regularly and systematically analyzing student work, more frequently providing feedback to students with specific strategies for improvement, and more consistently engaging in next-step strategies to scaffold student learning. Teachers also reported having a deeper understanding of the learning goals and success criteria for the science units studied. Additionally, this project, through classroom observations, interviews, and electronic teacher logs, suggests that small shifts in teacher knowledge may represent significant changes in formative assessment practices, a very encouraging sign that validates our belief in formative assessment as an agent to improve teaching and learning.

## 5. Conclusions and Next Steps

I began this paper by presenting a significant educational challenge: how can we improve the quality of teaching and learning in the U.S.? I proposed formative assessment as one approach to strengthening student learning, and improving the quality of instruction. Building teacher capacity to use formative assessment to increase instructional effectiveness is a challenging proposition. And yet, if we are to take seriously the charge of providing quality instruction to *all* students, formative assessment, clearly situated and grounded in the daily lives of students and teachers, remains an attractive and compelling approach to improving teaching and learning.

**References**

Bell, B., & Cowie, B. (2001). *Formative assessment and science education*. Dordrecht: Kluwer Academic Publishers.

Black, P., Harrison, C., Lee, C., Marshall, B., & Wiliam, D. (2004). Working inside the black box: Assessment for learning in the classroom. *Phi Delta Kappan*, 86(1), 9 - 21

Black, P., & Wiliam, D. (1998a). Assessment and classroom learning. *Assessment in Education: Principles, Policy and Practice*, 5(1), 7 - 74

Black, P. & Wiliam, D. (1998b). Inside the black box: Raising standards through classroom assessment. *Phi Delta Kappan* 80(2), 139 - 148.

Black, P., & Wiliam, D. (2004). The formative purpose: Assessment must first promote learning. In M. Wilson (Ed.), *Towards coherence between classroom assessment and accountability*. Chicago: University of Chicago Press.

Gearhart, M. & Osmundson, E. (2008). Assessment Portfolios as Opportunities for Teacher Learning. Educational Assessment: 14(1), 1 - 24.

Gearhart, M., Nagashima, S., Pfotenhauer, J., Clark, S., Schwab, C., Vendlinski, T., Osmundson, E., Herman, J., & Bernbaum, D. (2006). Developing Expertise with Classroom Assessment in K - 12 Science: Learning to Interpret Student Work Interim Findings From a 2 - Year Study. University of California Los Angeles: CRESST. Technical Report 704.

Gearhart, M., Nagashima, S., Pfotenhauer, J., Clark, C., Schwab, C., Vendlinski, T., et al. (2005). Developing expertise with classroom assessment in K - 12 Science: Learning to interpret student work. Interim findings from a two-year study. Educational Assessment: 11(3&4), 237 - 263.

Hattie, J., & Temperley, H. (2007). The power of feedback. *Review of Educational Research*, *77*(1), 81 - 112.

Heritage, M., Kim, J., Vendlinski, T., & Herman, J. (2009). From evidence to action: A seamless process in formative assessment? *Educational Measurement: Issues and Practice*, *28*(3), 24 - 31

Heritage, M. (2010). Formative Assessment: Making it Happen in the Classroom. Thousand Oaks, CA: Corwin Press.

Herman, J., L., Osmundson, E., & Silver, D. (2010). Capturing quality in formative assessment practice: Measurement challenges. (CRESST Report 770). Los Angeles, CA: University of California, National Center for Research on Evaluation, Standards, and Student Testing (CRESST).

OECD (2005), Formative Assessment: Improving Learning in Secondary Classrooms, Paris, ISBN: 92-64-00739-3, p.282.

Osmundson, E., Dai, Y., and Herman, J. (2011). Year 3 ASK/FOSS efficacy study. (CRESST Report 782). Los Angeles, CA: University of California, National Center for Research on Evaluation, Standards, and Student Testing (CRESST).

National Research Council. (2001). *Knowing what students know: The science and design of educational assessment*. Committee on the Foundations of Assessment. J. Pellegrino, N. Chudowsky, & R. Glaser (Eds.). Washington, DC: National Academies Press.

No Child Left Behind Act, 2002. U. S. Department of Education. Washington, D. C.: Author. Retrieved September 10, 2011, from http://www2.ed.gov./policy.

U.S. Department of Education (2009). Race to the Top program: Executive summary. Washington, D. C.: Author. Retrieved May 21, 2010, from http://www2.ed.gov/programs/racetothetop-assessment/index.html.

Ruiz-Primo, M. A., & Furtak, E. M. (2006). Informal formative assessment and scientific inquiry: Exploring teachers' practices and student learning. *Educational Assessment*, *11*(3 & 4), 205-235.

Shepard, L. A. (2000). The role of assessment in a learning culture. *Educational Researcher*, *29*(7), 4-14.

Shepard, L. A., Hammerness, K., Darling-Hammond, L., Rust, F., Snowdown, J. B., Gordon, E., Gutierez, C., & Pacheco, J. (2005). Assessment. In L. Darling-Hammond & J. Bransford (Eds.), *Preparing teachers for a changing world: What teachers should know and be able to do*. San Francisco: Jossey-Bass.

# 解读课堂中的形成性评价

Ellen Osmundson

【摘要】聚焦于解读课堂中的形成性评价，即一种促进学生学习的有效策略。首先，解释美国教育系统面临的主要问题，基于此提出一种有前景的解决方法——形成性评价。其次，简要概述形成性评价的研究背景，并呈现当前形成性评价过程的工作模式。再次，讨论我们和教师合作研究形成性评价的最新发现。最后，文章总结了今后解读形成性评价的步骤。

【关键词】形成性评价；工作模式；嵌入式评估系统

【作者简介】Ellen Osmundson/美国国家评价、标准及学生测试研究中心高级研究员

# 素质文化视野中的课堂评价理念

丁念金

【摘要】课堂评价理念应该具有素质文化视野，因为课堂评价要在一定的理念指导下进行，课堂评价理念应该基于文化，整个社会文化应该走向以素质文化为核心。素质文化视野中的课堂评价理念主要有：以素质发展为核心导向；师生共同成长；自主；个性化。体现课堂评价新理念的评价操作要领主要有：注重课堂评价的完整性；注重有效交往思路；形成自我评价与他人评价结合的完善机制；研制和使用多元化的课堂评价标准系列。

【关键词】文化；素质文化；利益文化；课堂评价；理念

【作者简介】丁念金/上海师范大学教育学院教授、博士生导师

在人的自觉意识达到高的发展水平的今天，人的行动都受理念的指导，课堂评价也不例外。课堂评价理念是很复杂的，它的形成需要多方面的视野，其中一个重要的视野就是文化视野。而在当今，人类文化应该走向以素质文化为核心，课堂评价是直接针对人的素质的，因此其理念尤其应该直接基于这一核心。在这里，"素质"取其广义，指人的身心发展水平和特征，包括知识、技能、智力、品德、创造力、价值观、性格、气质、身体素质等。本文就从素质文化的视野来探讨课堂评价理念，以及体现这些理念的课堂教学评价操作要领。

## 一、课堂评价理念的素质文化视野

### （一）课堂评价要在一定的理念指导下进行

课堂评价即指课堂教学评价，它包括对学生的学、教师的教以及此两者之间关系的评价。理念(ideology)，本是西方古代哲学中的一个重要范畴，在柏拉图那里，理念主要是指存在的普遍属性，它是绝对的永恒的存在，是现象世界的背后的深层的东西，是现象世界的本体、基础、来源和依据，并作为一种等级体系存在。现在，"理念"一词已经用于社会生活的各个领域，其基本含义是指基本的深层的观念。

课堂评价要以课堂评价理念为指导。人是有意识的，人的活动是在意识指导下的自觉的、能动的活动。马克思强调：人类的"特性恰恰就是自由的自觉的活动"[1]，这是强调人的活动由自觉意识所指导。在人的意识中，一个重要的层次是理念，这是基于对事物本质之认识的基本观念。人们正是以理念为基础，形成相关的方法论，并进而形成宏观的操作方略和微观的操作的具体方法。课堂评价作为人的一种自觉的活动，也要以一定的理念为指导，这里起指导作用

的理念就是课堂评价理念。课堂评价是对整个课堂教学的检验，课堂评价理念整合了整个课堂教学中的一个基本的理念，这些理念是形成课堂评价机制、制定课堂评价标准、选择课堂评价方式方法的重要依据。

### （二）课堂评价理念应该基于文化

人的任何活动都受到整个社会的文化的广泛而深刻的影响，都应该遵循社会文化中的精神、观念。文化作为一种包含着、积淀着人类精神的存在，它渗透于社会生活的各个方面。课堂评价作为社会生活的一个重要方面，尤其受到文化的重要影响。因为，课堂评价的核心是价值评判，而价值是整个文化的核心[2]，尤其是文化中的文化精神的核心。文化包含文化精神和文化形式两个大的层次，文化精神中包含价值。课堂评价首先要直接体现文化中的各种价值，其次受到整个社会的文化精神的影响，这些文化精神包括文化中的基本观念，另外，还要受到各种文化形式的影响。社会文化对课堂评价的影响，首先表现为影响着课堂评价的理念。因此，课堂评价理念应该基于文化。

### （三）整个社会文化应该走向以素质文化为核心

文化是非常广泛而复杂的，课堂评价理念所基于的文化的核心应该是素质文化，这主要是因为，整个社会文化应该走向以素质文化为核心，素质文化，就是人的素质发展为主导价值的文化。

漫长历史以来，人类社会文化的核心是利益文化，即以利益为主导价值追求的文化。这里的“利益”包括多个方面的内容，其中最显著的内容是财富和权力两个方面。在以利益文化为社会文化之核心的社会历史条件下，人们的行动、社会的风尚主要是受利益驱动的。关于长期以来人类社会文化以利益文化为核心的情况，许多思想家都认识到。例如，德国古典哲学家黑格尔的历史哲学的核心主题就强调：人对个人利益的追求是历史的原动力，并说：“如果没有利害关系，个人就不能做任何事情。如果把这种对利害关系的关切称为热情，我们可以说，没有热情世上任何伟大的事业都不会成功……热情，是指由私人的利益、特殊的目的而产生的人类活动。”[3]再如，马克思说：“人们奋斗所争取的一切，都同他们的利益有关。”[4]

过去历史中社会文化以利益文化为核心，一方面维系了人类的生存，另一方面又造成了极大的危害。利益文化强化人们对财富和权力的追求，财富和权力都是人类生存所必需的。首先，财富往往代表着生活条件，人们对财富的追求，满足了人们生活的需求，从生存条件上维系了人类的生存，并在一定程度上使得人们的生存质量走向美好。其次，权力在一定意义上代表着对社会秩序的维系，而社会秩序是人类生存的又一个重要条件。当然，在过去漫长的历史中，由于社会文化以利益文化为核心，许多人过度追求利益，包括过度追求财富和权力，而这种过度的追求导致了过多的争斗、过多的社会动荡，还导致了对地球资源的人类生存环境的过度破坏。在中国和在西方都是如此。应该说，在过去漫长历史中，人类社会的文化以利益文化为核心，是难以避免的。

当前，整个社会文化应该走向以素质文化为核心。这是因为：

第一，人类的社会生产力已相当发达，人类的生存已不成问题，在此条件之下，人们完全可以追求更高的文化理想了，这种更高的文化理想的核心就是对人类自身素质发展的文化自觉。在过去漫长的历史中，人类也有着自身素质发展的目的，事实上也不断地在实现人类自身素质的发展，正如马克思所说："人们的社会历史始终只是他们的个体发展的历史，而不管他们是否意识到这一点。"[5]当然，在过去的历史中，人们对素质发展的追求尚未达到高度的文化自觉。而今天，人们有条件达到素质发展的文化自觉了，基于这种文化自觉，整个社会应该走向以素质文化为核心。

第二，素质文化具有多方面的优越性，诸如：人的素质本身就是这个世界最美好的存在，因为人是这世界美好的存在，而人的内涵是人的素质；人的素质发展是人类社会发展的一项核心性的内容；人的素质发展是社会其他各个方面发展的一个重要条件，例如，是社会和谐的一个重要条件；人的素质发展是每个人都能够追求、能够获得成功的，因为每个人都具有达到高素质的潜力；对人的素质发展的追求，副作用很小，不会造成对地球资源的过度掠夺和对人类生存环境的过度破坏。文化的核心在于价值追求。人总是要有追求的，那么，什么东西最值得追求呢？是人的素质，因为人的素质最美好，积极效应最大，而消极效果最小，因此，在人类生存已不成问题的今天，整个社会文化应该走向以素质文化为核心，而不能继续以利益文化为核心，这是走向美好社会、和谐社会的根本。

## 二、素质文化视野中的课堂评价理念的构成

从素质文化的视野看，课堂评价理念主要包括以下几个方面：

### （一）以素质发展为核心导向

在过去较长的时间内，课堂评价的核心导向或者不够明确，即不知道为了什么而开展课堂评价活动，或者较多地以"资格"为核心导向。我们经常说的"应试教育"也是以获得某种资格为考试的主导价值追求。这里的资格有近期的，如获得"好学生"的资格；也有远期的，如获得升学机会并进而获得社会地位、社会职业的资格。

现在，从素质文化的视野看，课堂评价应该明确地以素质发展为核心导向。这是因为：第一，整个社会文化的核心将是素质文化，素质文化是以人的素质发展为主导价值的文化，由于社会文化是整个社会生活的基本体现和导向，因此社会生活的各个领域都应该体现素质文化这一核心，教育活动尤其如此。人类的社会活动是多种多样的，不同活动的核心职能不同，例如，经济活动的核心职能在于创造物质财富，同时也要促进人的素质发展，而教育活动的核心职能在于促进人的素质发展。第二，课堂评价是整个教育的一个有机的组成部分，而整个教育的核心职能在于发展人的素质，因此评价的基本宗旨也在于促进评价对象的素质发展。关于

评价应该成为整个教育中的一个有机的组成部分，许多学者已经明确地认识到，国际著名的教育评价专家格兰特·威金斯倡导的教育性评价体系就是一个典型的例子。[6]第三，评价的核心过程是一个价值评判的过程，价值评判的中心是价值，价值是文化的核心，而当前的文化应该走向以素质文化为核心，以素质发展为主导性的价值追求。

以素质发展为核心导向，其基本要求在于：其一，充分认识到人类社会文化的最重要的价值是人的素质发展，以促进人的素质发展为核心职能的教育活动是社会的中心[7]，而课堂评价又是教育的关键环节之一；其二，课堂评价的基本宗旨在于促进评价对象的素质发展，而不是为评价对象评分评等或赋予某种资格，这就真正将课堂评价与素质发展整合起来。

### （二）师生共同成长

过去的课堂评价在理念上往往是单方面的：或者是教师对学生进行评价，学生只是作为被动的评价对象；或者是管理部门对教师进行评价，教师只是作为被动的评价对象。从素质文化的视野来看，这种情况应该大为转变，即注重师生共同成长的理念。

为什么要树立师生共同成长的理念呢？这是因为：第一，从素质文化的视野来看，全社会各类成员都要不断地实现素质发展，所有社会成员的素质发展是整个社会文化发展的核心，就课堂而言，教师和学生这两类社会成员都是如此，都应该在各类课堂评价中共同成长；第二，课堂评价要评价学生的学、教师的教以及学与教的关系，学的活动和教的活动的主体分别为学生和教师，这两类主体都应该在课堂评价中成长，而且他们是相关联的，应该共同成长；第三，在课堂中，教师与学生构成一个学习共同体，学习共同体的基本使命是通过学习而共同成长；第四，过去，我们往往忽视了教师的成长，其实，教师的成长不仅具有其本身的意义，而且为学生的成长提供榜样示范和引领作用，这就与学生形成共同成长的态势；第四，课堂评价的部分活动是教师与学生之间相互评价，而按照第四代评价理论，评价是评价者与被评价者之间相互学习、彼此为师、共同建构、共同发展的过程[8]，具体到课堂评价，这应该是师生共同成长的过程。

师生共同成长的理念的基本要求在于：课堂评价的根本宗旨在于促进相关人员的素质发展；相关人员特别指教师与学生；教师的素质发展与学生的素质发展相互关联，相互促进；课堂评价中师生共同成长现象作为一种有代表性的社会现象，对全社会成员的成长起着示范和促进作用。

### （三）自主

在过去较长的时间内，课堂评价的一个重要特征是外在控制性，而缺乏评价对象的自主性。评价对象往往只是被动地接受评价：学生被动地接受教师和管理部门的评价，教师被动地接受管理部门的评价。从素质文化的视野来看，这种状况需要大为转变，即课堂评价应该注重自主。

课堂评价应该注重自主的理由主要有：第一，无论教师还是学生，他们作为评价对象，都具有自主的需要，正如莱恩·多亚尔和伊恩·高夫所强调的，对于人来说，自主是一种基本需要[9]，在课堂评价中，人的自主需要当然不会消失；第二，课堂评价的根本宗旨在于促进人的发展，而人的发展的一个重要方面是自主意识和自主能力的发展，自主性的发展是教育的一种重要目的，西方教育学界已经一致地认识到和强调这一点[10]，课堂评价也要促进教师和学生的自主性的发展，而要实现这一点，就必须增强课堂评价的自主性；第三，从根本上讲，人的素质发展是一个自主的过程，课堂评价要有效地实现促进教师和学生的素质发展的宗旨，就要增强课堂评价的自主性。

课堂评价的自主理念的基本要求为：课堂评价真正内化为评价对象（分别为学生、教师）的自身需要，使课堂评价成为满足评价对象的需要、促进评价对象之目的的实现的过程，并使评价对象充分地认识到和体验到这一点；第二，使课堂评价在总体上成为一个由评价对象自己主导的过程，虽然在评价的部分客观领域和环节也重视外在控制，但这只是评价的一个局部，而且这个局部要纳入到评价对象整体性的自主发展与评价的体系之中。

**（四）个性化**

过去，在多数情况下，课堂评价往往是整齐划一，即对于所有的评价对象来说，评价的目标、评价的内容、评价的标准、评价的方式方法等，都是一致的。从素质文化的视野来看，这需要实现大的转变，即转向较高程度的个性化。遵循和促进每个人的个性发展，不仅是个人素质发展的崇高需要，而且是民族和国家发展的需要，正如约翰·密尔（John S. Mill）所说的："一族人民是会在一定长的时期里前进一段而随后停止下来。在什么时候停止下来呢？在不复保有个性的时候。"[11]

课堂评价注重个性化的理由主要有：第一，素质文化是社会文化的一个领域，当今整个社会文化发展的一个重要特征是个性化和多元化，素质文化也应该如此，在课堂评价中，也应该体现个性化；第二，课堂评价的基本宗旨在于促进评价对象的素质发展，而人的素质发展应该是个性化的，人的个性化发展是马克思揭示的共产主义的一个最基本的理想，例如，马克思、恩格斯在其论著中曾至少六次阐述和强调"自由个性"的主张[12]，过去我们的整齐划一的课堂评价实际上严重地束缚了评价对象的发展，现在应该转变这一点；第三，在课堂评价中，每个评价对象的生活与学习目标、学习兴趣、知识基础、智力发展水平、性格等都是彼此不同的，课堂评价应该适应各个方面的个性差异，因此应该个性化；第四，课堂评价的基本宗旨是促进评价对象的素质发展，而不同评价对象存在不同的问题，对他们需要采取各不相同的促进对策，因此课堂评价应该个性化。

就课堂评价而言，个性化理念的基本要求有：课堂评价在具体目的上要促进评价对象的自由个性的发展，而不能束缚评价对象的个性发展；课堂评价的目标、内容、标准和方式方法的选择与使用，应该因评价对象个人的具体情况而异；课程评价采取的问题揭示与分析策略，也要因人而异；课堂评价要特别注重评价对象的创造性的发展，这是个人素质发展特别需要的，也是社会的丰富化、国家创新能力发展和强盛所特别需要的。

## 三、体现课堂评价新理念的评价操作要领

要体现素质文化的精神，体现上述课堂评价理念，就要在课堂评价上实行一整套的合理化操作，这个操作体系是非常复杂的，其中操作要领有如下几点：

### （一）注重课堂评价的完整性

由于素质文化是完整的，课堂评价是促进评价对象素质发展的过程，素质以及这种促进过程是完整的，因此评价应该是完整的。这里的完整性主要包括以下几层考虑：其一，在制定课程评价的目标时，要注重促进素质发展的完整性，即说，课堂评价要在具体的评价目标上促进评价对象之素质的完整发展，而不能仅仅注重某一个方面或少数几个方面，例如，不能仅仅注重知识再现的目标。为此，要制定一个完整的课堂评价规划，这个规划要对评价目标进行完整的设计。其二，在确定和分析评价对象时，要注重对象类别及其特征的完整性。课堂评价的一项具体的工作是分析评价对象，在分析评价对象时，要注意：既充分地注重学生又充分地注重教师，同时还要注重教师与学生之间的相互关联；要注意到各类不同的教师、各类不同的学生；要注意到教师的各个方面的特征、学生的各个方面的特征。其三，在制定评价标准时，要注重完整性，如各个方面都要考虑列入标准体系，在标准体系中占有适当的地位，从而形成一个完整的、合理的标准体系。其四，在分析问题和揭示解决问题的策略时要注重完整性。课堂评价要发现问题、针对问题和解决问题，在此，要防止陷入片面化，而注意考虑各个方面、各个层次、各个环节、各种具体情境。

### （二）注意有效交往思路

由于师生共同成长在一定程度上是通过交往而实现的，因此课堂评价在操作思路上要注重交往，尤其是师生交往。交往思路要求：将课堂评价过程纳入到教师的毕生发展过程和学生的发展过程，而这种发展过程的一个重要途径是交往——包括教师与学生的交往、教师与教师的交往、学生与学生交往等；认识到课堂教学在一定程度上是一个交往的过程，而课堂评价是整个课堂教学的一个部分、一个环节，要将课堂评价整合到整个课堂交往体系之中。具体而言，要注意：形成明确的交往意识，并让评价对象有意识地在交往中努力地实现自己的素质发展；注重遵循人际交往的礼仪，这有助于体现中国这个“礼仪之邦”的文化底蕴，有助于提高评价各方主体在评价活动中的舒适感和满意感，有利于更好地实现课堂评价深层地促进评价对象素质发展的作用，提高课堂评价的美好程度，因为，礼具有“释回，增美质，措则正，施则行”的作用；由于是交往过程，因此在评价过程中要充分地尊重每个人的尊严，评

价各方之间相互尊重；由于交往可以促进素质发展，为了充分实现这种作用，因此在课堂评价的操作中，各方之间要相互学习、相互吸收对方的优点、相互促进，实现第四代评价所追求的共同建构。

### （三）形成自我评价与他人评价结合的完善机制

课堂评价要有自主性理念，而自主性之作用的有效实现，需要在评价的操作机制上达到自我评价的完善结合。首先，应该以自我评价为主。注意：自我评价不等同于自主评价，前者是就操作机制而言的，而后者是就目的、动力、意愿而言的。课堂评价是非常复杂的，而且评价的核心内涵是价值评判，而价值评判不完全是主观的过程，它存在主观性与客观性关系之处理的难题[13]，仅仅靠他人的评价是根本无法完成的，大量的时候是需要评价对象自我评价。事实上，较长时间以来，人们就较高程度地重视自我评价。在当代社会中，存在个体自我认同的危机，为了促进个体自我认同感的形成，就更加需要注重自我评价，课堂评价也是如此。需要强调的是：有人可能会怀疑自我评价的客观性、普遍性和可靠性，笔者认为，只要设计巧妙，这是不必担心的，事实上，研究表明，自我评价活动同样是人类的本质特征的体现，自我评价活动同样具有普遍性和非私人性。[14]在课堂评价中，评价机制以自我评价为主，这是较为突出的，例如：教师的素质评价主要靠自我评价；学生的素质评价主要是靠自我评价；学生的学习过程评价很重要，而这主要靠自我评价。一般而言，只有那些容易客观化的内容才能有效地借助于他人评价，而这样的内容在教师的教、学生的学、教师和学生的素质发展中只占一小部分。

当然，不能仅仅注重自我评价，而应该尽量做到自我评价与他人评价的完善结合。这特别要注意如下几点：其一，在主观性较强的内容上以自我评价为主，而在客观性程度较高的内容上是他人评价为主，此两者形成一个总体框架；其二，增加自我评价与他人评价的交互作用，例如，适当地用他人评价来制约自我评价、检验自我评价的某些结果，而对于他人评价也要注重增加评价对象的自我体验，因为要通过自我体验才能增强评价对象对评价的认同，并进而促进评价对象的素质发展；其三，加强对自我评价的指导，包括加强对教师的自我评价的指导、对学生的自我评价的指导，指导者是多方面的。

### （四）研制和使用多元化的课堂评价标准系列

评价标准问题是评价的一个关键问题。为了体现课堂评价的个性化理念，就需要研制和使用多元化的课堂评价标准系列。具体来说，要特别注意以下几点：其一，尽量实现评价标准中体现的文化价值的多元性，因为文化价值的多元化已经成为当代文化发展的一个普遍而重要趋势。其二，尽量研制出多样化的、弹性的评价标准，这些标准形成一个系列或多个系列，为评价提供多元化的选择，并以实施评价时具有较充分的选择自由，从而为个人的素质发展提供广阔的自由空间。个人的自由发展不仅它本身具有重要性，而且是国家富强的一个重要条件、重要目的，人们早就有所认识，而当前，人们的认识更强烈了。[15]其三，有研制出的多个系列的评价标准中，要能够针对各个评价对象的具体情况，选择能完整地体现和促进其个性发展的标准系列。当然，有时可以考虑：针对不同个人的不同标准系列之间在评分水准上具有一定的平行性。


参考文献

[1] 中共中央马克思恩格斯列宁斯大林著编译局，编译．马克思恩格斯全集(第42卷)[M]．北京：人民出版社，1979：96.

[2] 张岱年．文化与价值[M]．北京：新华出版社，2004：8.

[3] 黑格尔．历史哲学(人对私利的追求是历史的原动力)[M]．张作成，等，编译．北京：北京出版社，2008：12.

[4] 中共中央马克思恩格斯列宁斯大林著编译局，编译．马克思恩格斯全集(第1卷)[M]．北京：人民出版社，1956：82.

[5] 中共中央马克思恩格斯列宁斯大林著编译局，编译．马克思恩格斯选集(第4卷)[M]．北京：人民出版社，1995：532.

[6] [美]Grant Wiggins．教育性评价[M]．国家基础教育课程改革"促进教师发展与学生成长的评价研究"项目组，译．北京：中国轻工业出版社，2005：12—13.

[7] 国际21世纪教育委员会．教育——财富蕴藏其中[R]．联合国教科文组织总部中文科，译．北京：教育科学出版社，1996：8—10.

[8] [美]H.J.沃尔博格．教育大百科全书：教育评价[Z]．张莉莉，译审．重庆：西南师范大学出版社，2011：61.

[9] 莱恩·多亚尔，等．人的需要理论[M]．汪淳波，等，译．北京：商务印书馆，2008：78.

[10] 詹姆斯·D·马歇尔，等．个人自主与教育[M]．于伟，等，译．北京：北京师范大学出版社，2008：75.

[11] [英]约翰·密尔．自由论[M]．程崇华，译．北京：商务印书馆，1959：76.

[12] 王盛辉．"自由个性"及其历史生成研究——基于马克思恩格斯文本整体解读的新视角[M]．北京：人民出版社，2011：47—55.

[13] [美]约翰·杜威．评价理论[M]．冯平，等，译．上海：上海译文出版社，2007：3—9.

[14] 陈汉新．自我评价论[M]．上海：上海人民出版社，2011：131.

[15] 崔宜明．个人自由与国家富强[M]．上海师范大学学报(哲学社会科学版)，2011(3)：21—22.

# The Ideology of Classroom Assessment in the Vision of Quality Culture

Nianjin Ding

**Abstract**: A vision on guality culture is indespensable for the idea of classroom assessment, because classroom assessment should be carried out under the guidance of the concept, the concept of classroom assessment should be based on culture, quality culture should be the core for the development of social culture. The concept of classroom assessment under the vision of quality culture mainly includes: quality-oriented development as the core; teachers and students grow together; independent; personalized. Key points of evaluation which reflect the new concept of classroom evaluation include: Attach great importance to the completeness of classroom evaluation: emphasis on the effective exchange ideas; Establish a comprehensive mecharism which combines self-evaluation and evaluation of others. Develop and use a wide range of classroom evaluation criterias.

**Key words**: culture; quality culture; classroom assessment; concept

# 课堂教学评价：描述取向

安桂清　李树培

【摘要】当前，由于量化取向的教学评价无法兼顾教学的整体性与发展性以及发挥评价的发展性功能，课堂教学评价亟待转型。描述取向的教学评价以倾听与观察、理解与解释、研究与改进为特征，能够有效的弥补量化取向教学评价的不足，从而为课堂教学评价改革提供了另一种可资借鉴的模式。学校层面在以教研组或备课组为基本单位推进这一新的评价方式时，可参考"进入现场，开展描述—解释现象，揭示主题—协商改进，提供建议—提炼结论，获得启示"这一行动框架。

【关键词】课堂教学评价；倾听与观察；理解与解释；研究与改进

【作者简介】安桂清/华东师范大学课程与教学研究所副教授

李树培/华东师范大学全国中小学计算机教育研究中心上海部讲师

## 一、当前我国教学评价的倾向与问题

20世纪80年代以来，随着教育统计学和教育测量学在我国的恢复与发展，中小学开始制定各种课堂教学评价量表，以求对课堂教学做出客观、公正的评价。当前我国中小学普遍使用的课堂教学评价标准，是从20世纪50年代初以来经过几十年教学实践的不断检验和修正，逐渐形成的一个包括教学目标、教学内容、教学方法、教学进程结构以及教师教学基本功等几个主要方面的评课要求。[1]进入21世纪之后，随着基础教育课程改革的推进，新的教育理念日益深入人心，相应地各级教育研究机构和学校开始调整和更新课堂教学评价标准，纷纷增加体现新课程思想的维度和内容，如"是否采用合作、探究的学习方式"、"是否应用多媒体教学技术"，等等。评课者根据评价量表中的每一指标分值进行判断和评分，最后算出得分或者给出等级，这种做法有效地推进了课堂教学评价的实践，提升了课堂教学的质量。但随着教育的发展和课程改革的要求，量化评判的教学评价愈益显露出其不足：

**第一，支离破碎的要素分解破坏了教育和人的整体性**

把课堂教学的评价要素分解为教学目标、教学内容、教学方法、信息技术等环节，使得教学容易为了迎合这些条分缕析的评价点而变得琐碎、机械。教师准备好丝丝入扣的教学设计方案，期望在流畅顺利的教学过程中如数实现，害怕或抗拒意外情况。这种求全责备的教学评价非常容易让本应个性盎然、师生精彩观念不断诞生、教学流程和教学内容可随时调整的课堂教学变得呆板、平淡甚至平庸，教师和学生都为求安全、保险、省心而舍弃了个性、情感和理智的全情投入，都仿佛在从事和完成一种不关涉自己内心的外在任务。教学是关涉师生对于学习内容的心智理解与情感体验的事情，不仅是一项认知性实践，更是伦理的、社会的、政治的实践。我们需要超越因素分解的教学评价，努力寻求教学生态中各存在者的生态关系，恢复教学评价的整体性，进而恢复教育和人的整体性存在。

**第二，浅表片面的评判标准消弭了课堂教学的复杂性**

依照当前多数学校所采用的课堂教学评判标准，教师更多考虑的是师生互动的频率、教学设备和手段的多样化、学生参与的人次和频次、课堂高潮的铺垫与迭起等形式化的东西，对于课程内容与学生理解、多媒体技术、课堂组织方式等之间的内在匹配度则无暇顾及，也无暇考虑何时互动、为何互动、采用多媒体技术的时机和方式、学生个体思维的状态等深层次问题。这种浅表片面的教学评价标准遮蔽了教学的本真意义，消弭了教学的复杂性和情境性，忽略了那些难以直接观测的动态生成的隐性教学要素。教学评价并非简单的因果对应阐释，而应秉持复杂、连续的动态思维，探寻体现教学复杂性的评价维度。

**第三，简单模糊的技术量化消解了教学评价的发展性**

教学评价对于教师的根本意义在于帮助教师提升课堂教学的质量和层次，能够实现促进学生发展的终极目的。传统的量化教学评价只能提供简单模糊的分数或等第，且不说这个分数或等第是否科学合理，更进一步说，这种教学评价实际上把教师置于被观看、审视、评判的被动地位，压抑了教师作为主体对自己教学行为的思考和辩解，忽视了教师在教学实践和专业成长方面所需要的时间和空间，对于教师的日常教学改善和专业发展并无太大益处。教师更为需要的是开诚布公、袒露心迹、直面教学问题的教学评价，这种教学评价能够激发教师对教学本身、对教材、对学生、对教者自己已有观念的反思和审视，进而出现新的教学认识和理解，并尝试不同的教学实践行为。这需要我们超越简单的量化评判和分类划等，追求和实现教学评价的发展价值。

综上所述，面对量化取向的教学评价所暴露的弊端，我们需要对当前的教学评价进行调整、转向，致力于恢复教学的整体性、复杂性以及评价的发展性，提高教学评价的问题聚焦度和反思深度。描述取向的教学评价有助于弥补量化取向的教学评价的不足，因此可以将其视为对量化评价方法的补充，用于丰富当前课堂教学评价的理论与实践。

## 二、描述性教学评价的内涵特征

“描述”是一种用语言界定、描绘、叙写或者表达教学情境的有关性质的尝试。它是现象学把握世界的一种方法。相应的，描述性教学评价作为一种质性评价形式，力图描绘课堂教学过程中教师和学生的认知实践、情感体验和人际交往，用心去理解和解释教师和学生教与学的行为、想法和状态，而后在此基础上对课堂教学做出非量化的评价与持续性的改进。描述性评价内在地被分为三个方面:倾听与观察、理解与解释、研究与改进。需要说明的是,三者之间并不是一个线性的、渐进的操作程序,恰恰相反,三者之间是相互融合、牵连的,倾听与观察时必然带着已有经验的痕迹,带着自己理解与解释的视角,而研究与改进的行为中必然纳入了倾听与观察、理解与解释的关注点。

### (一) 倾听与观察

在描述性教学评价中,评价者与课堂教学中的师生之间不是评鉴与被评鉴的对象化关系,而是一种欣赏与倾听的教育性关系,大家共同见证一段围绕学习内容展开的思想之旅,分享期间所遇到的种种问题。由于我们容易受到自己思维习惯和常识的遮蔽,有时候所听到的只不过是自己内心的声音,而无法听到言说者的真正意图。所以,在观察与倾听时,我们要努力搁置自己的思维定势,有意识地放慢节奏,调整呼吸、平静心情,减少急吼吼的结论和判断,这不仅是对所关注者的尊重和接纳,也是自我的调整和丰富。倾听与观察不是事无巨细或者一览无余的复制现象,而是有一定的选择或者情节,这与倾听观察者的经历或视角息息相关。好的倾听与观察视角必然内在地具有邀请性,引邀我们与文本与现象对话,让我们不由自主地进行"现象学式"的点头,仿佛身临其境般地看到、听到事件中的场景,想象和体味其所具有的可能性。

### (二) 理解与解释

理解是一种存在方式,因为教育本身不仅仅是传承知识,更重要的是精神的熏陶和滋养,因而教育中的理解"拓宽我们人类的经验,我们的自我知识,以及我们的视野,因为理解所传达的每一件事物都是被传达给了我们"。[2]只有通过理解,教育教学的意义和作用才能实现,学生才能实现其精神发展。教学是教师、学生、教材、环境之间的一种平衡和互动,其间涉及多种因素的相互交织与作用。"像教学这么复杂的、日常性长期性的沟通过程之中,眼睛看不见的因素和感化比看得见的行为拥有更重要的作用。"[3]只有在投入移情的理解与解释之中,我们才不会被表面现象所迷惑,我们才能更真切地理解师生话语中的真正意义,理解发言者的个性表现,理解他与他人之间的相互关系。为了避免过度阐释,我们应注意的是尽量不用主观预想的框框看待对方,而是以移情的态度体验课堂中教师和学生的语言、思想、情感和行为,设身处地的理解师生的内心世界、理解教学的真正状态。

### (三) 研究与改进

描述性评价直观形象、生动具体,它依赖的是"故事和日志,产生的不是答案或者解决办法,而是思考的空间……期望的是许多声音,对实际的课堂和真实的儿童的密切描述,以及对人类能力的一种深刻的重视"。[4]在描述性评价中,教师对人性、对自己的学生观和教学观进行重新审视,对师生之间、教学和评价之间的诸多问题进行反复观照和考量并付诸实践,因此,描述性评价实际上是对课堂教学事件和问题的研究与改进。通过研究和改进活动，描述性评价引导教师尝试不同的教学思路，提升教师对实践问题的理解和解决能力，丰富教师的实践性学识，最终有助于改善师生的课堂生存状态。由此，描述性评价的发展性功能可见一斑。

## 三、描述性教学评价的操作方式

从描述性教学评价的内涵特征出发，这种评价方式的现实形态更似教师群体对真实的课堂教学过程所开展的合作性研究。描述者通过对课堂的描述提供执教者有关课堂教学的信息，而执教者则通过对描述者的描述的反思，理解和改进教学现象。因此，描述性教学评价是执教者与描述者合作双赢的行为，在本质上它体现着一种教学、研究与评价一体化的课堂教学评价新取向。学校层面在以教研组或备课组为基本单位推进描述性教学评价时，可参考下列框架：

### （一）进入现场，开展描述

在任课教师执教时，其同事或其他专业人员作为描述者进入课堂，开始描述自身所体验的情境。同一般的课堂观察不同，对现象学持有承诺的描述不可能在一开始就设定明确的观察重点或描述对象。描述试图引导我们从理论抽象回归到真实的生活经验。换句话说，描述首要关注的是“课堂是什么样子的”这样的问题，而不是“课堂的特征是什么”。前者要求我们与现象直接接触，而不是钻入已有观念的框框去衡量现象。后者则试图对现象作出抽象和概括。从现象学的态度出发，后者的做法是对现象所作的有意或无意的克扣，只能造成课堂情境的被简化、被变形，把教师的教学从它发生的完整情境中撕裂开来。回顾教师对传统的量化教学评价的深刻抵制，其缘由概源于此。因此，作为课堂教学的描述者需要努力抵制对课堂教学现象进行抽象的诱惑。

让课堂教学展露和言说自身，不用理性的思维去分析，而是用质朴的心灵去际遇。要做到这一点教师需要不断学习并掌握描述的方法。描述期待着描述者运用自身的临场体验和直觉智慧，去理解、感受课堂情境的氛围以及师生的心态并将其记录下来。这看似简单，但由于被传统的各种观念包围着，描述者往往遗弃自己的体验。当我们在谈论一位教师的教学时，我们是不是经常会衡量“教学目标”实现的怎样，“师生互动”的状态怎样等类似的问题，有没有想过，如果不是被诸如“教学目标”、“师生互动”等给定的标准所束缚，我们岂会钻入已有的框框而不顾活生生的体验？掌握描述的方法需要教师不断的练习。首先用文字把当时在那一刻的感受记录下来，然后检讨这些文字，把含有“我以为，我认为”意义的句子去掉，去掉思考的东西，专心体味“课堂是什么样子的”。因为含有“我以为，我认为”意义的句子往往是描述者对现象所作的判断或规范，有违描述的精神。在进入现场开始描述的环节，描述性教学评价要求尽可能地以感性较强、直截了当的词汇描述当时的体验，而不作任何原因阐释或概括总结。描述的主题总是随后而生的，这是描述取向的教学评价的必然选择。

描述者可能存有困惑：存在于一定情境中的事情是如此之多，难道要事无巨细、面面俱到地将其描述下来吗？事实是我们无法也没有必要这样做。当描述者面对课堂教学的情境，自然会生发出感知的重点，恰当的做法是写出自己认为重要的东西，有倾向地选择的东西。在教学发生转折的时刻，在令人兴奋、烦闷、困惑、痛苦乃至平静的时刻，我们所际遇的行为、思想和体验是怎样的，描述就是将我们认为重要的具体情境或事件记录下来。从这一点也可以看出，一旦我们开始描述，就不可避免地在进行选择，即估价一系列情境的价值，所以评价自然地贯穿于描述之中。描述性评价的三个方面显然是相互融合的。下面是对一个教学片段所作的描述，以此为例，展示课堂运作的特殊品质：

在十年级的健康课上，教师提出了酗酒的主题，并出示了一个故事让学生们阅读。学生们要讨论的其中一个主题是喝酒的合法年龄。当谈论在班级展开时，教师给大家介绍了几个额外的概念和相关的酒消费的统计图。酗酒在青少年中并不普遍。教师强调酒精经常被认为是无害的，但实际上是非常致命的。为了证明自己的观点，教师谈到了一个十七岁的男孩两年前在一个派对后喝酒致死的事情。班上的讨论变得非常活跃。但主题发生了转变。学生们谈到成年人由于不负责任而为他们的孩子树立坏的榜样的故事。另一些人则认为适当饮酒确实有助于健康。教师静静地听着。这时，理查德，一个常在班上发呆的学生，忽然变地活泼起来。他不假思索地说，与从工作场所回到家中放松地饮酒的父母沟通太困难了。“我妈妈在她开始喝酒时就变得不像她了！”他说道。他突然的发话造成了惊人的影响。整个班级都静静地看着他。不过不是嘲笑的目光，而是似乎感受到了他所受到的危险。然后，其他人分享了他们喝酒的经验，以及因为喝醉后所发生的友谊毁于一旦的故事。当儿童们还在讨论时，我感到这是多么的不可思议，他们在一种接受和归属的氛围中分享着各自的脆弱和无助。[5]

**（二）解释现象，揭示主题**

在课后的群体研讨中，描述者首先需要汇报自己所记录的课堂教学现象，与群体分享自身的课堂体验。而后，教师群体经由反思对现象做出解释。对现象的解释可沿如下脉络展开：一是探寻执教者何以如此教学的原因；二是阐明描述者是如何看待这一教学现象的；三是发掘其他研究者对这类教学现象的解读。解释不是一个机械的过程，而是一个富有创造性的过程。之所以沿三个脉络展开，一方面是因为一、二两条脉络的交汇有助于让执教者与描述者在平等的协商中就课堂教学现象的意义达成一致，避免因单方面的“话语霸权”造成彼此缺乏认同的局面。另一方面，关注其他研究者的解释脉络，则是为了引导教师群体基于教育学或学科方面的专业知识对教学现象作出阐释，避免陷入对教学现象所做的自我经验性的分析。虽然对描述的解释并不排斥教师个体的日常经验，但对提升教师的专业实践而言，基于专业知识阐释教学现象具有更直接和更根本的价值。

解释的最终目的是揭示现象的主题。主题是经验的焦点和意义，对主题进行揭示就是明确现象的意义。因此主题不是通过概括或总结给所描述的现象加一个题目，而是试图阐明某种课堂教学经验的特质。通过揭示，我们将对课堂教学情境的运作方式、特点及对师生可能有的影响等问题有所明了。仍以上述教学片段为例：

这一片断展现了一个课堂教学发生转折的时刻。课堂讨论在不知不觉中滑入一场真正的对话。这一转折点是在怎样的情况下发生的呢？教师在组织学生讨论时，预定的讨论主题是喝酒的合法年龄。然而，主题发生了游离，计划好的课堂突然发生了转变。但教师似乎没有把学生拉回主题的意思，只是“静静地听着”，放弃了对课堂的控制。这似乎并不符合课堂讨论需要遵循的规则，比如不能跑题。表面上，教师的做法与片段一中教师的无所作为没有差别，然而，回到情境描述，我们看到教学随后的推进肯定了教师在这一时刻“无所作为”的意义。由理查德开始，谈话由外部世界转向了内心世界。学生们开始分享自己的秘密。被检讨的主题虽然开始变得缺乏逻辑和力量，但却更具有关心性和真实性。描述者也都体验到了主题讨论与心灵对话的细微区别。虽然两者都是“在一起谈论”的经验，但讨论的双方会产生观点的冲突乃至对立，而对话则把彼此带入一种共享的氛围中，学会相互理解和维系更深的联系。如果说讨论可以由教师施加控制，那么对话则不是按谈话者任何一方的意愿而进行的，它以个体间的亲密、脆弱和内在的约定为特征。正如加达默尔所言：“也许这样说更正确些，即我们陷入了一场谈话，甚至可以说，我们被卷入了一场谈话。……谈话的参加者与其说是谈话的引导者，不如说是谈话的被引导者。”[6]因此真正的对话绝不可能是那种我们意想进行的谈话。对话的发生需要建立共享的氛围和敞开彼此的心灵。

有时我们会发现上述主题作为一种共同特征反复出现于我们所收集到的描述中，由此也可以看出描述内在的具有启发性，虽然读者所际遇的现象同描述者所描述的情形并不完全相同，但不同现象所彰显的主题的要点可能是共同的，因此面对描述的现象，读者也便“心有戚戚焉”。这或许就是描述性评价的独特性或魅力所在，它引领我们在一种共通的人性中与他人建立联系，共同展开对世界的想象和思考。

**（三）协商改进，提供建议**

描述性教学评价不能随现象意义的揭示而完结。通过反思具体的教学现象来明确主题的方法有助于教师群体展开自我询问：“这样做对吗？”，这样的问题促使教师在认识到已凸显的主题时对具体现象（这个儿童、这种情形、这种行为）作出判断，明确自身局限并努力加以超越。课后研讨的最终目的是改进教学。以上述教学片断为例，旨在改进的协商仍在继续：

随着话语的推进，教师似乎忘记了自己作为教师负责组织班级讨论的身份。对于深具偶发性的对话而言，对课堂控制的适时放弃显示出教师极高的专业素养。它表明教师作为一个参与者融入教学之中，保持了一种深刻的在场，从而有机会倾听和理解学生的内在生活。如果说必须提供建议的话，在课堂对话发生的时刻，教师不仅仅作为倾听者，也可以开放自我并与学生分享他们的个人经验，通过表达自己有关喝酒的经验，与学生同享一个世界就如学生进入了教师的世界，并共同致力于转变这个世界。

由此观之，描述取向的教学评价实质上是对教师的日常教学不断加以改进的一种方式。需要强调的是，教学改进是一个长期的过程，"提供建议"不应随课后研讨活动的结束而结束。课后研讨活动的开展虽揭示出教学改进的可能方向，但有时并不能当场找到有效的改进策略，即使找到了也需要在实践中加以检验和不断修正。更何况教学改进永无止境，需要持续地进行研究，才可能不断诞生新的策略和方法。因此，教师需要持续地就某一主题展开探究。无论是描述者还是执教者在群体研讨后都应广泛地开展理论学习，吸取已有的教学经验，完善课堂教学改进的策略。另一方面也都应在自身的教学中积极尝试和应用改进策略，并不断反思和完善这些策略。

### （四）提炼结论，获得启示

虽然通过评价寻找到特定教学情境的改进路径已相当得完满，但为了获得对相关问题的一种高度警觉，描述取向的教学评价有必要进一步提炼评价的结论，总结情境的关键特征，以便指导教师感知其他的教学情境。如前所述，描述内在的具有启发性，尽管没有一个情境与其他情境是完全相同的，但在某个情境中提炼的结论，也许与其他情境中发现的结论有一定联系。回到上述教学片段：

相信所有的教师都会感慨那些触动学生的心灵而不仅仅是理智的课堂对话是多么的难以捉摸又是多么的弥足珍贵！虽然无法通过预设去达成这样的对话，但也并非无迹可寻。要点燃这样的对话，教师必须尊重教学生活的偶然性，知道什么时候该放弃控制。权力或控制的欲望往往成为教师专业实践的绊脚石。在教学的任一时刻，教师都应当去反思究竟是自己以作为教师的身份在主导着课堂，还是学生以自身涌动的力量在创造着课堂。

通过对结论的提炼，教师概括出特定情境的描述性评价所提供的经验和教训，这些经验和教训作为理解其他教学情境的一种方式，有助于发展教师对这类事件和对象的警觉性和敏感性，从而更为全面和深入地对其作出评价。

## 四、结语

描述性教学评价为课堂教学评价改革提供了另一种可资借鉴的模式，代表着课堂教学评价改革的新思路。在表现形式上，描述性教学评价的结果不再是简单的某个分数或某个等级，而是一个体现描述、研究与评价一体化的新文本。正如上述教学片段所展现的，描述、解释、改进、启示四个方面呈现着这个新文本的基本框架。透过这个新文本，我们不仅可以体会描述性评价的内在张力与启发性，更可以断定对教学本质的际遇很大程度上只能经由对具体情境的描述予以实现。

参考文献

[1] 裴娣娜.论我国课堂教学质量评价观的重要转换[J].教育研究,2008(1):17—23.

[2] [德]伽达默尔.科学时代的理性[M].薛华,等,译.北京:国际文化出版公司,1988:97.

[3] [日]佐藤学.课程与教师[M].钟启泉,译.北京:教育科学出版社,2003:344.

[4] [美]马格丽特.赫姆莉、帕特丽夏 F.卡利尼.从另一个视角看:儿童的力量和学校标准[M].仲建维,译.北京:高等教育出版社,2005:89.

[5] Max Van Manen (2002). *Writing in the Dark: Phenomenological Studies in Interpretive Inquiry*. London: The Althouse Press. Pp86 - 87,略有改动.

[6] [德]汉斯·格奥尔格·加达默尔.真理与方法——哲学诠释学的基本特征(下卷)[M].洪汉鼎,译.上海:上海译文出版社,1999:489.

## Classroom Teaching Assessment: A Descriptive Orientation

Guiqing An　Shupei Li

**Abstract**: Currently, classroom teaching assessment needs transformation because the quantitative oriented teaching assessment cannot pay attention to the integrety and complexity of teaching and the developmental function of assessment. The feature of descriptive oriented teaching assessment is listening and observation, understanding and explanation as well as research and improvement. It can make up for the shortcomings of quantitative oriented teaching assessment effectively. Therefore, the descriptive oriented teaching assessment gives us an alternative assessment mode which is worthy using for reference. Schools can refer to the following framework when descriptive oriented teaching assessment is carried out by teaching and research group or lesson preparing group: entering scene and giving description, explaining phenomenology and unfolding theme, negotiating improvement and offering suggestion, abstracting conclusion and getting enlightenment.

**Keywords**: classroom teaching assessment; listening and observation; understanding and explanation; research and improvement

# 促进学生学习的书面作业评价结果反馈研究

刘　辉

【摘要】寻求有效的书面作业评价方式是促进学生学习的实践诉求，也是一个需要解决的专业问题。通过对几种常用的书面作业评价结果反馈方式进行实证研究发现，评语式反馈是有效地促进学生学习的反馈方式。从促进学生学习的视角来看，必须要探索更规范的、更具有科学性的评语反馈技术。

【关键词】书面作业；评价结果；反馈

【作者简介】刘辉/上海市闵行区教育学院教育评价研究中心讲师

相比课堂理答受到的限制，如课堂时间和节奏，书面作业批改有更大应用空间，对学生反馈也更具有针对性，它对促进学生的学习有重要的作用。如果说改进课堂理答说明了口头评价反馈对促进学生学习的重要性，那么改进作业评价反馈形式则显示了书面评价反馈的重要性。"因为有研究显示，学生在某种程度上更喜欢与教师在书面反馈中进行交流，而不是口头反馈，因为教师的口头反馈有时可能会使学生觉得尴尬。"[1]

书面作业评价是教师评价学生学习情况时使用较多的方式之一。可是书面作业评价常常出现这样的现象：教师们往往花很多时间批改作业，给分数、写评语和作记录。但是，令人沮丧的是，我们经常会看到学生将批改过的作业扔到一边，看都不看一眼，更不用说花点时间来订正一下错题、反思自己的学习策略或者向教师、同学请求帮助。作业评价结果反馈似乎已经成为一种完成任务的行为，在某些情况下，作业似乎也是导致学生"学业负担过重"的一个元凶。因此，我们需要从促进学生学习的视角来剖析，书面作业究竟对于促进学生学习有何意义？书面作业评价结果如何反馈才能更有效地促进学生学习呢？

## 一、几种书面作业评价结果反馈方式的比较研究

日常的作业评价反馈形式最常用的有等级/分数，评语和评语＋等级/分数这三种方式。究竟哪种作业评价反馈方式能够更有效地促进学生的学习呢？心理学中有一些实验研究的结论可以作为借鉴。研究发现，教师提供的反馈信息将直接影响家庭作业效果，见表1。[2]

**表1　有关"作业批改"的综合研究结果**

| 作业采用的反馈形式 | 原始研究个数 | 平均效应值 | 百分点得分 |
| --- | --- | --- | --- |
| 有教师批语作为反馈的作业 | 2 | 0.83 | 30 |

续　表

| 作业采用的反馈形式 | 原始研究个数 | 平均效应值 | 百分点得分 |
| --- | --- | --- | --- |
| 有批改分数的作业 | 3 | 0.78 | 28 |
| 布置了作业，既没有批改分数，也没有批语 | 47 | 0.28 | 11 |

表1说明，布置了作业但没有批改，其效应值只有0.28。但当批改出分数时，效应值就会增加到0.78。最后，教师给学生的家庭作业做出书面批语，效应值达到0.83。

英国心理学家巴特勒(R. Butler)曾就作业的反馈形式进行了研究。在一个有关小学作业的反馈实验中，对分成三组的学生分别给予评语、等级、评语＋等级三种不同的反馈形式，实验结果显示，在仅是给予评语的小组中的学生的学习成绩提高是明显的，而给予其他两种形式反馈的小组中的学生学习成绩并没有明显的变化。[3]

美国心理学家佩奇(E.B. Page)曾对74个班的2000多名学生的作文进行过研究。他把每个班的学生分成三组，分别给予三种作文记分方式。第一组的作文只给甲、乙、丙、丁一类的等级，既无评语也不指出作文中存在的问题。第二组给予特殊评语，即不仅给予等级，而且给评语，但获得同一等级的作文的评语是一样的，不同等级的评语不一样。例如，对甲等成绩，评语为“好，坚持下去”；对乙等成绩，评语为“良好，继续前进”等。第三组除评定等级外，还给予顺应性评语，即针对学生作文中存在的问题加以个别矫正，根据每个学生的表现给予相应的建议和指导。结果表明，三种不同的评语对学生后来的成绩有不同的影响。开学时，学生作文水平差不多。到期末时，发现作文水平的提高程度不一致。[4]

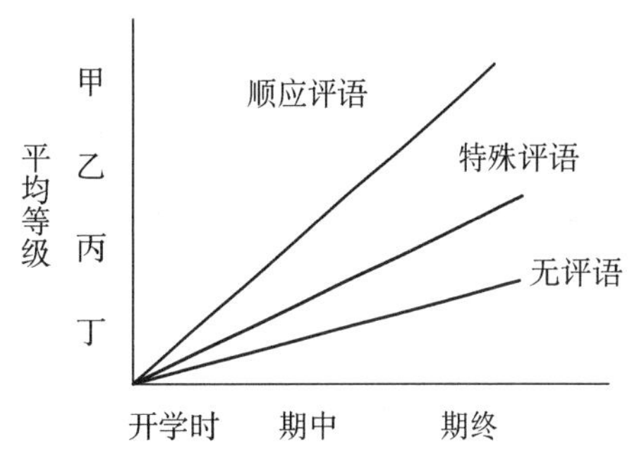


**图1　不同类型的评语反馈对学生成绩的影响**

由图1中的学生成绩可以看出，顺应性评语针对学生的个别差异进行针对性的反馈，效果最好；特殊评语虽有激励作用，但由于未针对学生的个别特点进行详细、具体的反馈，所以效果不如顺应性评语；而无评语的成绩则明显低于前两者。

## 二、对改进书面作业评价结果反馈方式的思考

### （一）有效的书面作业评价结果处理是评语式反馈

由心理学实验研究可以证明，反馈是必要的，关键在于采用什么方式进行学习信息反馈。通过评定等级可以表明学生进步的大小，即评定的分数或等级并非表明个体的能力而是其进步快慢的指标。想要有效地促进学生的学习，帮助学生纠正错误，指引改进方向和方法，还需要教师给予有针对性的评语，向学生提供详细的反馈信息。

作业中的等级或分数反馈形式，使学生喜欢把自己与他人进行比较，而使他们忽视了对自己学习的思考，以及自己怎样通过评语改进学习。这样，分数或等级就使学生的注意力集中于他们的“能力”上，而不是集中在自己努力的重要性上，同时也易于使成绩差的学生的自尊心受损。当学生作业的反馈是评语＋等级的形式时，他们拿到作业本后，喜欢做的第一件事是比较彼此的等级，而很少阅读评语，可见等级影响了评语的反馈作用。分数高低并不会告诉学生怎么去提高，评语才真正能让学生和父母知道该如何进步，从而调整学习。学生忽视评语使教师的建议不被认真接受，间接妨碍了学习。

英国评价专家布莱克(Paul Black)通过实证研究也发现，“在促进学习的评价中，教师通过有效的作业反馈方式使学生理解当前水平与学习目标之间的差距，并为他们提供一系列改进的建议以缩小学生表现与目标之间的差距，帮助学生形成改进的策略。相对于简单的分数或等级来说，详细的含有改进建议的作业评语对于改进学生学习有重要作用”。[5]由此可见，评语式的书面作业评价结果反馈对于促进学生学习是最有效的。

### (二) 高质量的反馈评语的标准

但在布莱克等人进行的促进学习的形成性评价研究(King's — Medway — Oxfordshire Formative Assessment Project, KMOFAP)中对教师评语的调查显示，教师的评语一般是不具体的、不精确的，而且评语多为类似于表扬的一些用语，如“你很优秀，很棒”、“好样的，这次更整洁了，说明你在努力”等。这些评语所反馈的信息已经脱离了学生具体科目的学习目标，而且有时候评语过分的关注学生的情感、意志品质方面，而忽视了作业是用来促进学生学习这一本质的目的。因而，经常有些教师花费了很长时间去写评语，但是评语却远离了自己布置作业的初衷。[6]另外教师在课堂上很少给学生时间来阅读写在学生作业上的评语，也很少有学生回家后阅读教师的评语。

通过对实验研究结果的反思和教学实践中的观察，我们找到了改进作业评价结果反馈方式的方向。能够促进学生学习的作业评价反馈是一个以改进学习为目的，教师、学生共同参与，对评价信息进行分析、判断和反馈、交流，进而提出改进教与学措施的过程。“在促进学习的评价中，作业评语要提供积极的反馈并且要与学习的目标相关联。有效的作业反馈应该包括三个元素：明确学生哪些是做的很好的，哪些是需要改进的，简明的暗示应该如何改进。”[7]所以，在作业评价结果反馈的环节中，必须给予学生针对性的、具体的反馈，对学生需要改进的地方给予详细建议。

#### 1. 有效的评语不等于表扬

我们并不反对教师在评语中对学生的鼓励与表扬，表扬学生很重要，表扬经常让学生觉得很满足，也会鼓励学生进步。但是表扬必须依赖于学生已经做的特别的事情而不是依赖于他们大体的行为，某种程度上说更要注重细节——应该鉴别被表扬的具体的行为是什么，以致学生了解他们作业的哪方面是被单独的挑出来被表扬。在作业评价中，单纯的表扬或者批评并不能有效地促进学生的学习，促进学生逐渐改正缺点，获得发展，这主要是因为教师在反馈中并未给予学生有关表现的重要信息。反馈时要告诉学生你做了什么，或者没做什么，可以让学生进行自我调整。

2. 有效的评语要清晰阐述哪些是正确的和错误的

有效的评语反馈能用学生理解的语言描述出为什么一个答案是正确或是错误的。学生也可以通过把自己的作业和教师提供的样本相比较来概括自己的描述性反馈。这样，他们就可以把自己的想法与教师给出的反馈作比较。评语反馈应该能用清晰的、指导性的语言告诉学生改进学习的途径。比起简单地给学生贴上错误的标签，有效的反馈指导学生在学习过程中怎样表现得更好。

3. 有效的评语要提出改进建议

评语必须指出哪方面仍需要改进，并对如何改进提出建议；为学生根据评语提高自己创造机会，将需要改进之处纳入学生总体学习进程。有效的评论一次只针对某一个方面提出改进意见。促进学习的反馈通过告知学生他们与学习目标之间的距离来描绘更远的图景，即教师希望他们最终达到的目标。通过给学生建议，缩短学生的实际学习情况和需要达到的成绩之间的差距，教师可以帮助学生学会概括自己改进学习的策略。

## 三、基于学情的书面作业评语式反馈的建议

### （一）评语式反馈要激发学生学习动机

通过详细的、含有改进建议的评语来进行作业情况的反馈，向学生加强“只要努力就可以不断提高”的信念。这种评价不仅是帮助所有的学生改进学习，更重要的是帮助学习困难的学生取得良好的成绩。使所有的学生都参与到评价中来，并相信每个学生都可以成功。通过采取评语反馈，弱化等级和分数的评价结果处理办法，让学生的关注点从分数、等级转移到自己的薄弱之处，并对“为了达到标准下一步该如何做”有了清晰的认识。这种方式有助于激发全体学生，尤其是学习困难学生的学习动机，并且使他们受到积极的鼓励，提高了自信。

教师评语要关注于学生的学习策略或学习思维，以激发学生自我构建知识为上策。“教师应基于学习任务本身给予反馈，正面的学习反馈包含了一个连续系统，其中让学生自我建构知识，获得高质量学业成就为最高级别。”

### （二）评语式反馈要师生互动交流

改变单纯由教师批改的评价方式，让学生参与作业评价结果处理过程，能使学生在参与中学会学习方法，加深对所学习知识的理解，使学生变得更自信。学生参与作业评价结果反

馈，可以采用以下方法：

一是师生互相交流，共同对作业进行评价，学生可以发表见解，提出困惑。这种方式有助于教师更加及时、准确地获得信息，了解教学中存在的问题，调整教学的策略，根据学生学习中的问题给予更多个性化的帮助。我们在教学实践中发现，学生从胆怯看教师评语到勇于向老师提问。举例来说，有学生从老师的评语中已经悟出了自己在英语学习策略的不足："老师，我的英语成绩为什么总是提高得不快？单词和课文的内容我总是记不住，老师你有什么好办法？老师你能把改变句型的顺口溜写给我好吗？"；有的学生还会对教师的教学工作提出建议："老师，我觉得除了默写词汇表后的单词外，课文中你上课划出的重点单词和词组也应该默写，这样我们才能加深印象。"

二是学生的自我反馈。为了减轻教师批改作业的工作量，学生可以进行自我反馈。教师对作业提供反馈确实能起到提高成绩的作用，而现实情况却是，有时候教师没有足够的时间对所有的作业都给予同样的注意。许多教师尽力给每一份作业打分和下批语，但当不胜负荷时，教师应当采用一些有助于减轻工作负担、但能尽量增进反馈效果的策略。例如，让学生对作业进行自我反馈。如果连续几天的作业都是有关同一个主题的话，学生可以在完成作业后的第二天上午自己批改和讨论他们的作业，然后把作业放到教室的一个文档筐里。老师会经常翻阅这些作业，给他们写些特别的批语。当老师布置练习性作业来提高学生的速度和精确性时，可以让学生做一些自我反馈。教师要事先制定好评价标准，要求学生跟踪自己的速度和精确性。如果有学生想从老师那儿得到特殊反馈，教师可以抽出时间和大家一起讨论练习进展的情况。

### （三）评语式反馈要促进学生的自我调节学习

当前学生对作业的一个普遍态度是完成作业上交就万事大吉了。学生对教师批改后的作业并没有给予足够重视，对其中的错误及其原因也懒得去分析。因此，作业对于促进学生学习的作用也就没有充分实现。"从自我调节学习原理出发，正确的做法是教师或家长要求学生每次或每隔一段时间对老师批改完后发回的作业进行分析和自我评价，找出作业中的不足，进行错误分析，不断进行反思，而不是做完作业交差，应付了事。"[8]通过这种不断循环的反馈"学生可能认识到检查他们的作业不需许多额外的时间从而导致更高的准确性"[9]，并最终形成自我监控和自我调节的学习。

让学生学会对自己的作业评价结果进行反思，分析评价结果的原因并调整自己的学习。正确的归因是改进学生学习的关键。学习成就归因是影响成就动机、影响学业成绩的重要因素。对于学生来说，他们也经常感到困惑："我的作业上为什么得到的是 B 而不是 A 呢？""我还有哪些方面是需要改进的？我要如何去改进自己的学习？"因此，我们必须把学习者看作积极的信息处理者和修订者，让学生能够在评价结果信息的反思中学会学习。自我调节的学习者能够"为其学习设置目标，然后尽力监控、调节、控制他们的认知、动机和行为，并受他们的目标和环境特点的指导和约束"。当学生的成绩没有达到学习标准时，教师帮助学生分析其完成任务的方法与策略是否是合适的，以便调整策略。学生也要认真地领会和分析教师反馈的内容，修正自己的策略清单，改进学习。

教师之间还可以相互交流、分享能给学生留下深刻印象而且容易让学生理解接受的评语。教师为了让学生更关注作业评语，可以采用一些强调作业评语重要性的方法。例如，在上课时有选择性地分析作业和评语，强调评语可以用于提高学习，创造一个关注评语的氛围，同时提高学生对课堂学习和作业的期望。

评语式反馈方式已有一定的理论研究作为基础，也已在实践中探索出有效的、简便易行的方法。如果进行更深入的理性思考，经过总结和提升已有经验，形成更清晰、规范，更具有科学性的评语反馈技术，会成为改进学生学习、实现减负增效的重要手段。

参考文献

[1] Education Development Plan Group (EDP). (2009). *How Am I doing? — Assessment and Feedback to Learners*. http://www.slannet.org.uk, 2010-05-30.

[2] Robert J. Marzano, & Debra J. Pickering. 有效课堂—提高学生成绩的使用策略[M]. 张新立，译. 北京：中国轻工业出版社，2003：79.

[3] R. Butler. (1988). Enhancing and Undermining Intrinsic Motivation: the Effects of Task-Involving and Ego-Involving Evaluation on Interest and Performance. *British Journal of Educational Psychology*, 10-14.

[4] 冯忠良. 教育心理学[M]. 北京：人民教育出版社，2000：248—249.

[5] Black, P., & Wiliam, D. (1998). Inside the Black Box: Raising Standards Through Cassroom Assessment. *Phi Delta Kappan*, 80(2).

[6] Black, P., & Harrison, C., & Lee, C., & Marshall, B., & Wiliam, D. (2003). *Assessment for Learning: Putting It into Practice*. Maidenhead: Open University, 43.

[7] 张文慧. 学习性评价方法研究[D]. 北京：首都师范大学，2006.

[8] 杨宁. 从自我调节学习的角度看家庭作业[J]. 课程·教材·教法，2004(11)：36.

[9] Paris, S. G., & Paris , A. H. (2001). Classroom Applications of Research on Self-regulated Learning. *Educational Psychologist*, 36(2), 91.

# Study on Feeding Back the Written-Assignments Assessment Results: Facilitating the Students' Learning

Hui Liu

**Abstract**: The effective feedback of the written-assignments assessment results is the demand of both the practice and professional area. The demonstration research about the feedback of written-assignments assessment results proved that, written-assignments remark is an effective method of feeding back the assessment results to student. To facilitatte the student' learning, we must search better canonical attachments of feeding back the assessment results.

**Key words**: written assignments; assessment result; feedback

# 中日小学生数学学业能力评价[①]

孔企平　杨　莉

【摘要】发现并改善当今我国数学教育中的问题点，提高全国义务教育阶段的学生学业能力及综合应用能力水平，是我国义务教育阶段的重要任务之一。日本自2007年以来，在这一方面，针对义务教育阶段的学生实施了"全国学力调查"，以分析把握学生的学力状况。在日本教育经验的启发下，我们对我国部分地区小学生数学学力进行调查，帮助我国教师学者了解学生目前的学业能力和思维发展现状，以此提供对学生有益的补救性教学。同时，对中日两国学生进行评价分析，通过比较了解不同文化背景下学生的数学表现的相似和差异性，帮助我们拓展教育视野，帮助教师思考教师课堂教学的创新的途径和方法。

【关键词】学业能力；学力评价；中日比较；数学教育

【作者简介】孔企平/华东师范大学课程与教学研究所教授、博士生导师
杨莉/华东师范大学课程与教学系硕士研究生

为了发现和改善当今学校教育的问题点，提高全国性的义务教育的水准，日本实施了"全国学力调查"，以分析把握中小学生的学力状况。在日本经验的启发下，我们课题组结合自己的实际研究进行了此次调查。

## 一、调查概述

调查测试题选用了日本"全国学力调查"小学六年级数学试卷部分，内容和问题典型可靠。此次调查意在①调查中国六年级学生的数学基本知识、基本技能的掌握及问题解决能力；②比较中日两国小学六年级数学成绩，了解不同文化背景下数学表现的相似和差异，帮助我们了解数学思维发展的现状，提供诊断和决策信息；③对学生进行认知诊断评价，了解考生认知过程和技能的强弱，从而进行有针对性的补救教学；④通过现状分析与比较，思考教师课堂教学创新的途径和方法。

## 二、中日两国调查信息概要

### （一）被试

调查包含中国五个地区5个不同学校，各地区的学校及人数分布见表1。表2为日本教

① 本文为教育部人文社会科学重点研究基地研究项目"基于理论与实践对话的数学创新研究"（批准号为07JJD880233）和"义务教育阶段数学学科核心能力模型与测评框架研究"（批准号为79641022）阶段性研究成果。参加本文讨论的还有课题组成员来玉超和周芳芳，孔天睿参与了数据收集与统计工作。

育课程研究中心提供的调查信息。

**表1　中国五个地区不同学校的信息及学生人数分布**

| | 新疆某小学1 | 吉林某小学 | 广东某小学 | 辽宁某小学 | 新疆某小学2 | 总体 |
|---|---|---|---|---|---|---|
| 人数 | 49 | 55 | 60 | 37 | 69 | 270 |

**表2　日本全国各地区学校信息和学生人数分布[1]**

| | 公立学校 | 国立学校 | 私立学校 | 合计 |
|---|---|---|---|---|
| 实施学校数(校) | 21,889 | 75 | 108 | 22,072 |
| 人数 | 1,125,585 | 7,631 | 6,276 | 1,139,492 |

### (二) 试题

试题分为两部分:检测学生基本知识和基本技能的试卷A、检测学生知识应用和问题解决能力的试卷B。试卷A、B分别从"知识"和"灵活运用"两个层面来考察学生。具体地说,"知识"是指"不掌握就会对今后的学习内容产生影响"、"希望时常能够灵活运用"的知识、技能,就是"学年相应的基础性知识"和"为了培养生存能力的实践性知识";"灵活运用"是指"将知识、技能灵活运用到实际生活的各种各样的场合的能力"和"为了解决各种各样的课题而建立构想、进行实践、评价、改善的能力"。它不仅是获得知识,而且是有效地运用自如的能力。

试卷A包含计算题和简单常规问题,共7大题;试卷B为复杂的问题,共6大题。题型为选择题和问答题,选择题有单项和多项,问答题允许学生写下自己的解答过程。

测试时间数学A为20分钟、数学B为40分钟。

## 三、总体分析

### (一) 中国测试总体分析

表3给出了五个地区学生在试卷A、B中得分的平均数。明显看出:

**表3　中国五个地区学生在试卷A和试卷B中得分的平均分分布**

| | 新疆某小学1 | 吉林某小学 | 广东某小学 | 辽宁某小学 | 新疆某小学2 | 总体 |
|---|---|---|---|---|---|---|
| 试卷A平均分 | 94.84 | 91.84 | 72.63 | 81.24 | 84.06 | 84.67 |
| 试卷B平均分 | 78.45 | 72.91 | 55.37 | 64.7 | 66.33 | 67.21 |

(1) 试卷A得分的平均分远高于试卷B,其中新疆某小学1在试卷A、B中得分的平均分相差最小,但也超过16分。

(2) 五个地区学生在测验中的表现差异性大,新疆某小学1学生表现最好,吉林某小学表现欠佳,两个地区在试卷A、B中得分差距极大,超过18分。

(3) 试卷 A、B 相关程度高,试卷 A 中得分平均分高的地区,试卷 B 也相对高,反之亦然。运用 SPSS,对五个地区 270 名学生在试卷 A 和试卷 B 中得分进行相关分析。在显著性水平为 0.01 的条件下,结果显示试卷 A 和试卷 B 之间的 Pearson 相关系数为 0.548,概率 P 值为 0.000。二者呈现出显著的正相关,如表 4 所示。

**表 4　五个地区 270 名学生在试卷 A 和试卷 B 得分的相关性检验**

| | | 总体试卷 B |
|---|---|---|
| 总体试卷 A | Pearson Correlation | .548** |
| | Sig. (2 - tailed) | .000 |
| | N | 270 |

**. Correlation is significant at the 0.01 level (2 - tailed).

### (二) 日本测试总体分析

**表 5　日本小学生在试卷 A 和试卷 B 中的正答数及正答率分布[2]**

| | 人数 | 平均正答数 | 平均正答率 | 正答中位数 | 标准偏差 |
|---|---|---|---|---|---|
| 试卷 A | 1,139,492 | 15.6 问/19 问 | 82.10% | 17.0 问 | 3.4 |
| 试卷 B | 1,139,492 | 8.9 问/14 问 | 63.60% | 9.0 问 | 3.0 |

据日本教育课程研究中心"全国学力・学习状况调查"结果显示,在算术 A 测试中,日本小学生整体的正答数的分布为 J 字型的单峰分布(如图 1 所示)。算数 A 测试总题数为 19 题,其中全国平均正答数为 15.6 问,中位数为 17 问,众数为 19 问。

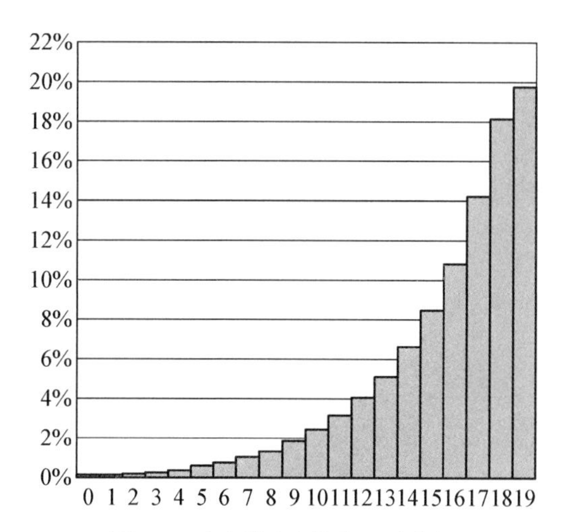


图 1　日本小学生在算数 A 测试中总体正答数分布[3]

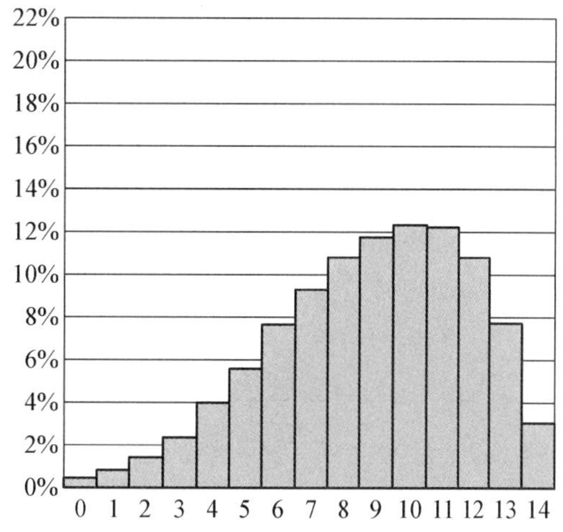


图 2　日本小学生在算数 B 测试中总体正答数分布[4]

(注:横轴为正答数,纵轴为小学生人数的占比)

在算术B测试中，日本小学生整体的正答数分布形为负偏态分布(如图2所示)。算数B测试总题数为14题，其中全国平均正答数为8.9问，中位数为9问，众数为10问。

由此，从算数A测试(基本知识和基本技能)的整体来看，日本小学生的平均正答率为82.1%，也就是相当多的学生对学习内容的理解和掌握较好；对于算数B测试(基本知识技能与灵活运用)，学生的平均正答率为63.60%，在7到12处成绩分布相对较为集中和均衡，未出现多数极端的差或好，过半数的学生能够正确作答8问及更多的问题。

## 四、对试卷的分析

为了进一步考察学生在不同题目中的表现及所存在的差异，找出问题所在，接下来分别对试卷A、B进行分析。

### (一) 对试卷的分析(中国)

1. 对试卷A的分析(中国)

图3中给出了五个地区270名学生在试卷A中(每大题各个小题)作答正确率百分比分布情况。第一大题包含了7道小计算题，考察学生的加减乘除四则运算能力。其中的第5、6小题答题正确率低，主要是因新疆地区试卷印刷错误，学生作答无效，最终以零分统计。其他地区在5、6小题作答正确率的百分比见表6：

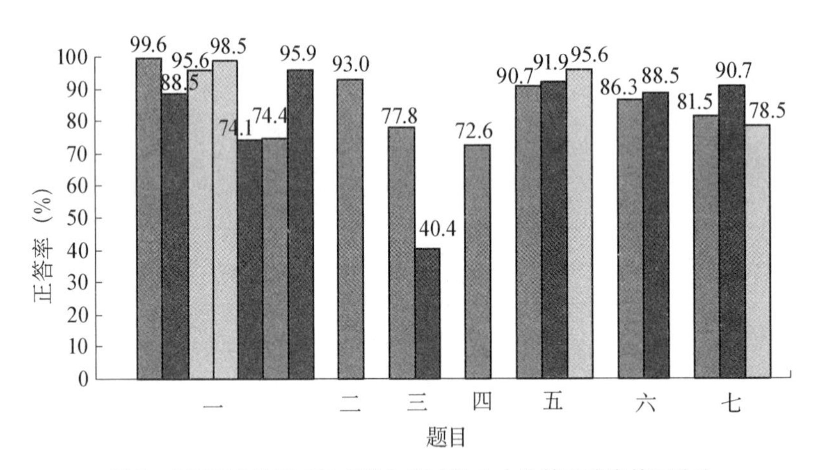


**图3　中国五个地区270名学生在试卷A中作答正确率的百分比**

**表6　中国四个地区270名学生在试卷A第一题5、6答题正确的百分比**

| | 新疆某小学1 | 吉林某小学 | 广东某小学 | 辽宁某小学 |
|---|---|---|---|---|
| 试卷A 一(5) | 100 | 100 | 98.33 | 100 |
| 试卷A 一(6) | 100 | 100 | 100 | 100 |

从图 3 中还可明显看出，第一、三、四、七大题除外，其余大题各小题大部分作答正确率都超过 80%以上。其中第二题分数的图形表示及第四题平行四边形、三角形、圆的面积计算答题正确率高，均达到 90%以上；第三题数线上表示分数、分数的比较大小及第四题简单的文字题作答正确率低。第三题的第 2 小题只有 40%左右，主要原因可能是学生并没有理解题意。表 7 中给出了各个地区在每题目中作答正确率百分比分布情况。可以看出各个地区小学生的作答表现情况。

**表 7　中国五个地区学生在试卷 A 中(第一题除外)作答正确率的百分比分布**

| 题目<br>正答率(%) | 二 | 三 | | 四 | 五 | | | 六 | | 七 | | |
|---|---|---|---|---|---|---|---|---|---|---|---|---|
| | | 3.1 | 3.2 | | 5.1 | 5.2 | 5.3 | 6.1 | 6.2 | 7.1 | 7.2 | 7.3 |
| 新疆某小学 1 | 91.8 | 87.8 | 57.1 | 93.9 | 100 | 100 | 100 | 93.9 | 95.9 | 98 | 100 | 95.9 |
| 吉林某小学 | 94.6 | 96.4 | 61.8 | 72.7 | 100 | 96.4 | 98.2 | 92.7 | 100 | 94.6 | 100 | 90.9 |
| 广东某小学 | 88.3 | 60 | 23.3 | 56.7 | 78.3 | 90 | 90 | 78.3 | 58.3 | 65 | 65 | 41.7 |
| 辽宁某小学 | 94.6 | 73 | 16.2 | 70.3 | 86.5 | 78.4 | 89.2 | 89.2 | 97.3 | 73 | 94.6 | 70.3 |
| 新疆某小学 2 | 95.7 | 89.9 | 39.1 | 72.5 | 89.9 | 91.3 | 98.6 | 81.2 | 95.6 | 78.3 | 97.1 | 92.8 |

2. 对试卷 B 的分析(中国)

图 4 中给出了五个地区 270 名学生在试卷 B 中(包含每题中的各个小题)作答正确率百分比分布情况。每大题各小题大部分正确率都低于 80%，第三题看统计图回答问题、第四题复杂的算术文字题、第五题复杂的图形文字题中均有小题作答正确率不超过 60%，如第一题中第 1 小题有关长方形公式在实际中的应用作答正确率也较低。第三题中的第 3 小题正确率只有 20%左右，表明了学生的读图能力和判断能力存在较大问题。表 8 中，可看出各地区小学生的作答表现情况。

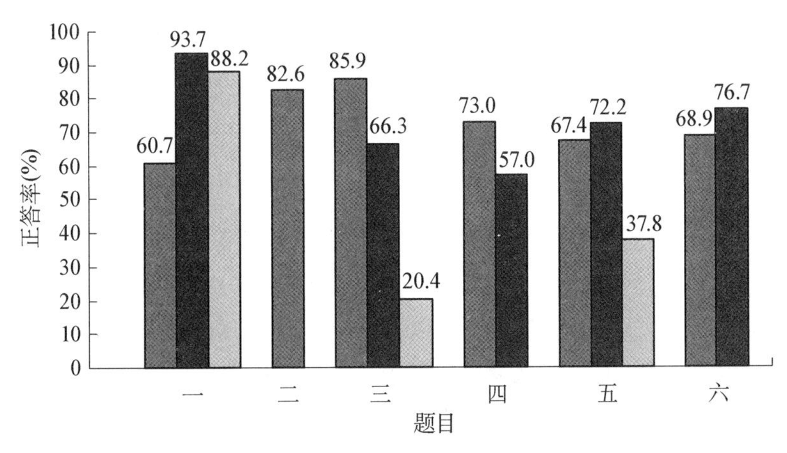


**图 4　中国五个地区 270 名学生在试卷 B 中作答正确率的百分比**

表 8　中国五个地区学生在试卷 B 中作答正确率的百分比分布

| 题目 | 一 | | | 二 | 三 | | | 四 | | 五 | | | 六 | |
|---|---|---|---|---|---|---|---|---|---|---|---|---|---|---|
| 正答率(%) | 1.1 | 1.2 | 1.3 | | 3.1 | 3.2 | 3.3 | 4.1 | 4.2 | 5.1 | 5.2 | 5.3 | 6.1 | 6.2 |
| 新疆某小学 1 | 77.6 | 95.9 | 100.0 | 100.0 | 99.0 | 53.1 | 34.7 | 91.8 | 69.4 | 65.3 | 98.0 | 40.8 | 75.5 | 95.9 |
| 吉林某小学 | 81.8 | 100.0 | 92.7 | 72.7 | 84.5 | 80.0 | 14.6 | 78.2 | 70.9 | 72.7 | 67.3 | 58.2 | 76.4 | 80.0 |
| 广东某小学 | 53.3 | 90.0 | 78.3 | 73.3 | 75.8 | 56.7 | 15.0 | 51.7 | 38.3 | 51.7 | 58.3 | 31.7 | 61.7 | 55.0 |
| 辽宁某小学 | 46.0 | 83.8 | 89.2 | 73.0 | 89.2 | 70.3 | 18.9 | 75.7 | 56.8 | 83.8 | 70.3 | 32.4 | 56.8 | 78.4 |
| 新疆某小学 2 | 46.4 | 95.7 | 84.1 | 91.3 | 81.2 | 71.0 | 20.3 | 72.5 | 53.6 | 69.6 | 71.0 | 27.5 | 71.0 | 78.3 |

### （二）对试卷的分析(日本)

通过上述的整体分析，我们来对两份试卷进行逐一分析，以便能分析出日本小学生作答时所产生的问题，以便与我国学生的情况进行比较。

1. 对试卷 A 的分析(日本)

试卷 A 的构成是：共分为七大题，其中，一题含 7 小题、三题和六题均含 2 小题、五题和七题均含 3 小题。第一大题中，第 4 小题(考察整数与小数的除法运算)和第 7 小题(考察四则运算的顺序)正答率相对较低；第三大题中，第 2 小题(考察分数、小数的大小、意义及在数轴上的表示)正答率很低，为 55.9%；第四大题(考察对小数的乘法的理解)，正答率为 54.3%；第五大题第 3 小题(考察对圆的面积求解公式以及求解圆面积)，其正答率相对较低，为 73.2%。

2. 对试卷 B 的分析(日本)

试卷 B 的构成是：共分为六大题，其中一、三、五大题均含 3 个小题；第二大题只含一题；四、六大题均含 2 个小题。图 5 与图 6 相比，总体正答率明显下降，主要是由于试卷 B 考察的是基本知识和技能灵活运用的能力。正答率较低的题目分别有：第一大题第 1 小题(67.5%)和第 3 小题(68.1%)，其分别考察对长方形周长的理解及求解方法、理解长方形面积的意义并会求解、说明及使用；第二大题(59.0%)，其考察学生对计算方法的理解并能用语言对其进行阐释；第三大题第 3 小题(54.1%)，其考察学生理解并会看条形统计图及其所表达的内容；第四大题第 1 小题(29.5%)和第 2 小题(59.3%)，第 1 小题考察使用百分数求解问题，第 2 小题考察学生基于已给条件来选择信息并能做到思维和作答有条理；第五大题第 3 小题(18.2%)，其考察学生能够基于已给条件来观察发现图形形状(如正方形、长方形等)，能够比较图形面积的大小并给出合理说明。第六大题第 1 小题(65.1%)和第 2 小题(51.4%)，其考察学生根据给出的数学的语言和记号，通过直观观察进行求解计算，并与实际表中记录的数据进行计算后，二者进行比较。

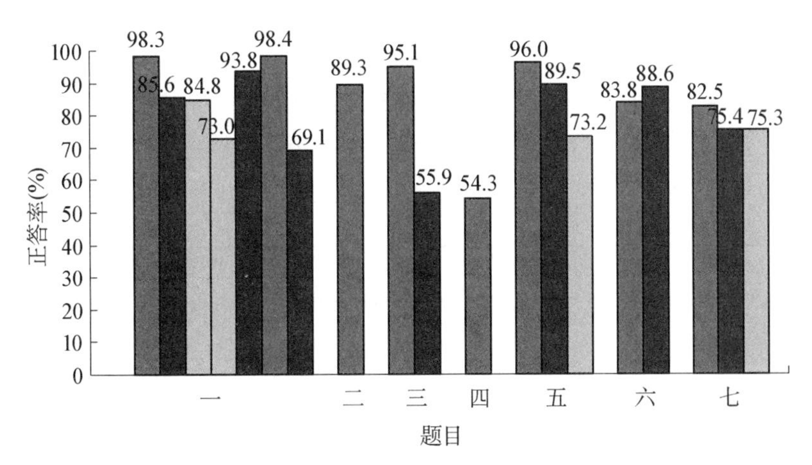


**图 5　日本全国小学生在试卷 A 中作答正确率的百分比[5]**

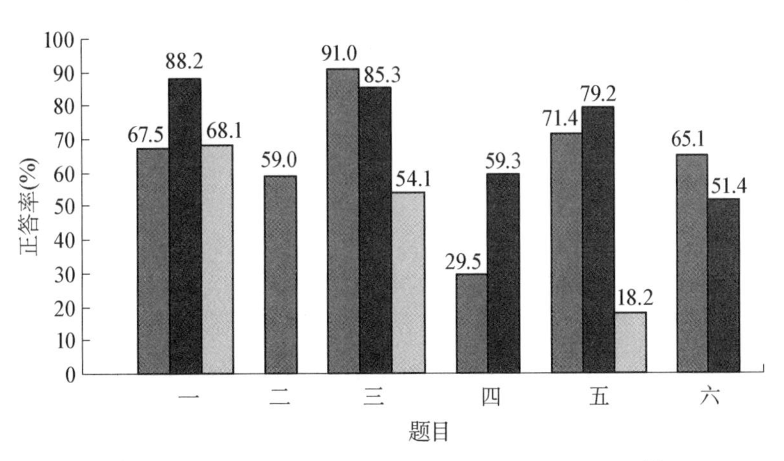


**图 6　日本全国小学生在试卷 B 中作答正确率的百分比[6]**

## 五、中国各地区小学生在试卷中出现的错误分析

上面主要侧重试卷的定量分析，在此基础上进行定性分析，揭示不同地区学生作答错误出现的原因及认知表征。

1. 试题 A 中第三题第 2 小题(分数比较大小及坐标上表示数)的错误分析

总体上有 77.78%的人数正确解答了 2.1(在 0.5，$\frac{7}{10}$，$\frac{4}{5}$中，最大的数是哪个?)，但 2.2(从 A—M 中选出 1 个表示最大数刻度的记号，并写出来)的作答正确率只有 40.37%，参见表 7，可以发现各地区在 2.2 上的表现最好为 61.82%，最差只有 16.22%。表 12 中给出了五个地区学生在试卷 B 在第三题 2.2 中每个错误的分布及错误类型的描述。从表 9 中我们可以看出，对第三题 2.2 未能正确作答，很大程度上取决于学生对问题的误解和忽视。总体统计，分别有 21.48%、16.67%的学生选择 M、未作答，充分说明了这点。

**表 9　中国五个地区学生在试卷 A 在第三题 2.2 中每个错误的分布及错误类型的描述**

| 错误类型 | 学生错误类型的百分比 | | | | | |
|---|---|---|---|---|---|---|
| | 总体 | 新疆某小学 1 | 吉林某小学 | 广东某小学 | 辽宁某小学 | 新疆某小学 2 |
| 选择 M | 21.48 | 20.41 | 12.72 | 21.67 | 32.43 | 11.59 |
| 未作答 | 16.67 | 12.24 | 12.72 | 33.33 | 5.41 | 14.49 |
| 其他 | 21.48 | 10.20 | 12.72 | 21.67 | 45.95 | 23.19 |

2. 试题 A 中第四题(简单文字题)的错误分析

总体上有 72.59%的人数作答正确,但相比试卷 A 中其他题目作答偏低。从表 10 中可以看出,未能正确作答中过半数(以总体为例,选择答案 4 的百分比为 11.48% + 2.96% = 13.44%,而未作答及其他为 2.96% + 10.00% = 12.96% )是因为选择了 4(3 为正确答案)。可见,学生观察力比较薄弱,出现审题偏差。

**表 10　中国五地区学生在试卷 A 在第四题中每个错误的分布及错误类型的描述**

| 错误类型 | 学生错误类型的百分比 | | | | | |
|---|---|---|---|---|---|---|
| | 总体 | 新疆某小学 1 | 吉林某小学 | 广东某小学 | 辽宁某小学 | 新疆某小学 2 |
| 选择 4 | 11.48 | 4.08 | 20.00 | 11.67 | 16.22 | 7.25 |
| 选择 3、4 | 2.96 | 0 | 3.64 | 6.67 | 0 | 4.35 |
| 为作答 | 2.96 | 0 | 3.64 | 3.33 | 0 | 5.80 |
| 其他 | 10.00 | 2.04 | 0 | 21.67 | 13.51 | 10.14 |

3. 试题 B 中第一题 1(有关长方形公式在实际中的应用)的错误分析

总体上只有 60.74%的人数作答正确,参见表 11 各个地区作答正确的百分比,辽宁某小学和新疆的都未过半。3 和 5 是正确答案,从表 11 中可以看出学生主要错误在于思维定式导致的漏选,因为答案 3 为 5 + 3 + 5 + 5,答案 5 为 (5 + 3) × 2,而学生耳熟能详的长方形周长公式为(长 + 宽) × 2。

**表 11　中国五地区学生在试卷 B 在第一题 1 中每个错误的分布及错误类型的描述**

| 错误类型 | 学生错误类型的百分比 | | | | | |
|---|---|---|---|---|---|---|
| | 总体 | 新疆某小学 1 | 吉林某小学 | 广东某小学 | 辽宁某小学 | 新疆某小学 2 |
| 选择 5 | 25.93 | 12.24 | 18.18 | 25.00 | 32.43 | 39.13 |
| 选择 3 | 2.22 | 0 | 0 | 5.00 | 2.70 | 2.90 |
| 未作答 | 0 | 0 | 0 | 0 | 0 | 0 |
| 其他 | 11.11 | 10.20 | 0 | 16.67 | 18.92 | 11.59 |

4. 试题 B 中第三题(看统计图回答问题)的错误分析

这题在总体人数上,2 的正确率不高,只有 66.30%;3 的正确率在试卷 B 各题目中为最低,只有 20.37%。题目 2,大部分作答错误归结为,只对统计图做了一般表面上描述,没有根据其中隐含的数量关系进行计算，做出总结性的表述。例如大部分同学是这样回答的“1983年到2003年，男性15—39人数减少，男性40—59人数减少，男性60—人数增加，女性人数减少”。可见学生图形概括的能力偏低。对于题目3，从表12中可以看出，选项1和5严重干扰学生的作答，可见学生对比例的理解存在问题。

**表12 中国五地区学生在试卷B第三题3中每个错误的分布及错误类型的描述**

| 错误类型 | 学生错误类型的百分比 | | | | | |
|---|---|---|---|---|---|---|
| | 总体 | 新疆某小学1 | 吉林某小学 | 广东某小学 | 辽宁某小学 | 新疆某小学2 |
| 选择1 | 9.63 | 0 | 14.55 | 20.00 | 8.11 | 4.35 |
| 选择1、2 | 22.59 | 22.45 | 25.45 | 11.67 | 27.03 | 27.54 |
| 选择2、5 | 10.37 | 12.24 | 10.91 | 5.00 | 5.41 | 15.94 |
| 选择2 | 10.37 | 6.12 | 12.73 | 15.00 | 13.51 | 5.80 |
| 未作答 | 1.85 | 0 | 0 | 3.33 | 0 | 4.35 |
| 其他 | 24.81 | 24.49 | 21.82 | 33.33 | 27.03 | 21.74 |

5. 试题B中第四题(解决复杂的算术文字题)的错误分析

这题的第2题，参见表8，总体人数上作答正确率为57.07%，但因各个地区各学校很少写做题过程，因此错误类型分布情况无法统计。但根据第1小题可以推断出这两个小题错误出现的原因：(1)对题目情景的不理解；(2)对周四、周日的优惠政策不理解；(3)无法从题目情景中构建出一个合理的数学模型。

6. 试题B中第五题(解决复杂的图形文字题)的错误分析

这题在总体人数上，1的正确率不高，只有67.40%；3的正确率也极低，只有37.38%。从表13中可以看出学生对1的为做出正确回答主要集中在画成右下直角，还有一些未作答。可见学生空间观点比较薄弱，对空间图形距离的估计出现偏差。令人惊奇的是总体中画成右下直角的同学有41人，竟然有21人做对了第二道题目(3路线为左上直角)。

**表13 中国五地区学生在试卷B在第五题1中每个错误的分布及错误类型的描述**

| 错误类型 | 学生错误类型的百分比 | | | | | |
|---|---|---|---|---|---|---|
| | 总体 | 新疆某小学1 | 吉林某小学 | 广东某小学 | 辽宁某小学 | 新疆某小学2 |
| 画成右下直角 | 16.67 | 14.29 | 12.73 | 16.67 | 13.51 | 23.19 |
| 未作答 | 15.19 | 20.41 | 14.55 | 31.67 | 2.70 | 4.35 |
| 其他 | 0.74 | 0 | 0 | 0 | 0 | 2.90 |

从表14中可以看出，3作答正确率极低主要集中于对中央公园的面积计算错误。从图7中可以看出中央公园是一个平行四边形，因此主问题转化为平行四边形的面积计算问题；而对试卷A第五题第1小题也是平行四边形面积的计算(见图8)，学生总体上的作答正确率百分比超过90。可见，出错不在于对平行四边形面积公式的掌握，而是不能准确把公式运用到

具体的情境中。

**表 14　五个地区学生在试卷 B 第五题 3 中每个错误的分布及错误类型的描述**

| 错误类型 | 学生错误类型的百分比 | | | | | |
|---|---|---|---|---|---|---|
| | 总体 | 新疆某小学 1 | 吉林某小学 | 广东某小学 | 辽宁某小学 | 新疆某小学 2 |
| 用算式 160 × 70 = 1120 计算中央公园面积，东公园面积正确 | 35.93 | 51.02 | 16.36 | 38.33 | 13.51 | 49.28 |
| 用算式 160 × 70 = 1120 计算中央公园面积，110 × 110 = 1210 计算东公园面积，误打误撞 | 12.59 | 10.20 | 10.91 | 15.00 | 18.92 | 10.14 |
| 未做 | 7.41 | 4.08 | 10.91 | 15.00 | 2.70 | 2.90 |
| 其他 | 18.89 | 8.16 | 14.55 | 15.00 | 51.35 | 20.29 |

（注：大连开发区金石汉佳中心小学大部分作答错误的同学理由空白。）

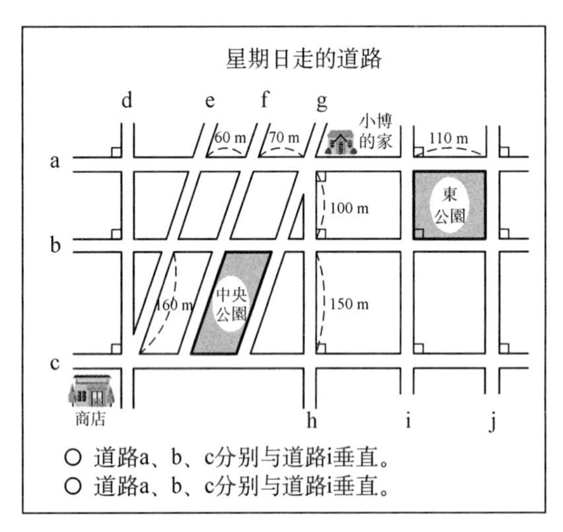


**图 7　试卷 B 中第五题第 3 小题**

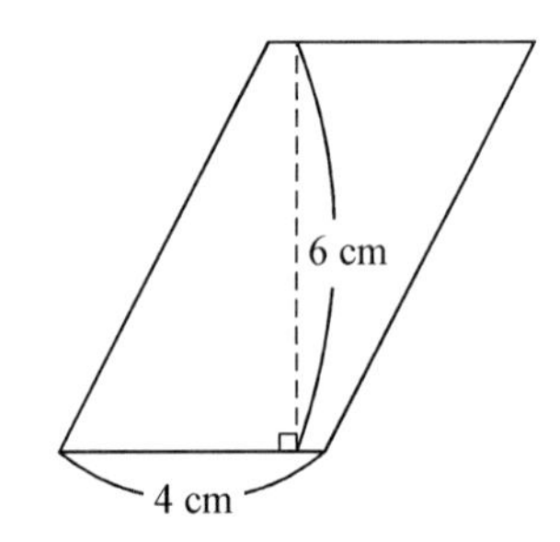


**图 8　试卷 A 中第五题第 1 小题**

## 六、中日两国小学生数学学力比较（基于试卷正答率）

### 1. 基于试卷 A 的比较分析

在上述分析中，已经分别对中日两国的试卷 A 的题目设置进行了简要分析，由图 9 中，从整体上可以看出中日两国小学生的数学学力状况具有相似性（中国第一大题的第 5、6 小题除外：由于新疆地区试卷印制错误，均分较低，除去新疆地区的均分后，其他几区均分水平与日本相当）；但是局部还是有一定差异性，如在第一大题第 3、4、7 小题、第四大题、第五大题第 3 小题、第七大题第 2 小题，中国小学生的数学学力表现更加出色，高出日本小学生 10 分到 30 分之多。与此同时，日本小学生在第三大题的学业能力表现要高于中国，高出 11 到 15 分之多。

此外，两国小学生基于试卷的 A 的具体正答率见表 15 和表 16。

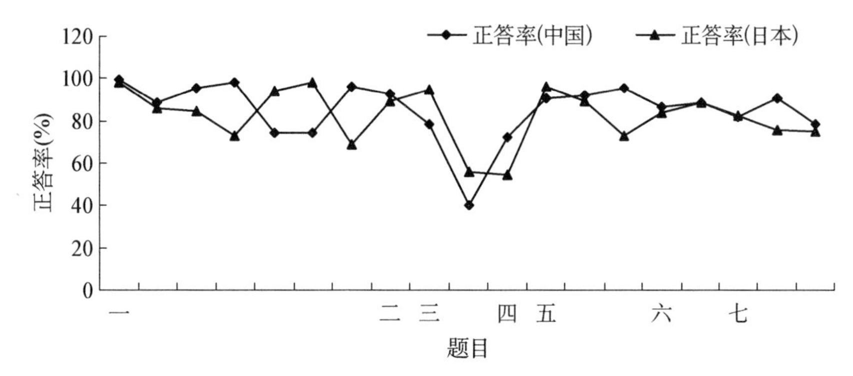


**图 9 中国与日本小学生试卷 A 正答率分布**

**表 15 中日两国小学生基于试卷 A 的正答率分布**

| 题目<br>正答率(%) | 一 | | | | | | | 二 | 三 | |
|---|---|---|---|---|---|---|---|---|---|---|
| | 1.1 | 1.2 | 1.3 | 1.4 | 1.5 | 1.6 | 1.7 | 2 | 3.1 | 3.2 |
| 中国 | 99.6 | 88.5 | 95.6 | 98.5 | 74.1 | 74.4 | 95.9 | 93.0 | 77.8 | 40.4 |
| 日本 | 98.3 | 85.6 | 84.8 | 73.0 | 93.8 | 98.4 | 69.1 | 89.3 | 95.1 | 55.9 |

**表 16 中日两国小学生基于试卷 A 的正答率分布(续)**

| 题目<br>正答率(%) | 四 | 五 | | | 六 | | 七 | | |
|---|---|---|---|---|---|---|---|---|---|
| | 4 | 5.1 | 5.2 | 5.3 | 6.1 | 6.2 | 7.1 | 7.2 | 7.3 |
| 中国 | 72.6 | 90.7 | 91.9 | 95.6 | 86.3 | 88.5 | 81.5 | 90.7 | 78.5 |
| 日本 | 54.3 | 96.0 | 89.5 | 73.2 | 83.8 | 88.6 | 82.5 | 75.4 | 75.3 |

2. 基于试卷 B 的比较分析

基于试卷 B 的意图，中日两国小学生在灵活运用基本知识和技能上，某些内容面上较为薄弱，从图 10 中可以清晰地看出两国学生在知识灵活运用的薄弱点。此外，对中日两国的正

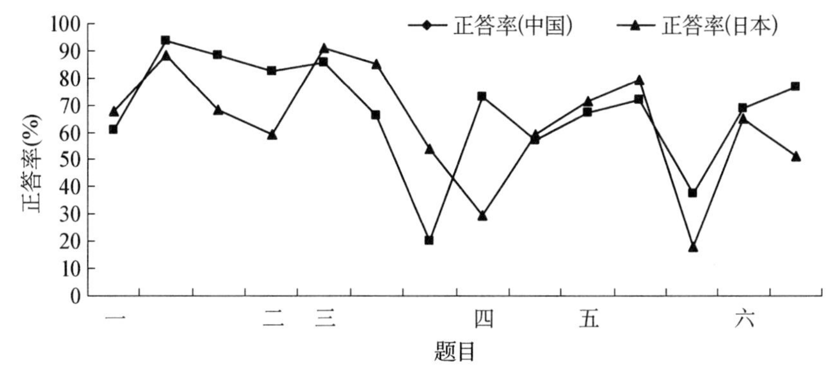


**图 10 中国与日本小学生试卷 B 正答率分布**

答率进行对比，基本上具有相似性，但也存有较大差异处，如在第一大题第 3 小题、第二大题、第四大题第 1 小题、第五大题第 3 小题、第六大题第 2 小题，中国要高出日本 20 分左右；同时，日本小学生在第三大题的表现要好于中国小学生，大致高出 20 到 30 分左右。两国小学生基于试卷的 B 的具体正答率见表 17 和表 18。

**表 17　中日两国小学生基于试卷 B 的正答率分布**

| 题目<br>正答率(%) | 一 | | | 二 | 三 | | |
|---|---|---|---|---|---|---|---|
| | 1.1 | 1.2 | 1.3 | 2 | 3.1 | 3.2 | 3.3 |
| 中国 | 60.7 | 93.7 | 88.2 | 82.6 | 85.9 | 66.3 | 20.4 |
| 日本 | 67.5 | 88.2 | 68.1 | 59.0 | 91.0 | 85.3 | 54.1 |

**表 18　中日两国小学生基于试卷 B 的正答率分布(续)**

| 题目<br>正答率(%) | 四 | | 五 | | | 六 | |
|---|---|---|---|---|---|---|---|
| | 4.1 | 4.2 | 5.1 | 5.2 | 5.3 | 6.1 | 6.2 |
| 中国 | 73.0 | 57.0 | 67.4 | 72.2 | 37.8 | 68.9 | 76.7 |
| 日本 | 29.5 | 59.3 | 71.4 | 79.2 | 18.2 | 65.1 | 51.4 |

## 七、结论与建议

从上述总体分析及试卷分析，我们可以总结出：

（一）总体来讲，小学六年级学生综合应用的能力弱于基本的知识和基本的技能，不同地区差异性显著。

（二）实证得出小学六年级学生综合应用的能力与基本知识和基本技能显著正相关。可见在课堂教学中两者并不相冲突，而是互相的促进。基本知识、基本技能的巩固是综合能力提高的前提，而综合能力的提高反而能加强学生对基本知识、基本技能的掌握。

（三）小学六年级学生数学阅读能力有待提高。这主要表现在两方面：1. 从统计图中获取、收集信息能力差，以试题 B 中第三题为例。2. 在应用问题情景中存在理解的障碍。这是学生在试卷 B 中成绩不高的原因之一，其中最典型的是试卷 B 中第四题(解决复杂的算术文字题)。

（四）小学六年级学生不能把数学的概念公式正确合理地运用到具体的情境中。这一点突出表现在试题 B 中第五题(解决复杂的图形文字题)第 3 题——一道融入情境的图形面积计算。对比试卷 A 第五题，不含情境的图形面积计算，学生表现迥然不同。在试卷 A 中大部分同学都作答正确，而在试卷 B 中大部分同学都作答错误。

针对总结，建议在教学中：

（一）在教学中，注重提高学生问题解决的能力。问题解决是指学生将他们的数学知识应用于新的问题情境中的能力，它要求学生能识别所遇到的问题，根据已知条件构造和选择恰当的策略、综合所学知识去解决所碰到的问题。同时能对解题过程及答案做出评价，判断解题过程和答案的正确性。它反映了学生将所学知识综合应用于新的问题情境中的能力。

（二）在平时的教学中，注意引导学生理解问题的情境，建构合理的数学模型。实际上，数学的问题情境可以有很多方面，比如和学生日常活动有直接关联的个人情境、与学生学校生活或工作环境有关的教育情境、要求学生观察身边更广阔的环境中一些方面的公共情境等等。

（三）在课堂教学中，巩固基本知识和基本能力的同时，应该更关注学生综合运用能力的培养。寻找、发现导致学生综合应用能力不高的问题所在，从而进行创新性的课堂教学，为学生综合应用能力的发展提供更好的学习环境，更多的机会。

## 附录

### 小学第6学年算术A

**1.** 完成下面的计算。

(1) $28+72$

(2) $27\times 3.4$

(3) $9.3\times 0.8$

(4) $12\div 0.6$

(5) $1-\frac{5}{8}$

(6) $\frac{3}{7}+\frac{4}{7}$

(7) $6+0.5\times 2$

**2.** 在下面的正方形中，涂色部分是整体的$\frac{2}{3}$的，是哪个图形？从下面的1～5中选择一个答案，写出它的编号。

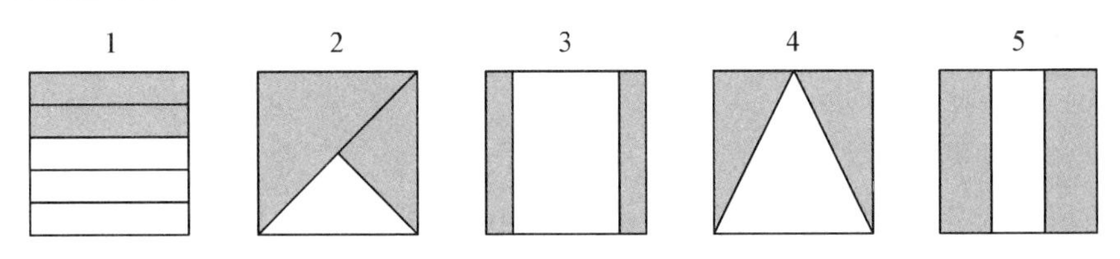


**3.** 在下面的数射线上，相邻的两个整数之间分成10等份，并标上刻度。回答下面的问题：

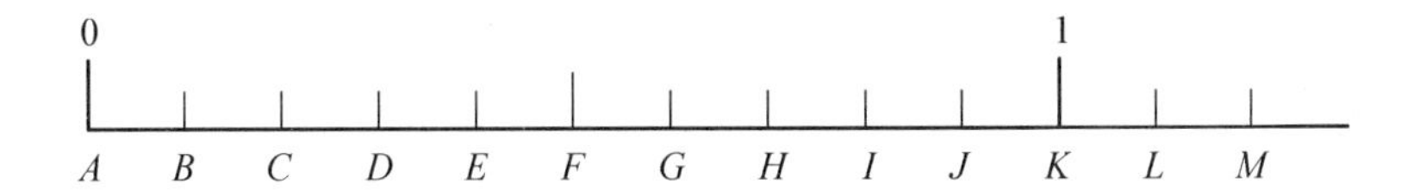

（1）从 A～M 中选出 1 个表示$\frac{7}{10}$刻度的记号，并写出来。

（2）在 0.5，$\frac{7}{10}$、$\frac{4}{5}$中，最大的数是哪个？从 A～M 中选出 1 个表示最大数刻度的记号，并写出来。

**4.** 从下面 1～4 的问题中，选出一个答案可以用 210 × 0.6 这个算式求出的问题，并将它的标号写出来。

（1）买 0.6 kg 砂糖，付了 210 日圆。1 kg 这种砂糖的价格是多少？

（2）将 210 kg 的大豆分成每袋 0.6 kg 的小袋，总共需要多少个袋子？

（3）一种缎带每米 210 日圆，买 0.6 米这样的缎带需要多少日圆？

（4）红彩带的长度为 210 cm，红彩带的长度是白彩带的长度的 0.6 倍，白彩带的长度是多少米？

**5.** 写出求下面图形面积的计算公式和答案。

（1）平行四边形

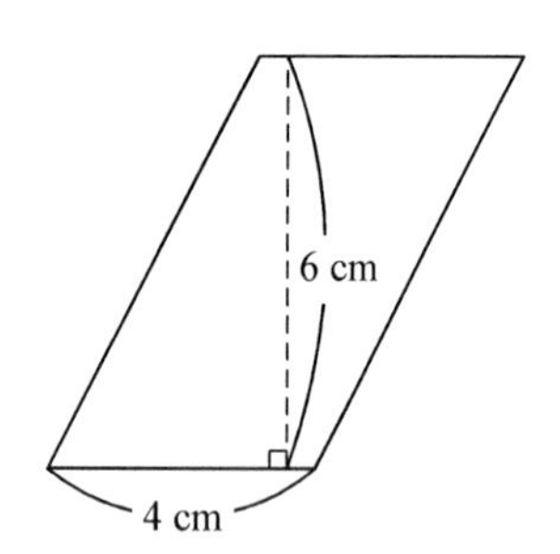


（2）三角形

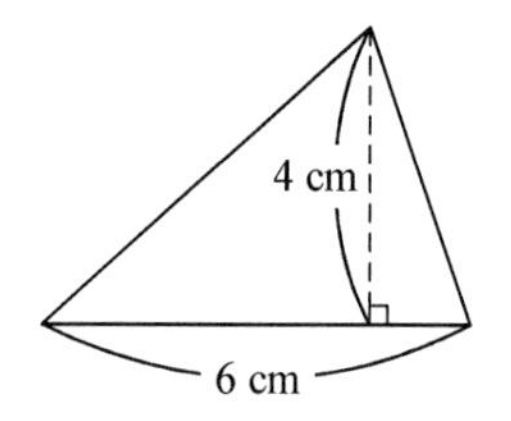


（3）圆（圆周率使用 3.14）

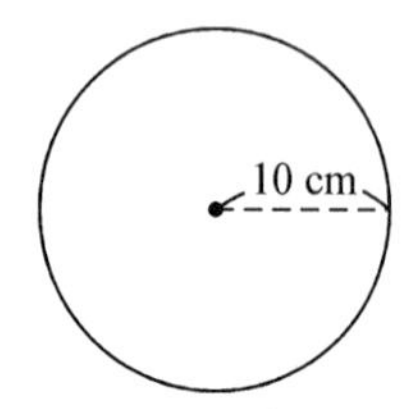

**6.** 回答下面的问题

（1）下面三角形的角 a 的大小是多少度？

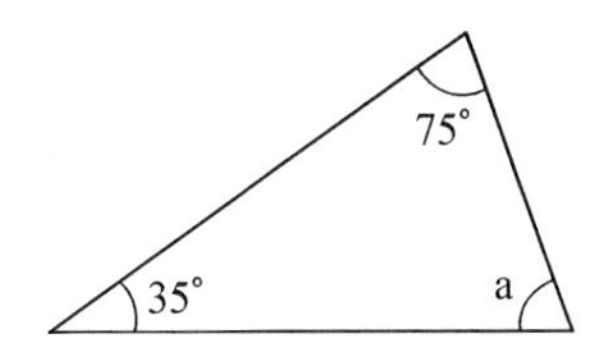


（2）要在下面的方格纸中画一个平行四边形。另外一个顶点在哪里？从标号为 1～5 的点中选一个点，并写出它的标号。

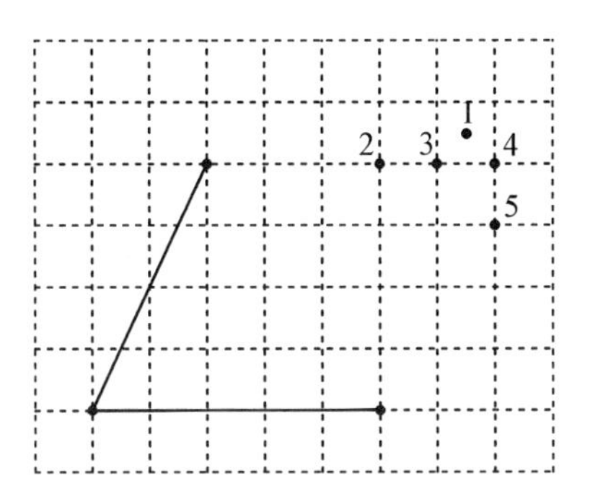


**7.** 向下面那样使用长度为 16 cm 的绳子，围长方形或正方形。

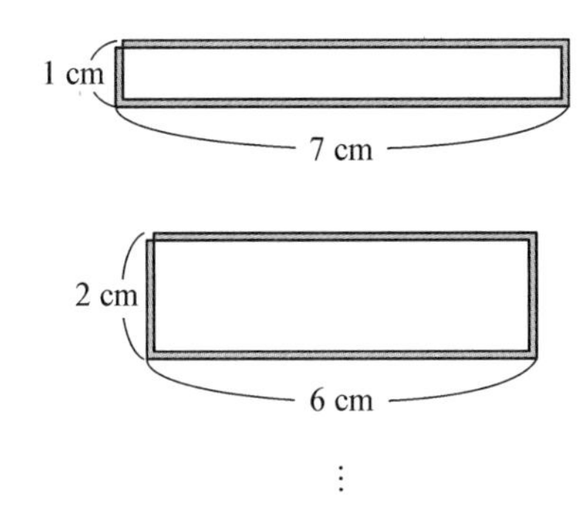


（1）当长方形的宽为 3 cm 的时候，这个长方形的长为多少 cm？写出答案。

（2）将围成的长方形或正方形的长与宽的关系汇总到下表中（在表的空白处填上数字）。

| 宽（cm） | 1 | 2 | 3 | 4 | 5 | 6 | 7 |
|---|---|---|---|---|---|---|---|
| 长（cm） | 7 | | | | | | |

（3）长方形或正方形的长每增加 1 cm，宽怎样变化？

## 小学第 6 学年算术 B

**1.** 有一个像图①那样的长 9 m、宽 6 m 的长方形花坛。在这个花坛中有一个长 5 m、宽 3 m 的长方形阴影部分。

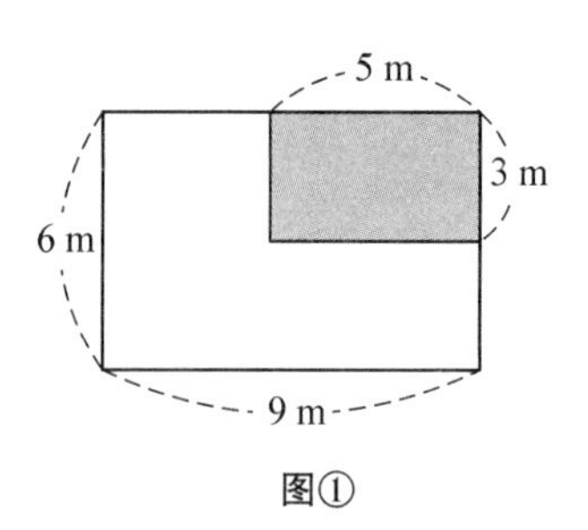

图①

(1) 要用围绳将阴影部分围起来,围阴影部分的围绳的长度,用怎样的公式求出?

从下面的①～⑤中选出两个,写出它们的标号。

① 5＋3

② 5×3

③ 5＋3＋5＋3

④ 5×3×2

⑤ (5＋3)×2

(2) 三崎先生要在花坛的白色部分种植郁金香。白色部分的面积,用怎样的公式求出?

从下面的①～④中选出一个,写出它的标号。

① 5×3＋3×9

② 3×6－5×3

③ 6×9－3×5

④ 3×9－3×5

(3) 如下面的图 A、图 B、图 C、图 D 所示,有一个长 9 m、宽 6 m 的长方形花坛。在这个花坛中有一个长 5 m、宽 3 m 的长方形阴影部分。

图 A、图 B、图 C、图 D 中的白色部分的面积与图①中白色部分的面积是相同的。为什么这些白色部分的面积是相同的?使用文字或算式或图说明理由。

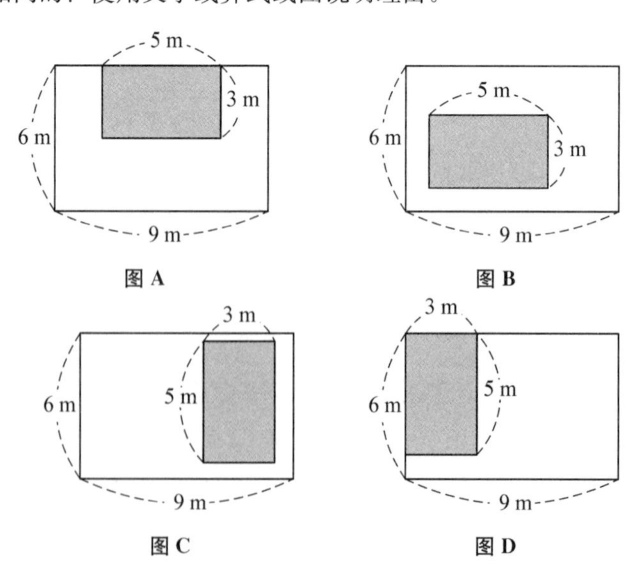

**2.** 1 块巧克力 25 日圆，要买 12 块这样的巧克力，总共需要多少日圆，幸代想用笔算来计算。

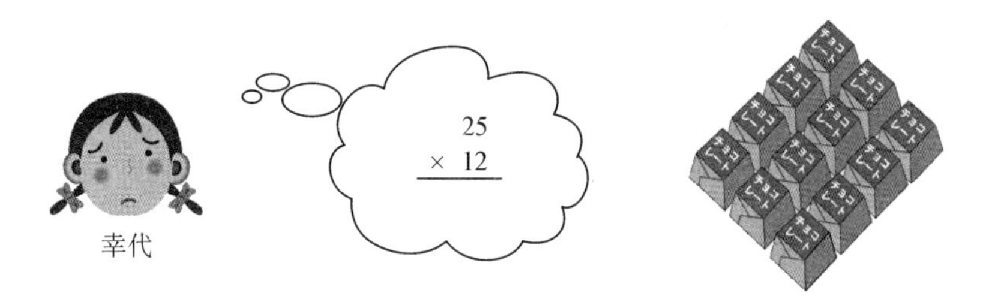


听到这个消息，隆志和悦子想到了不用笔算就能算出 $25\times12$ 的简单方法。

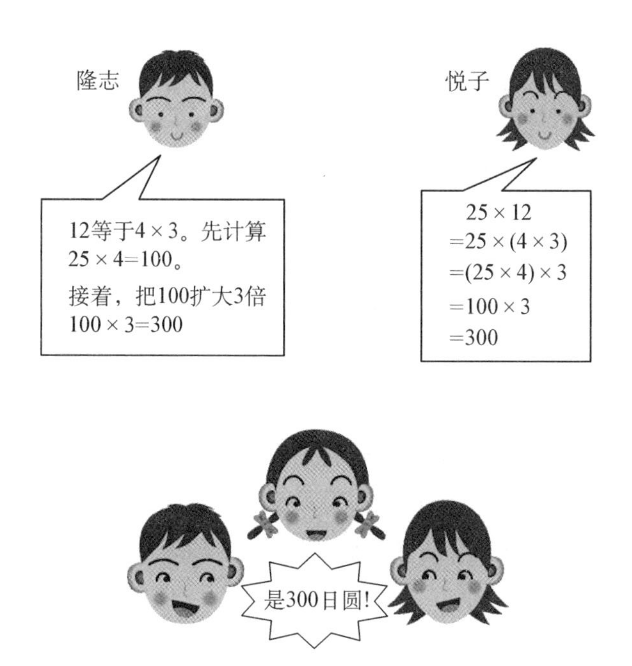


接下来，幸代想知道买 32 个这种巧克力需要多少日圆。

你能像隆志和悦子那样，巧算 $25\times32$ 吗？

使用文字或算式写出巧算的方法。

**3.** 秋子在学习日本的渔业时，看到下面的条形统计图。这个条形统计图将从事渔业的人员按照男性的年龄层和女性进行分类：

**从事渔业的人数**

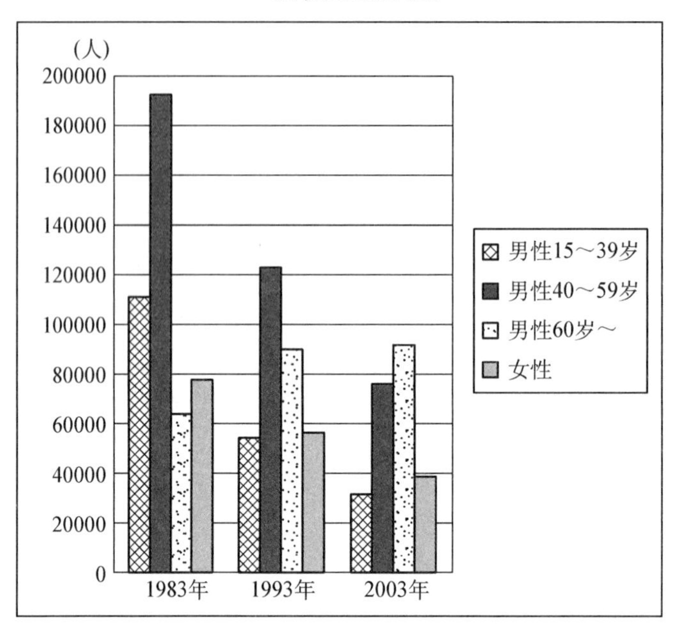


（1）在 1983 年，从事渔业最多的是哪一群人？在 2003 年，从事渔业最多的是哪一群人？从下面的①～④中分别选出一个，写出它的标号。

① 男性 15～39 岁　　② 男性 40～59 岁

③ 男性 60 岁～　　④ 女性

（2）看这个条形统计图，可以知道从事渔业的总人数的变化情况。写出从 1983 年到 2003 年从事渔业的总人数是怎样变化的。

（3）接着秋子根据条形统计图将从事渔业的各种人群的比例画成了下面的百分比条图。

**从事渔业的各种人群的比例**

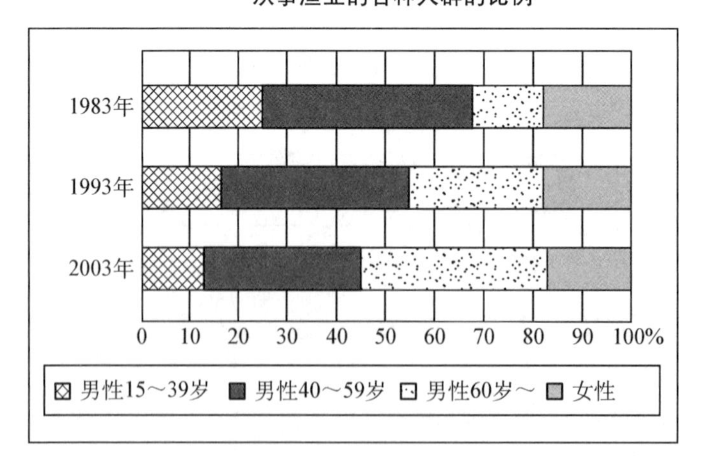

读上面的百分比条图，你能够知道从 1983 年到 2003 年有什么变化？

从下面的①～⑤中选择两个正确的，写出它们的标号。

① 从事渔业的人数在减少

② “男性 15～39 岁”从事渔业的人数的比例在减少

③ “女性”从事渔业的人数的比例大约占一半

④ “男性 60 岁～”从事渔业的人数的比例比原来的 2 倍还多

⑤ “男性 60 岁～”从事渔业的人数比原来的 2 倍还多

**4.** 隆志家附近有一个蛋糕店。这个蛋糕店中有蛋糕卷、奶酪蛋糕、草莓蛋糕、巧克力蛋糕，价格如下：

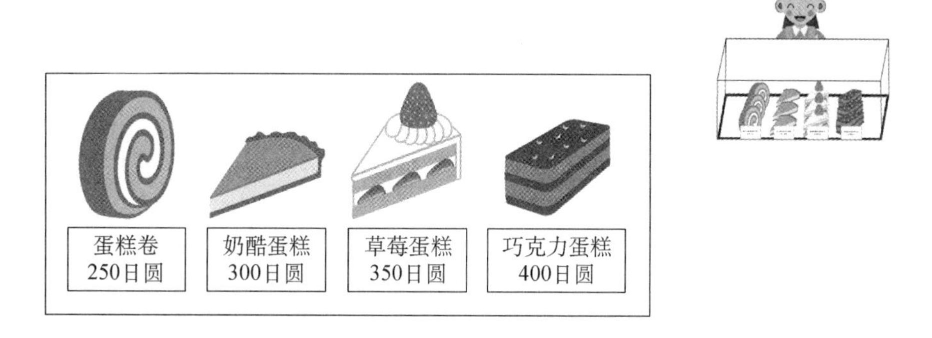


| 星期四 | 星期日 |
| --- | --- |
| 所有的蛋糕降价 20%进行促销。如：定价 250 日圆的蛋糕降价 50 日圆，卖 200 日圆。 | 定价低于 320 日圆的蛋糕一律卖 200 日圆。 |

这个蛋糕店星期四和星期日进行促销活动。星期四和星期日按照下面的方法促销：

(1) 隆志想买 1 个奶酪蛋糕和 1 个巧克力蛋糕。

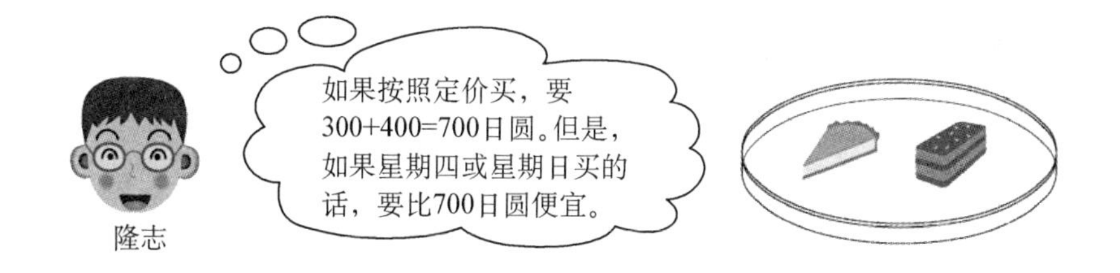


星期四或星期日，隆志哪天买的话比较便宜？分别写出求解的算式和答案。

(2) 隆志星期日想买 5 个蛋糕。他想 5 个蛋糕的总价刚好为 1500 日圆。隆志首先选了 1 个蛋糕卷、1 个草莓蛋糕和 1 个巧克力蛋糕。

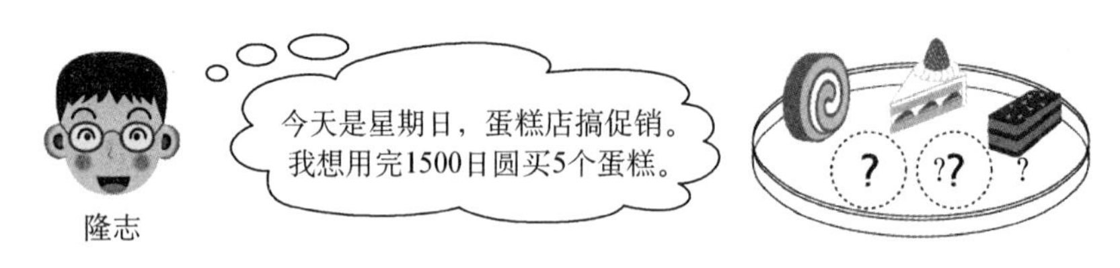


剩下的两个蛋糕，在蛋糕卷、奶酪蛋糕、草莓蛋糕、巧克力蛋糕中，怎样选择？写出一种答案。

**5.** 小博星期六出门去商店购物。他沿着下面地图中标有  的道路从路口Ⓐ到路口Ⓑ。

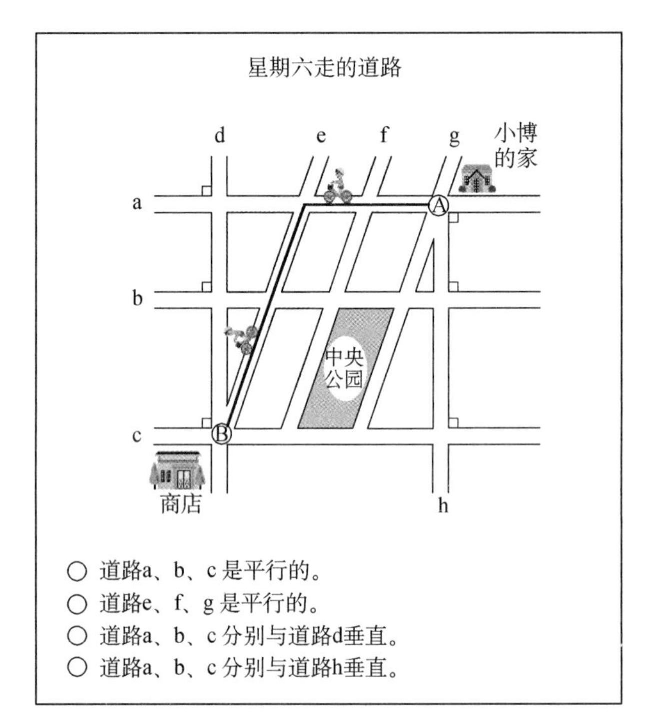


（1）小博购物后，想从路口Ⓑ返回到路口Ⓐ。

要想不走来时经过的道路，重新选择一条路，并且这条路的路程与来时的路程相等，小博选择哪条路合适？选择一条道路，在图中画出来。

（2）小博在第 2 天星期日，从路口Ⓐ经过路口Ⓒ到路口Ⓑ。

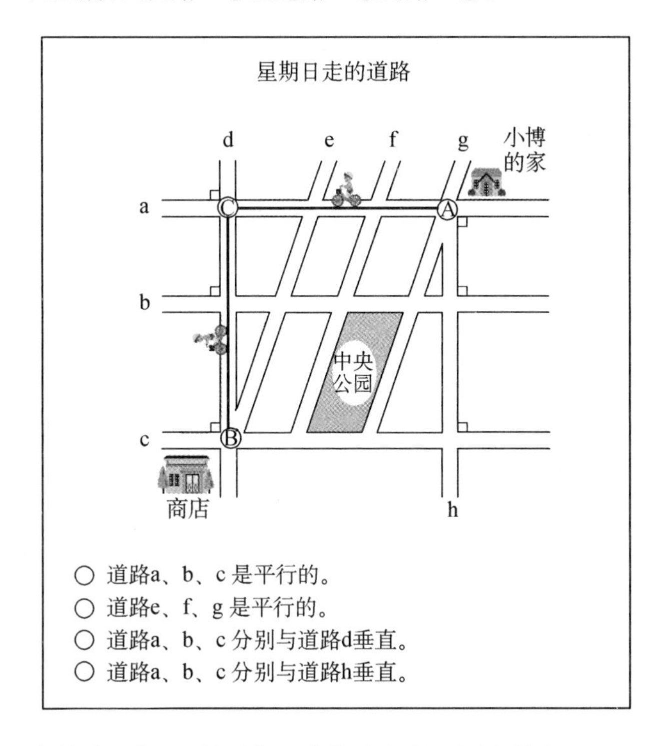


小博星期六走的路程长，还是星期日走的路程长？写出答案。

（3）小博家附近有个东公园。

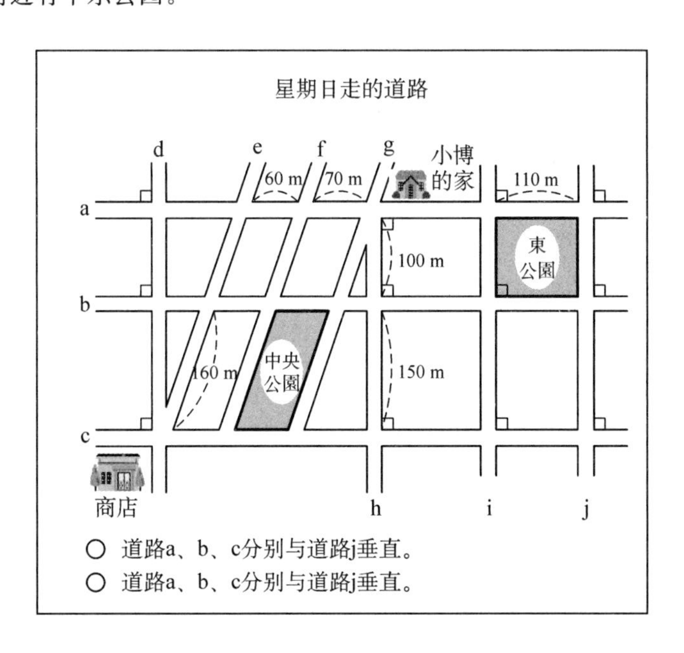

东公园与中央公园相比，哪个的面积大？用文字或公式等说明理由。

**6.** 体育课上正在学习跳高。据说一个人跳高能跳过的高度与他的身高及他的 50 米跑的成绩有关系。通过下面的算式，就可以计算出一个人能跳的目标高度是多少厘米。

**求所跳的目标高度(cm)的计算公式**

| 身高(cm)的一半加上 120，减去 50 米跑的成绩(秒)的 10 倍<br>(身高÷2)+120−(50 米跑的成绩×10) |
|---|

健太

良夫

**健太与良夫的身高与 50 米跑的成绩如下表所示：**

| | 身高(cm) | 50 米跑的成绩(秒) |
|---|---|---|
| 健太 | 140 | 8.0 |
| 良夫 | 160 | 8.0 |

(1) 健太使用上面的公式计算了他能跳的目标高度。但实际跳跃后，他跳过了115 cm。这个成绩与健太能跳的目标高度相比，可以说明什么？从下面的①～③中选择 1 个正确的，写出它的标号。

① 所跳的成绩刚好与他能跳的目标高度相同

② 所跳的成绩比他能跳的目标高度高

③ 所跳的成绩比他能跳的目标高度低

(2) 良夫也想使用上面的公式计算了他自己能跳的目标高度。健太看了自己和良夫的身高与 50 米跑的成绩后，说了下面的话：

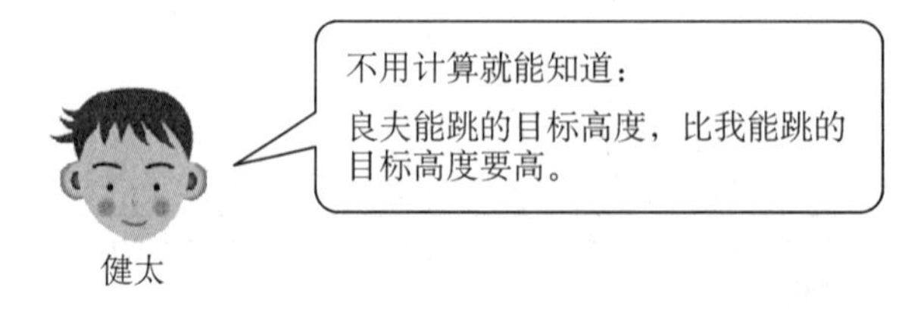


健太为什么不计算就知道良夫能跳的目标高度比自己能跳的目标高度高？使用文字或算式说明理由。

参考文献

[1][2] 日本国立教育政策研究所.平成19年度全国学力・学習商況調査——調査結果のポイント.2007(10):1,4.

[3][4][5][6] 日本国立教育政策研究所.教科に関する調査の結果.2007(10):16,18,17,19.

# A Comparative Study of Mathematics Academic Ability in Primary School between China and Japan

Qiping Kong　Li Yang

**Abstract**: One of the most important tasks in compulsory education stage in China is to discover and settle problems existed in mathematics education in order to improve the students' academic ability and synthesis application ability. Since 2007, in this regard, Japan has implemented the National Assessment of Academic Ability for students of the compulsory education stage to analyze the performance of the students' academic ability. We implemented the Assessment of Academic Ability which was inspired by the practice of Japan to help our teachers and scholars to grasp the students' current academic ability of mathematics and the current situation of intellectual development in order to provide a useful remedial teaching for students. Meanwhile, we compared between China and Japan in the findings of the assessment to understand the students' performance of similarities and differences in mathematics in different cultural backgrounds. The purpose is to help us broaden the educational horizons and to help teachers find the ways to design better classroom teaching.

**Key words**: Academic ability; assessment of academic ability; Sino-Japan comparison

# S－P表法的改进和应用

许志勇　丁树良

【摘要】传统的S－P表法只能提供粗糙诊断信息，不能为改进教学提供明确的指向。而改进的S－P表法结合认知诊断测量理论，不但可以为改进教学提供明确指向，而且为认知诊断分类提供了更多的定性分类的信息。试验表明，教师对于改进的S－P表法诊断分类结果认同率可达到69%。因此改进的S－P表法可以成为教师进行诊断分类的重要辅助手段。

【关键词】S－P表法；认知诊断；马氏距离

【作者简介】许志勇/天津市教育招生考试院助理研究员
丁树良/江西师范大学计算机信息工程学院教授博士导师

## 一、引言

S－P表(Student Problem Chart)是学生的答题得分表，它是由日本学者佐藤隆博(Takahiro Sato)于1970年所创立，通过计算每位学生及每道试题的作答反应模式的注意系数，以及整份测验的差异系数和同质性系数，教师可以借助这些统计指标来诊断学生表现、测验品质、以及教学成果，并作为改进教学、命题、与辅导学生的参考。[1] S－P表法的基本过程是，把使用选择题题型的测验分数变成1(答对)或0(答错)的数据，并按学生得分总分的高低，由上向下的顺序排列，试题按照答对人数的多少，由左向右排列，然后画出学生得分曲线，称S(student)线，画出问题答对人数曲线，称P(problem)线，这就得出一个S－P表。[2]

S－P表法最大的优势是计算方便，教师易掌握，而且依据计算学生及每道试题的作答反应模式的注意系数，将学生的学习类型和试题类型进行定性分类[1]，根据定性分类信息，可以为改进教学和命题质量提供有效信息。但是由于对学生的学习类型分类较粗糙，只是将学生的学习类型分为六种类型，不能指出学生学习中存在的不足，以及不能指出学生某个概念或者某些学习材料是否真正掌握。而且S－P表法只适应用于小样本数的班级人数之形成性评量的测验资料分析。[3][4] 因此本文着力探讨如何借助现代认知诊断测量理论的优势，使得现代认知诊断测量理论和技术与S－P表法相结合，提供更加准确有效的反馈信息，并且适用于大规模教育考试的分析。

## 二、S－P表法改进的基本思路

现代认知诊断测量理论是近几十年发展起来的新的测验理论，其最大的特征是强调宏观和微观、能力水平和认知水平的评估并举，将被试在测验上的反应进行加工，以揭示个体所知道的和所能做的事实，更着重告诉利益分担者（stakeholder）被试所不知和不能之处，以便于有针对性地进行补救，而不是局限于能力的特质水平的概念。该理论实现的途径是借助于认知心理学与心理和教育测量学，通过认知心理学研究方法对测量任务所涉及的知识、技能、策略、加工过程与成分等各认知变量做认知分析，获得测量任务的实质性的心理模型。然后依据设计好的心理模型进行测验设计，将各种认知变量直接融合入测量模型，借助现代统计方法揭示个体认知变量的特征。[5]现代认知诊断测量理论由于大多使用复杂的心理计量模型，只有专业人员才能理解和运用，而普通的中小学教师通常认为心理计量模型过于艰涩、深奥、难懂，影响到现代认知诊断测量理论的推广和运用[6]，而且过于复杂的心理计量模型使得参数也变得难于估计，估计方法也可能影响到后期认知诊断的精度。改进 S－P 表法的基本思路是不借助于复杂心理计量模型，以经典测量理论为基础，吸取现代认知诊断理论相关知识，达到改进 S－P 表法后期分类过于粗糙的目的。

## 三、S－P 表法改进的基本步骤

结合认知诊断理论的相关知识，S－P 表法改进的基本步骤如下：

（1）确定所欲测内容的认知属性及属性间的层次关系；

（2）根据步骤（1）给出可达阵 R 及被试 Q 矩阵 $Q_s$ 阵，并进行测验蓝图设计（即给出测验 Q 矩阵 $Q_t$ 阵），计算出理想反应模式（ideal response pattern，IRP）以及对应的知识状态（即属性掌握模式）（knowledge state，KS）；

（3）对学生的测验总分成绩和观察反应模式（observed response pattern，ORP）用 S－P 表法进行分析；

（4）对任意一个被试 i 的 ORP，记之为 ORP（i），根据测验的标准误，计算 ORP（i）总分的置信区间$[a_i, b_i]$；

（5）寻找总分成绩落在$[a_i, b_i]$的所有 IRP，这些 IRP 构成的集合，记为 $IRPS_i$；

（6）应用马氏距离法从 $IRPS_i$ 中找出一个 IRP，使之与 ORP(i)的距离最小；

（7）根据步骤（6）中获得的理想反应模式（IRP），可以知道学生的知识状态（即属性掌握模式）（KS）；

（8）重复第（4）步到第（7）步，一直到得出所有的被试的 KS；

（9）由步骤（3）到步骤（8）导出的 S－P 表分析与 KS 的综合，就是改进 S－P 表法分析结果。

设计步骤（1）、（2）、（4）、（6）的理由在于，一是给出认知诊断模型（cognitive diagnostic model），达到改进 S－P 表法前期缺乏测验设计的不足之处；二是设计很好的认知诊断测验（即可达矩阵 R 作为 $Q_t$ 的一部份），保证理想反应模式（IRP）与知识状态（KS）一一对应[7]；三是观察反应模式（ORP）的总分成绩是随机变量，可以波动；四是使用马氏距离法可以吸取学生作答表现的整体信息,有利于保证诊断分类的准确性。

## 四、S-P表法改进的试验

### (一) 数据来源

为了了解改进S-P表法的效果,以某市小学五年级诊断测验的数据作为分析的基础数据,从中选取了四所学校的数据作为分析对象。四所学校参加诊断测验数据如表1所示。

表1 四所学校参加诊断测验不同类型试卷考试的人数分布

| 学校代码 | A卷 | B卷 | C卷 | 小计 |
|---|---|---|---|---|
| 103 | 27 | 28 | 25 | 80 |
| 104 | 80 | 82 | 83 | 245 |
| 105 | 62 | 60 | 60 | 182 |
| 106 | 72 | 72 | 69 | 213 |
| 合计 | 241 | 242 | 237 | 720 |

### (二) 测验的基本属性

该测验以认知诊断理论作为编制测验的理论指导,选取小学数学五年级下学期简单分数(不含带分数)加、减运算作为测验的内容。该测验确立的认知属性及属性层级关系以及约简的关联矩阵 $Q_r$,如图1和表2所示,表2中包括可达矩阵对应的七种基本类型,它们是第1、2、3、5、9、11、16类型。

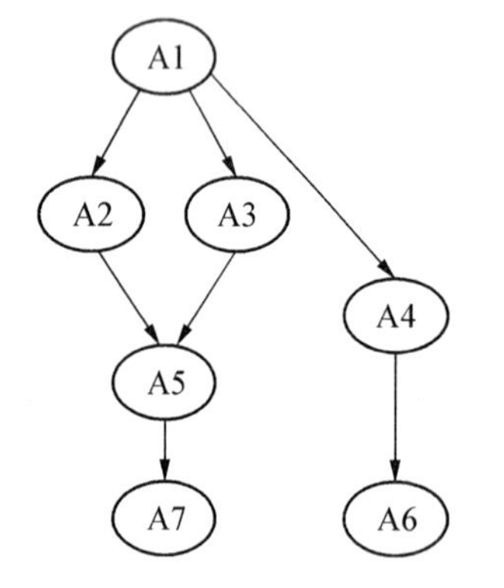


A1:基础知识(分数单位、分数性质、加减混合运算顺序)

A2:同分母分数加减方法

A3:通分

A4:约分

A5:异分母分数加减方法

A6:化成最简分数

A7:分数加减混合运算方法

图1 小学数学五年级分数简单加减法认知属性及层级关系

表2 十八种类型考核的认知属性

| 类型 | A1 | A2 | A3 | A4 | A5 | A6 | A7 |
|---|---|---|---|---|---|---|---|
| 第1类型 | 1 | 0 | 0 | 0 | 0 | 0 | 0 |
| 第2类型 | 1 | 1 | 0 | 0 | 0 | 0 | 0 |

续 表

| 类型 | A1 | A2 | A3 | A4 | A5 | A6 | A7 |
|---|---|---|---|---|---|---|---|
| 第3类型 | 1 | 0 | 1 | 0 | 0 | 0 | 0 |
| 第4类型 | 1 | 1 | 1 | 0 | 0 | 0 | 0 |
| 第5类型 | 1 | 0 | 0 | 1 | 0 | 0 | 0 |
| 第6类型 | 1 | 1 | 0 | 1 | 0 | 0 | 0 |
| 第7类型 | 1 | 0 | 1 | 1 | 0 | 0 | 0 |
| 第8类型 | 1 | 1 | 1 | 1 | 0 | 0 | 0 |
| 第9类型 | 1 | 1 | 1 | 0 | 1 | 0 | 0 |
| 第10类型 | 1 | 1 | 1 | 1 | 1 | 0 | 0 |
| 第11类型 | 1 | 0 | 0 | 1 | 0 | 1 | 0 |
| 第12类型 | 1 | 1 | 0 | 1 | 0 | 1 | 0 |
| 第13类型 | 1 | 0 | 1 | 1 | 0 | 1 | 0 |
| 第14类型 | 1 | 1 | 1 | 1 | 0 | 1 | 0 |
| 第15类型 | 1 | 1 | 1 | 1 | 1 | 1 | 0 |
| 第16类型 | 1 | 1 | 1 | 0 | 1 | 0 | 1 |
| 第17类型 | 1 | 1 | 1 | 1 | 1 | 0 | 1 |
| 第18类型 | 1 | 1 | 1 | 1 | 1 | 1 | 1 |

该测验由进行了等值设计的A、B、C三份平行试卷构成，每份试卷共40题，包含两种题型，分别为选择题和填空题，其中选择题20题，填空题20题。每份试卷考核的认知属性一样，位置和顺序基本一致，而且题型内部将考核属性较少的试题放在前面，考核属性较多的试题放在后面。

## 五、数据分析及结果

### （一）S-P表分析结果

使用自编S-P表分析程序，对数据进行S-P表分析，数据分析结果如表3。

**表3 S-P表诊断分类各学校不同类别学生的人数**

| 学校代码 | | A | A' | B | B' | C | C' | 小计 |
|---|---|---|---|---|---|---|---|---|
| 103 | A卷 | 9 | 14 | 1 | 3 | 0 | 0 | 27 |
| | B卷 | 7 | 18 | 1 | 0 | 0 | 2 | 28 |
| | C卷 | 19 | 6 | 0 | 0 | 0 | 0 | 25 |
| | 小计 | 35 | 38 | 2 | 3 | 0 | 2 | 80 |
| 104 | A卷 | 33 | 36 | 4 | 6 | 0 | 1 | 80 |
| | B卷 | 26 | 47 | 2 | 5 | 1 | 1 | 82 |
| | C卷 | 33 | 37 | 4 | 3 | 6 | 0 | 83 |
| | 小计 | 92 | 120 | 10 | 14 | 7 | 2 | 245 |
| 105 | A卷 | 20 | 31 | 2 | 6 | 0 | 3 | 62 |
| | B卷 | 26 | 28 | 3 | 3 | 0 | 0 | 60 |
| | C卷 | 27 | 25 | 3 | 3 | 0 | 2 | 60 |

续　表

| 学校代码 | | A | A' | B | B' | C | C' | 小计 |
|---|---|---|---|---|---|---|---|---|
| | 小计 | 73 | 84 | 8 | 12 | 0 | 5 | 182 |
| 106 | A卷 | 25 | 32 | 6 | 5 | 0 | 4 | 72 |
| | B卷 | 30 | 26 | 6 | 8 | 0 | 2 | 72 |
| | C卷 | 31 | 21 | 7 | 5 | 3 | 2 | 69 |
| | 小计 | 86 | 79 | 19 | 18 | 3 | 8 | 213 |
| 合计 | | 286 | 321 | 39 | 47 | 10 | 17 | 720 |

注：根据余民宁书《教育测验与评量—成就测验与教学评量》的分类标准，A为学习稳定型，A'为粗心大意型，B为努力不足型，B'为欠缺不足型，C为学习不足型，C'为学习异常型。

表3的数据表明，有607名学生被分类为A和A'类型，占总人数的84.31%(＝(286＋321)/720)；有39名学生被诊断为B类型，占总人数的5.42%；有47名学生被诊断为B'类型，占总人数的6.53%；有27名学生被诊断为C和C'类型，占总人数的3.75%。

**(二) 认知诊断结果**

由于S－P表法分析不能为改进教学提供更加详细的信息，不利于补救教学，因此使用改进后的S－P表法进行分析。根据改进后S－P表法的基本过程，首先通过表2的18种类型考核的认知属性可以得到18种IRP，然后按照马氏距离法，对考生的实际作答模式进行诊断分类，分类结果如表4所示。

**表4　改进后S－P表法诊断分类的结果**

| 类型 | 属性掌握模式 | A | A' | B | B' | C | C' | 小计 |
|---|---|---|---|---|---|---|---|---|
| 第1类型 | 1000000 | 0 | 0 | 0 | 0 | 0 | 3 | 3 |
| 第4类型 | 1110000 | 0 | 0 | 0 | 0 | 0 | 1 | 1 |
| 第6类型 | 1101000 | 0 | 0 | 0 | 0 | 0 | 1 | 1 |
| 第7类型 | 1011000 | 0 | 0 | 0 | 0 | 1 | 1 | 2 |
| 第8类型 | 1111000 | 0 | 0 | 0 | 0 | 1 | 2 | 3 |
| 第9类型 | 1110100 | 0 | 0 | 0 | 0 | 0 | 4 | 4 |
| 第10类型 | 1111100 | 0 | 0 | 1 | 5 | 4 | 2 | 12 |
| 第13类型 | 1011010 | 0 | 0 | 0 | 0 | 1 | 1 | 2 |
| 第14类型 | 1111010 | 0 | 9 | 18 | 28 | 0 | 0 | 55 |
| 第15类型 | 1111110 | 129 | 163 | 14 | 8 | 0 | 0 | 314 |
| 第16类型 | 1110101 | 0 | 0 | 0 | 0 | 0 | 2 | 2 |
| 第17类型 | 1111101 | 0 | 1 | 6 | 6 | 3 | 0 | 16 |
| 第18类型 | 1111111 | 157 | 148 | 0 | 0 | 0 | 0 | 305 |
| 合计 | | 286 | 321 | 39 | 47 | 10 | 17 | 720 |

表4的数据表明，全部的学生分属于13种类型，其中第2类型、第3类型、第5类型、第11类型、第12类型缺少学生分布。绝大部分学生(619名)，占全体学生总人数86%的学生被诊

断为第18类型和第15类型，与S－P表法诊断的结果，绝大部分学生被诊断为A和A'类型，较为一致。其他91名学生多被诊断为第10类型、第14类型和第17类型。

表4的数据还表明，S－P表法分类为B类型和B'类型，属性掌握模式多为第14类型和第15类型。分类为C类型，属性掌握模式多为第10类型。分类为C'类型，属性掌握模式多为第1类型、第9类型。因此改进的S－P表法达到了对原有分类更加细分的目的，而且通过学生属性掌握模式的确定，可以了解学生是否掌握某种属性，然后对未掌握属性进行针对性的补救教学。

## 六、诊断结果的有效性

为了了解改进后S－P表法的有效性，采用让有经验的教师对诊断结果进行评判的方法，具体过程如下。

### （一）学生作答试卷的抽样

根据表4的诊断结果，采取按不同属性掌握模式所占总体比例随机抽样的方法，对于每种属性掌握模式至少保证抽取一份试卷，共抽取了36份试卷，其中还保证了不同卷别所考核的人数一致，均为12人。抽样结果如表5所示。

表5　抽样学生考查试卷所属卷别及诊断为不同属性掌握模式的人数分布表

| 类型 | 掌握属性模式 | 试卷类型 | | | 小计 |
|---|---|---|---|---|---|
| | | A卷 | B卷 | C卷 | |
| 第1类型 | 1000000 | 1 | 0 | 0 | 1 |
| 第4类型 | 1110000 | 1 | 0 | 0 | 1 |
| 第6类型 | 1101000 | 0 | 1 | 0 | 1 |
| 第7类型 | 1011000 | 0 | 0 | 1 | 1 |
| 第8类型 | 1111000 | 0 | 1 | 0 | 1 |
| 第9类型 | 1110100 | 0 | 0 | 1 | 1 |
| 第10类型 | 1111100 | 0 | 0 | 2 | 2 |
| 第13类型 | 1011010 | 0 | 0 | 1 | 1 |
| 第14类型 | 1111010 | 0 | 2 | 2 | 4 |
| 第15类型 | 1111110 | 5 | 4 | 1 | 10 |
| 第16类型 | 1110101 | 0 | 0 | 1 | 1 |
| 第17类型 | 1111101 | 1 | 0 | 1 | 2 |
| 第18类型 | 1111111 | 4 | 4 | 2 | 10 |
| 合计 | | 12 | 12 | 12 | 36 |

### （二）教师对诊断结果的一致性

为了了解教师对改进后S－P表法诊断结果的认同性，邀请了三名教学经验丰富的教师对改进S－P表法诊断结果进行评判，其中两名为小学教研员，一名为在职教师。在教师进行评判之前，首先对教师进行了相关知识培训，让教师熟悉和了解诊断考试的认知属性及属性之间的层级关系，并熟悉三份平行试卷的考核内容。然后组织教师讨论如何判断学生是否掌握了某些属性以及学生掌握了某些属性后，与传统 S－P 表法学生作答反应方式分类的关系。在此基础上，教师分别对 36 份抽样试卷进行诊断，确定学生是否掌握某些属性以及作答反应方式，最后让教师对改进后 S－P 表法的诊断结果进行评判，判断是否认同改进 S－P 表法诊断结果，如表 6 所示。

**表 6　三名教师对改进 S－P 表法诊断结果的评判结果**

| | 同意 | 基本同意 | 不同意 | 小计 |
|---|---|---|---|---|
| A 教师 | 25 | 0 | 11 | 36 |
| B 教师 | 18 | 4 | 14 | 36 |
| C 教师 | 21 | 7 | 8 | 36 |
| 小计 | 64 | 11 | 33 | 108 |

表 6 的数据表明，三名教师对诊断结果基本同意及以上的比例达到 69%，说明教师对于改进 S－P 表法的诊断结果较为认可，可以成为辅助教师开展诊断评价工作的工具，达到减轻教师工作量的目的。

## 七、讨论

改进的 S－P 表法有着比传统 S－P 表法更加精细的诊断分类结果，能够为改进教学和命题提供较多的改进信息，也比一般的认知诊断提供更多的定性分析信息。教师对改进后 S－P 表法诊断分类结果有着较高的认同性(一致性 69%)，说明可以成为辅助教师开展诊断评价工作的工具。但是在使用该方法过程中，有以下问题值得关注。

### (一) 属性及属性层次关系确定的重要性

按照 Leighton，Gierl，Hunka 的说法[8]，属性和属性之间的层级关系构成认知模型。改进的 S－P 表法是以认知模型的建立为前提。目前认知属性的确定一般由学科专家、口语报告、回顾文献等方法来确定，对于基础教育实践者来说，通过学科专家或一般教师来确定认知属性是可行的，但是必须注意到认知属性及其层级确定的复杂性，以及认知诊断模型的准确性对后期诊断分类的影响。另外还需注意的是，确立了认知属性及层级关系以后，进行测验设计时，须将可达矩阵放入测验蓝图之中，才能保证 IRP 与 KS 一一对应[7][9]，后期诊断分类精度才有保证，否则就可能因为多个 KS 对应一种 IRP，而影响认知诊断的准确率。

### (二) 诊断分类方法对诊断分类的影响

认知属性大多存在层次关系，Leighton 等人认为[8]，通常有着四种基本类型，分别为线性型、收敛型、分支型和无结构型，更复杂属性层次关系由四种基本层级关系组合而成。如果诊断分类方法能够考虑属性层级，分类精度可能提高。

改进的 S－P 表法分成两步：S－P 表分析法和运用马氏距离法进行诊断分类，这个分类方法并没有充分考虑属性之间的层次关系的信息。如果采用其他一些认知诊断模型，比如 AHM、DINA，分类效果可能更好。

**（三）改进 S－P 表法的局限性**

改进 S－P 表法应用了现代认知诊断理论和经典测量理论，计算方便、推广容易，同时还弥补了传统 S－P 表法不能对大规模考试数据进行诊断的不足。但是改进 S－P 表法没有给出个体属性掌握概率，也没有给出可能错误诊断的概率，这些都值得进一步讨论，使这个辅助诊断方法更加有效。

参考文献

[1] 余民宁. 教育测验与评量——成就测验与教学评量[M]. 台北：心理出版社，2009：332—358.

[2] 刘新平，刘存侠. 教育统计与测评导论[M]. 北京：科学出版社，2003：232.

[3] Takeya, M. (1980). Construction and Utilization of Item Relational Structure Graphs for Use in Test Analysis. *Japan Journal of Educational Technology*, 93－103.

[4] Tatsuoka, K. K. (1984). Caution Indices Based on Item Response Theory, *Psychometrika*, 95－110.

[5] 刘声涛，戴海崎，周骏. 新一代测验理论—认知诊断理论的源起与特征[J]. 心理学探新，2006(4)：73—77.

[6] 涂冬波，漆书青，戴海琦，蔡艳. 教育考试中的认知诊断评估[J]. 考试研究，2008(4)：4—14.

[7] 丁树良，杨淑群，汪文义. 可达矩阵在认知诊断测验编制中的重要作用[J]. 江西师范大学学报(自然科学版)，2010(5)：490—494.

[8] Leighton J. P., Gierl M., & Hunka S. M. (2004). The Attribute Hierarchy Method for Cognitive Assessment: A Variation on Tatusuok's Rule-Space Approach. *Journal of Educational Measurement*, 205－236.

[9] 丁树良，祝玉芳，林海菁，蔡艳. Tatsuoka Q 矩阵理论的修正[J]. 心理学报，2009(2)：175—181.

## Application and Improvement of S－P Chart Method

Zhiyong Xu, Shuliang Ding

**Abstract**: The traditional S－P chart method can only provide rough diagnostic information for teaching, but cannot provide clear direction for improving teaching. While improved S - P chart method combined with cognitive diagnosis theory, not only can provide clear information for improving teaching, but also provide more qualitative information than cognitive diagnosis only. Experiments show that about 69 percent teachers in our program favour the results provided by the improved S - P chart diagnostic classification method, for the improved method can serve as a good supplementary means.

**Keywords**: Student-problem chart; Cognitive diagnostic; Mahalanobis distance

# 新课程改革以来学生评价改革的回顾与思考

丁朝蓬

【摘要】分别从学生评价理念的变革、日常学生评价实践的改变与研究、高利害评价体系的实践探索与研究、大规模教育考试的改进与研究四个方面回顾了新课程改革以来学生评价改革情况,并提出一些思考。应真正澄清学生评价的价值追求,并遵循学生评价的一些原则。

【关键词】学生评价;新课程改革;回顾;思考

【作者简介】丁朝蓬/人民教育出版社

文本将集中回顾新课程改革十一年来学生评价改革的实践探索,并提出学生评价改革进一步努力的方向。按照评价对学生所起作用来分,学生评价可分为日常学生评价和高利害学生评价。新课程的学生评价改革,对这两类学生评价都进行了探索。

## 一、学生评价理念的变革

从20世纪末的新课程改革开始至今,我国教育学者大量借鉴研究了西方学生评价近二三十年来的新进展,使我国教育界学生评价理念有了根本性的转变。传统的评价观念把评价等同于纸笔考试,考试的作用只是检测学习结果以及甄别、选拔学生。新课程改革彻底扭转了这种肤浅功利的认识。新的学生评价理念是,学生评价的根本目的是促进学生发展,而不是把学生分成三六九等;评价的本质功能是为教和学提供反馈,是为了帮助促进学习,筛选、选拔只是其一部分功能。评价应有利于提高学生的自我概念,而不是让大多数学生体验挫败感。在教学与评价的关系上,评价是为改善教学而采用的策略、工具,而不应是教学的指南,因为能够评价的总是少于能够学习的。促进学习的评价应整合于教学活动中,使评价过程成为学习过程的一部分。评价并非只能以纸笔测验方式进行,纸笔测验所能评价的发展目标和内容是有限的,表现评价、成长记录等评价方法是真实评价,能够评价纸笔测验所不能评价的发展目标。

## 二、日常学生评价实践的改变与研究

日常学生评价是在学校日常教学活动中进行的学生评价,其作用主要是为学生的学和教师的教提供反馈,促进学与教的水平的提高。日常评价更强调评价的发展性(有利于学生发展)、丰富性(多方面、多角度提供反馈信息)。

新课程学生评价理念的变革集中体现在教育部2002年印发的《关于积极推进中小学评价与考试制度改革的通知》中。广大中小学教师在文件精神的指导下逐渐树立了新的评价观念。

如教师普遍认同评价是为了促进学生的发展，应发挥评价的激励功能；认同评价内容要全面，应将学生的情感、态度、价值观、个性心理品质等纳入学生评价体系中。[1]教师们认识到评价标准应该多元，“多一把尺子就多一批好学生”，很多学校采用多种多样的评价形式(如一个学科分多次考试、设立多种学生奖励)，让每个学生体验成功。[2]很多教师在教学活动中鼓励学生之间相互评价和学生自我评价，促进学生评价能力的发展。一些教师逐渐了解并尝试使用非纸笔测验的评价方法，如表现评价、成长记录袋、展示性评价等，通过这些新的评价方法评价学生的高层次思维能力、合作能力、交流表达能力以及情感态度的发展。[3][4][5]在小学阶段，大多数教师采用“平时表现为主，参考考试成绩”的评价方法，[6]对学生的成绩报告普遍采用了等级制，不根据分数给学生排名。[7]

随着新课程实验的推进，教育理论界和学校教师对教学和评价应基于课程标准的认识更加明晰和深入，相应的研究和探索不断增多。如人民教育出版社课程教材研究徐岩领衔的国家社科基金“十一五”规划国家课题“中小学生学业评价标准的研究与开发”依据各科课程标准研究开发了各学科学业评价标准，同时开发了各类评价样例(包括纸笔测验样例和表现评价样例等)，帮助教师实施基于标准的日常教学与评价。[8][9]华东师范大学崔允漷教授的团队开展了“基于课程标准的学生学业成就评价研究”，研究了课程标准分解、表现标准开发等问题，为教师分解细化课程标准、进行基于课程标准的学生评价提供方法指导。[10]

如何评价学生情感态度价值观仍是实践中尚未解决的问题。一些研究者在研究了情感、态度、价值观的概念内涵基础上，提出了情感态度价值观评价的实施方法建议。[11][12]一些研究者研究探索了如何在学科中评价学生的学业情感[13]和价值观。[14]

## 三、高利害评价体系的实践探索与研究

在当前我国的基础教育阶段，最重要的两大高利害评价是初中毕业升入高中时的评价和高中毕业升入大学时进行的评价。高利害评价更强调评价的准确性(准确评价学生的发展水平，特别是在群体中的相对水平)、公平性(评价内容、评价方式、评价结果的利用对所有学生是公平的)。

长期以来，我国的高利害评价被窄化为高利害学业考试，即中考和高考。学生的前途命运系于一次考试的一分半分，导致学校教学围着考试指挥棒转，大搞强化训练、题海战术，增加学生负担，背离了促进学生身心健康发展的教育宗旨。新课程改革志在改变这种极不合理的高利害评价体系。

### (一) 高中毕业及升学评价体系的探索与研究

我国高考方案的改革可追溯到20世纪80年代中后期，上海、湖南、云南、海南率先进行高中毕业会考改革，1992年全国开始了“3＋2”的高考方案，1999年，广东省率先探索“3＋X”高考方案，2000年，全国各省陆续实施“3＋X”方案。[15]2004年，高中新课程首先在海南、广东、山

东、宁夏开始，新一轮高考方案改革随之启动。

2008年颁布的《教育部关于普通高中新课程省份深化高校招生考试改革的指导意见》提出的改革任务是“促进高校招生考试改革与高中课程改革相结合，促进国家统一考试改革与高中综合评价改革相结合，促进考试改革与高校录取模式改革相结合，逐步建立和完善在国家统一考试录取基础上的全面、综合、多元化的考试评价制度和高等学校多样化的选拔录取制度”。改革的主要任务涉及三方面：建立和完善高中学生的综合评价制度，包括由各省份组织实施的普通高中学业水平考试和学生综合素质评价，并逐步纳入高校招生选拔评价体系；进一步深化统一考试内容的改革；进一步推进高等学校选拔录取模式和方式改革。依据这一精神，实施高中新课程的各省份相继探索了新的高考改革方案。很多省份都将学生综合素质评价以电子档案的形式被计入，同时作为高校录取新生的重要参考。山东、宁夏、福建、辽宁、安徽、天津、北京，统考科目都设置为“3＋文综/理综”。山东采取了“3＋X＋1”的统考模式，“1”指基本能力，内容涉及高中课程的技术、体育与健康、艺术、综合实践等以及运用所学知识解决实际问题的能力。广东实行“3＋文科基础/理科基础＋X”的统考模式，X为专业选考科目，由高校根据各自专业情况进行设置，由考生自行选择。但是，广东在2010年又退回了“3＋文科综合/理科综合”，取消了X。[16]海南、广东、江苏、浙江将学业水平考试的成绩纳入了高考录取，海南实行“3＋3＋基础会考”，基础会考卷面成绩的10%计入高考总分。广东省2009年开始实行学业水平考试，2010年起将考生的学业水平考试等级与报考不同层次高校的资格联系起来。江苏实行“3＋学业水平测试＋综合素质评价”，除了语文、数学、外语三门统考外，政治、历史、地理、物理、化学、生物、技术七科进行学业水平测试，学生的学业水平测试达到某个等级才具备报考相应层次高校的资格。浙江实行“3＋X”基础上的多种变式，进行全科会考，在会考基础上分类测试、分批选拔。北京是将高中会考成绩以等级形式记入学生电子档案。综观这些高考方案，各省市在改变“一考定终身”、促进高中生各科学业和综合素质的全面发展、促进高中学校实施素质教育方面进行了非常有益的探索，但在为学生提供更多选择性以及为高校选拔适合专业要求的新生方面，还显得改革力度不够。

对于如何改革高考方案(即评价体系中包含哪些评价内容，作为高校选拔新生的依据与标准)，学理层面的研究从未停止过。有的研究者认为，高考科目设置，应该采用分类设计的策略，即报考不同层次不同类型高校的学生考不同的科目组合，科目组合可分文理两大类，文和理内部最多区分两种科目组合，以满足各种不同层次、不同类型高校选拔新生的需要。[17]有的学者则提出高中课程和高考科目设置都应超越文理分科或文理合科的思路，走专业分化的道路，[18]要充分认识学生在兴趣和能力倾向方面的个体差异，“在适量的共同基础上，提供专业分化科目供学生选修选考，从而培养和选拔各类通才、各类专才”。[19]有学者分析介绍了国际上很多国家和地区将表现性评价纳入高校升学考试的做法和经验，提出将表现评价纳入我国高考是必要而且可行的。[20]有学者介绍了我国香港、英国、澳大利亚、美国等国家如何将校本评核（其中有一部分是表现评价）的成绩与统一考试成绩进行合成，建议我国高考的计分方式改革势在必行。[21][22]特别值得一提的是，民间教育研究机构"21世纪教育研究院"发布了一个高考方案设想，主要的两个特点是实行多轨道、分层次的统一考试和举行"全国学业能力水平测试"。[23]

### （二）初中毕业及升学评价体系的探索与研究

2002年教育部印发的《关于积极推进中小学评价与考试制度改革的通知》提出"初中升高中的考试与招生中，要综合考虑学生的整体素质和个体差异，改变以升学考试科目分数简单相加作为唯一录取标准的做法"。2004年，第一批义务教育新课程实验区面临新中考。《国家基础教育课程改革实验区2004年初中毕业考试与普通高中招生制度改革的指导意见》指出了明确的改革方向："本次初中毕业考试与普通高中招生制度改革要改变以升学考试科目分数简单相加作为唯一录取标准的做法，力求在初中毕业生学业考试、综合素质评定、高中招生录取三方面予以突破。""普通高中招生要坚持综合评价、择优录取的原则。学业考试成绩和综合素质的评价结果应成为普通高中招生的主要依据。"

各实验区的中考方案都包括学业考试和综合素质评价两部分。普遍的做法是将初中毕业考试与高中升学考试合并为一个学业水平考试，这是与我国高中教育更加普及的发展形势相适应的。学业水平考试是以课程标准为依据的标准参照考试，为了淡化分数对高中录取的影响，很多实验区将学业考试的结果以等级制表达；也有实验区同时采用等级制和百分制两种形式，等级结果用于毕业决定，百分制结果用于高中录取。[24]

与各省高考方案中对综合素质评价具体实施办法规定不多相反，各实验区对于如何实施初中学生的综合素质评价提出了具体的评价指标体系。大多数实验区根据教育部《关于积极推进中小学评价与考试制度改革的通知》所提的基础性发展目标（道德品质、公民素养、学习能力、交流与合作能力、运动与健康、审美与表现）构建了综合素质评价的一级指标，有的实验区还确定了二级指标以及每个指标所对应的关键表现和评价证据。各实验区都要求综合素质评价要坚持评价主体多元，即学生自评、学生互评和教师评价相结合。

各实验区采用了不同的方式，使综合素质评价结果作为高中招生的依据。有的实验区采用"硬挂钩"方式，就是将综合素质评价的等级视同一门考试科目的成绩，将之与其他科目成绩相加后作为高中录取的依据；有的采用"部分挂钩"方式，即规定各科考试总分在某一区间内的学生按照综合素质评价结果录取；还有的是"分层挂钩"，规定报考不同性质和水平高中的学生要在综合素质方面达到不同的等级标准。[25]

比起学业水平考试，综合素质评价面临的挑战更大，特别是当其结果要纳入到高利害的升学评价体系中。最根本的一个挑战是，综合素质的内涵到底是什么？综合素质评价的内容、维度到底应该是什么？在教育部"初中毕业与高中招生制度改革"项目组提供的《关于2005年基础教育课程改革实验区初中毕业生综合素质评价工作的实施建议》中，是把6个基础性发展目标作为综合素质评价的主要内容，其中的“学习能力”与学科发展目标之间的关系尚不清晰；有的研究者提出，在实际操作中，绝大多数实验区是把综合素质评价等同于非学术能力的评价，而“综合素质”理应包括学术能力和非学术能力，建议把综合素质评价在概念层级上提升一级，把它作为整个评价体系的一个基本理念。[26]在大多数实验区关心如何使综合素质评价的内容更具体更规范更公平的同时，却有学者提出了不同的意见，高凌飚认为综合素质评价不要有过细的标准、太固定的视野，不要过分强调管理，要还原综合素质评价的本质功能。[27]当多数教育工作者探索综合素质评价如何给分并计入中考成绩时，有研究者却提出综合素质评价与高中招生“硬挂钩”导致评价成为选拔适合教育的学生的工具，为选拔不为发展，是舍本逐末，进而提出综合素质评价应该“育”“评”统一，学校应有目的有计划地加强学生综合素质的培养，而不是只给学生一个短暂而终结性的“评判”。[28]

## 四、大规模教育考试的改进与研究

大规模教育考试是由专业考试机构统一设计组织、在较大范围内实施的测试，大规模教育考试对公平性、信度、效度等测量学特征有更为专业的要求。从目前我国学生评价实践看，大规模教育考试有初中毕业和高中毕业的学业水平考试、用于高一级学校升学的统一考试、省级和国家级的教育质量监控考试(实际也是学业水平考试)、用于比较不同国家学生学业成就的国际评价项目(如PISA、TIMSS)。其中学业水平考试和教育质量监控考试都属于标准参照考试，另外两类考试则是常模参照性质的考试.

我国从20世纪80年代起开始对大规模教育考试的改进和研究，近一二十年来，愈益呈现出两个主要特征，一是紧密配合基础教育的改革，发挥“指挥棒”作用，促进中小学素质教育的实施；二是不断借鉴和运用现代教育测量理论与技术，推动教育考试的标准化、科学化。大规模教育考试的改进和研究主要涉及以下几个方面的问题：考试内容和试题编制、考试计分方式及其解释、考试结果的利用。

### (一) 紧密配合基础教育改革，促进素质教育

从2004年起，高考开始实行“统一考试，分省命题”，与此相适应，教育部颁布了《普通高等学校招生全国统一考试大纲》。该考试大纲遵循课程改革的方向，更新了命题理念，“强调综合能力测试；强调考查创新意识和实践能力；强调理论与实践相统一；强调关心科技、社会、生活等内容”。[29]高中新课程改革的方向是突出课程的选择性、多样性，每个学科包含必修模块和选修模块，近几年的高考相应设置了“选做题”，考生根据自己高中所学的选修模块选择作答。

本次新课程改革是以课程标准为核心的改革，学业水平考试(无论是用于学生毕业还是用于教育质量监控)是检测学生能否达到课程标准的大规模考试，对课程改革有着最直接的影响。有学者指出，学业水平考试内容改革的基本原则是保证考试内容规范与课程标准的内

容要求的一致性，包括内容领域或主题的一致性、知识深度水平适应性、内容主题中知识范围对应性、内容主题或知识点的平衡性和学科知识的建构。[30]有学者借鉴美国的“标准与评价匹配度”的分析方法研究了我国学业水平考试与课程标准的符合程度，发现了这些考试中与课程标准不一致的地方。[31]有研究者在广泛研究了世界多国学业水平考试设置体系、考试内容、考核方式、管理模式与组织实施的基础上，[32]也对当前我国学业水平考试存在的问题进行了中肯的分析，这些问题包括：缺少作为命题依据的学业标准，考试内容改革思路欠清晰，试题编制和组卷未能遵循基本的教育测量原理，分类决策的过程欠科学，分数报道不能提供有用信息[33]；尚未形成一套规范的学业评价体系，缺乏对考试信息的深度挖掘，未能体现考试的诊断和发展功能[34]；全国各省份普通高中学业水平考试的考试性质、考试科目与功能定位均不统一[35]。

PISA、TIMSS、NAEP、SAT、ACT，这些都是国际上著名的、发展成熟的大规模教育考试，对我国大规模教育考试的发展具有重要的借鉴意义。我国学者对这些考试的研究成百上千，研究的范围也非常广泛，如考试框架、试题设计、评分、实施管理等。我国大规模教育考试内容一直在探索变知识立意为能力立意的具体方法和途径，研究者们研究了国外成熟的学生评价项目如何评价学生的各种能力，包括问题解决能力[36]、思维能力[37]、创新精神和实践能力[38]以及学习方法[39]。同时，研究者也试图借鉴国外教育考试如何评价学生的情感态度发展。[40][41]

近年来，一种超越布卢姆教育目标分类学和皮亚杰认知发展理论的SOLO理论（structure of the observed learning outcome）引起了研究者的兴趣，这种理论对于学生回答问题质量的分类具有独到之处，并可以此为基础编制能够区分学生不同思维质量的开放性试题。[42]这对于改进考试的命题很有价值。

大规模教育考试也正在向多元化发展，除传统的纸笔测试外，也可以有口试、实验操作以及以实验报告、论文、调查报告、实验设计完成的“课程作业”。研究者也在探讨将表现评价作为大规模教育考试的一部分。[43]

### （二）运用现代测量理论和技术提高考试质量

现代大规模教育考试是建立在心理与教育测量理论和技术基础上的，20世纪50年代至今，在经典测验理论之后又发展出了概化理论、项目反应理论、认知测验理论，并促进了测验应用的发展，如标准参照测验的编制、题库建设、计算机化自适应测验、测验等值、测验偏差侦查等。[44]与国际上著名的标准化教育考试相比，我国大规模教育考试的专业化程度还比较低，近年来研究者不断学习、研究、借鉴现代测量理论、测验编制的技术以及国际相关经验，以提高我国大规模教育考试的质量。

教育部考试中心从2006年启动教育考试国家题库建设，其目标是“把教育考试国家题库建设成有现代教育测量理论支持的，操作灵活、科学合理、快捷高效、安全保密的计算机管理的试题管理系统、试卷生成系统和命题教师的管理系统，使之成为我国国家级教育考试的工作平台，为我国各类学校选拔合格的新生提供科学、准确、有效的测试试题和分数依据”[45]。

教育部考试中心从2006年开始实施PISA中国试测研究项目，实施了PISA测试工具翻译和预试调整、学校样本和学生样本选取、评价实施、编码阅卷、数据整理、统计分析和结果报告全环节的评价工作。“其目的在于通过PISA2006和PISA2009两轮中国试测研究实践，掌握和借鉴PISA先进的评价理念、理论和技术，为构建符合中国国情的、基于现有大规模考试的教育质量评价体系奠定基础、积累经验和锻炼队伍。”[46]

有研究者运用多元概化理论分析了综合能力测试上海卷（文科卷），探讨单科试题和综合试题在综合能力测试中的作用，探讨是否可以用综合试题取代单科试题。[47]

“对考试分数进行等值处理不仅是保证测验信度和公平性的重要环节，也是建立题库和实现计算机化自适应性考试的核心环节。”我国很多重要的考试尚未实现等值。[48]等值问题也是我国学者关心研讨的一个主题。

增值评价是一种考试结果的新的解释方法，“采用统计分析技术，通过对学生一定时期内的学业成绩（或非学业成绩）变化情况进行分析，并与预期结果进行比较，得到该学生在这一时期内的‘增值’，进而通过学生的‘增值’得到学校和教师的‘增值’”。有的省探索使用这种方法对不同区县的教育质量进行评价。[49]

近几年，认知诊断理论进入我国学者的视野。认知诊断理论是认知心理学与测量学相结合而产生的新一代测验理论，“强调对个体认知优势和弱势的细致诊断，并对个体当前发展状况进行反馈和提供补救建议，从而有针对性地促进个体认知发展”[50]。我国学者对这一前沿理论进行了分析介绍。[51][52]

总的看来，当前我国仍处于对现代测量理论和技术的引进介绍阶段，离真正将这些理论和技术应用于我国的教育考试还有不小的距离，我国大规模教育考试专业化任重而道远。

## 五、学生评价改革的思考

### （一）关于学生评价的价值追求

整体回顾新课程改革以来的学生评价，笔者认为，教师的学生评价观念确实发生了很大变化，比如多数教师认识到并尽力做到尊重学生、鼓励学生、展示学生的优势和特长，教师在实践中也倡导学生自评和互评，也尝试使用多样的评价方法。但是，由于多元化的高利害评价体系尚未形成，整个社会应试教育的氛围依然强烈，学校评价和教师评价仍然以应试分数、升学结果为最重要的标准，因此教师在重重压力下仍旧最看重考试分数，他们觉得最得心应手、最能有效应对升学考试的评价方法就是纸笔考试。为了让学生在激烈的考试竞争中获胜，教学和考试的难度不断提高，以至很少考虑大多数学生在这个年龄段所能达到的认知能力。虽然这十几年来国家一直在倡导素质教育，三令五申减轻学生学习负担，但现实的状况却不容乐观：学生的学习负担日益加重，身体和心理都承受着巨大压力，中小学生因学业压力而自杀的事情时时见诸媒体。看着那么多孩子戴着小眼镜、背着沉重的书包、表情凝重、面色疲惫，听到本该无忧无虑、意气风发的少年儿童竟然选择死亡，我们这些成年人特别是教育工作者怎能不痛心疾首！

当下的学生评价，亟待澄清其价值追求——教学和评价的根本目的到底是什么？是让学生获得高分、升入名牌学校吗？我们总在抱怨当今社会急功近利，但却在学校里天天向学生示范着急功近利；我们向往人人平等的理想社会，但在学校却用不尽合理的分数制造着不平等；我们教导学生要过有意义的人生，但却将学生阶段的人生意义限定为唯一——考高分，而高分预示着世俗公认的成功。对学生来说，学校是他/她除家庭之外最重要的生活场所，学校生活直接影响着他/她对人生的体验、对社会的认识。家长以为，牺牲童年的快乐就可以换来幸福的人生，其实，一个未感受过童年特有的纯真快乐的人，成年后即使获得世俗眼中的成功，也未必能感受到真正的幸福，弗洛伊德早已告诉我们童年情感经验对人生的重大影响。

我们国家的经济发展水平已经大大提高，我们的高等教育已经大众化，我们有足够的经济基础为未成年人创造一个和谐从容的生活和教育环境，让每一个儿童快乐幸福地成长，但我们的社会文化却是以成年人的所谓成功标准压迫着儿童承受超负荷的学习压力。现代社会已经是一个终身学习的社会，我们的教育却使儿童很早就丧失学习的兴趣和愿望。现代社会是需要创新的社会，但在考试分数禁锢下的儿童却难以发展创造性。

我们的社会文化、学校、教师、家长都应该静思教育的价值追求、评价的价值追求。教育的目的是帮助儿童成为一个身体、认知和个性协调发展的、完整的人，儿童能够感受社会的美好同时也愿意为社会创造更多的美好，只有儿童感觉到人生的幸福，这个世界才会充满幸福。评价是教育的工具和方法，这个工具的价值追求应该是与教育的价值追求相统一的，评价是为了帮助学生，而不能异化为伤害学生的“紧箍咒”。

### （二）关于学生评价应遵循的原则

为了实现评价促进学生发展的价值追求，笔者认为，学生评价应遵循如下原则。

首先，评价应促进每个学生的发展，不让一个学生掉队。所有的学生都是处于发展的过程中，是在前进的道路上，由于先天与后天各种因素的影响，学生的发展会有不同的速度、不同的特点。学校和教师应给予每个学生同样的关注和标准。评价的作用就是了解每个学生当前处于什么样的发展水平、具有什么样的优势和不足，判断学生下一步可能前进的方向和距离。评价应提高学生的自我概念，增强其自信心和自我效能感，而不应使学生体验挫败感，丧失学习的兴趣和动力。

第二，日常学生评价应重在实现其诊断功能，而不是如何准确地给学生下结论、贴标签。

国外一种不同于传统静态测验的动态评价对我们的学生评价改革极具启发意义。动态评价对学生智力和认知的认识、对学生现有水平和发展潜力的认识、对学生低成就水平原因的认识，都与传统观念截然不同。动态评价的突出特点是能对学生的学习障碍进行诊断，并通过互动干预有针对性地指导学生的认知策略。动态评价启发我们应关注学生的元认知能力，元认知能力与学习成就具有密切关系，也关系到学生能否进行自主学习。[53][54]

参考文献

[1] 李亮.普通中学教师的学生评价观研究[D].石家庄：河北师范大学，2009.

[2] 贾相忠，华明艳.转变观念关注全程评价[J].人大复印资料《小学各科教与学》，2004(1).

[3] 程淑华，赖配根.多元客观开放——记河南省濮阳市子路小学展示性评价研究[J].人民教育，2003(1).

[4] 陈碧波.成长记录袋，想说爱你不容易——小学语文教师应用成长记录袋的调查研究[J].上海教育科研，2009(1).

[5] 明成满.学期档案袋在历史教学评价中的运用[J].人大复印资料《中学历史、地理教与学》，2004(2).

[6] 马云鹏，唐丽芳.对新课程改革实验状况的调查与思考[J].中小学管理，2004(1).

[7] 闫瑞祥.绍兴市小学新课程改革实验的调查及问题思考[J].绍兴文理学院学报，2007(11).

[8] 徐岩，丁朝蓬.建立学业评价标准促进课程教学改革[J].课程·教材·教法，2009(12).

[9] 孙新，彭征.中学物理学生学业评价标准的研制[J].课程·教材·教法，2010(9).

[10] 崔允漷，夏雪梅.试论基于课程标准的学生学业成就评价[J].课程·教材·教法，2007(1).

[11] 蒋奖，丁朝蓬，段现丽.学生情感态度价值观的评估：给教师的建议[J].课程·教材·教法，2009(11).

[12] 李吉会.如何评价情感、态度和价值观[J].教育科学研究，2006(2).

[13] 汤慧丽.学生学习情感评价研究[D].郑州：河南大学，2009.

[14] 何明祥.学业水平考试中尝试对科学情感态度与价值观的评价[J].教学管理，2008(11).

[15] 臧铁军.高考30年考试技术改革的路线解析[J].中国考试，2008(12).

[16] 李力.新课改视野中的高考改革方案述评[J].中国考试，2009(12).

[17] 周军，周轩，郑启跃.关于高考科目设置改革的思考[J].中国考试，2004(1).

[18] 冯生尧.论高中课程和高考招生专业分化的必要性[J].全球教育展望，2011(1).

[19] 冯生尧.论专业分化的高中选修、高考选考和院系分招制度[J].课程·教材·教法，2011(4).

[20] 冯生尧.表现性评价纳入高考制度的必要性和可行性[J].全球教育展望，2007(9).

[21] 温忠麟，罗冠中.高考方案：考试方式与计分方式[J].中国考试，2008(3).

[22] 蔡筱坤.香港公开考试的校本评核设计与推行[J].考试研究,2010(6).
[23] 21世纪教育熊丙奇教授:高考改革方案宣讲[EB/OL]. http://edu.sina.com.cn/l/2009-06-14/2329172841.shtml,2011-10-3.
[24] 张亚宁.新中考改革能否超越应试功利之现实[J].中国教师,2006(6).
[25] 赵德成.初中毕业生综合素质评价实践的问题与思考[J].中国教育学刊,2007(7).
[26] 方檀香.综合素质评价实施面临的挑战及突破——访华东师范大学崔允漷、柯政[J].基础教育课程,2011(4).
[27] 高凌飚.对综合素质评价的几点思考[J].基础教育课程,2011(4).
[28] 朱福荣.对初中学生综合素质评价的思考[J].当代教育论坛,2007(4).
[29]《高考的内容、形式与能力考查关系的研究》课题组.高考的内容、形式与能力考查关系的研究[J].中国考试,2006(4).
[30] 雷新勇.基于标准的教育改革背景下学业水平考试内容改革的思考[J].上海教育科研,2008(8).
[31] 王磊,黄琼,刘东方.中考命题与化学课程标准的一致性研究——基于九省市中等学校招生考试概念原理知识的比较[J].基础教育课程,2010(3).
[32] 杨向东,崔允漷.关于高中学业水平考试的比较研究[J].全球教育展望,2010(4).
[33] 雷新勇.我国学业水平考试的基本问题及反思[J].教育测量与评价,2010(1).
[34] 辛涛.新课程背景下的学业评价:测量理论的价值[J].北京师范大学学报(社会科学版),2006(1).
[35] 刘决生.我国普通高中学业水平考试存在的问题与对策[J].上海教育科研,2010(3).
[36] 贯洪芳.关于问题解决能力测试的研究[J].考试研究,2007(10).
[37] 任子朝.思维技能测验的测量目标与技术——剑桥评价的思维技能测验评介[J].中国考试,2011(11).
[38] 常桐善.学生创新和实践能力考核在大学招生中的价值:美国"彩虹项目"的启示[J].考试研究,2009(2).
[39] 朱小虎.PISA对学生学习方法的研究及启示[J].外国中小学教育,2010(9).
[40] 陆璟.PISA学习参与度评价[J].上海教育科研,2009(12).
[41] 黄颖,骆红山.对科学态度的评估及启示[J].科普研究,2010(1).
[42] 吴维宁,李佳,孔惠斯.SOLO试题的编制与质量检测[J].教育测量与评价,2009(3).
[43] 冯生尧,谢瑶妮.英国高考中的表现性评价:中心评审课程作业[J].比较教育研究,2006(8).
[44] 漆书青,戴海崎,丁树良.现代教育与心理测量学原理[M].南昌:江西教育出版社,1998.
[45] 教育部考试中心题库工作小组.谈教育考试国家题库建设[J].中国考试,2008(4).
[46] 王蕾.基于大规模考试的教育质量评价[J].教育科学研究,2010(11).
[47] 雷新勇.用多元概化理论研究综合能力测试(上海卷)改革的必要性[J].中国考试,2005(1).
[48] 谢小庆.考试分数等值的新框架[J].考试研究,2008(4).

[49] 许志勇.运用增值评价,促进教育均衡发展——以某省教育招生考试院的实践为例[J].教育测量与评价,2011(4).

[50] 蔡艳,涂冬波,丁树良.认知诊断测验编制的理论及方法[J].考试研究,2010(6).

[51] 余娜,辛涛.认知诊断理论的新进展[J].考试研究,2009(5).

[52] 关丹丹.认知诊断理论与考试评价[J].中国考试,2009(4).

[53] 丁朝蓬.动态评价对学生评价改革的启示[J].教育测量与评价,2009(8).

[54] 罗贵明,蔡水清.国外动态测验的理论与应用及其对我国考试评价改革的启示[J].教育测量与评价(理论版),2008(11).

## Review and Thoughts about Student Assessment Reform Since New Curriculum Reform

Zhaopeng Ding

**Abstract**: This paper focuses on student assessment reform since New Curriculum Reform launched at the end of 20th century. In addition, some ideas and suggestions about student assessment are proposed. The philosophy of student assessment has been changed radically. New approaches are used in classroom assessment practice. Scholars investigate accademic performance standards to promote the standard-based reform. High-stake student assessment system is being explored. New plans for college entrance exam and senior high entrance exam are proposed, aiming at promoting multiple admission reform. Large-scale educational exams are studied and reformed to adapt to and promote quality education. Futhermore, new theories and techniques of psychological measurement are used to advance the quality of our exams. The value pursuit of student assessment should be clarified. The student assessment should abide by some principles.

**Keywords**: student assessment; New Curriculum Reform; review; thoughts

# 第三部分

# 学习进展、学生发展与课堂评价系统的设计

# Assessment and the Improvement of Learning

Joan L. Herman

National Center for Research on Evaluation, Standards, and Student Testing (CRESST)
UCLA Graduate School of Education and Information Studies

**Abstract**: This paper presents an overview to the role of classroom assessment in improving student learning. It begins with a general model of the relationship between assessment and learning, and then presents three distinct perspectives: Assessment of learning, Assessment for learning and Assessment as learning. Then, the paper summarizes how each is thought to operate, share research on both how it influences learning and what design features and characteristics can maximize its effects, and provide examples from work done at the National Center for Research on Evaluation, Standards and Student Testing. Closed by stressing the importance of coordinating these different types of assessment toward the same goals, the paper is concluded with a few challenges in bringing vision to reality.

**Keywords**: Assessment of Learning; Assessment for Learning; Assessment as Learning

## A General Model: The Role of Assessment in Improving Learning

Some think of assessment as a tool, an instrument for measuring what students know and can do. Others think of assessment as a process, a process of eliciting and using evidence to serve various purposes. Figure 1 synthesizes both definitions to provide a model of how assessment can influence learning.

The model follows what we think good teachers do:

- they start with goals for student learning
- they administer assessments that will help them understand where students are relative to these goals
- they interpret the results of the assessment-student responses or scores to understand how students are actually doing, and they use their interpretations to improve their teaching.

The use of results to improve as subsequent instruction is one key way in which assessment can improve learning but as we will see, there also are others.

The figure also implies some of the core elements of good assessment. A good assessment:

- is well aligned with learning goals,
- elicits student responses that correspond to the expected learning,
- includes appropriate scoring mechanisms to reliably interpret student responses relative to the goals, and provides reliable and valid evidence for subsequent improvement action.

As we shall see, the subsequent action varies with the type of assessment.

## Assessment Of Learning

Assessment of learning is the historical perspective on testing. In fact, you may know that the roots of standardized testing go back to the imperial examinations of China's Han Dynasty (220 - 206BC). These exams are credited as the first use of standardized testing and the idea that gathering standard information on individuals' capabilities could lead to better decisions, in this case decisions about coveted civil service appointments. One can imagine that faced with the exam, elite, would-be candidates would prepare for the test and engage tutors to do so, a first instance of the impact of assessment on learning. Used for purposes of selection, the Han Dynasty assessments also are a first example of how an assessment of past learning can be very influential in individuals' futures.

Although they can have important future consequences, assessments of learning look backward, after learning has occurred over the course of a unit, a semester, an academic year, and a K - 12 career. They answer questions such as:

- What did students learn?
- What grade should students receive?
- Did students reach proficiency?
- Should students be selected or admitted to special programs, schools, and universities?

Assessments of learning also are called "summative" assessments. Summative assessments are used to make judgments about individuals—students or teachers— and/or collectives—e.g., schools, and often have important consequences.

Effects of assessments of learning. Because they have important consequences-think about your secondary school or college admissions tests, people pay attention to what is on them. Tests motivate behavior because students want to do well on the tests and teachers want their students to do well. Research around the world shows this effect of important tests. Tests communicate what is important for students to know and be able to do, and what is tested is what teachers and students concentrate on teaching and learning. This is as true for typical classroom tests as they are for really high visibility, high consequences tests. In the United States, for example, students will frequently ask their teachers: "What's going to be on the test, teacher?" They then study what's going to be on the test and ignore that which is not going to be on the test.

Moreover, research in the United States suggests that teachers not only concentrate on the content of the test, but their teaching also models the test formats. If state accountability tests are comprised of multiple choice items, students get lots of multiple choice exercises. The same is true of test preparation schools and services.

In other words, tests of learning send a strong signal about what and how to learn, and this signal has strong influences on learning.

Tests of learning also have influence on learning when the results are used to make decisions that influence subsequent learning opportunities. Results for example, can be used to analyze curriculum strengths and weaknesses or to provide special services for some children. These decisions also increase the match between what is tested, opportunity to learn, and actual learning.

*Cognitive principles for maximizing learning effects*. If what gets tested is what gets taught and studied, then it is important that tests address both the most important learning goals and how well students understand and can use their knowledge. Modern learning theory suggests that expertise comes not from mindless memorization and accumulation of facts, but from the active construction and organization of their knowledge relative to new challenges. Tests can incorporate the same instructional principles and characteristics research shows increases learning. These are things like asking students to show how they represent their knowledge, how they see the relationships between the big ideas of the field, how they relate subsidiary and super—ordinate knowledge, through, for example, knowledge mapping. Teachers can assess students by asking them to use multiple representations to explain their thinking or to justify their response to a question. Teachers can ask students to apply schema they've learned in instruction: for example, how to approach word problems and how to apply linear equations to new situations. These kinds of intellectual activities support transfer-students' ability to apply their knowledge in novel situations, and students' ability to combine their knowledge in new ways to solve novel problems.

*An example: CRESST's Integrated Learning Assessment*. CRESST's Integrated Learning Assessment provides an example of an assessment for learning that embodies some of these characteristics. The assessment tests reading, writing, and thinking in subject matter, for example, literature, US history, world history, biology, chemistry, and physics. The assessment tasks ask students to read a variety of texts, selected to examplify the common text types in the discipline. For example, in history, the text may include maps and charts; primary sources such as journal entries, debates, newspaper articles, as well as more traditional types of tests. Students are asked questions about the texts that test their ability to comprehend the materials, synthesize across ideas, and compare and contract perspectives. The assessment models the important ways in which students are expected to comprehend, draw inferences from, and synthesize ideas from written materials. The same ideas could be applied to video or web-based materials.

As a culminating activity, students are asked to use what they've read, in combination with what they've previously learned, to explain an application of a major subject matter principle or concept, or to take and argue the position on an important issue. Based on the research on writing, students are given an authentic audience and purpose for the piece—e. g., write a letter to the editor advocating position X, explain to your friend the forces that led to the civil war.

The writing task encourages students to organize their knowledge relative to major disciplinary ideas and to employ standard schema in expressing their view points, which include being clear on the main idea, substantiating major arguments, and the evidence which supports them. The rubric for scoring students' responses extends the schema development by making explicit important features of explanation and/or argument. For example,

- Summary dimensions:

O Content quality

O Communication quality

- Rhetorical structure:

O Focus/organization

O Argument development

O Support for claims/Use of evidence

- Language use

O Mechanics and conventions

O Word choice and sentence variety

Each of these elements is scored on a-four point scale, with clear criteria and exemplars for each score point. We also have extensive training and checking regimens to assure that scorers are consistent in their scoring-that is, that two scorers or two teachers looking at the same student essay would give it essentially the same scores on each dimension. Rubric scores can provide feedback to students and teachers on general areas of strength and weakness and have implications for revising curriculum and instruction and potentially for providing some students remedial assistance.

These tasks and the general specifications that underlie them were developed to serve accountability purposes—for example, as part of annual tests to certify student proficiency or to evaluate schools. We also believe that teachers can use this same general framework to develop classroom activities and assessments that can help their students build their capacity in content based reasoning, argumentation and explanation. The framework and specifications support the alignment between expected goals, classroom instruction and assessment, and accountability testing.

## Assessment For Learning

While assessment of learning looks backward at what has been learned, assessment for learning looks forward to immediate, next steps in the teaching and learning process that will help students accomplish the expected learning goals. Assessment of learning occurs after learning is supposed to have happened. Assessment for learning occurs during the process of instruction and is on-going with it. Assessment for learning is often called "formative assessment."

The questions that formative assessment-or assessment for learning-answers essentially involve diagnosing students' learning progress and taking appropriate action based on it. Among the questions:

- Where are students' relative to my immediate learning goals? What stands in their way of accomplishing the goals?
- Have students progressed as I expected? Has their thinking advanced as I had planned? If not, what misconceptions or learning obstacles do they evidence?
- How can I help students bridge the gap between where they currently are and where I want them to be, i. e., accomplishing immediate and subsequent learning goals, and progressing toward mastery?
- Based on the data, what are the next steps for teaching and learning? What kinds of

instructional activities will best respond to individual students' learning needs?

Figure 2 graphically displays this general process of assessment for learning, courtesy of my colleague, Margaret Heritage:

Teachers start by making their learning goals clear and knowing how that learning is expected to develop. Teachers collect evidence of where students are relative to that progression by asking students questions, observing student activity and analyzing student work. Teachers' analysis of student responses enables them to interpret the status of student learning and to identify the gap between where students are and where they need to be. Teachers then use these interpretations to provide feedback to students and to analyze what they [teachers] need to do to help students surmount the misconceptions or obstacles to learning they are encountering. Based on this inquiry, teachers then take instructional action to help students bridge to new learning to close the identified gap, and the process starts all over again. It is on-going and dynamic.

*Research on learning effects*. Theory and research on formative assessment suggest a number of components that are essential for success:

- Be clear on learning goals and clearly communicate them to students.
- Make clear to students what the success criteria are for achieving the goal, so that they will know when they have reached the goal and how their success will be judged. For example, the rubric for the Integrated Learning Assessment, mentioned above, specifically defines the criteria by which student work will be judged.
- Use questions that will elicit evidence of students' understanding and the quality of their thinking, so that misconceptions and other obstacles to learning can be identified. There are implications here as well for the kinds of learning goals which assessment for learning addresses-but we'll come back to those.
- Probe student thinking to clarify where students may be having difficulty and use prompting to help students bridge from current to more sophisticated levels of understanding and expertise.
- Provide descriptive feedback to enable students to understand where their difficulties lie. Research clearly shows that feedback is more effective when it is focused on the task the students are engaged in and provides the student with suggestions, hints or cues, rather than simply communicating that a response is right/wrong, grading, or offering praise.
- Finally, assessment is formative only when the data are used to take action, to inform

subsequent teaching and learning activities. Diagnosis does not help unless it is used to productively influence immediate instruction.

Research also shows some pretty dramatic effects when these kinds of processes are in place:

- Black and Wiliam's (1998) landmark review concluded that formative assessment has strong effects on student learning, particularly for low ability students.
- At the same time, it changes teachers' roles and changes the kinds of learning that are valued. Formative assessment goes hand in hand with goals for deeper learning, complex thinking, and problem solving.
- There also is theoretical evidence that formative assessment increases student efficacy and motivation for learning. Through formative assessment students come to see themselves as capable and effective learners.

*Assessment for learning example: CRESST Powersource Project.* CRESST's recently completed Powersource Project provides one successful example of the use of formative assessment (Dr. Yunyun Dai will be talking more about this project). Here the focus was on major principles in middle school mathematics whose understanding was thought essential to success in Algebra, a critical course for US students' college readiness. A series of three, brief assessments, was developed for each of the major principles, e. g., rational number equivalence and properties of arithmetic. The first in the series was considered a pretest, and teachers were expected to use results from that assessment to plan their initial instruction. A first post test was then given to check on student understanding and those results used to see where students were and additional instruction provided as needed prior to a second post test.

Teachers were provided a number of supports to help them implement the Powersource approach: professional development dealing with the content, assessment approach, and common obstacles to student understanding; and instructional guides for prescribing subsequent instruction based on assessment results.

We conducted a randomized field trial to test the effects of Powersource on student learning. Teachers were randomly assigned to Powersource and a "business as usual" control group. Initial findings showed some promise: Powersource had positive impact on student learning, but only for some students.

After three years of implementation, we observed main effects for Powersource, that is, Powersource students uniformly outperformed comparison students. We think these findings are important for a number of reasons: #1, they show the impact of formative assessment on student learning, but #2, they suggest that it takes time for teachers to really learn how to use formative assessment, an implication that fits with a lot of other research we've done at CRESST, including that of Dr. Ellen Osmundson who will discuss later. It takes time for formative assessment to take hold. It takes time for teachers to learn and apply new practices. Formative assessment is a complex endeavor.

## Assessment Of and For Learning and Working Together

To this point, I've discussed assessment of and for learning as being distinct and different. However, it is really important that they work together and reinforce one another in coherent systems of assessment. Most critical is that both types of assessment address the same significant learning goals. The idea is that assessment for learning- formative assessment-propels students toward the larger goals of assessment of learning-summative assessment. Formative assessment is smaller grain size, diagnostic, on going, while summative is less frequent, at a much larger grain size and thus doesn't provide detailed diagnosis.

Figure 3 pictures the intended process. Students and learning goals for them are the center of the system. Starting from these goals, formative assessment provides evidence that enables teachers to develop their students learning so that they will do well on summative assessments and over the year build to end-of-year achievement. The whole process is highly interactive, with prior assessments providing evidence to inform subsequent teaching and learning, and the goal being all students achieving high levels of competency; and, in the US, it means being on track to being prepared for success in college.

## Assessment As Learning

Assessment of and for learning focus on student learning, but exist outside of the student, led by policy makers, administrators, and teachers. The concept of assessment as learning makes students the central agent in the learning and assessment process.

Assessment as learning uses the same concepts as the prior assessment types, but focuses on

- Students developing as independent learners, self aware of what and how they learn, monitoring their own learning progress, and being proactive in overcoming obstacles and misconceptions.
- Classrooms as learning communities, where learning is socially mediated, and students and teachers work together cooperatively and interactively to support individual students.

• Self and peer assessment, where the students themselves are the principal assessors and users of data; teachers are guides.

Figure 4 shows a similar figure to the formative assessment model, but with the student rather than the teacher as the driver, and in a collaborative community with other students. Here too the process starts with clear goals for learning and a good sense of what success looks like, but it is the student who analyzes the evidence, interprets his/her performance and draws inferences on learning gaps that may exist, conducts inquiry and solicits feedback from teacher and peers to understand how to move forward, and takes action to do so, closing the identified gap and reinitiating the process toward additional goals — a continuous process of assessment, reflection, and learning.

We have less evidence on assessment as learning then we do on the prior conception, other than that we know that students' meta-cognition is very important to their performance. We see examples of assessment as learning in more inquiry-oriented instructional methods, such as project-based and problem-based learning and in portfolio assessment. Central in these models is that students are expected to understand the learning goals, establish personal goals, assess their progress, analyze their strengths and weaknesses, and find solution paths for attaining success.

## Concluding Thoughts

I've covered a lot of territory in describing assessment of, for, and as learning. Common to all three is the importance of being clear on learning goals and of measuring what is important. Because they signal to students and teachers what is important to know and be able to do and what kinds of learning are valued, assessment should reflect the most significant learning goals for students. In assessments of learning, what gets measured is what gets taught and what gets studied. In assessment for learning, what gets taught is what gets assessed. In both cases, the assessments need to be in sync and should focus on the capabilities that students need for future success. Many leaders in the United States and in other countries of the world believe that to be prepared for success, students need not to be crammed full of knowledge but instead need to develop deep understanding of central principles, to be able to reason and think critically, solve problems, and be lifelong learners.

Secondly, common to all three is the use of evidence to inform subsequent improvement efforts. In the case of assessments of learning, grain size is large, timing is after the fact, and the frequency of assessment limited, so assessment results provide only general indications of curriculum and/or student strengths and weaknesses that can guide future planning. In the case of assessment for and as learning, the assessment is on-going, yields detailed diagnosis, and results can be used to inform immediate next steps.

Thirdly, assessment of learning, as previously mentioned, has existed for eons. The concepts of assessment for and as learning are conceptions that are more recent and tend to be new for many teachers. The concepts are more easily described than accomplished. Based on research in the United States, they are not likely to occur without critical supports for change in teacher practice. CRESST research, for example, suggests the need for both sound methods and tools for collecting formative evidence and professional development to help teachers engage in a formative process.

Finally, formative assessment, assessment for and as learning, are not concepts that apply only to students. They also apply to teachers: Teachers can become more adapt at formative assessment if they are clear on the goals and success criteria for the practice, get descriptive feedback on their performance, and are supported in their actions to close the gap between their current assessment practices and those of formative assessment. Similarly, assessment as learning would suggest the value of teachers taking responsibility and being the central agents in any expected change.

**References**


Assessment Reform Group 2002, *Assessment for Learning: 10 research-based principles to guide classroom practice*, Assessment Reform Group, London, United Kingdom.

Black, P., McCormick, R., James, M. & Pedder, D. (2006) Learning how to learn and assessment for learning: A theoretical inquiry. *Research Papers in Education*. 21: 2. 119 - 132.

Black & Wiliam (1998) Inside the Black Box: Raising Standards Through Classroom Assessment *Phi Delta Kappan*, 80, 139 - 148.

Dwyer, C. A. (ed. 2007) The Future of Assessment: Shaping Teaching and Learning. Mahwah, N.J.: Lawrence Erlbaum Associates, 2007.

Cheng, L., & Watanabe, Y. with Curtis, A. Eds. (2004) *Washback in language testing: Research contexts and methods*. Mahwah, NJ: Lawrence Erlbaum Associates.

Earl, L. (2003) *Assessment as learning: Using classroom assessment to maximize student learning*. Thousand Oaks, CA: Corwin Press.

Gardner, J. (Ed) *Assessment & Learning*. London: Sage Publications.

Harlen, W. (2006) The role of assessment in developing motivation for learning. In J. Gardner (Ed)

*Assessment & Learning*. London: Sage Publications. 61 - 80.

Heritage, M. (2010) *Formative assessment: Making It Happen In the Classroom*. Corwin Press: Thousand Oaks, CA.

Herman, J. (2010) Coherence: Key to next generation assessment success. Los Angeles, CA: CRESST. Available at http://www.cse.ucla.edu/products/policy/coherence_v6.pdf

Herman, J. L. (2008) Accountability and assessment in the service of learning: Is public interest in K - 12 education being served? In L. Shepard and K. Ryan (eds). *The future of test-based accountability*. New York: Taylor and Francis

OECD/CERI 2005, *Formative Assessment, Improving Learning in Secondary Classrooms*, OECD Publishing, Paris, France.

Sadler, D. R. (1989). Formative assessment and the design of instructional systems. *Instructional Science*, *18*, 119 - 144.

Shepard, LA. (2006). *Classroom assessment*. In Brennan, RL (Ed.), *Educational measurement*. (4). (p. 623 - 646). Washington, DC: National Council on Measurement in Education and American Council on Education/Praeger.

Stiggins, R 2007, 'Assessment through the Student's Eyes', *Educational Leadership*, vol 64, no 8, pp. 22- 26.

Wall, D. (2005) The Impact of High-Stakes Examinations on Classroom Teaching. Studies in Language Testing 22. Cambridge University Press.

# 评价与学习的促进

Joan L. Herman

【摘要】本文总述了课堂评价在提高学生学习中的作用。首先介绍了评价与学习之间关系的普遍模式,并呈现"关于学习的评价"、"促进学习的评价"、"作为学习的评价"这三个截然不同的方面。随后,文章总结了这三个方面的具体实施,分享了其如何影响学习以及如何设计使其效果最佳的研究,并提供美国国家评价、标准及学术测试研究中心的研究样例。文章最后强调为了实现促进学生学习这一目标,协调不同类型的评价的重要性以及可能遇到的挑战。

【关键词】学习的评价;为了学习的评价;作为学习的评价

【作者简介】Joan L. Herman/美国加州大学洛杉矶分校教育与信息科学学院、美国国家评价、标准及学术测试研究中心(CRESST)主任

# 促进学习理念下对NRC考评观及考评模型的发展研究

冯翠典

【摘要】促进学生的学习，是当下学习考评领域的“大观念”。探讨促进学习的考评模型，可以给相应的理论探究和实践操作提供基本框架。以美国国家研究协会NRC的考评观为逻辑起点，在促进学习的理念下，对NRC考评观进行了两次发展。NRC认为“考评是基于证据的推理过程”，通过逻辑演绎把NRC的考评观发展为“考评是基于证据进行推理并做出反馈的过程”，而通过来自教师的观念，考评观进一步发展为“考评是基于证据共同建构的过程”。同时，NRC的考评模型也得到发展。

【关键词】考评促进学习；考评本质；考评模型

【作者简介】冯翠典/浙江台州学院教师教育学院教师

本研究在促进学习的理念下，以美国国家研究协会NRC的考评观为逻辑起点，对NRC考评观进行了两次发展，期望对促进学习的考评的理论思考和实践操作提供一些讨论。

## 一、促进学习:学习考评的大观念

对学生的学习评价，主要有两种功能:“为了选择的评价和为了教育的评价。”[1]这两种评价现在更多地被称作“对于学习的考评”(assessment of learning)和“为了学习的考评”(assessment for learning)。[2]前者是为了满足教育问责的需要;后者是为了满足促进学习的需要:这两个方面都是重要的。但整个20世纪的教育考评，更多地是满足问责的需要，而不是作为推进教与学的工具。“为了学习的考评”是相对缺失的。[3]所以，许多理论家主张重视评价促进学习的功能，比如，麦克米尔(McMillan, J.)提出，“应该认识到，考评从广泛意义上讲，是教学的必要一部分，不仅是记录学习的工具，也是促进学习的工具”。[4]一些国际权威机构，如美国国家研究协会(NRC)也声明了同样观点:“近年来，有关考评的观念发生了重要的变化。在新的观念中，考评和学习是同一枚硬币的两面。”[5]我国崔允漷教授也指出:“当前，对学习的关注已经成为教育评价改革的一个大观念(big idea)。评价不再被看成是教学过程终结之后的一个环节，或凌驾于教学过程之上的活动。相反，评价要被当作镶嵌于教学过程之中的一个成分，与教学、学习一起构成了三位一体的整体。”[6]

可见，促进学习在当下学习考评领域已成共识。探讨促进学习的考评模式，可以给相应的理论探究和实践操作提供基本框架。以美国国家研究协会NRC的考评观为逻辑起点，在促进学习的理念下，本研究对 NRC 的考评观及考评模型进行了两次发展。

## 二、NRC 的考评观及考评模型

2001 年，NRC 在《知道学生所知的：教育考评的科学和设计》中提出了对考评本质和考评模型的看法，影响深远。NRC 是采取比较上位和宏观的视角来讨论考评的，指明其“既关注对学校学习的考评，也关注对学校成就的考评”。[7] 并强调“本报告讨论的很多理论基础是适用于任何目的下的考评的”。这说明 NRC 期望首先从一般性的本质化视角来看待教育中的考评，这种视角可让我们看到所有形式和所有目的下的考评的共同机制和规定性法则，也使其可以作为探讨促进学习的考评观念和考评模型的逻辑起点。

### （一）NRC 的考评本质观：从证据中推理的过程

NRC 指出，任何考评都是一种工具，其设计是用来观察学生的行为并产生数据，这些数据是用于得出关于学生知道什么的合理性推理的。这种收集证据来支持考评主体做出推论的过程被称为从证据中推理（reasoning from evidence）。[7]42 这是借用梅斯雷弗（Mislevy，R. J.）的观点。这种关于学生学习的推理过程是所有考评具备的特征，包括课堂小测验、标准化成就测验、计算机辅助教学、学生在进行实验时和教师进行的交谈。

通过追溯梅斯雷弗的观点[8][9]，可以发现，梅斯雷弗是从考评活动的本质特征，即所有考评都遵循的一般原则来阐述的。所有形式的教育考评实质上都是对学生知识、技能和成就的推理，这种推理需要证据作为支持；这种逻辑适用于任何形式和任何理念下的考评，无论是传统行为主义范式下的测验理论，还是新兴认知主义和建构主义范式下的质性考评。

当然，梅斯雷弗用来重新认识考评本质，用来打通不同考评实践之间沟壑的出发点的是测验理论。测验理论无疑是关乎推理的，即测验理论所研究的是学生对某些测试题的回答情况和学生所具有的能力特点之间的关系，其实是基于数据进行推理的过程。所谓的概率，本质上不是关乎数字的，而是关乎推理的。测验理论所处理的是行为主义心理学概念下的关于学生能力和特点的证据。而认知主义和建构主义的兴起会要求关注和行为主义心理学所不同的学生能力和特点的模式，或要求采取不同的收集证据的策略。但不管怎样，推理的一般原理——推理是数据性概率下的概念——是可以应用到更为广泛的对话中的。

### （二）考评三角：NRC 关于考评本质的模型

对于考评是“从证据中推理的过程”这句简短的命题，NRC 又做了进一步解读。[7]43 推理过程的第一个问题是“关于什么的证据？”考评中收集到的数据（data）只有在确立了与所考虑的假设之间的关系时才会变成证据（evidence）。数据本身并不能提供它们的意义；它们作为证据的价值只有通过一些解释的框架才能体现，即这些数据是关于什么的，是为了什么而收集的。在教育情境中，教育性考评会提供一些数据，比如书面论文、在答题卡上的分数、小课题的汇报，或者学生对他们问题解决的解释。但这些数据只有与学生如何获得知识和技能的假设联系起来才是证据。

第二，考评接下来是考虑关于什么样的证据或观察可以帮助做出关于学生能力的推理。一个人对学习本质的理解会影响到其期望收集的考评数据的种类，以及得出推论的过程。比如，认知主义的研究者就会寻求关于学习者如何处理问题的证据，包括他们如何理解他们需要解决的问题，以及他们用来解决问题的策略。

另外，考评也依赖于什么样的框架可以使得这些证据有意义，即对证据作出解释的过程。测量科学提供了很多方法来通过收集的证据做出关于学习者能力的推论。例如，一些考评使用概率模型来处理样本或者交流不确定性。而现在开始重视使用质性的框架来进行解释，但不管怎样，推理的过程决定了要在学生所说、所做或所提供的东西上关注什么，从而可以形成关于学生知道什么和能做什么的证据。

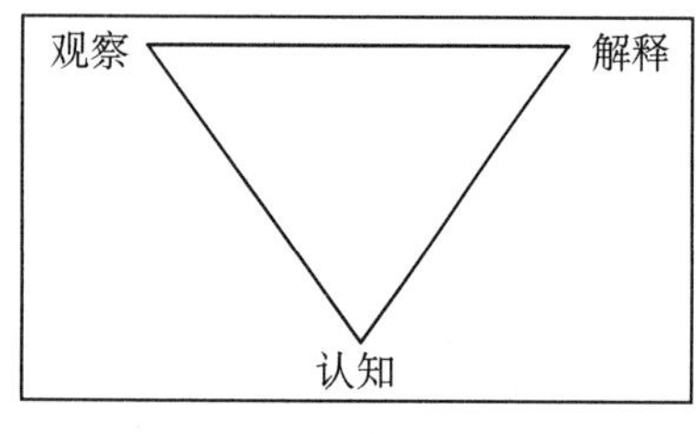


**图 1　考评三角(资料来源:NRC,2001)**

在这种解读基础上，NRC 顺理成章地提出了"考评三角"(assessment triangle)的考评模型，如图 1。三角的顶点代表所有考评所具备的三个成分：学生在某领域中认知(cognition)和学习的模型，一套关于哪些种类的观察(observations)能够给学生的能力提供证据的信念，以及使证据获得意义的解释(interpretation)过程。[7]43

这三个要素，在具体的考评中可能是明显的或者是隐含的，但任何考评若不考虑这三个方面，都不能进行设计和实施。考评三角提供了分析现有考评和未来设计的工具和框架。

### (三) 根据"考评三角"提出的"五要素"考评模型

可以看出，考评三角涉及的是在考虑考评本身的内在逻辑时必要的要素，使用的"认知"、"观察"、"解释"都是从抽象意义和概括意义上说的。具体的考评实践中，这些术语的所指是有具象表现的。这三个顶点其实是对应"考评什么(考评目标)"、"如何考评(考评方法)"和"如何解释(参照标准)"的问题。从"考评是基于证据的推理过程"这种观念来看，这三个方面又分别对应三个连贯性的问题："需要什么证据?""如何获得证据?""如何理解证据?"可以理解的是，考评参照是和考评内容、考评方法紧密相连的，并不具备独立存在的实体意义，从而可把"考评方法"和"考评参照"整合成一个考评要素："如何考评"，其具备实体性意义的要素是"考评方法"。

在具体的操作中，考评还必须有指导性的目的性要素和支持性的条件性要素。如 NRC 指出，在考虑考评的设计和实施时，还有一个必须而且是首要考虑的要素"考评的目的"[7]2，即要回答"为什么考评"的问题，考评的目的贯穿并制约着整个的考评过程。针对考评目的的重要地位，吉普斯（Gipps，C. V.）在1994年就提出：考评首要地是“要与目的相适应（fitness for purpose）”。[10]厄尔（Earl，L. M.）在2003年也提出，对于考评活动来讲，“目的就是一切（purpose is everything）”。[11]可以看出，考评目的成为考评系统的要素，而且是规定性的要素，是得到共识的。考评还必须考虑一些条件性的要素保障实施，即“参与的主体”和“发生的情境”，回答“谁参与考评”和“在何时发生”的问题。

这样，围绕考评的实施，就可以发现考评系统是一个五个要素形成的系统，分别是：为什么考评（考评目的）、考评什么（考评目标）、如何考评（考评方法、考评解释）、谁参与到考评中（考评主体）、在何时发生考评（考评情境），这样五个要素所组成的考评系统可简称为“五要素考评模型”，见图2。

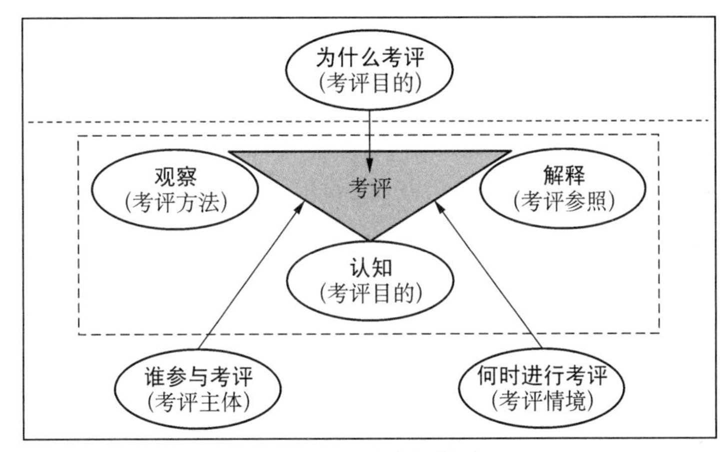


**图2　五要素考评模型**

## 三、促进学习理念下对NRC考评观及考评模型的第一步发展

NRC的“考评三角”及由其引申出的“五要素”考评模型都是针对一般性或总体性的考评活动的，即可以解释和应用到任何情境下的考评实践，比如，大规模考试或课堂考评。但具备这种一般性视角的同时，还是需要理解到不同形式和不同目的下的教育考评之间的差别、区分的关键等问题，来更为针对地理解教育考评。这种进一步的区分是必要的，NRC本身也承认，教育考评还是服务于不同的目的的，也具备不同的形式，具体来说，课堂情境中的考评和大规模情境下的考评主要完成三个方面的目的：“促进学生学习、测量个体学生成就、考评教育项目。”本研究更为关注的是促进学生学习的考评应是什么样的。对NRC考评观及考评模型的第一步发展是在文献研究基础上通过逻辑思维的工具完成的。

### （一）促进学习理念下对NRC考评观的第一步发展

1. 促进学习理念下的考评对反馈的强调

谈及用考评促进学习，人们往往会想到“形成性评价”。但重要地是要看到，“形成性评价”

概念原初并不是为了“促进学习”的，使用形成性评价“促进学习”经历了一个过程。在笔者一篇关于形成性评价涵义演变的综述中，清晰地呈现了这样一个过程。[12]

斯克里文（Scriven，M.）1967年首次提出“形成性评价”（formative evaluation）的概念，初衷是着眼于有效的课程开发而对学生进行的评价，[13]和学生的学习本身其实是没有关系的。布卢姆（Bloom，B.）1968年把“形成性评价”的观点用于学生的学习，将其作为“掌握学习”基石。[14]但深究起来，掌握学习的理念是在学生学习的形成性阶段对学习结果进行检测，从而教师可以决定是否给予矫正性或补救性教学。只是关注学习困难的学生，并不涉及全体学生的学习需要，以及教师必要的调整。

评价促进学习的观念是源于对反馈的强调，这种观念在80年代末开始凸显。克鲁克斯（Crooks，T.J.）1988年指出，在当时的年代里，学生考评更多的“放在了考评的评分功能上而不是促进学生的学习的功能上”。他强调，学生“应能得到实践和使用作为项目目标的技能和知识的常规性的机会，以及获得对他们表现的反馈”。[15]塞德勒（Sadler，D. R.）1989年首次提出“形成性考评”（formative assessment）的概念，并强调反馈的必要性以及自我监控的概念。[16]对反馈的强调，是形成性考评文献的基本特征。而对学习进行反馈的核心本质——使用学习的证据来调整教学——在2000年左右得到更清晰地论述。例如，布莱克和威廉姆指出“形成性考评并没有一个严谨的定义和广为接受的涵义”，但这些定义都有一个共同的目的，即对教学活动提供反馈，并促进学生学习。[17]2002年，布莱克等人又对形成性考评以“为了学习的考评”（Assessment for Learning）的名义进行了强调：“为了学习的考评是任何其设计和实施是为了促进学生学习的目的的考评，这种考评是和为主要服务于教育问责、学生分等以及颁发证书等目的而设计的考评不一样。如果一个考评活动能够在教师和学生对学生个体或群体进行考评时提供反馈信息用于调整教学和学习活动，那这种考评活动就能真正地帮助学生学习。这些考评只有当考评证据切实地用于教学调整来满足学习需要时才是‘形成性考评’。”[18]

可以看出，强调通过考评对学生和教师提供反馈，并进而导向学习的深入和教学的调整，是促进学生学习的考评的基本特征。

2. 促进学习理念下对NRC考评观的第一次发展

通过文献研究，可以发现“反馈”是促进学习的考评的必要条件，没有反馈，就没有改进，甚至没有最基本的连贯性动作。作为一项考评，并不是“知道收集什么证据”、“收集了相关的证据”、“理解了证据的意义”就结束了，最重要的是要采取相应的决策来解决“如何应对证据”，从而达到改进教学和促进学习的目的。促进学生学习的考评，应是教师和学生在学习证据的基础上不断互动和决策的过程，反馈的存在是这种考评的基本特征；没有反馈是可以发生考评的，只是没有反馈不能发生“促进学生学习”的考评。从而，促进学习的理念下，反馈应是考评机制的基本要素。

坚持把“反馈”作为考评的要素，可以重新来看考评的本质，对于“考评是基于证据进行推理的过程”的观点，笔者是认同的；但应清楚，进行“推理”后应该采取一定的措施或行为来应对这种推理，这些措施或行为就是反馈。没有反馈的考评对于内部性的主体，即教师和学生，没有丝毫意义；没有反馈的考评必然是无益于学习的。从而，考评可更为准确地定义为“基于证据进行推理并作出反馈的过程”。

### （二）促进学习理念下对 NRC 考评三角的第一步发展

对 NRC 考评观发展后，考评三角也应进行发展。NRC 的“考评三角”是能够解释和适用于一切类型和所有情境下的考评，是比较概括化的。而就课堂情境下为促进学生学习进行的考评而言，“反馈”是必要要素。如前所述，考评三角中“认知”是规定“考评什么”的，即“考评目标”或“需要什么样的证据”；“观察”和“解释”其实都属于“如何考评”的要素中，即“如何收集到所需的证据”（考评方法）和“如何解释收集到的证据”（参照标准），可以用“考评活动”统称。这样，“观察”和“解释”两个顶点就合二为一。为了彰显反馈的重要和必要地位，笔者把“考评反馈”作为三角的另一个顶点，即“如何利用考评证据”的问题。并表达立场：是否存在有效的考评反馈是区分“内部性目的”的考评和“外部性目的”的考评的核心标志，也是标识了是“为了学习的考评”还是“对于学习的考评”的重要标志。还需指出，“考评目的”是考评一以贯之的核心要素。图 3 是发展后的“考评三角”。

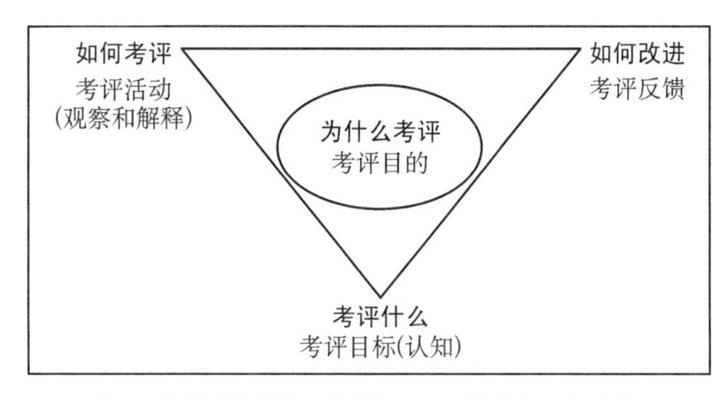


**图 3　发展后的考评三角（基于 NRC 的考评三角发展）**

### （三）促进学习理念下对五要素考评模型的第一步发展

根据对考评三角的发展，可以把根据考评三角引申出的“五要素考评模型”也进行相应的发展，如图 4。

可以理解到的是，在“五要素考评模型”的实际运作中，真正运转起来的就是作为其核心的“发展后的考评三角”，但实体性要素还是考评三角所涵盖的“考评活动”和“考评内容”。“考评反馈”虽是必要要素，但并不是实体性或独立性的，只是存在于“考评活动”和“考评内容”运转

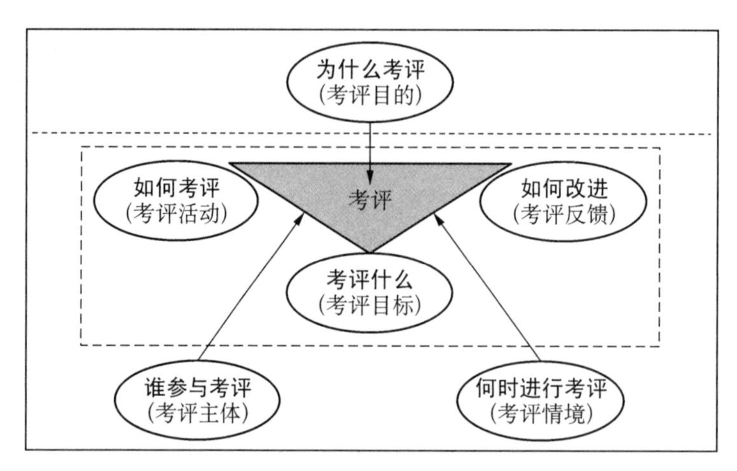


**图 4　发展了的五要素考评模型**

起来的关系中。关于其他三个必要要素，在具体的实施中，“考评目的”会是一种内隐的贯穿性的要素，而“考评主体”和“考评情境”是考评的支持性要素，也是由于“考评什么”和“如何考评”两个要素所引发的，是必然存在的。

## 四、促进学习理念下对 NRC 考评观及考评模型的第二步发展

### (一) 促进学习理念下对 NRC 考评观的第二步发展

本研究在对 NRC 考评本质观及考评模型做出第一步发展后，把研究的结果通过教师访谈检验其合理性。而在模型检验过程中，很重要的研究结果是对考评观的第二次发展。在研究过程中，虽然笔者已经具备了这样一种意识：促进学习的考评是师生之间共同建构的活动。但在考评本质的定义中并没有明确提出来，通过教师访谈发现，教师们对“考评是一种基于证据进行推理并提供反馈的过程”的定义争议很大，根据实际的教育经验，教师们质疑关于考评实践的线性单向逻辑，而倾向于以建构的观念来理解考评。下面几位教师的观点清晰地呈现了这样一种理解。

“我觉得考评是贯穿全课的，是穿插在你说的这几个环节中的。方法也很多，你可以通过表扬什么的。再比如探究，各个小组的情况怎么样？要及时给他们反馈。比如，你们小组做的最好啦，哪一个同学的意见最科学，或者学生把作业汇报一下，这也是一种考评。就是说，考评是贯穿全课的过程的。”

(101019.I.QQQ.40:00—42:00)

“这个考评啊，不是一个独立的环节，不是分开的，实际上所有的教学过程都伴随着这个考评，是伴随发生的，比如，上午的那个老师，她讲了一个内容，她讲压缩空气，空气挤出来，被压缩了，然后产生一个力量。这个教学和体验的过程中，通过学生的回答，这个怎么理解的，那个

怎么理解的，回答的时候其他的同学有看法，这就是在进行考评啊。这个过程是伴随着考评的，不管是老师评，小组评，个人评等等，都是在过程中发生的。”

（101020.I.HSG.01：11：00—01：13：00）

“我一上课看到学生的表现，就是一个考评，比如，‘你坐的很端正’、‘你今天的精神非常棒’、‘你的知识面这么宽啊’，这些，其实就是老师对学生的考评，听到以后，学生就想，老师表扬我哦，说我视野开阔哦，知道很多东西哦，那他就有个冲动，把自己想知道的东西滔滔不绝地说出来。就是说，学生就能根据你的引导走，这其实也就是一个互动，我觉得考评的过程就是这样的。”“然后，他们思考，去设计实验，去做实验，或者讨论，这就是他们的学习过程，在这个过程中，老师有个巡视。嗯，这一组表现的很好，我就会停下来倾听，倾听的过程，以及倾听中对他们的解释，我觉得也是一种考评。因为他们做的好，你才会走过去倾听；或者他们做的不好，你才会走过去指导。”“那么学生，在这个过程中，就会意识到：‘哦，原来是这样啊。’他就会在你的暗示下进行修正。然后呢，在汇报的过程中，老师、同学之间的一个讨论，还有表扬啊，就是一个总结性的考评。”

（101027.I.RLY.40：00—43：00）

这说明促进学习的考评本质上是建构性的，是贯穿在整个的教学过程中的。基于此，笔者进行了对考评本质的第二次发展，把考评定义为“**考评是基于证据进行共同建构的过程**”，在这种意义上，对学生学习的考评和学生的学习以及教师的教学本质上都是融为一体的。

关于考评的建构性和互动性而非线性本质，早在 1988 年，墨菲和托里斯（Murphy, R. & Torrance, H.）就指出了：我们最为关注的并不是说考评必须是纯粹的心理测量学意义上的，以及必须绝对可信的；而是，考评应该在教育过程中扮演一种建构性的角色，以及能够提供关于某一阶段教育成就的有效信息。这些教育成就可能是不容易测量的（not ealily measurable），但却是很重要的教育目标（desirable）。[19]这种观念预示着对考评新的强调，即应提供学生知道什么和能做什么的有用的图景。或者说，考评应该关注整体性的学习和鼓励质性的理解。从这种观点看，考评就应该是建构性的，其目的是帮助学生而不是宣判学生。强调的是个体的成就与其本身原有水平的比较，或者是和既定的标准相对照，而不是强调和他人进行比较。[20]这意味着考评的目的有了新的转变：从根据既定的课程和教学材料来给学生分类转变到使教学材料适应学习者的个体需要，并让学习者之间有互惠性的学习经验。这就有必要关注学生的学习，因为每个人特定的学习需求是不一样的。考评中的平等不再意味着不切实际地追求同等水平的成就和给全体学生提供相同的经验，而是意味着考评的实践和结果的解释对每个人来说都是公平和公正的。实现每一个人的潜能的要求反映了考评应改变和学习的关系——即从“测量学习”转变到“促进学习”。

说到考评的建构性本质，不得不提及古巴和林肯的第四代评价的观念。1989 年《第四代评价》中，他们鲜明地提出了评价的建构性本质，把评价定义成“人的心理建构”。[21]并把第四代评价描述为这样一种图景：评价相关者的理想、目标和问题作为收集评价信息的组织范畴，评价的实施过程是在建构主义者的探究范式（constructivist inquiry paradigm）的方法论下进行的。[21]古巴和林肯关于评价的建构性本质的论断自提出后，引起广泛关注。但笔者坦言，单纯就其理论阐述而言，让笔者能充分理解，并拿来观照实践是不容易的。在笔者原初的观念中，古巴和林肯的观念似乎太过“后现代”，很难与现实的考评联系起来。而通过本研究的理论推演和实践检验，考评的建构性本质以通俗易懂的方式显现出来，这本身也算是对古巴和林肯观念的一种呼应或验证。更重要地，对笔者来讲，在这种过程中，笔者能把考评的建构性本质放在实然的实践中来理解，而不仅仅看作一种似乎不可及的应然。

**（二）促进学习理念下对 NRC 考评模型的第二步发展**

在把考评本质进一步定义为“**考评是基于证据进行共同建构的过程**”之后，重新来审视考评模型。应该能够得出的结论是，不应把考评只看作一个静态的结构，或者是线性的实施，而应看作是互动建构的过程，这个过程是围绕“证据”进行的：“需要什么证据”、“如何获得和解释证据”、“如何利用证据”，图 5 是把发展后的考评三角运转起来的模型。

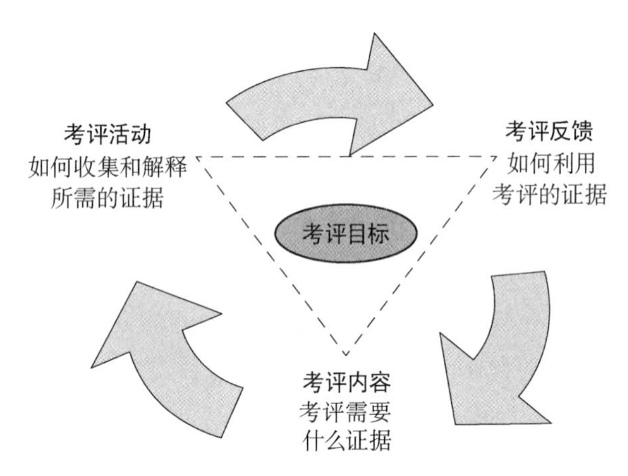


**图 5　发展后的考评三角的程序化图**

这样，促进学习的考评活动就是在促进学习的考评目的下，基于学习证据进行的共同建构的活动。考评目的贯穿在整个的考评活动之中，并指导学习证据信息流的运转，呈现出顺势起转的建构性特征。图 6 是促进学习的考评活动的运行模型，该模型与图 5 的不同体现在已经超越了对各个考评要素孤立的理解，而是把各个要素整合起来，在“考评目的”的指引下围绕“考评证据”进行。这个模型既可以说是对 NRC 考评模型的第二次发展，也可以说是对五要素考评模型的动态化理解。

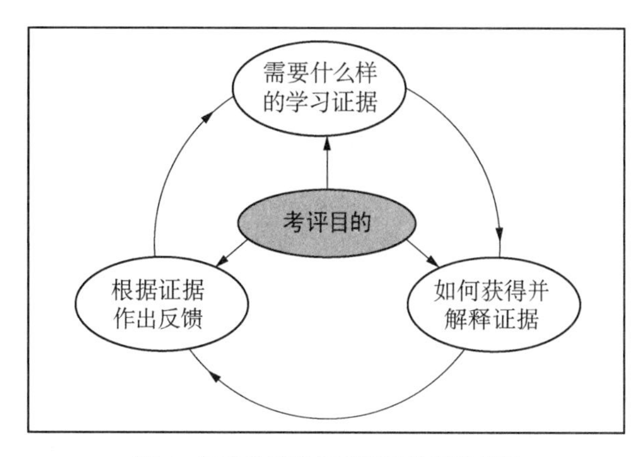


**图 6　促进学习的考评活动的运行模型**

## 五、本研究的意义

### （一）引导在学习评价的整体性领域思考评价的问题

本研究是从理解和讨论评价活动的基本特征和必要组成开始的，最初的问题域是指向整体性的学习评价的。总体来说，学习评价有两种实践样式，一是注重对学习结果进行鉴定的评价（evaluation），典型的表现是大规模考试；二是注重对学习整体予以促进的考评（assessment），典型的表现是课堂考评。但应该理解到的是，这两种实践样式不可能进行非此即彼的对话和转换，二者共同承担了学习评价的基本功能，也存在着共通的一般性法则，应该互相协同，彼此借力。本研究的视角可以引导从整体上考虑对于学生学习的考察，在对不同形式和不同目的的评价活动“同”的思考下思考“不同”，才是有意义的。

### （二）明确了促进学习的考评的本质特征和核心机制

本研究首要地是明确了促进学习的考评本质。就一般性的评价活动来讲，是一种基于证据的推理过程。而促进学生的学习，应涵盖反馈的要素，即考评是基于证据进行推理并作出反馈的过程。而且，反馈并不是存在于考评活动的最后环节，而是贯穿在整个的学习和教学过程中，从而考评是基于证据进行共同建构的过程。由此可以看出，促进学习的考评的核心机制是“基于证据”运行的，即“需要什么证据”、“如何获得和解释证据”、“如何利用证据”。

### （三）有利于思考如何融通不同形式不同目的的考评

基于本研究，笔者期望教育者意识到的是，应思考不同形式的考评的本质不同是什么？比如，学段测验、大规模测验等传统纸笔测试必然是阻碍学习的吗？课堂评价、档案袋评价等“另类”的形式必然是促进学习的吗？在这种思考的基础上，更重要地是要思考如何融通不同形式和不同目的的考评，从而发挥学习评价整体上服务于学生学习的功能。期望本研究会对这样关键性的思考提供一些思路。

参考文献

[1] Biggs, J., & Watkins, D. (1995). *Classroom Learning Australia*. Prentice-Hall.

[2] Black, P., & William, D. (1998). *Inside the Black Box: Raising Standards Through Classroom Assessment*. Phi Delta Kappan.

[3] Stiggins, R. (2002). *Assessment Crisis: The Absence of Assessment for Learning*. Phi Delta Kappan.

[4] McMillan, J. (2008). *Assessment Essentials for Standard-based Education (2nd edition)*. California: Corwin Press.

[5] National Research Council. (1996). *National Science Education Standards*. Washington. DC: National Academy Press.

[6] 崔允漷.促进学习:学业考评的新范式[J].教育科学研究,2010(3):11-15,20.

[7] NRC. (2001). *Knowing What Students Know: The Science and Design of Educational Assessment*, NRC.

[8] Mislevy, R. J. (1994). Evidence and Inference in Educational Assessment. *Psychometrika*, 59 (4), 439-483.

[9] Mislevy, R. J. (1996). Test Theory Reconceived. *Journal of Educational Measurement*, 33(4), 379-416.

[10] Gipps, C. V. (1994). *Beyond Testing: Towards a Theory of Educational Assessment*. Oxford: Routledge Falmer.

[11] Earl, L. M. (2003). *Assessment as learning: Using Classroom Assessment to Maximize Student Learning*. California: Corwin Press.

[12] 冯翠典,高凌飚.从"形成性评价"到"为了学习的考评"[J].教育学报,2010(6):49-54.

[13] Scriven, M. (1967). The Methodology of Curriculum Evaluation. In Taylor, R., Gagne, R., & Scriven, M. (Eds.). *AERA Monograph Series on Curriculum Evaluation* (pp. 39-83). Chicao, IL. Rand McNelly.

[14] Allal, L., & Lopez, L. M. (2005). Formative Assessment of Learning: A Review of Publications in French. In OECD(Ed.), *Formative Assessment: Improving Learning in Secondary Classroom* (pp. 241-264). France: OECD Publishing.

[15] Crooks, T. J. (1988). The Impact of Classroom Evaluation Practices on Students. *Review of Education Rresearch*, 58(4), 438-481.

[16] Sadler, D. R. (1989). Formative Assessment and The Design of Instructional Systems. *Instructional Science*, 18(2), 119-144.

[17] Black, P., & Wiliam, D. (1998). Assessment and Classroom Learning. *Assessment in Education*,

5(1), 7-74.

[18] Black, P., Harrison, C., Lee, C., Marshall, B., & Wiliam, D. (2002). *Working inside the Black Box*. London: Kings College.

[19] Murphy, R., & Torrance, H. (1988). *The Changing Face of Educational Assessment*. Milton Keynes: Open University.

[20] Gipps, C., & Murphy, P. (1994) *A Fair Test? Assessment, Achievement, and Equity*. Buchingham: Open University Press.

[21] Guba, E. G., & Lincoln, Y. S. (1989) *Fourth Generation Evaluation*. California: Sage Publications.

## The Development of NRC's Concept of Assessment Nature and Assessment Model Under the Idea of Promoting Learning

Cuidian Feng

**Abstract**: Promoting student learning is the "big idea" of educational assessment. Inquiring the assessment model under the idea of promoting learning will provide basic framework corresponding theory and practice. Take NRC's concept of assessment nature as the logical start point, this study developed the concept twice. First, in NRC's view, "assessment is process of reasoning from evidence". Then, through logical deducation, this wiew is revised into "assessment is process of reasoning from evidence and feedback". Last, as the outcome of teacher interview, assessment is redefinded as "assessment is process of evidence-based collaborative construction."

**Keywords**: assessment for learning; assessment nature; assessment mode

# “教—学—评”一体化教学的探索与实践

## ——以初中语文为例探究“课堂评价”的有效途径

卢　臻

【摘要】为提高课堂评价的有效性，从设置明确、可操作的学习目标，到实施教学评一体化教学，再到开展对课堂评价进行再评价的课堂观察活动，我们围绕“教学评一致性”展开了一系列的试验研究，澄清了影响课堂教学效益的诸多问题，也在一定程度上提高了语文教学效益。

【关键词】课堂评价；分解课标；课堂观察

【作者简介】卢臻/河南省郑州市教育局教学研究室教研员

崔允漷主编的《基于标准的学生学业成就评价》一书指出，没有良好的课堂层面的评价，就没有良好的教学实践；课堂层面良好的教学实践在很大程度上取决于课堂层面的评价实践。[1]课堂评价贯穿课堂教学始终，既是促进学生学习的重要教学手段，又是诊断、调控、引导课堂教学的重要工具。然而，正如该书所说，评价是课程改革中的短板，它严重制约着素质教育的推进；同样，课堂评价也是课堂教学中的短板，流弊已久的庸俗的课堂评价使课堂教学成为一本“有教无凭”的糊涂帐，严重影响着课堂教学效益的实现。

### 一、课堂评价的四种怪现状

#### （一）有评无效，评价不具针对性

课堂评价具有很强的目标参照性，在围绕某一学习目标学习之后即针对目标适时、适当评价，以获取学生的达标信息从而调节教学；如果偏离学习目标或学习活动，课堂评价就会丧失其应有的效度而失去评价功能。有教师执教《郭沫若诗两首》，学习目标为：了解联想和想象的区别，能初步使用联想与想象。在学生讨论过“《天上的街市》哪部分写实？哪部分为想象？”等问题之后进行评价：仿照“天上的明星现了，好像点着无数的街灯”句，发挥联想与想象续写句子“1.牵牛花开放了，好像……；2.月光照在地上，好像……”。首先，评价与学习目标不匹配，例句是个仅用联想而未用想象的句子，依照其“发挥联想与想象续写句子”只能更加模糊学生对联想与想象的理解；其次，评价与学习活动不吻合，“写实”与“联想”是两个概念，执教者不仅将其混同且未引导学生区别“联想”与“想象”的不同，这个评价难以考量出学生“这一时段”的学习。

### （二）有评不判，评价不具诊断性

前苏联心理学家阿莫纳什维利指出，评价的本质在于激励学生学习，帮助其纠正错误，树立信心。新课改之后，许多教师对有关“激励”、“赏识”的理念多有误解，在课堂评价上不敢对学生说“不”，只要有答，就是“好”、“很好”、“非常好”。“好”在哪里？“好”的标准是什么？如此妄评不能为学生的后续学习提供任何指导，不能让答者明确自己的学习状况，以期提高；也不能让听者明白自己的程度，以期完善。有教师执教文言文《童趣》一课，上课伊始就提问三个学生“用自己的话翻译一遍”，评语分别为：“翻译得非常好”、“非常流利地翻译出来了”、“翻译得真棒”。到底怎么个棒法？是把重点实词翻译准确了，还是把虚词翻译到位了，还是把特殊句式翻译顺畅了？客观指出优劣，既引导不能者学习的方向，又提高能者的学习能力，如此不加诊断的“好好评价”等同于无评价。

### （三）有评无价，评价不具指导性

对于表现性任务，只有依据一定的量规才能客观评判学生达成目标的表现、在达标过程中的位置以及目前位置与目标之间的差距等。就语文而言，对学生习作的评价需要量规，课堂上学生的朗读、仿写、演讲等活动也需要一定的标准，才能“因价”有层次地诊断学情，有区别地指导学生，有目标地进行后续教学。然而，语文课堂上“说”“写”活动成灾，有标准的评价少有；学生的读写能力不是在“标准”中提升，而是在“好评”或“无评”中原地打转。有教师在执教《端午的鸭蛋》一课的最后10分钟时间里，让学生仿照其语言特点描写自己家乡的特产。这个任务设计的很好，能力与情感、思维与逻辑、旧知与新知均可考查，但因没有明细的描述性的标准，写得好的学生不知其好处，写得差的学生不知其差处，当然更不知道自己的差距与发展空间：学习的劳动因为“无价”之评而丧失了应有价值。

### （四）有评无人，评价不具促进性

常见的课堂评价有四种形式：教师讲，教师评，评即测试，教师“一统课堂”；学生学，教师评，评即讲解，课堂由“学生学”转而为“教师讲”；教师定标准，学生自评价，评即对答案；学生学，学生评，评即固定模式，千人一面。以后者为例，有学校推行“先学后教”的学习模式，将学生的评价语固定为：“这个小组/这个同学学习认真，条理清楚，字体工整，声音宏亮，我们都要向他们/他学习。”这些评价只见整体不见个人，只见结果不见过程，只见老师不见学生，不能针对每个学生学习的障碍点给予一定的指导，也不能促使学生为自己学习正确定位而寻求发展空间。评价的多元性不仅在于评价主体的多重性，更在于适配目标开发多种评价工具以促进学生学习。

## 二、课堂评价缺失的原因

课堂评价在教学中长期“不作为”的现象背后隐藏着深刻的原因：

课堂评价意识的缺失。从根本上说，中国的教育信仰实用主义，从来很少在“什么是”问题上深入探究，总是将注意力集中在“怎么做”上。这种实用理性的教学论对课堂评价的直接影响是：未能严格定义课堂评价的内涵及功能，致使长期存在“评价即考试”、“评价即‘不准学生到那儿去’的禁令”；以行政推进手段代替可操作性的课堂评价指导，以致在新课程强调评价并倡导多元评价之后，课堂上就轰然刮起上述评价形式的“歪风”。

课堂评价技术的缺失。我们是在意识觉醒之后才蓦然发现课堂评价种种不足的，其最大的不足除了对课堂评价的理性认知之外，更在于对课堂评价技术的掌握：如何保证评价与学习目标的一致性？如何匹配与学习目标一致的评价工具与量规？如何针对不同的表现性任务设计表现性评价？

目标/课标意识的缺失。课堂评价意识和技术的缺失直接导致教师评价素养的缺失。评价基于课程标准，课堂评价基于学习目标，学习目标来自于对课程标准的分解，分解课标的能力是课堂评价素养的根。因此，评价意识的缺失源自课标意识/目标意识的缺失，这是语文教学效益低下的根。

如何唤醒教师的目标意识？如何在课堂教学活动中实现目标？怎样寻找到目标达成的有效信息？如何促使教师提高评价的实用性？在几经实践与探索之后，我们决意用“教-学-评一体化”的教学思想及教学策略促进教师目标意识的复苏与评价技术的掌握。

## 三、“教—学—评”一体化教学实践

受皮连生“目标导向教学”的启发[2]，结合崔允漷“有效教学”的思想[3]，我们尝试构建“教-学-评一体化”课堂教学运作系统（如图1）：

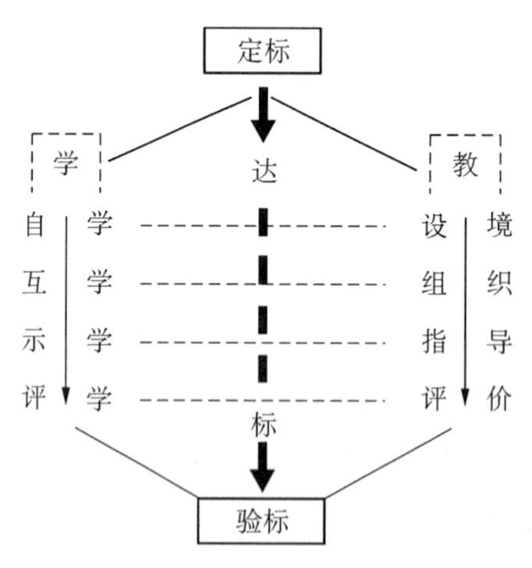


**图1　“教-学-评一体化”课堂教学运作系统**

教学目标是课堂教学的灵魂，它主导并决定着学习活动与课堂评价的跟进，学习活动与课堂评价围绕学习目标有机互渗，达成并验证学习目标，形成“定标—达标—验标”课堂教学转轴；同时调控并决定着学生“学”与教师“教”，“学”与“教”围绕学习目标双线并行并相机合作，形成“师促生学”课堂教学两翼。

具体来说，教学评一体化教学的整体格局为“三环四步”。“三环”指教学的三个主要环节(1)依据课标，参考学情，师生共同定标；(2)围绕目标，依托文本，师生合作达标；(3)基于学习，及时评价，师生共同验标。“四步”主要指达标、验标环节的四项教学活动：(1)教师设置情境，学生依标自学；(2)学生合作探讨，教师指导学习；(3)小组展示学习结果，教师组织学生完善；(4)学生互评学习结果，教师提炼、总结、评价。整个教学过程中，“学”为主，“教”为从，学而后教，教师始终是站立在学生身旁适时指导的共学者；自学为主，互学为辅，先自学后合作，学生始终是以独立的个体进行学习的生命体。

从教学设计的角度上讲，教学评一体化教学的实质是常规教学的科学化——有效设置教学目标，科学设计课堂评价，合理设计教学活动。对于凭经验设计教学、跟着感觉实施教学的大多数教师来说，“科学化”与其固有的教学观念发生了极大冲突，实践起来可以说步履维艰。鉴于此，我们采取了“分阶段——小步调”的实施策略，有步骤地开展教学评一体化教学实践工作。

**(一) 分解课标，制定明确、可操作的教学目标**

“具体化”是分解课程标准的重要手段，将教育目的、课程目标、单元目标等不加“具体化”地直接作为学习目标，是学习目标含糊的首因。知难行易，认识到这一点并逐步制定、落实、验证学习目标是我们着力进行的工作。

1. 剖析案例实证含糊目标的无效性。对于沿袭模糊目标历时太久的多数教师来说，认识目标的模糊性是困难的。我们以退为进，深入课堂，选取典型案例现场剖析，让含糊目标造成教学低效的事实撞击教师的观念，从而促使教师审视自己的教学，追问分解课标的方法，激发制定明确目标的意识。

2. 团队合作撰写学段/学期课程纲要。脑中没有教学知能网络，手下就难以进行课标分解。我们采取迂回策略，暂停“分解课标-制定课时目标”工作，转向以教研组为单位“分解课标—撰写学段或学期课程纲要”，从整体上构建7—9年级教学内容，这样，打破了教师“各念各的经”的教学分散状态，形成了在统一的知能体系下“上下一盘棋”的教学形态，为制定明确的课时目标打下基础。

3. 根据实际教学情境确定学习内容。(1)进行学习前测，寻找学生的能力起点。根据学生原有知识基础进行教学，这是有效教学论的重要思想。因此，分析学情，找到学生的能力起点，是分解课标的第一要务：篇章教学之前，针对基本学习内容进行检测，把握学生学习上的已知点、疑惑点、困难点，据此确定认知重心，使教与学在某种程度上达成统一。(2)深入阅读文本，把握文本的核心内容。根据《语文有效教学》(华东师范大学出版社，郑桂华著)我们设计了四个问题让教师思考:这篇课文具备哪些只有在语文课上才能学到的知识?这篇课文具有哪些明显的特征或代表性?哪一特征具有统领性以便于整体把握文章内涵?哪一特征具有迁移性以便于理解同一文章或同一语言现象?据此确定教学目标的认知内容。

4. 简化分解课标程序制定学习目标。分解的核心即"呈验",用外显的可观察的行为动词呈现认知心理动词,用具体可描述的知识名词呈现笼统的整体知识,用与行为动词相匹配的行为条件呈现教学活动,用先于教学活动的评估任务验收目标达成程度。在上述学情与文本分析的基础上以此四要素呈现课标内容,制定出具体、明确、可操作的学习目标。

### (二) 围绕目标,实施教学评一体化教学

我们仍从课堂教学做起,在澄清认识的同时,逐步渗透教学评一体化思想。

1. 教学反思,分析教学活动的低效性。语文教学的最大问题在于过多关注"怎么教"而很少关注"教什么",以致教学过程浮泛,教学目标不能有效达成。为使教师认识到教学的无效性,我们围绕"教、学、评的适配性"进行同课异构,观课,评课,促使教师领悟到课堂教学低效的原因所在,逐渐确立教学评一体化教学的理念。

2. 任务分析,分三课型构建教学模式。不同的学习目标需要不同的教学支持条件及与之匹配的评估方式,教、学、评保持内在的匹配性,这是目标分类学的重要思想。通过编制学段课程纲要可以得知,初中语文教学主要包括有关课文内容知识、通过对字词句的解码获取意义的技能和理解作者思路、构思与表达技巧方面的技能等三方面内容,据此,我们尝试将语文教学分为词语积累课、文本解读课、语言品味课、手法鉴赏课等四种基本课型,并分别制定以学生自主学习为主的教学策略。

3. 围绕目标,设计评价方式与教学活动。原则上评价设计先于教学活动设置,为简化教学设计程序,我们指导教师将评价设计镶嵌在教学活动设置之中。其基本教学思路为:实现目标 1 的教学活动——评价目标 1 的方式及标准——调整或补救教学;以下目标 2、目标 3 与此相同。如此,学习目标是课堂教学的支点,评价则是驱动课堂教学的原动力,驱动着"教"与"学"指向目标的达成并为达成目标而努力,同时又因评价反馈而激发起继续学习的动力,课堂"教"与"学"的质量呈现螺旋上升的趋势,从而实现课堂教学效益。

### (三) 课堂观察,建立三级教学评价机制

为激发教师和学生为"教"、"学"的成功(达标)而教、学的责任感,我们除进行目标激励之外,还运用评价理论与技术建立了三级目标评价机制。

1. 开发"课堂评价的评价量表",关注教师对学习的评价方式及评价效果,指导教师开展过程性、情境性、有效性评价,我们尝试对教师评价实施再评价,将评价纳入对教师评价的范围之内,制定"课堂评价的评价量表"(见表 1),供教研团队通过对评价的实施与观察进行反思,促使其把评价纳入有意识、自觉的、可控的范围之内,增加有效的评价行为。

表 1　课堂评价的评价量表

| 目标 | 评价方式 | 目标适配度 | 评价标准 | 达标程度 |
| --- | --- | --- | --- | --- |
| 目标一 | | | | |
| 目标二 | | | | |
| …… | | | | |

2. 开发“小组目标学习评价量表”(见表 2),关注每一个学生的学习,督促小组成员互学、助学,我们开发此量表让学生自主评价学习行为,实现“以评促学”的评价目的。

表 2　小组目标学习评价量表

| 组别 | 组员 | 自主学习 | | | | | 小组讨论 | | | | | | | 组间交流 | | | | |
| --- | --- | --- | --- | --- | --- | --- | --- | --- | --- | --- | --- | --- | --- | --- | --- | --- | --- | --- |
| | | 学习状态 | 学习方式 | | | | 参与人次 | 是否完成分工 | | 有无充分交流 | | 有无完善 | | 参与人次 | 听取方式 | | 有无争论 | |
| | | 积极 | 消极 | 圈点勾画 | 旁批 | 其他 | | 是 | 否 | 是 | 否 | 有 | 无 | | 只听 | 笔记 | 有 | 无 |

6 人一小组,A 层两人,为学习优异者;B 层三人,为学习进取生;C 层一人,是所谓的后进生——“差生”。这样,在促使“差生”在同学监督之下以良性行为进行学习的同时,促使同学之间互助学习,形成所谓“兵教兵”、“兵助兵”的学习生态。

3. 开发“班级目标学习评价量表”(见表 3),关注整体学生学习质量的提高,从发言质量、课堂检测、作业等多个层面评价小组学习情况,及时反馈评价信息,以激励小组之间展开良性的学习竞争,实现“以评助学”的评价目的。

表 3　班级目标学习评价量表

| 目标 | 评价方式 | 组别 | 达标情况 | | | | | |
| --- | --- | --- | --- | --- | --- | --- | --- | --- |
| | | | 质疑情况 | | 发言情况 | | 课堂检测 | 作业 |
| | | | 质疑次数 | 问题质量 | 发言次数 | 发言质量 | | |
| 目标一 | 第一组 | | | | | | | |
| | 第二组 | | | | | | | |
| | 第三组 | | | | | | | |

另外,我们还建立了“一评二测制度”。“一评”即课堂评价,一目标一落实,一落实一评价,一评价一促进,促使每个学生在学习上都有所进步。“二测”即学习前测与学习后测:前测的主要目的在于测故问新,借以了解学情,确定学生学习的起点;后测主要为篇章或单元测验,考查学生阶段性目标达成情况及延伸迁移的能力,为下阶段学习奠定基础。

评价手段的介入,加强了学科建设,促进了教师专业化发展,增强了教师学生本位意识,使教师之间、学生之间、师生之间形成一个互助、共赢、良性的生态系统,同时,在很大程度上改变了语文教学无目的状态,大大提高了课堂教学效益。2011年4月11日,我们在试点学校郑州市52中举行了"教学评一体化教学展示课"活动,由实验教师苗苗、王芳分别执教《端午的鸭蛋》文本解读课与语言赏析课,引起了与会者的巨大反响,一致反映:教、学、评围绕一个目标展开,课堂教学扎实、有效;学生自学、合作与教师的讲解有机结合,真正做到了先学后教;学生是学习的主人,讨论、探究的学习氛围激发了学生学习的自主性。

然而,教学评一体化教学仍然面临诸多问题,如分层次实施教学及课堂评估的问题、小组内量化评价的合理性及操作性问题、研究性团队的构建问题,等等,都在提醒我们在教学评一体化教学的道路上走得再谨慎一些,理性一些,科学一些;同时,也敦促我们走得更快一些,想得更多一些,做得更实一些。

参考文献

[1] 崔允漷.基于标准的学生学业成就评价[M].上海:华东师范大学出版社,2008.

[2] 皮连生.学与教的心理学[M].上海:华东师范大学出版社,2009.

[3] 崔允漷.有效教学[M].上海:华东师范大学出版社,2009.

## Exploration and Practice of "Instruction-Learning-Assessment Alignment

— Taking Junior High School Chinese Subject as an Example to Explore Effective Ways of the "Classroom Assessment"

Zhen Lu

**Abstract**: In order to enhance the validity of classroom assessment, we have tried a series of experimental researches on "instruction-learning-assessment alignment" from learning aims, classroom observation to reassess classroom assessment. Questions on influences of class outcomes have been clarified, and Chinese teaching outcomes to some extent have been improved.

**Keywords**: classroom assessment; disintegration of curriculum standards; classroom observation

# 课堂评估范式的演进和趋势

## ——从标准化测验到真实性评价

岳刚德

【摘要】课堂评估范式由课堂评估范围、课堂评估技术以及课堂评估功能构成。本文对20世纪初盛行的标准化测验到中后期兴起的真实性评价之间的课堂评估范式转换进行了考察，揭示了课堂评估从过去对学习结果进行量化评定、分级和甄选，开始关注教学情境下以完成真实任务为目的的过程评估范式，以支持、促进和引导学习的发生，指导学生积极建构与真实世界有意义联系的个人经验。基于此，提出以学习为中心的课堂评估范式，通过对课堂教学全程信息的收集、评估和解释，实现课堂评估与教学和学习过程的自然整合，旨在促进学习发生，诊断学习结果，监控学习进展，为制定教学目标以及科学地进行教学决策提供可靠的数据。

【关键词】课堂评估；标准化测验；真实性评价；范式转换

【作者简介】岳刚德/杭州师范大学学科教育研究所副教授

### 一、标准化测验的范式危机

20世纪初，出于对教育评价的客观性的追求，西方国家出现了教育测验运动，其方法论基础和依据是借鉴自然科学研究领域里的统计方法。这一运动的最大成就是开发了“标准化测验（Standardized test）”技术以及诞生了测验行业和一门新型学科——心理测验学。这种以大规模生产选择题的标准化测验，它的每一个题目都有两个核心指标：一是效度，即测验的有效性，也就是测验达到预期的程度；一是信度，即测验的可靠性，测验结果在不同时间和不同情境下的一致性。标准化测验的信度和效度是建立在对测量结果进行统计分析的基础上而得出的，它实际上只有事后的校正意义，而无法在测试前提供其可靠性和有效性的合理依据。

#### （一）标准化测验的评估范围

20世纪初，由于科学主义和行为主义盛行，使得对“刺激—反应”的客观化和精确化追求成为编制智力测验量表的理论和实践动力。随着适龄儿童人数的剧增，儿童需要通过甄别、区分，被公平地安置在一个适当的地方，这无疑扩大了智力测验量表的社会需求，使得该量表由过去通过心理测验辨别智力落后的人，逐渐成为测量学校所有儿童智力的主要工具，许多学校因此成立了“测验部”。[1]早期教育测验的研究侧重于测验的客观化与标准化。其中客观化主要体现在两个方面：一是标准客观化；二是定分客观化。[2]旨在防止人为的主观因素影响评估结果的客观性。于是，通过各种量表的编制，严格地测量学生的各种心理品质，并给予精确的指标，成为各种类型心理测验共同遵守的编制指导原则。为此，美国心理学家詹姆斯·麦基恩·卡特尔指出："心理学若不立根于实验与测量上，决不能达到自然科学之准确；如果我们有一个普遍的标准，使在不同时间和地点得到的结果可以比较的话，那么测验的科学性和实用性的价值必然会大有提高。"[3]他主张建立常模，制定标准，力求使教育测验理论得到进一步完善和发展。到了20世纪二三十年代，心理学家开发了越来越多的标准化测验，一时间学生成绩测验风靡全国。

标准化测验就是对所有不同的被试，不考虑测验的时间和地点，按照相同标准进行有目的的控制、评分和解释，最后，通过对学生的分数进行比较，实现甄别、分级和安置的评估目的。这种把被试通过测验得到的分数作为其学习结果的量化评定，可能影响对课堂教学的认识和评价：一是这种相对于学习发生的滞后延迟性反馈机制，无法从根本上观照儿童的学习过程，并进行合理干预，造成教学和评估的剥离与脱节；二是把被试的学习过程简单化，承认教师的课堂教学行为和学生的学习结果之间的线性因果关系，强化了教师在课堂教学中对学生学习控制的合法性。因此，通过研究教师的课堂教学行为，合理推测学生的学习结果，拓展了课堂评估研究的新视野。

在研究课堂教学中教师行为与学生学习相关性时，弗兰德斯采用"社会相互作用模式"分析教师的课堂教学行为对学生的学习态度和学习效果的影响。他从教师语言、学生语言和无效语言三个维度十种情况提出了"弗兰德斯互动分析系统"，并用量表、评分标准和矩阵定量分析课堂中师生的言语互动行为。通过大量的研究，他指出，教师的直接影响较多时，会导致学生参与的不足；教师间接影响较多时，学生的参与就更多。因此，教师应该更多地对学生施加间接影响，多提问少讲授，要用更多的接纳和表扬来激励学生，在教学中要充分的考虑学生所表达的想法和感情。在后来的研究中，他还发现教师行为的变化与学生成效的关系是非线性的，认为教师在不同的情境中的最理想行为是：较低水平的间接影响更适合于事实类和技能类的学习任务，较高水平的间接影响则更适于抽象推理类和创造类的学习任务。[4]

**（二）标准化测验的评估技术**

标准化测验具有规范的标准，它在各个环节按照系统的科学程序组织，对误差进行严格控制，是一个系统化、科学化、规范化的施测过程。作为一种课堂评估技术，标准化测验的显著特征是测验全过程的标准化，即按照标准确定测验的目的和计划，实施项目编制标准化、测验管理标准化、评分记分标准化、分数解释标准化等。

首先，标准化测验根据测试目的，将教学目标中的知识目标分解为许多知识点，并选择重点内容进行测试，以考察学生对知识的理解、掌握和熟练程度。由于学生在某一领域中所要学习的知识有很多，如果对一个领域进行全面的测试，那么试卷就会很长。因此，标准化测验经常只测试其中的一小部分知识。这样测验的知识点经常只能覆盖该领域的40%—50%，有时会更少，而且为了提高试题的区分度，通常试题编制者编制题目的难度一般是让大约一半的学生答对。这样，出题者就会避免那种让绝大多数或少数学生答对的题。为了编制这样的试题，标准化测验就会避免出一些学生都掌握的内容，而这些内容往往由于其重要且被教师在教学过程中反复强调，学生们也就掌握了它们。这样，标准化测验将教师和学生的课堂教学带入一个怪圈：即教师们越是强调重要的知识或能力，标准化测验就越不会考；而教师为了提高学生学习成绩不得不对许多可能被测试到的、并不重要的知识点猛下功夫，随意增加大量课外习题。不仅在课业上增加了学生的负担，同时也容易引起师生的应试过程中出现过度的心理焦虑。

其次，为了防止测验过程中出现人为主观的因素干扰，题目设计者在命制试题时，力求从以下三个方面予以克服：一是对题干部分要求结构良好，以保证问题结果的唯一性；二是采用选择题、是非题、匹配题和填空题等题目类型；三是采用计算机读卡技术判卷。并以信度、效度、难度和区分度四个指标作为监控试题编制的质量标准，为标准化测验结果的解释提供合理依据。

第三，测验之所以要实现标准化，目的在于提高测验的科学性，保证测验对测验目的的有效性以及测验结果的可靠性。因此，标准化测验的组织和管理必须遵循一套标准化的程序：(1)标准化测验须经预测；(2)对测验的条件要求严格；(3)计分方法标准化；(4)必须编制常模。[5]

第四，为了进一步提高标准化测验的信度，考试机构对测验后的原始分数进行处理，用平均分数、标准分数和T分数对测验结果进行校正和解释，并以此作为建立考试常模的重要数据，为不同地区、不同学校、不同班级的测验结果进行比较提供依据。

**(三) 标准化测验的评估功能**

20世纪20年代末，美国经历了一场严重的资本主义经济危机。这场经济危机同样给教育带来了深刻的影响。教育资金的匮缺、青年的失业等等，促使人们对教育的社会价值、社会效果进行深入的反思。人们认识到虽然教育测验运动对学力测验的研究和教育成就的定量客观化方面取得了一定成效，但由于它不可能将学生的价值观、情感、态度、人格等因素全面纳入评估范围进行评定，从而引起了人们对教育测量的深刻反思和批判。

作为一种诊断工具，标准化测验多数使用常模参照标准测验，教育工作者和家长可以根据或参照全国常模、地区常模或学校常模，对学生的学业成就进行推断。因此，常模参照标准测验通过测验结果的比较和使用，实现其甄选、区分和安置的功能。

首先，标准化测验承担着学生分流的工作，从小学的能力分组到高中不同程度进阶课程的设置，测验的成绩经常被教师和学校视为对学生采取不同指导的相对客观的依据。但是，仅凭一次的测验成绩就用以诊断学生的学业成就，这不仅夸大了标准化测验的功能，实际上也忽视了测验的公正性和公平性。正如格兰特·威金斯指出的那样，"测验分数只不过是成绩的一个指数而已，将它看得比成绩本身还重要并不是理智的，这就像一位医生，只注意体温计的读数而不在意病人的真正身体健康，而这一点恰恰是很容易被模糊的，因为人们经常将测验的分数当作'真正的成绩'"。[6]

其次，标准化测验的结果是教育管理部门考察学校绩效责任的重要指标。教育管理部门根据标准化测验的结果，建立绩效评估指标体系，以此作为考察学校教学质量的评估手段。由于对影响学生学习的复杂性估计不足，对学生智力结构的认识缺陷，以及标准化测验评估范围的局限性，使得这一评估手段运用的合理性、有效性和公平性普遍遭致广泛的诉议。

第三，作为一种延迟性课堂评估技术，标准化测验以学生的学习结果为评估对象。虽然这种评估技术已经与课堂教学和学习的过程剥离，但是其结果却可能决定或影响学生一生的命运。许许多多在学校成绩平平后来却在社会不同领域表现卓越，由于标准化测验设计的测验结果与实际效果之间存在的反差或不一致性，使得该评估的效度和信度均遭到质疑。

综上所述，标准化测验采用分数量化评定技术，从测验计划实施到结果解释的全程质量标准指标监控，显而易见，这种课堂评估范式可以为决策和教学提供有用的信息，但对教师并没有什么特别价值。这种评估范式自身存在的危机，集中体现在"认分不认人"、评估技术与课堂教学和学习过程剥离、评估延迟等，已经遭遇来自方方面面的质疑和批判。于是，寻求一种新的替代性课堂评估范式，成为课堂评估范式演进、转换的根本动力。

## 二、真实性评价的兴起

在对课堂教学的结果进行标准化测验的同时，课堂中发生的师生互动行为进行量化编码研究也在进行。与此同时，对课堂中发生的事情进行"经验性、质性和诠释性的研究活动也在展开"。[7]这种研究范式的转型表明，当数据既不简单也没有共同标准时，教育情境的复杂性遭遇已经不可避免。它要求评估与生活结成比与个人成绩更温和、更复杂、更密切的联系。美国课程专家埃利奥特·W.艾斯纳提出真实性评价及特征，重新诠释和评估教育实践中新的评定活动。这种基于适应情境学习或背景认知而提出的评估技术，不仅用于评定学生在学校完成的学习任务，而且要反映学生在校外真实世界中遭遇的任务；它所评定的学生作业不仅反映了学生当下的学习状况，还揭示了学生解决问题的过程，而且一个问题拥有一个以上可行的解决方法或答案，允许学生选择一种表现形式展示自己的学习成果。由此可见，在真实世界中，个体创造自己真实的反应，并在对经验的反应中创造自己喜欢的方式。

### （一）真实性评价的评估范围

作为一种替代标准化测验的课堂评估范式，真实性评价暗示了一个评价发展的趋势：评价同构于课程和教学，随时迎接真实性任务的挑战并支持和促进真实情境下的问题解决。于是，评估学生的真实学习需求，收集学生知识掌握过程的信息，设计真实性任务，以及学生学习过程中问题解决能力和批判性思维能力的发展，成为探讨真实性评价不能绕开的问题。

真实性评价以学生的学习过程为中心，它通过让学生完成真实性任务，积极主动地参与整个教学过程，同时在厘定评估范围时，关注学生的个体差异和不同学习需求。由学生参与制定标准，可以清楚地了解通过教学自己应当知道什么以及自己能做什么。学生对学习目标的认识、态度以及伴随学习过程中开展的自我评价和同伴评价，不仅有利于激发学生学习动机，评估个人的学习进展，而且在教学过程中，通过评估随时捕捉学生的学习需求。

学生的学习需求因人而异，即使是同一学习者，在不同的学习情境下，当遭遇相同的学习任务时也具有不同的表现形式。这不仅意味着影响学生学习的因素多种多样，而且在学生的学习过程中，教学发生的机制本身是复杂而非线性的。因此，准确地评估学习者的学习需求以及学习过程中学习者之间的相互关系，既是教学决策的先决条件，也是实现学习目标的首要前提。

众所周知，当学习者在遭遇真实的学习任务时，会运用个人经验尝试性地表征、分解、组合和描述活动对象，提出自己的解释性框架。而真实性学习任务的非结构良好特征，对学习者的日常思维提出新的挑战，并要求其具备一定的问题思维能力。因此，确立课堂评估的质量评价标准，评估学习者的思维层次或水平，对于发展学习者的思维能力，提高学习者的问题解决能力，为实施真实性评价提供了学习进展评估的参照性框架。

问题解决能力的培养既是学校创新教育实践的目的之一，也是真实性评价的评估对象。首先，对问题来源、问题属性以及问题域进行类比分析，确定问题提出的背景或情境，问题的焦点以及问题范围；其次，根据问题解决能力的培养层次，可以从三个层面制定评估标准：一是学习者提出问题的能力，着重评估学习者的问题意识；二是学习者分析和综合问题的能力，着重评估学习者的经验、思维能力和问题域；三是学习者解决问题的能力，着重于学习成果的评估。第三，对问题解决方案进行评估、记录，并将相关评价材料和反馈信息装入学习者成长档案袋。

### （二）真实性评价的评估技术

真实性评价的兴起并不意味着标准化测验的终结。相反，测验在真实性评价中仍然是一种非常有力的评价工具。真实性评价对标准化测验的否定源于对传统测验标准的唯一性质疑，因此，倡导评估技术的多元化是真实性评价的基本理念和指导原则。

标准化测验对真实性评价的贡献主要体现在两个方面：一是把事实性知识作为工具，运用测验手段判断学生对描述性内容理解的水平；二是制定质量评估标准体系，确立评估标准及其能被测量的达成情况和熟练性水平之间的内在对应逻辑，即应该达到的质量标准与通过测量实际达到的熟练性水平之间的量化效应关系。其中，测验技术在确定二者之间效应关系中起到了评价工具的作用。

在选择和描述真实任务的具体评价标准时，需要遵守一套既定的程序：首先要制定评估计划，明确评价的重点、具体任务以及学生需要掌握的结构性较强的知识和技能；其次，将与真实任务相关的知识技能和学习过程分成不同类型和层次；第三，描述学生学习取得成功的可以观察的具体行为和过程。[8]第四，对与评价标准相符的学习成果和行为表现评分，并及时记录。显而易见，真实性评价不仅要求学生将学到的知识应用到与教材呈现的类似情境之中，而且还要求其建立与生活世界的联系，解决日常生活中遭遇的、真实的类似情境中发生的、更具复杂性的问题。因此，根据评价标准运用课堂观察、成长记录袋和自我评价等课堂评估技术，对于学生在学习过程中的行为表现、学习成果以及学生之间因完成学习任务形成的伙伴关系进行整体评估，凸显真实性评价替代标准化测验的发展趋势。

课堂观察是收集课堂教学信息反馈的有效评估技术，它包括对教师教学行为的观察、学生学习表现的观察以及对“教”与“学”之间相互作用机制的课堂呈现的记录。Albikoff 和 Gittelman 把儿童的课堂行为分为指向任务的行为、脱离任务的行为和与任务不相关的行为共计十类，建立了儿童行为观察的十分法系统。[9]Jerome & Robert 对教师课堂言语行为进行了编码，首先，教师根据学生行为与真实任务的关系表现为言语认同和言语不认同两类教学行为；其次，根据学生在任务中的表现做出表扬、提示与批评的反馈；第三，对学生的总体表现表达出学习认同和不认同、社会认同与不认同、不恰当的认同与不认同，无认同或不认同等行为。[10]Greenwood 等建立了班级里学生和教师的观察编码系统，对在课堂教学情境中发生的教学行为进行归类观察记录。[11]此外，国内有学者围绕“学生学习”，从“课程性质，教师教学和课堂文化”与“学生学习”之间的关系构建“4 个维度，20 个视角，68 个观察点”的课堂观察框架和工具。[12]

成长记录袋是真实记录学生成长过程的学习作品，在某一具体层面反映学生的学习兴趣、成长经历以及进步发展的路径。通过研究和评估成长记录袋，可以及时对学生的学习与发展提供专业反馈和指导。同时，根据学习与发展之间的逻辑关系，成长记录袋可以分为以下三种类型：一是成果类成长记录袋；二是过程类成长记录袋；三是阶梯式成长记录袋。由此可见，成长记录袋不仅反映了课堂教学情境下学生完成真实任务的行为表现，而且，它本身为课程标准的研制和教学标高的确立提供了可靠的实证资料和原始数据。

自我评价是个体成长过程中对自身行为表现的接纳和反思，通过自我反馈进行校正，通过持续学习努力达到较高标准。正如 Hein 和 Price 指出的那样，“学生的自我评价为教师提供了独特的信息，也激励学生自我反思。尽管有时学生的自我评价过高，但是他们对自己所完成的学习、思考如何改善个人学习、自己从事的活动以及不理解的东西都写出了坦率的评论”[13]。在评价过程中，自我评价与同伴评价之间组合形成良性互动，可以进一步帮助学习者在学科课堂学习中完善自我，建立良好的学习效能感。因此，自我评价主要采用以下四种常见的方法：一是反思性日志；二是核查表；三是同伴互动；四是反馈商讨和目标设置。[14]

### （三）真实性评价的评估功能

与传统标准化测验不同的是，真实性评价直接面向与生活世界相联系的真实性任务，这种结构不良问题的解决是对学生思维能力的挑战。因此，从该种意义上讲，真实性评价的实施有助于在学校场域中培养具有创新精神和实践能力的人才。

情境的模拟性、任务的真实性以及评价的过程性和开放性是真实性评价的四个特征，正是基于上述特性，使得真实性评价在促进学生学习的过程中发挥了引导、提升和监控的作用，主要体现在以下三个方面：一是模拟生活世界的真实学习情境，有利于儿童沟通科学世界和生活世界的对话，建构知识的个人意义；二是真实性任务的复杂性对儿童分析或解构问题提出了新的挑战，有助于促进思维能力的发展和问题解决能力的提高；三是评价与标准、教学和学习自然地整合，使得宏大的课程目标、真实的评价标准和可以观察、测量的学习结果在课堂教学过程中一起呈现，评价本身成为促进学生学习发生的技术，而且真实性评价面向生活世界开放，其评价主体的多元化成为拓展学习者学习资源的新路径。

正如前文所述，标准化测验与课堂教学和学习的过程是剥离的。作为一种延迟性评估技术，标准化测验只以学习的结果为测量对象，建立一套标准化的评估体系监控教学质量。这种课堂评估范式虽然在某种意义上发挥诊断教学的功能，但它在本质上是对教学内容的选择性适应，实际上却无法实现对学习的干预，难以对学校课程改革、教学变革和学习方式转变产生影响，因而它必然遭遇被替代性评价取缔的范式危机。真实性评价以真实的教学情境为脉络，以真实性任务的完成为评估对象，通过教学为学习者提供问题解决的机会，把课程标准转化为质量评价标准，以监控学习者达到的学习层次和水平。简言之，在真实性评价过程中，标准、教学和评估是三位一体的。由此可见，在学校层面实施真实性评价，对传统课程范式、教学模式和学习方式提出了挑战，从而促进学校层面的课程变革、教师课堂教学行为的更新和学生学习方式的转变。

真实性评价的实施改变了学习者与评价的关系，过去学习者成为评价的对象即被试，而在真实性评价过程中，学习者被赋予充分的自主性而成为评价的主体，从评价标准的制定，成长档案袋的记录，学习进步的描述到学习成果的交流，学习者全程参与学习和评估过程，激发了学习者内在的学习动机，学习者因此感受到学习的意义，并乐意对学习负责。由此可见，在课堂教学中通过真实性评价的实施，重新建立了学习者与学科之间的关系，在某种意义上帮助学生在学科教学中认识自我，并通过对成功学习的体验建立学习自信。

## 三、一种平衡的课堂评估范式：以学习为中心

通过对课堂评估范式从标准化测验到真实性评价的考察，不难发现，标准化测验的范式危机不仅源于标准单一、缺少多元，而且缺失对评估本身的检视和修正；真实性评价设计的真实性任务受到课堂教学物理空间边界的限制，只能以教学情境的模拟性取代真实性，虽然实

现了对传统课堂评估范式的超越，开始关注对学习过程及进展的监控，但是对于构建促进学生学习的课堂评估质量标准体系而言，真实性评价仅仅是该质量体系中的构成要件之一。因此，开发以学习为中心的课堂评估技术，对学习者的学习需求、参与学习过程和习得的学习结果进行整体评估，这是未来课堂评估范式演进的趋势。

### （一）以学习为中心的课堂评估范围

作为一种旨在促进学习发生的课堂评估范式，以学习为中心的课堂评估主要对学习者的学习需求、学习过程、学习情感、学习方式和学习结果等五个要素进行评估。首先，教师需要使用清晰、友好、直接的语言陈述课堂教学目标，了解和评估学生对学习目标的预期，以及与学习目标相关的知识经验准备；其次，对学生参与课堂教学过程的机会、回答问题的质量、小组合作学习的表现以及课堂交流的内容组织及表达等进行评估；第三，对学习者参与课堂教学的情感进行评估，通过考察学习者学习情感、态度与价值观之间的关联性，对评估结果提出合理的解释；第四，了解学习者的学习方式，发展一种适应学习者的课堂评估技术，以及运用课堂评估引导学习者尝试新的学习方式；第五，抽样对学习者的学习结果进行诊断，使用清晰的语言交流和反馈评估结果，并对学习者如何改进学习以及具体在某方面改进提出专业建议。

对于不同的课堂评估类型，其评估范围也不同。Richard I. Arends & Ann Kilcher 根据课堂教学的目标、过程、结果以及评估的目的、意义和功能把以学习为中心的课堂评估分为以下三类：一类是促进学生学习的评估（Assessment for learning），以诊断性评估和形成性评估为主要技术，其中，诊断性评估重点对学生的先前知识、兴趣、性向、需求和迷失概念（misconceptions）进行评估，形成性评估旨在对学习过程进行评估，监控学习进展，为教师教学决策和学生学习提供有效的信息反馈；二类主张评估即学习（Assessment as learning），以自我评价和同伴评价为主，其中自我评价有利于学生自我导向和自主管理，同伴评价使得同伴之间的相互交流和学习更容易；三类是关于学习的评估（Assessment of learning），即总结性评估，通过评估学习结果对学生的学习进展做出专业诊断，有助于教师了解学生的学习进展，及时调整教学计划。[15]

### （二）以学习为中心的课堂评估技术

课堂评估技术的发展总是受到课堂评估范围的限制。因此，对于以学习为中心的课堂评估而言，如何收集关于学习者学习需求、学习情感、学习方式和学习结果的信息并进行评估，对评估结果提出合理解释，是开发评估技术面临的首要问题。

学习者在学习上存在的问题非一日之寒，而是长期累积而成。因此，合理运用课堂观察，对学生的学习习惯、学习态度和学习方式进行跟踪观察、记录，并结合学习结果评估信息，对学生进行个性化的学习指导，有助于促进学生反思个人的学习范式，不断改进和解决学习过程中存在的问题。

思维能力的发展是课堂教学的核心目标之一，而课堂提问是激发学习积极思考、引导学生正确思考、评估学生思维品质的有力评价工具。在课堂教学过程中，课堂提问的设计、师生、生生之间通过思想对话、智慧碰撞形成的教学理答、学生疑惑的提示或点拨、问题边界拓展及延伸，涉及课堂提问评估技术的合理开发与运用，这个问题在当下课堂评估技术研究领域还未引起足够重视。

合作学习是中小学课堂教学中对学生成长与发展十分具有意义的学习方式。通过异质分组、合作研讨、汇报结果，学生学会了领导、协作、表达与交流，体会了责任和义务的情境意义，习得在真实世界中解决问题需要掌握的知识和技能。因此，分组合作学习的组织与管理工作显得十分必要，特别是关于邀请学生参与分组规则的制定，在合作学习过程中指导学生学会自主管理，有助于训练和培养学生在公民社会中应具备的基本素质和技能。

**（三）以学习为中心的课堂评估功能**

以学习为中心的课堂评估范式秉持一个基本信念：教育影响只有通过自我学习才有可能发生。因此，促进学习发生，诊断学习结果，评估学习情感，通过激发学生积极思考，鼓励学生表达与交流，不断更新自我学习，既是课堂评估追求的目标，也是课堂评估的基本功能。

学习发生的条件是学习者以学习主体的身份和角色介入学习过程。换言之，学习在本质上属于学习者非常具有私人意义的个人事件，只有学习者介入学习过程之后才能感受和体会学习与个人的意义，并通过选择性适应愿意承担学习责任，且对学习结果负责。因此，通过实施课堂评估建设学生参与的课堂评估文化，使学生以学习主体的身份和角色参与课堂评估过程，促进学习发生，是学校落实以学习为中心的课程评估的主要抓手。

信度、效度和公正是评价课堂评估可靠性、有效性和公平性的三个重要指标，以学习为中心的课堂评估立足于课堂教学过程，建立质量评价标准体系，全程收集评估信息和数据并及时反馈、交流评估结果，有利于支持课堂教学，对于教师而言，教师可以根据评估不断调整教学计划，而学生则可以修正当下的学习策略或技能。

学校主要是学习发生的地方，也是学生生活的地方。学生在学校参与的各种活动内容和方式在很大程度上受到学校评估范式的制约。因此，建立以学习为中心的课堂评估质量体系，在促进学生有意义学习发生的同时，促进学生身心健康发展，这是学校教育的职责，也是教育评估的使命。

参考文献

[1] 郭文博，缪丽娟.美国教育标准化测验动因的历史考察[J].集美大学学报，2010(1).

[2] 陈玉琨.教育评估的理论与技术[M].广州：广东高等教育出版社，1986：19.

[3] 陈如平.效率与民主：美国现代教育思想管理研究[M].北京：教育科学出版社，2004：13.

[4] Wittrock (1986). *Handbook of Research on Teaching*. NewYork: macmillan publishing company. 198.

[5] 王汉澜.教育测量学[M].河南:河南大学出版社,1987:173—175.

[6] 王玉衡.美国标准化测验的问题与质疑[J].比较教育研究,2002(9).

[7] [美]埃利奥特·W.艾斯纳.教育想象——学校课程设计与评价[M].李雁冰,主译.北京:教育科学出版社,2008:204.

[8][14] [美]Kathleen Montgomery.真实性评价——小学教师实践指南[M].董奇,等,译.北京:中国轻工业出版社,2004:91,154—162.

[9] Abicoff, H., & Gittelman, R. (1985). *Classroom observation code: A modification of the Stony Brook Code*. Psychopharmacology Bulletin, 21,901-909.

[10] [美]Jerome M. Satter, & Robert D. Hoge.儿童评价[M].陈会昌,等,译.北京:中国轻工业出版社,2008:279.

[11] Greenwood, C. R., Hops, H., Walker, H. M., Guild, J. J., Stokes, J., Young, K. R., Keleman, K. S., & Willardson, M. (1979). Standardized Classroom Management Program: Social Validation and Replication Studies in Utah and Oregon. *Journal of Applied Behavior Analysis*, 12,235-253.

[12] 沈毅,等.课堂观察框架与工具[J].当代教育科学,2007(24).

[13] Hein, G., & Price, S. (1994). *Active assessment for Active Science*. Portsmouth, NH: Heinemann. 31.

[15] Richard I. Arends, & Ann Kilcher. *Teaching for Student Learning: Becoming an Accomplished Teacher*, Routledge Taylor & Francis Group, 2010:136.

## Trends and Evolution of Classroom Assessment: From Standardized Test to Authentic Assessment

Gangde Yue

**Abstract**: The paradigm of classroom assessment is composed of scope, technology and function. This paper has studied the paradigm shift from standardized test to authentic assessment, it is discovered that standardized test used quantification assessment to evaluate learning outcomes in order to grade and arrange the subjects. Authentic assessment is implemented in context of real world, it aims to evaluate the learning process by completing real task from everyday life, and to promote student's learning, to direct to an active learning about how to construct the meaning of real world. On the basis of comparative studies on two paradigms above, the researcher has advanced a balanced classroom assessment focused on learning, which collect information about the whole process of teaching and learning in classroom, and evaluate the assessment through interpreting information. It is discovered that balanced assessment has offered the data to draw up teaching plan and to decide when or how to teach next step.

**Keywords**: classroom assessment; standardized test; authentic assessment; paradigm shift

# 让评价引领教学

## ——基于课程标准的学生学业成就评价探索

佟 柠

【摘要】课程改革的核心问题是教学与评价的变革。如何让教学与评价的变革切实依循新课程改革的方向推进？如何让体现着国家意志的学科课程标准在教学与评价中得到落实？江苏省锡山高级中学从探寻有效教学的技术路径为突破口，与华东师范大学课程与教学研究所合作，把改革的着力点放在了基于课程标准的教学实践探索上。锡山高中基于课程标准建构从模块到单元的教学目标体系、评价体系，努力让每一个教学活动都有明晰的指向、确定的标准，让教学行为与策略的改进有明确的依据。学校以课题研究为依托，探索各学科课程标准分解路径；以必修科目为试点，学评结合，推进标准、教学与学业水平测试的一致性；以变革课堂为目的，基于标准，促使课程标准与日常教学有效衔接。基于课程标准的教学实践探索，使锡山高中收获了教学质量的大幅提升、教师专业的蓬勃发展和学生的全面而有个性的发展。

【关键词】基于课程标准；学生学业成就评价

【作者简介】佟柠/江苏省锡山高级中学中教高级教师

众所周知，教学与评价的变革是课程改革的核心问题。如何让教学与评价的变革切实依循新课程改革的方向推进？如何让体现着国家意志的学科课程标准在教学与评价中得到落实？这是深化课程改革必须关注也应该解决的难题。从教学大纲到课程标准是一场重大的变革。新课程以课程标准的形式规定了学生应达到的学业目标，并以此引导和规范着学生的学业成就评价，它意味着学校课堂教学真正要从关注教的行为转向关注学生学习后的变化，意味着教学评价要从关注结果转向促进后续学习。正是基于这样的认识，我们把改革的着力点放在了基于课程标准的学生学业成就评价的探索上，并希望通过评价来引领课堂教学的变革。

2005年秋，在江苏整体进入新课程改革的时候，我们曾尝试改变教学目标的叙写方式，要求教师站立于学习者的角度，选用外显行为动词，陈述学生学习后的变化，以此作为改变我们的课堂、提升教学有效性的一个切入点，引导教师在对"是陈述学生学习后的行为变化吗?""如何检测、观察这种变化?"的不断追问中，澄清教学目标、规范叙写目标。为了评估教学目标的达成状况，我们集中探索"目标导引教学"的课题，并借鉴华东师范大学崔允漷教授指导研发的课堂观察技术，改进课堂教学。应该说，这些变革都使得课堂发生了变化，都富有成效，但都还没有系统地、全面地、根本性地变革我们现有的课堂；而且随着探索的深入、思考的深入，面临的问题也就越来越明晰地呈现出来:不基于课程标准,如何科学确定每一课时的教学目标?又如何建构科学的评价体系?如果将评价的指向集中于学习的结果,那对于学习者的后续学习又有多大的益处?[1]

2008年11月,通过与崔允漷教授等专家多次的交流、探讨,改革的话题也越来越集中到一个关键词上:评价,为了促进学习的评价。

基于课程标准的学生学业成就评价,它不是简单地对学习结果进行评定或比较,而是在发现学生与课程标准要求的差距的过程中,不断调整教学、反馈信息以促进后续学习,其价值指向不仅是"对学习的评价",更是"为了学习的评价",属于促进学习的评价范式。然而,我们清醒地看到:身处教学一线的教师,对评价范式的转型还了解甚少,对促进学生学习的评价的基本技术还不甚熟悉,实践层面的探索也刚刚起步,国内也还缺少可资借鉴的成熟经验。这一切都提醒我们,这种探索注定需要一个长期而艰苦的过程。[2]

三年多来,我们以课题研究为依托,逐步进入教学评价的实质性领域,主要是基于课程标准建构从模块到单元、到知识点的教学目标体系、评价体系,努力让每一个教学活动都有明晰的指向、确定的标准,让教学行为与策略的改进有明确的依据。

## 一、以课题研究为依托,集智求解,探索各学科课程标准分解路径

从学校层面上构建基于课程标准的学生学业成就评价是一个系统工程,它不仅需要学校、专家、教师形成合力展开探索,行政力量与学术力量的相互协调保证研究实效,更需要集中力量突破"如何使学生学业成就评价建立在课程标准之上"这一关键问题,而解决这个问题的前提是科学分解课程标准。

2009年1月,崔允漷教授为我校教师开设讲座,系统介绍了基于标准的学生学业成就评价的理论基础、促进学习的课堂评价框架以及国外的相关经验。崔教授提出了让老师们眼前一亮的话题:"评价不仅仅是证明学生当前拥有什么,更重要的是让学生知道一次考试与后续学习的关系,今后努力的方向,使得后续学习表现得更好……"与此同时,由崔允漷教授和他的团队撰写的《基于标准的学生学业成就评价》一书中的许多内容,如"基于标准的学生学业成就评价的含义、模式;基于标准的命题;基于标准的表现性评价"等问题不断激发着教师们对自己的日常教学以及评价行为进行思考,助燃了研究的热情。因此,近40位骨干老师自愿组织研究团队,期望选择一个子课题深入研究。经过三次选题沙龙,学校形成了27个子课题组,160余名教师主动参与到课题研究中来,一个空前庞大的课题团队在锡山高中形成。虽然各学科的课程标准有差异,但分解课程标准成了老师们研究的重点。以数学组为例,大家认为现在的《高中数学课程标准》中只有模块课程目标,而单元目标和知识点目标必须明确和细化。为此,数学组将课题锁定为"高中数学必修1、4模块课程目标分解与评价研究"。[3]

探索的帷幕从课程标准的分解拉开。经过课题组的前期探索,锡山高中开始全员参与探

寻各学科课程标准分解的路径。2009 年 9 月，全校在报告大厅举行集体备课展评大会，展评的内容是从课程标准到教学目标的分解以及相应的评价手段、评价方法。所有教研组长一一走上主席台，展示备课成果，并随机抽取一个“样本”进行现场点评。在大会上，主持人和报告人说得最多的一个词就是:课程标准。课题进入到了以教研组为单位的全员参与研究阶段。

为什么要开展全员参与式的研究，而且是广泛的、深入的和真实的全员参与式的课题研究？我们认为，基于标准的学生学业成就评价进入到了课程的核心领域，我们的经验还不多，不同的学科有不同的特点，所以不能完全照搬某一学科的标准分解路径来分解所有的学科课程标准，我们需要各学科独立开展真实的探索。因此，让更多的老师加入进来，让更多的思想展开碰撞，让课题研究活动与教师的教研活动紧密融合起来，才能够达成开展真研究、实现真发展的目的，也才能够确保各学科课程标准分解的科学性与可操作性。

因此，学校建立了每两周一次的以“课程标准分解与教学目标设定”为主题的教研活动新机制，教研组和课题组共同成为课题推进的主体，采用集体教研形成《模块课程纲要》的方式，分学科按模块研究制订模块学习目标、教学内容及进度安排，重点要求形成模块学习评价方案。在此基础上，各学科进一步将模块学习目标分解为单元、知识点教学目标，形成配套评价方案，使之成为学科教学的法典。

当然，我们也遇到了不少困难。比如，由于有些学科的课程标准过于凸显过程与方法，对知识与技能的表述不够明晰，让老师感觉无从下手实施标准分解，或者简单处理、照搬照抄其他学科的分解技术，从而引发教师对课程标准分解技术科学性与有效性的怀疑；还有些学科老师感受到在课程标准分解的过程中，关注知识与技能的分解比较容易，而对情感态度价值观、过程与方法等方面的重视与关照则比较困难……这些问题都在研究的过程中逐一暴露出来了，但是，这也让我们进一步看到，只有经历全员参与这样一个研究的过程，研究的成果才会更加客观、科学，也才可能被广大教师所采纳与接受，研究的成果才会不仅仅属于少数教师，而是属于广大教师。

2010 年 1 月 16 日，带着历经一年的探索，语文、数学、英语、物理、地理、体育等课题组代表带着案例向专家介绍课程标准的分解路径。

语文学科分析了《语文课程标准》呈现方式特点、苏教版教材编写的个性特点，剖析了语文教学所面临的无序、随意以及文本多解的实际教学困难，提出了“基于文本、寻向定格、构建目标”的标准分解路径。英语学科介绍了“基于文本、回溯标准、构建目标、运用表现性评价来设计表现性任务、制订评分规则”的标准分解路径案例。崔允漷教授等专家对两个学科的标准分解路径表示认可，认为两个学科在标准分解的路径上有一定的相似性，即依据特定的文本，回溯对应的标准要求，确定具体的教学目标，并认为从文本出发定目标是可行的。

数学组、地理组、物理组、化学组、信息技术组等主要采取根据课程标准、教学要求、考试说明，并基于学生已有的认知水平开展标准分解的技术路径，构建本学科的模块目标、单元目标以及知识点教学目标。专家对以上学科的标准分解思路基本认可，认为对于内容标准已经写得比较清晰的学科，在基本的分解流程与路径确定之后，可以在分解标准、确定目标后进入基于目标的课堂教学与评价的探索。[4]

## 二、以必修科目为试点，学评结合，推进标准、教学与学业水平测试的一致性

基于标准的内涵是要实现标准、教学与评价的一致。[5]一致性是国家课程标准被有效执行的体现，是引导教学目标回归课程标准内在要求、使评价活动指向学习内容标准的必要保证。因此，让教师自编的检测建立在课程标准之上，就能够减少教学过程中的“无用功”。

2009年我校高二必修学科教师正是在“基于标准”的理念指导下，重新审视自己的教学观念与行为，不断追问：每节课的目标来自何处？这些目标对于教师、对于学生都清晰吗？可检测吗？教师在编制这些目标时的依据充分吗？与国家课程标准的关系有多大？与学业水平测试要求有何关系？我们平时的教学主要是基于经验、基于教科书还是基于标准？在教之前，我们真的清楚该内容面对这样的学生应该“教到什么程度”吗？[6]

教师们重新研究学科《课程标准》与《江苏省普通高中学业水平测试（必修科目）说明》，尝试清晰地勾画出学生学习必修模块之后预期的学习结果，并对学生所达成的学业水平等级做出了统一和明确的要求，努力使每一位备课组教师都去思考课程标准、教学与评价的一致性问题，真正沿着有效教学的方向前进。

如何将内容标准转变成学习表现标准是生物学科选择的突破路径，这在基于标准的学生学业成就评价中是一个极为关键的问题，也是基于标准的评价中的瓶颈问题。生物教师在高二生物学业水平测试的复习中，解读《普通高中生物课程标准》中规定的内容标准和《江苏省普通高中学业水平测试（必修科目）说明》的范围和要求，将《课程标准》要求和《说明》中的知识点整理和细化为学习表现标准，学评结合，基于学习表现标准设计评价试题，检测复习效度。

地理学科遵循“目标来源于课程标准；评价设计先于教学设计；评价设计嵌入教学流程……”这些基于标准的教学与评价的特征，力求实现教学与评价相融合，确定出“研读课程标准（测试说明），理解课程标准（测试说明）；重构教学目标，确定学习表现标准；设计评价方案，嵌入教学流程；实施课堂教学，反馈评价结果；改进教学策略，支持后续学习”的基于标准的教学与评价流程。[7]

2009年江苏省学业水平测试成绩揭晓：锡山高中高二考生全员通过学业水平测试；参加生物学科学业水平测试的13个班中有7个班达A率为100%；参加地理学科学业水平测试的13个班级中有4个班级A率达到了100%。在总结与反思学生在学业水平测试中所取得的成绩的过程中，各备课组教师们深感实施基于课程标准的教学与评价，摒弃仅仅基于经验或教材来判断学生学习效果的评价行为，通过设计科学的评价方案和有效的“评价样题”，不断获得与目标紧密联系的、教师教到什么程度、学生在学业上进步的“证据”，是引导学生走向学业成

功的关键。2010 年学校学业水平测试必修学科达 4A 的人数达至江苏省第一。

一位老教师的感触也许从一个侧面朴素地揭示了这种变革的价值:一辈子捧着《大纲》教书,心里只想着教什么、教多少;课改有了新"课标",心里才真正装进了学生,教学才做到了"目中有人,胸中有底"。而锡山高中的课堂正因为对"人"的关注、对"底"的把握才变得生动而有效,才呈现出"教得得法、学得轻松、考得满意"的景象。

## 三、以变革课堂为目的,基于标准,促使课程标准与日常教学有效衔接

在推进基于标准的学生学业成就评价的过程中,我们始终以一系列问题的追问来保持研究不偏离航线,那就是,我们的研究变革课堂了吗?我们促使课程标准与日常教学有效衔接了吗?

基于标准的学生学业成就评价不是一个凌驾于教学之上的独立系统,而应当是教学的一个组成部分,[8]它在本质上是教学的一种思想。评价是获得设计、调整教学所必需的信息和推进学生学习的手段,是教—学过程中不可分割的一部分,评价与教学应该是一体化的。[9]

应该说,促进课程标准与日常教学无缝衔接的关键是教学与评价的有机融合。因此,我们不仅自上而下将课程标准分解为教学目标,在标准与教师的教学设计之间建立实质性的联系,将标准纳入教学设计;而且自下而上,通过设计与目标紧密联系与匹配的评价方法获得学生学业进步的过程性证据,让教学目标成为教学与评价相互融合的纽带。我们进一步扬弃把评价等同于标准化考试的观点,大力倡导表现性评价等更能体现学生综合学习结果的评价方式。例如,体育、艺术、校本课程等的教师不断探索基于目标的表现性评价,转变评价方式,让学生参与到评分规则的制订中去,切实地从关注教师的教转到关注学生的学。学校也通过组织课堂教学展示、教学设计评比等活动持续推进基于标准的教学与评价的有机融合。

我校教师曾参加"无锡—新加坡中小学校长论坛"的教学展示活动。新加坡教育部学校司督导陈碧娴女士这样评价说,"教师把课程标准的要求转化为长长的问题链,用不断提问的方式带领学生层层深入探讨新知识,是一堂高效的课"。嘉诺撒仁爱会小学张孝琼校长则认为"教师让学生对自己的活动表现进行评价,有利于形成学生的自我概念,促进教学目标的达成"。

## 四、以发展教师为宗旨,创新机制,提升教师评价素养与职业幸福感

在基于课程标准的学生学业成就评价实践探索过程中,我们把发展教师做为重要的宗旨和价值追求,大力倡导"让教师真正过上学习的、研究的、合作共进的专业生活",并将之作为组织各项研究活动的原则,不仅致力于教师的评价素养和研究品质的提升,更要使教师不断体验到职业的幸福感,收获专业发展的乐趣。为此,我们不断创新校本教研机制,探索出了课题组深度汇谈、教研组专题研讨以及读书交流沙龙等制度。这些制度不仅确保了实践探索的深入、持续与有效开展,而且使教师享有了具备研究品质的专业化生活。

在一次对课题组教师的访谈中，几个关键词成为教师发自内心的感受：合作、踏实、判断、专业、一致性、基于证据……

老师们认为，在进行基于标准的评价设计与实施的时候，必须要学会合作。无论是课程标准的分解、教学目标的确定还是表现性评价的开发等都需要教师群策群力。可以说，基于标准的学生学业成就评价只能是专家、教师、管理者和社会人士长期合作的成果。

教师教到什么程度，学生学到什么程度，是教师必须面对的一个专业判断。做出科学判断，需要一定的工具支撑，需要基于证据。

踏实是教师高质量履行教育职责后的心安，是一种专业感觉，也是一种专业自信。踏实的核心问题是教师有了明确的评价依据，把握住了学生的学习状态，心里有了底。[10]

一年多来，全校老师共同阅读交流了《基于标准的学生学业成就评价》、《有效教学》、《促进学习的学生参与式评价》等有关学术著作，并将之运用于教学实践。在全校的读书交流大会上，一位青年教师就曾与大家分享研究的喜悦，讲述了她如何运用《促进学习的学生参与式评价》一书中的相关理论，设计并运用"物理探究学习评价方案"，并将成果发表在核心期刊上的故事。

在衡量教师专业发展的诸多指标中，课题组成员均显示出了很强的专业发展势头。这些教师的课堂教学以教学与评价相融合为特色，在全国、省、市频获一等奖；围绕着"基于标准的学生学业成就评价"主题所撰写的二十多篇学术论文发表在核心期刊上；2010 年两位课题组成员被评为江苏省特级教师，6 位成员入选为无锡大市学科带头人，3 位成员入选江苏省 333 工程第三层次培养对象。

基于课程标准的学生学业成就评价实践探索，我们收获的不仅是教学质量的大幅提升、教师专业的蓬勃发展，更重要的是坚定了这样的信念：有效来自科学，科学基于标准。

参考文献

[1][2] 唐江澎.带着信念，我们启程[J].基础教育课程，2009(3).

[3] 佟柠.课堂评价研究，原来别有一番天地[J].基础教育课程，2009(3).

[4] 佟柠.全员参与课程标准分解[J].基础教育课程，2010(4).

[5] 崔允漷，等.基于标准的学生学业成就评价[M].上海：华东师范大学出版社，2008：110.

[6][7] 佟柠.我们的教学基于标准吗[J].基础教育课程，2009(7).

[8] 崔允漷，等.基于标准的学生学业成就评价[M].上海：华东师范大学出版社，2008：207.

[9] 崔允漷，等.基于标准的学生学业成就评价[M].上海：华东师范大学出版社，2008：208.

[10] 佟柠.路是对的，就不怕走不通[J].基础教育课程，2009(8).

# Let Assessment Lead Teaching

## —— Exploration of Students' Academic Achievement Evaluation Based on the Curriculum Standards

Ning Tong

**Abstract**: The core issue of curriculum reform is the reform of teaching and assessment. How can we push forward the reform of teaching and assessment according to the new curriculum reform? How can we implement the subject curriculum standards which embody the will of the state in teaching and assessment? Jiangsu Xishan senior high school cooperating with the Institute of Curriculum and Teaching of East China Normal University, takes the seeking for effective teaching techniques as the breakthrough point and puts the focus of the reform on the exploration of teaching practice which is based on curriculum standards. Xishan senior high school constructs a module to unit system and an assessment system on the basis of curriculum standards, aiming to provide every teaching activity with clear instructions and specific standards as well as to provide the improvement of teaching behavior and teaching strategy with a clear basis. The school explores the ways to decompose the curriculum standards of each subject, relying on theme study. It combines learning and evaluation and at the same time promotes the consistency of standards, teaching and academic proficiency test, by taking compulsory subjects as the experiment target. Based on the standards, the school also promotes the effective convergence of curriculum standards and daily teaching in order to reform the class. And the exploration of this kind of teaching practice has made Xishan senior high school improve its teaching quality dramatically, teachers' professional development as well as students' overall and individual development.

**Keywords**: on the basis of curriculum standards; students' academic achievement assessment

# 第四部分

# 课堂评价与教师专业发展

# Standardized Student Assessments: Which Appropriation by Teachers? Which Effects on Their Practices?

Jean-François Chesné

Chef du bureau de l'évaluation des actions éducatives et des expérimentations

**Abstract**: PACEM (Project for acquisition of competencies by students in mathematics during compulsory schooling) is a project of the DEPP (French national Directorate of Evaluation, Prospective and Performance) which integrates four main dimensions: student assessment, teachers' training, observation of individual practices in classrooms and study of the dynamics between teachers within the same school. Its main objective is to bet on changes of practices induced by a training course based on the results of students of a test taken at the start of school year. Two other tests measure pupils' progress: the first one at the end of the first year, and the other one at the end of the second year.

The design of the experimentation is built on a theoretical frame linked to the theory of activity: that of the so-called "double approach", didactic and ergonomic (Robert and Rogalski). This frame allows analysis of teachers' practices relative to students' results while considering proposed tasks and the constraints linked to the teachers' daily practices, in order to determine what could vary in these practices. In a second phase, hypothesis on teachers' training work in a "Zone of Proximal Development of practices" lead to elaborate training elements.

The project started in September 2010 and will end on June 2012. It has been implemented at two levels of compulsory schooling, in two different "academies" (regional education authorities) and on two different themes: the last two years of primary school (grades 4 and 5) on Magnitudes and measurements in the city of Marseille, with most schools located in underprivileged areas, and on the first two years of lower secondary school (grades 6 and 7) on Numbers and calculation in the "académie of Créteil" (near Paris), on a sample of classes among which 40 belong to underprivileged areas status.

After the first year experimentation we can say that, compared to the progress in control groups which did not follow the experimental protocol, the performance of participating students is significantly better for grade 6 and very significantly better for grade 4. This would tend to show that a relatively small but specific investment in training and coaching teachers leads to a significant improvement in school performance.

**Keyword**: PACEM; student assessment; teacher training; experimentation

## Introduction

PACEM is a "Project for Acquisition of Competences by Students in Mathematics" during compulsory schooling. This project is a middle scale project piloted by the DEPP (Directorate of Evaluation, Prospective and Performance) for the French Ministry of Education.

I have designed this project from one background hypothesis, one evidence and two questions.

My hypothesis is that national and international assessments are more and more important in the management of education systems, but in the same time, most teachers don't seem to be concerned by them, as if they were only external measuring instruments.

The evidence is, as a recent OECD report reminds us, that "of all the school factors that can influence students' achievement, teachers in the classroom have by far the biggest impact".

So my first question is: in what extent is it possible for teachers to appropriate the contents and the results of such assessments? And the second one is: which effects can this appropriation have on teachers' practices?

PACEM is a project integrating several dimensions: student assessment; teachers' training and effects of a specific training on individual and collective practices within schools.

After this short preamble, I will begin by the national foundations and issues of the project, and then I will describe how it has been implemented. I follow by a presentation of some results (in grade 4), then we will see how the project will develop during this school year, and at last, I will outline my first conclusions.

## Foundations and issues of the project

Let me give you a quick overview of the structure of the French education system:

**Primary schools structure**

<table>
<tr><td rowspan="8">Primary<br>( école primaire )<br>3 - 11 years old</td><td rowspan="3">Nursery school<br>( école matemelle )<br>3 - 6 years old</td><td>Petite section</td><td rowspan="3">cycle 1</td></tr>
<tr><td>Moyenne section</td></tr>
<tr><td>Grande section</td></tr>
<tr><td rowspan="5">Elementary school<br>( école élémentaire )<br>6 - 11 years old</td><td>Cours préparatoire ( CP )</td><td>cycle 2</td></tr>
<tr><td>Cours élémentaire $1^{ère}$ année ( CE 1 )</td><td rowspan="4">cycle 3</td></tr>
<tr><td>Cours élémentaire $2^{e}$ année ( CE 2 )</td></tr>
<tr><td>Cours moyen $1^{ère}$ année ( CM 1 )</td></tr>
<tr><td>Cours moyen $2^{e}$ année ( CM 2 )</td></tr>
</table>

( *Source*: *School Education in France 2010*, *French Ministry of Education* )

Teachers teach all subjects in primary school.

**Secondary schools structure**

<table>
<tr><td rowspan="5">Secondary<br>( secondaire )<br>11 - 18 years old</td><td rowspan="4">Lower secondary<br>( collège )<br>11 - 15 years old</td><td colspan="2">$6^{e}$</td></tr>
<tr><td colspan="2">$5^{e}$</td></tr>
<tr><td colspan="2">$4^{e}$</td></tr>
<tr><td colspan="2">$3^{e}$</td></tr>
<tr><td>Upper secondary<br>( lycée )<br>15 - 18 years old ( * )</td><td>Generale route Technological route<br>Seconde<br>Première<br>Terminale<br>Baccalauréat généralet technologique</td><td>Vocational route<br>Seconde<br>Première<br>Terminale<br>Baccalauréat professionnel</td></tr>
</table>

( *Source*: *School Education in France 2010*, *French Ministry of Education* )

Teachers generally teach one subject in secondary school.

All that concerns teaching staff and curricula is under the responsibility of the State.

**Devolved powers in the management of the school system**

| Overview of competencies | Nursery and primary | Low secondary secondary ( *Collège* ) | Upper secondary ( *Lycée* ) |
|---|---|---|---|
| Investment ( construction, reconstruction, equipment, functionning) | Municipality | *Département* | *Région* |
| Teaching materials | Municipality | State | State |
| Teaching staff ( recruitment, training, postings, pay) | State | State | State |
| Curriculum | State | State | State |
| Awarding diplomas | — | State | State |

( *Source*: *School Education in France 2010*, *French Ministry of Education* )

The teachers are recruited by competitive exams, they become State civil servants. From 2011, candidates must have a two-years master diploma. After their success, candidates become trainee teachers: they are assigned to a school for a year. They obtain a permanent status at the end of their first year of teaching, if their appraisal is positive.

To monitor the educational system, the DEPP collects information from representative samples by combining:

- a *comparative view* on students' knowledge and skills according to international assessments as PISA;
- a *national view* with assessments according to national objectives, based on French curriculum standards;
- a *national and a comparative view* on aspects of teachers' beliefs, attitudes and practices.

In parallel, national exhaustive assessments have been implemented to enable:

- schools, *départements* and *académies* to have local results;
- teachers to do individual diagnosis in their own classes from which they can implement pedagogical actions appropriated to each situation. I am aware of a number of aspects that will make the final analysis difficult, as:
- PACEM is a multidimensional study: assessment, training and teaching.
- Other variables are involved: school effect, class effect, teacher effect.
- Shall we speak of good practices or effective practices?
- What about the effects over time?

To design this project, I used a double approach theorical framework that allows a cross-analysis of the mathematics teacher's activity (A. Robert, J. Rogalski, 2005): it gives a methodology for analyzing the teacher's activity in the classroom, based on concepts used in the fields of the didactics of mathematics (that included content knowledge and pedagogical content knowledge) as well as in cognitive ergonomics.

This frame allows analysis of teachers' practices relative to students' results while considering proposed tasks and the daily constraints linked to the teachers, in order to determine what could vary in these practices. In a second phase, a hypothesis on teachers training in a "Zone of Proximal Development of Practices" led me to elaborate training elements.

The project builds on research in several areas. Among the works on which I have based my approach, let me quote:

- Knowing and teaching elementary mathematic (Liping Ma, 1999);
- Teaching in underprivileged areas (Peltier and al, 2004; van Zanten, 2001);
- Teacher effects on student achievement (Gautier and Dembélé 2004; Nye and al, 2004; Konstantopoulos, 2007);
- Teacher use of student performance (Hyler, 2011);

## Description of the project

The main objective of PACEM is to change teaching practices through training based on the results of students from a test at the beginning of the school year.

From the results at a pre-test in the beginning of a school year, I design a teachers' training session for only some teachers (not all of them), from which I expect a feedback in the schools, that I call percolation (i. e. a combination of diffusion and transformation) and a then a change of individual and collective practices.

Two post-tests measure the progress of students: the first one at the end of the first year, and the other one at the end of the second year. These two tests will be used to evaluate the experimentation itself.

**General organization of the project**

The project was started in September 2010 and will end in June 2012. It has been implemented at two levels of compulsory schooling, in two different "académies" (regional education authorities) and on two different themes.

In fact, the project has two parts: one is implemented in the last two years of the primary school (ISCED 1, grades 4 and 5) about Magnitudes and measurements, in the city of Marseille, in schools almost entirely located in underprivileged ("priority education") areas. The other is implemented in the first two years of the lower secondary school (ISCED 2, grades 6 and 7); about Numbers and calculation, in the "académie of Créteil", on a sample of classes 50 % of which are from underprivileged areas. The two themes have been chosen by the local inspectors.

At this phase of the project, we have only cleaned up and treated the data for grade 4, so that is the part of the project that I will present in this article.

52 teachers (districts of Marseille11 and Marseille 12) form an experimental group: 25 teachers who have received training (the《 project correspondents 》) and 27 teachers have not been trained. 34 teachers (from Istres) form a comparison group.

About 1560 students are involved in the project for the first year: the experimental group is composed with 11 schools, 24 classes, 450 students for Marseille 11 and 14 schools, 28 classes, 470 students for Marseille 12 and the comparison group (Istres) is composed with15 schools, 34 classes and 640 students.

**Distribution of students**

30,0%
40,8%
29,2%
■ Istres
□ Marseille 12 ■ Marseille 11

The students enrolled in schools from underprivileged areas (or EP for "Priority Education") are not distributed in the same manner, and that could have been a real problem for the experiment.

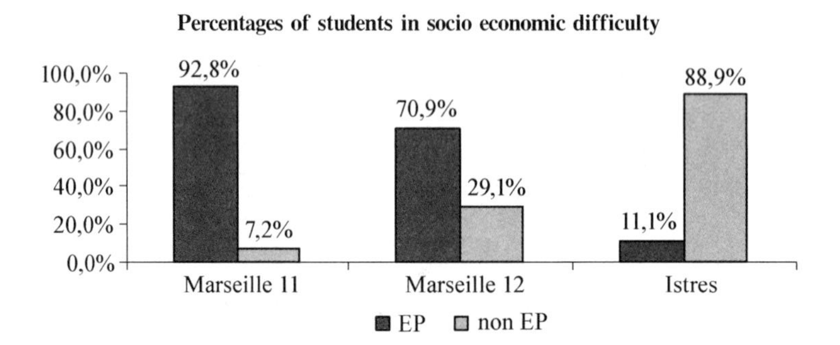


The assessment booklets are divided in two parts:

- 1st part (8 or 9 exercises, 31 or 32 items, it depends on the test):
  - ➢ the subject is measurement units
  - ➢ MCQ and production of short responses
- 2nd part ( 9 to 12 exercises, 12 to 15 items):
  - ➢ The exercises are relating to problem solving
  - ➢ MCQ

Most of the items come from formal national assessments, and some have been added for the experimentation. 7 items are the same in the two tests: they are anchoring items that will permit to compare the difficulties of the tests.

## Teachers' training

Between the two tests, as I said earlier, some teachers have been trained, and as a teacher trainer, I already used released items of national or international assessments or the results of these items to:

- make teachers aware of the tasks that can be given to students, in France and abroad;
- suggest teachers other ways of assessing;
- make teachers aware of the level *a posteriori* of tasks given to students;
- propose teachers answers to students' errors;
- suggest teachers ways so that students do not make these mistakes;

Partly based on this experience, the spirit of the project has an individual dimension in the classroom) and a collective dimension (in the school). Individually, teachers are expected to:

- take into account student success;
- understand the difficulties of students and develop strategies to deal with them;
- design new organizations of teaching;
- adapt every day teaching to the classroom;
- distinguish what belongs more to classroom time or more to after-school hours.

Concerning their implication in a team work, they are expected to:

- reflect, exchange knowledge and practices with their colleagues;
- discover their practices in the classrooms;
- implement a common teaching project in their school.

To try to achieve these objectives, teacher training for grade 4 has 3 components:

- A minimum face-to-face training: a half day for launching the project in September 2010 for all teachers, and 2 days in October 2010 only for 《correspondents》;
- A collaborative platform;
- A local support by inspectors and pedagogical advisors.

The adopted strategy is in four steps:

- Prepare the place for something new;
- Introduce something new;
- Give time to appropriate new knowledge (by giving examples of what doing better means in practice);

• Organize, structure and contextualize (before teachers go back to their classrooms and have to do this entire work of every day by themselves).

What I call "something new" is:

• Statistical national and international data( objectivation of the difficulty of a task);
• Basic content knowledge and pedagogical content knowledge;
• Explanations, eliciting about the curriculum standards;
• Examples of tasks;
• Possible lesson plans related to the proposed tasks;
• Examples of lessons sequences (progressions)

## 2010 - 2011: first results for grade 4

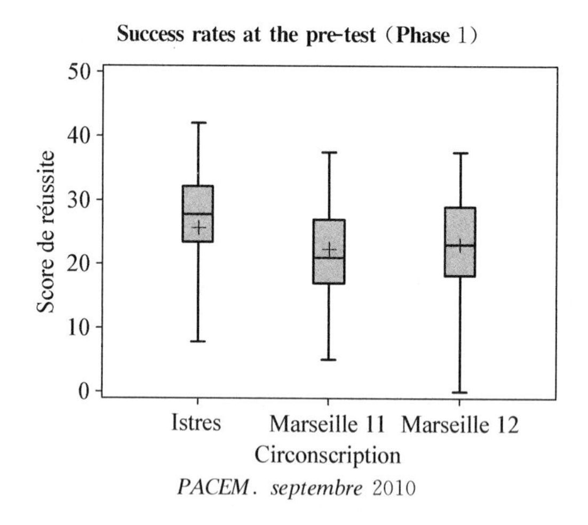

*PACEM. septembre* 2010

We can see that the first quartile of the comparison group (Istres) is above the mean of the two experimental groups and the mean is above the third quartile.

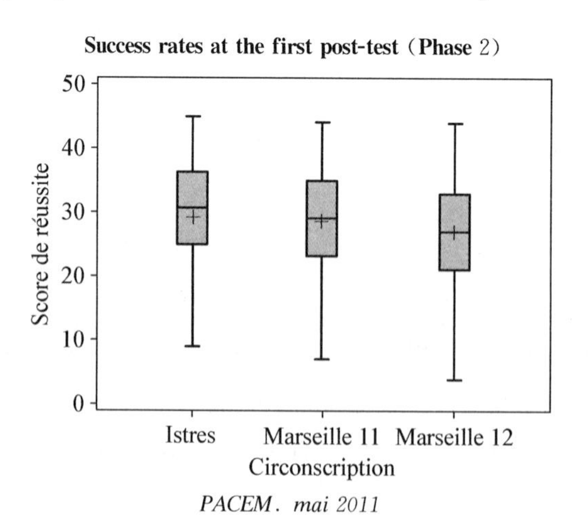

*PACEM. mai 2011*

As we can see on the above diagram, the difference between the experimental group and the comparison group is significantly reduced, mainly for one of the two experimental groups.

## PACEM 2011 - 2012

The project is continuing and extended in 2011 - 2012 in two directions: on one hand, with teachers of grades 4 and 6 with a similar protocol to the one of 2010 - 2011; on the other hand, with teachers of grades 5 and 7. For these grades, there were no initial tests in September 2011, and the post-tests at the end of the school year are planned to be national large scale assessments. That will offer two levels of analysis: effects of the experimentation over 2 years for the grades 4 and 6, and effects of the experimentation over 2 years for 2 student cohorts.

## Conclusion

After the first year experimentation, the performance of participating students to the project is significantly better compared to the progress in control groups which did not follow the experimental protocol. We are aware that a Hawthorne effect may have occurred and another possibility is that teachers may have produced a possible imbalance in favor of the chosen subject. Though we must be very careful at this phase of the analysis of the results, this would tend to show that a relatively small but specific investment in training and coaching teachers, integrating results of standardized assessments, leads to a significant improvement in school performance.

### References


Chesné J.-F. (2010) Les acquis des élèves en calcul à l'école primaire, *Education et Formation n°79*, pp. 21 - 27.

Chesné J.-F., Pariès M., Robert A. (2009) *Partir des pratiques en formation professionnelle des enseignants de mathématiques des lycées et collèges Petit x n°80*, pp. 25 - 46.

Ma L. (1999). *Knowing and teaching elementary mathematic: teachers' understanding of fundamental mathematics in China and the United States*.

Robert A. and Rogalski J. (2005) A cross-analysis of the mathematics teacher's activity. An example in a French 10th-grade class, *Educational Studies in Mathematics*, volume 59, 1 pp. 269 - 298.

Peltier M.-L. and al, (2004) Dur, *dur d'enseigner en ZEP - Analyse de pratiques des professeurs des écoles*, La Pensée Sauvage.

Nye B., Konstantopoulos S., Hedges L. (2004) How Large Are Teacher Effects? *Educational Evaluation and Policy Analysis*, Vol. 26, No. 3, pp. 237 - 257.

Gauthier C. and Dembélé M. (2005) *Qualité de l'enseignement et qualité de l'éducation: revue des résultats de recherche*, UNESCO Report, 2005/ED/EFA/MRT/PI/18.

Hyler J.-H. (2011) *If you build it will they come? Teacher use of student performance data on a web-based tool*, Working Paper 17486, http://www.nber.org/papers/w17486.

Van Zanten A. (2001) *L'école de la périphérie - Scolarité et ségrégation en banlieue*, PUF.

# 标准化学生评价：哪种适合教师采用？ 实践效果如何？

Jean-François Chesné

【摘要】PACEM(义务教育阶段学生数学能力习得项目)是DEPP(法国国家评估、规划和绩效董事会)所主持的一个项目，该项目集合了四个主要维度：学生评价，教师培训，个体活动的课堂观察以及学校内部教师之间的互动。此项目的主要目标是验证培训课程引发的变化，该课程基于学生在学年开始时的测试中取得的成绩设置。另外还有两次测试用来衡量学生的进步：第一次是在第一年的年末，第二次是在第二年的年末。

这个实验的设计是基于与活动理论相联系的理论框架："双重方法"理论，即说教式方法和人机工程方法(Robert and Rogalski, 2005)。为了寻找出在实践中可能会变化的因素，考虑到与教师日常行为相关的一些限制，研究者可以在此框架里分析与学生行为结果相关的教师行为。在第二个阶段，研究者将基于在最近发展区开展教师培训的假设进行一系列精细的培训。

该项目于2010年启动，将于2012年6月结束。此项目在两所不同水平的义务教育学校，两个不同的研究院(区域教育当局)以及两个不同的主题上实施：其一是关于数量和测量，选取马赛市的一所初等教育学校的最后两个年级(四年级和五年级)，这里大部分学校位于落后地区；其二是关于数字和计算，选取一所中等教育学校的前两年(六年级和七年级)，地点是"académie of Créteil"(巴黎附近)。样本中的有40个班级处于落后地区。

第一年的实验结果显示：较没有参与培训的控制组来说，实验组6年级的学生表现要更好，实验组4年级的学生表现更是卓越。这也进一步表明，在教师培训上的相对小，但很具体的投资可以很客观的提高教师在学校中的表现。

【关键词】PACEM；学生评价；教师培训；实验

【作者简介】Jean-François Chesné/法国教育活动和实验评估办公室主管

# What Students Know, what Teachers Know: Theories-Tools-Outcomes

Michael Neubrand

Carl-von-Ossietzky-University in Oldenburg Mathematical Institute

**Abstract**: Assessment-in what forms ever it takes place-has to be grounded on theoretical considerations of different levels and qualities. Among them most salient is that the content domain tested has been structured according to processes of teaching and learning. Then, tasks are the essential tool to assess the relevant content structures. The classification of tasks by appropriate marks and features is therefore a relevant issues and a big challenge when setting up educational assessment in mathematics.

This paper focuses on the studies PISA (an International Comparison taking mathematical literacy as target, including an ample national option in Germany) and COACTIV (a representative study in Germany on teachers' knowledge in mathematics and mathematical pedagogy). Both studies aim to realize differentiated assessment, taking aspects of content and task analysis into consideration. Differentiated outcomes of that kind allow getting information which is suitable for developing the teaching and learning in the classroom further, in two respects: Students' knowledge can be assessed in categories that point directly to issues of the teaching and learning in the classroom, and the influence teachers' knowledge has on students' learning progress can be tapped in a way that shows which didactical actions in the classroom could be effective.

**Keywords**: PISA; classroom assessment; theories; tools; outcomes

## Introduction

Assessment has different functions — and accordingly there is a variety of issues. On what I concentrate here is that assessment and evaluation often define the mathematics that is valued and worth knowing. This claim covers many aspects of assessment: large scale studies as well as evaluations of student thinking, assessment of teachers' knowledge as well as of their activities in the classroom. These large scale and local forms of assessment are tied together in various ways. One is the path from teachers' knowledge towards students' learning progress, and a second one is the path from recognizing the results of large scale studies towards analyzing students' thinking at exactly these tasks. The first path was carried out in the German study COACTIV (Baumert & al., 2010; Kunter & al., 2011), the second was elaborated quite recently in a doctoral thesis (Ulfig, 2011).

Both approaches are grounded in the theoretical study of task characteristics under a decisive mathematics education perspective, since tasks are the tools to get information about students' achievement, about their ways of thinking and learning, and also about how teachers build lessons and react to students—these all always under a mathematics content perspective. And—conversely—tasks are a good means to influence the further development of mathematics education in the large and the small scale, and they are also a good means to communicate mathematics education issues with teachers. Finally, tasks also allow a profiled description of the results of empirical studies, provided the characteristics of the tasks are set up close to issues of teaching and learning mathematics (Neubrand, 2004 a).

## 1. What is a task in mathematics?

"Using tasks as units of analysis [in that case: the tasks of the lessons in the TIMSS Video Study; MN] makes sense, since features of mathematical tasks can be a rather objective means of analysis, provided the features taken into consideration are related to cognitive processes of mathematics learning. Furthermore, mathematical tasks unify two different strands in the teaching and learning process: They serve the teacher to construct his or her lesson, and they serve as well the students to construct their mathematical knowledge" (J. Neubrand, 2006, 294f). In similar ways many authors talk about tasks in mathematics education (e.g. Bromme, Seeger & Steinbring, 1990; Stein, Grover & Henningsen, 1996; J. Neubrand, 2002). Therefore, a consideration of tasks under content and cognitive aspects is useful for the purpose of setting up assessments in what contexts ever.

One general orientation is often used to set up a model of tasks (really an apriori "model", not a post-hoc description), the so-called cycle of modeling (cf. Blum & al., 2007). It should show that the process of solving a mathematical task—let aside those tasks which only need to carry out a known procedure from a known starting point (we call it "technical tasks" later)—can be viewed as a cycle consisting of considering a situation, finding or constructing a suitable piece of mathematics which corresponds to that situation, the "model", working out that model in the realm of mathematics, and finally interpreting or even validating and revising the model according to how well is fits to the situation. In this general form the cycle of modeling is not only applicable to tasks that mathematize real world situations (where it originally came from) but also to the solving processes of tasks which are settled as problems in inner-mathematical contexts. (Fig. 1; in this form drawn from Klieme, Neubrand & Lüdtke, 2001, p.144.)

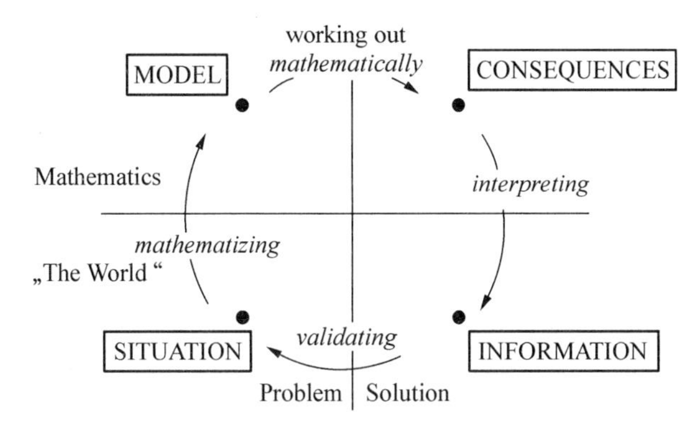


**Figure 1. The cycle of mathematical modeling**

Taking the cycle of modeling as a background, the German mathematics group for the PISA-study (cf. Neubrand, 2004 b) developed a "model of tasks" that consists of a "kernel" (the inner four shades rectangles in Fig. 2) and a "periphery" (the outer ellipse). The kernel contains those four central aspects which determine the characteristic of each task: if procedural or conceptual thinking (in the sense of Hiebert, 1986) is intended, if more the one step in the modeling cycle is required, if the solving of the task is done in a single step or if a chain of steps is necessary, and in which context, within mathematics or from the "real" world, the task is set. The periphery is build of a number of features (thought of as an open list) which all turned out (taking regression analyses in the PISA-study) to contribute specifically to the difficulty of the task (cf. various articles in Neubrand, 2004 b). (Fig. 2)

The four central aspects in the "kernel" address qualitatively different kinds of cognitive activities incorporated in a task. In a condensed form, one recognizes "Three Types of Mathematical Activity" according to which aspects are present or not (Neubrand & Neubrand, 2004):

(1) *Technical tasks*: Procedural thinking only; one or multi-step; no problem solving or modeling activity needed; all activities within mathematics.

(2) *Procedural modeling and/or problem oriented tasks*: Mathematizing and/or problem solving is necessary; the origin can be a situation in a real world context (modeling), or a

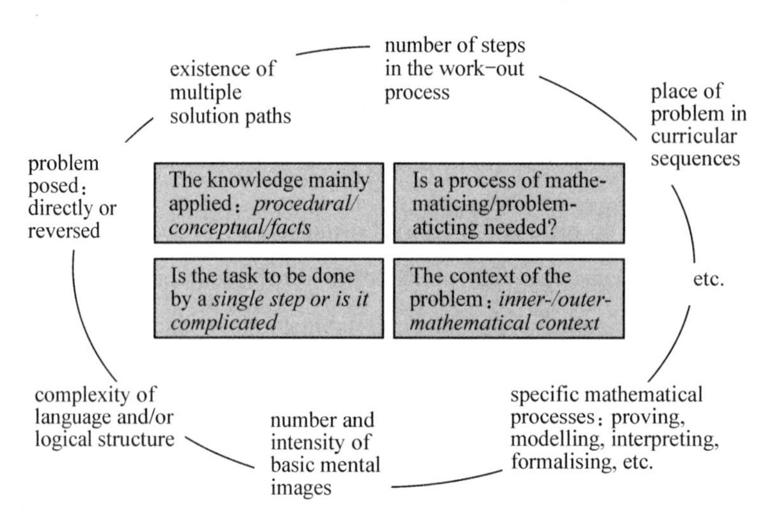


**Figure 2. The "Model of Task" constructed for the German interpretation of PISA-2000 (Neubrand, 2004 b:37).**

mathematical situation with problem solving activities; mostly procedural thinking during the work-out process; one or multi-step.

(3) *Conceptual modeling and/or problem oriented tasks*: Mathematizing and/or problem solving is necessary; the origin can be a situation in a real world context (modeling), or a mathematical situation with problem solving activities; mostly conceptual thinking during the work-out process; one or multi-step.

Since mathematics is characterized by the both ways of thinking, procedural as well as conceptual (Hiebert, 1986; Kilpatrick, 2001), an overall test on mathematics should have a roughly equal distribution over these three classes, at least over the two classes for modeling / problem-solving if a mathematical literacy test is constructed. PISA roughly fulfilled this claim, but many other tests don't (Neubrand, 2001; Neubrand, 2011/2012).

## 2. What students know: Profiles and international differences

The "Three Types of Mathematical Activity" lead to understand deeper what information a large scale achievement study can also deliver. This holds on the national as well as on the international level. In both cases a separation into the types of mathematical activity shapes the information in such a way that it can be interpreted as advices to a further development of mathematics teaching.

### 2.1 Profiles of mathematics achievement

PISA-2000 showed in Germany (where we had an extensive national option to PISA, and thus data about many additional tasks) that students' achievement differed in specific ways according to what school system the students come from. This is a crucial problem in Germany since the educational system in Germany is characterized by its heterogeneous federal structure. The 16 Federal States in Germany have not only different curricula, but also different school structures, different distribution of students to the various school types and final exams, and consequently the traditions and ways mathematics is taught differ (see e.g. a comprehensive description in the forthcoming English COACTIV book (Kunter & al., 2012)). Thus, the fact that the students in the 16 States show different achievement scores is of high political interest, however from the standpoint of mathematics education, the more interesting question is if one can exhibit different patterns in the achievement. This would allow detecting if the achievement in a State shows characteristic content related advances and weaknesses. Indeed by taking the "Three Types of Mathematical Activities", one finds "profiles" which could be traced back to several curricular decisions. E.g. one striking effect seen by a differentiated assessment is the emphasis on technical performance in the Eastern German States (the right side in Fig. 3), while the Western German States mostly show here their weakest results. (Neubrand & Neubrand, 2004; Neubrand, 2011/2012). (Fig. 5)

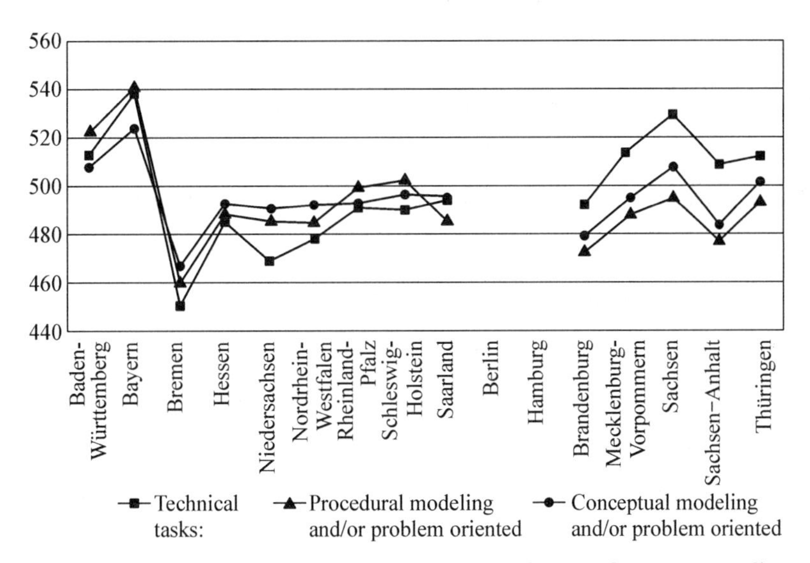


**Figure 3: Profiles in the mathematical achievement in the States in Germany, according to the "Three Types of Mathematical Activity". Data PISA-2000 (Neubrand & Neubrand, 2004).**

## 2.2 International differences

Also in the field of international comparisons a characterization of the tasks is fruitful.

E.g. to explain on a content basis in which features the both countries Japan an Germany differed in the PISA-2000 test, we added some additional features to the "periphery" in Fig. 2 of the task model (Neubrand & Neubrand, 2003). For a regression model we used some aspects of the modeling process and modes of representations. Then one could conclude by a regression analysis of the differences of the scores (transformed into logits) on the PISA-tasks what the main reason of those differences was. It depended on the class. At items with "procedural modeling" the representation mode "geometric drawing" in the task explains 44% of the Japan-Germany difference, with a (standardized) regression coefficient of .696 to the advantage of Japan. Even clearer was the picture in the field of "conceptual modeling". Three variables tapping aspects of visual information processing (geometric drawing, tables and schematic drawing) explain 76 % of the variance, with regression coefficients up to .880. Conceptual understanding on the basis of visual information seems therefore to make the crucial difference between the two countries. The item-characteristics therefore point clearly to those content areas and learning-teaching styles in mathematics that could be strengthened in Germany.

## 3. What students know: Tests and students' thinking

Alone from the scores of the tasks one cannot see how the students think when they solve the task. However, without the scores on a sufficiently large basis one is not secure if the observed students only bring out an idiosyncratic solution or if their solution stands for a bigger group of students. In a recent doctoral dissertation (Ulfig, 2011) therefore some original tasks from the PISA studies were given to students who solved the problem, and then were forced to think aloud and later to reflect in an interview their solving processes. The different data sources influence each other, so that a final coding allowed the identification of certain characteristic thinking mode of the students. The students were deliberately drawn from Hauptschule, the lowest track in the German school system, and the track with the most educational problems. These students often bring the lowest achievement; the data of the Gymnasium students, i.e. those who attend the academic track in the school system, serve as the sharpest contrast.

As an example the PISA item "Carpenter" is chosen, an international item occurring in both, the PISA - 2000 and PISA - 2003 test. According to the short analysis in the international PISA report (OECD, 2004:113) the item requires decoding visual information and see similarities and differences. The students have to use argumentation skills, only a few technical geometrical knowledge, however geometrical insight. In our system it is a "conceptual modeling" item, since no numerical procedure is applicable, but qualitative arguments. The scoring in PISA underlined this view, successful students have to answer all four designs correctly (Design A: Yes; B: No; C: Yes; D: Yes), thus capitalizing that the item is about understanding the concept perimeter in various mathematical situations. PISA reported (OECD, 2004, p 113) that the most successful countries on this question were Hong Kong & China (40% correct), Japan (38%) and Korea (35%); Germany however brings only 20% correct solutions, splitting into 8% in Hauptschule and 33% in Gymnasium (Ulfig, 2011: 178). Even these striking data alone pose the question: why.

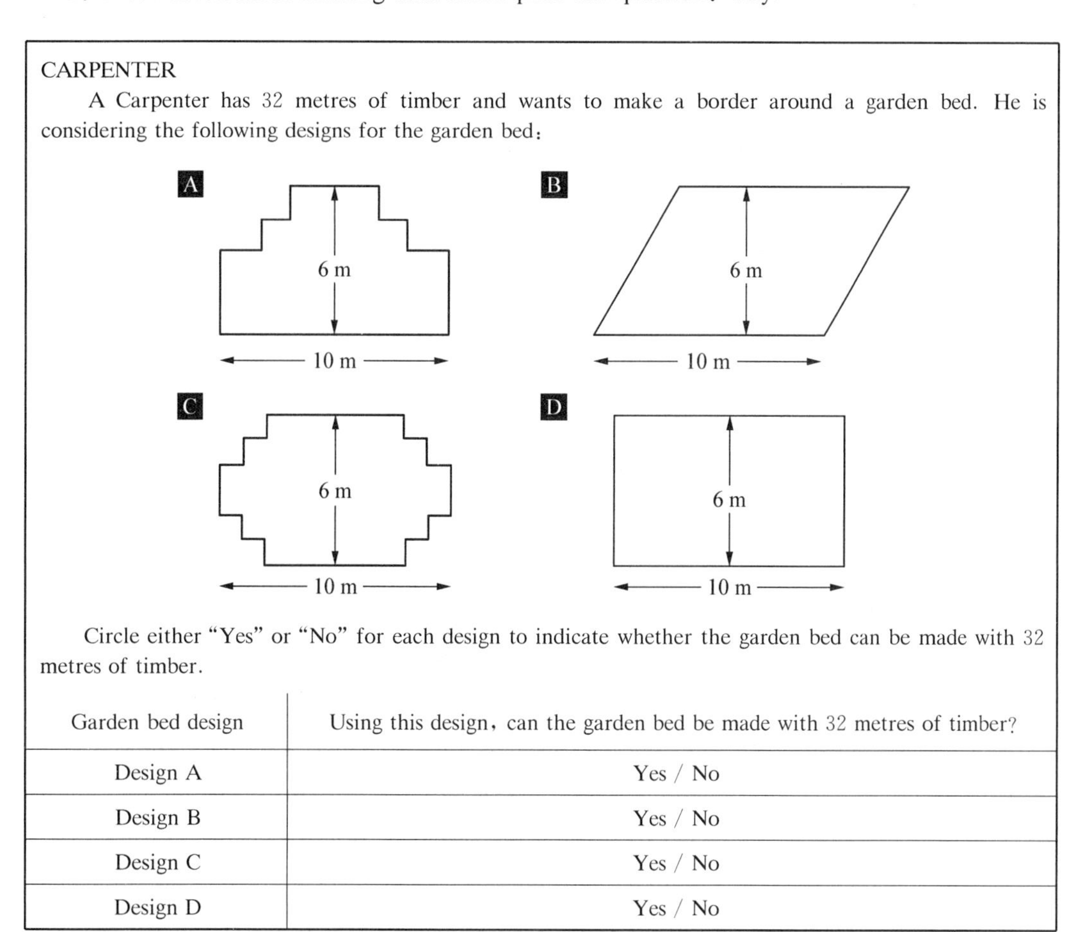

CARPENTER

A Carpenter has 32 metres of timber and wants to make a border around a garden bed. He is considering the following designs for the garden bed:



Circle either "Yes" or "No" for each design to indicate whether the garden bed can be made with 32 metres of timber.

| Garden bed design | Using this design, can the garden bed be made with 32 metres of timber? |
|---|---|
| Design A | Yes / No |
| Design B | Yes / No |
| Design C | Yes / No |
| Design D | Yes / No |

**Figure 4: The task CARPENTER of PISA - 2003, also contained in PISA - 2000 (OECD 2004 p. 112)**

The first approach to answer the why-question is to differentiate the answers into the answers on each design separately. One recognizes that the rectangle design (D) doesn't cause bigger problems, at least in Gymnasium. But even this design had—surprisingly—one third wrong answers in Hauptschule. However the Zick-Zack designs (A and C) and the parallelogram design (B) make things considerably harder even for the Gymnasium students. (Fig. 5) Thus, a closer look seems promising.

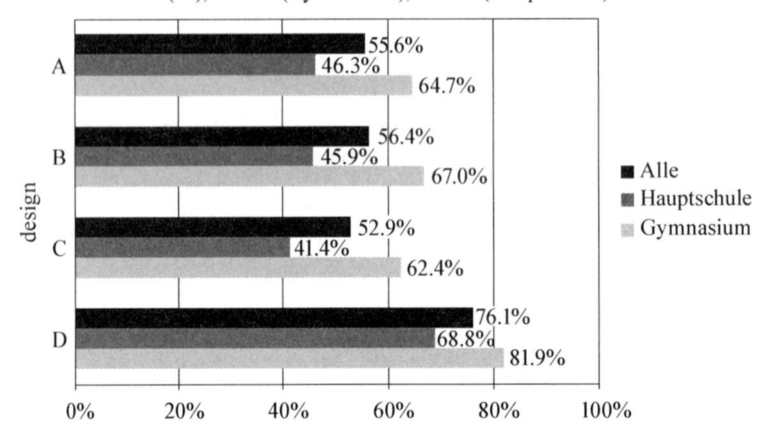


**Figure 5: Percent of correct answers at any design in the PISA item "Carpenter": Data from Germany PISA-2003. N=2980 (all); N=983 (Gymnasium); N=581 (Hauptschule) (Ulfig, 2011:178)**

The thinking aloud technique and the interviews exhibited that really conceptual shortages are the reason for the limited success in Hauptschule. "What kind of things are these designs [the Zick-Zacks; MN]?" a student expressed. "I know the rectangle and the parallelograms, however these do not properly exist! They lack something!" (after Ulfig, 2011, p. 222). This shows that the concept "figure" itself is shortened onto "figure with a name I've learned". Other utterances reveal that the concept of perimeter is not a geometrics one but just a formula, so that it fails to be applied to unknown geometric drawings. Ulfig derived from interviews like these characteristics of a phenomenon she called "limitation of geometric thinking" which can be seen from being bounded to only to the known figures, from overemphasizing calculations or from the attempt to measure the unknown quantities. (Ulfig, 2011, p. 226ff).

In that way, the analysis of tasks from the large scale tests give hints how to further develop mathematics teaching in certain classrooms and for certain populations of students. The tests makes explicit where the problem zones are, the interviews give insight into the thinking, and the test results can assure that this thinking is shared by many students. Assessment in that view leads to directed and realistic advices for the use in the mathematics classroom.

## 4. What teachers know: Concepts, models, outcomes

Taking the opportunity of the PISA-2003 test also a study on the professional knowledge of teachers in mathematics was conducted, actually the knowledge of the "PISA-teachers", i. e. of those teachers who taught the classes from which the international PISA data were drawn in Germany (Baumert, Blum & Neubrand, 2004). Therefore the first time we had a representative sample over German mathematics teachers in all school types and over the whole country. The study "COACTIV", an acronym for 'Professional Competence of Teachers, Cognitively Activating Instruction, and the Development of Students' Mathematical Literacy' could take the PISA data for the students (with one extra longitudinal survey in Germany to observe the learning progress), and developed a new assessment test for mathematics teachers.

The leading idea was to come as close as possible to the core business of the teachers, i. e. the teaching of mathematics in the classroom (Kunter & al., 2007, 2010, 2012). The basic model is the well known and often used distinction of Shulman between three fundamental dimensions of teacher knowledge: content knowledge (CK), pedagogical content knowledge (PCK), and generic pedagogical knowledge (Shulman, 1986).

Indeed, Shulman's model is characterized by its close connection to topic specific thinking in pedagogy, mathematics education in our case. As Content Knowledge he declares: "The teacher need not only understand that something is so; the teacher must further understand why it is so, on what grounds its warrant can be asserted, and under what circumstances our belief in its justification can be weakened and even denied. Moreover, we expect the teacher to understand why a given topic is particularly central to a discipline whereas another may be somewhat peripheral." (Shulman, 1986, p 9). He distinguished further: "Within the category of pedagogical content knowledge I include the most useful forms of representation of a subject area's ideas, the most powerful analogies, illustrations, examples, explanations, and demonstrations in a word, the ways of representing and formulating the subject that makes it comprehensible to others. Since there are no single most powerful forms of representation, the teacher must have at hand a veritable armamentarium of alternative forms of representation, some of which derive from research whereas others originate in the wisdom of practice. Pedagogical content knowledge also includes an understanding of what makes the learning of specific topics easy or difficult: the conceptions and preconceptions that students bring with them." (Shulman, 1986, p 9). Finally he also adds the component of generic pedagogical knowledge.

Behind this CK and PCK view stands what is often condensed in mathematics education in the picture of the "didactics triangle: topic — teacher — student". Essentially teaching deals with making a topic accessible to students via a deliberately prepared trajectory.

To assess the various aspects of PCK, COACTIV focused on three aspects: knowledge about presentations and explanations, knowledge about students' thinking and failures, and knowledge about the potential tasks have as tools to construct lessons so that cognitive activation can take place. Again, tasks given to the teachers are the tool to assess their professional knowledge, but now they are mostly "tasks over tasks"; compare e. g. Ma (1999) or Ball, Lubienski & Mewborn (2001) for that format of assessing teachers' professional knowledge. E. g. for the aspect "explanation / instruction" we asked:

> A student says: I'm not able to understand why $(-1) * (-1) = +1$. Please sketch as many ways as possible to make that equation clear for the student.

Roughly one third of the teachers, and still 20% of the Gymnasium teachers couldn't provide a sufficient answer, i. e. deeper than "that is just a case for memorizing". For the aspect "awareness of students' cognition" we asked e. g.:

> The area of a parallelogram is calculated as baseline * height.
>
> 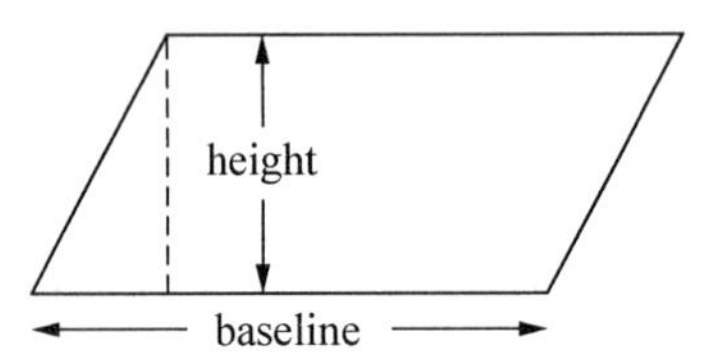
> 
>
> Please give an example of a parallelogram which causes difficulties with that formula when presented to students.

A possible answer could be a parallelogram like this:

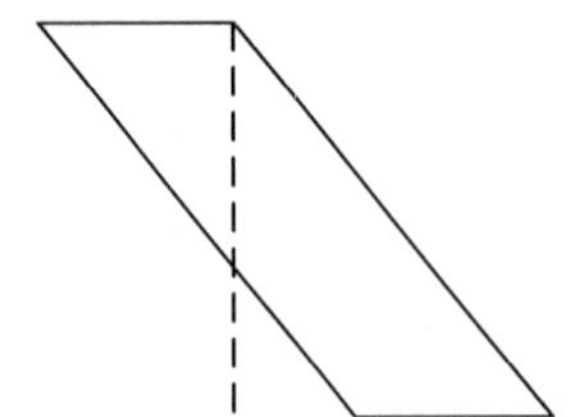

But also a square, in which the "height" is commonly seen as a "side", can affect students' problems in understanding.

The knowledge test in COACTIV had two components. The first is a test over Content Knowledge (CK), conceptualized as those elements of knowledge which are the relatively close mathematical background knowledge of the topics that occur in the middle grades of schools (e.g.: Is $(2^{1024}-1)$ a prime number? — Why is $0.99999... = 1$ ?). The second is a test over Pedagogical Content Knowledge (PCK) with the above mentioned facets explanation / student thinking / cognitive potential of tasks (e.g. multiple solutions). See more details about test construction and test properties in Krauss & al. (2011). Both tests correlate, however as the scatter plot shows there are interesting outliers.

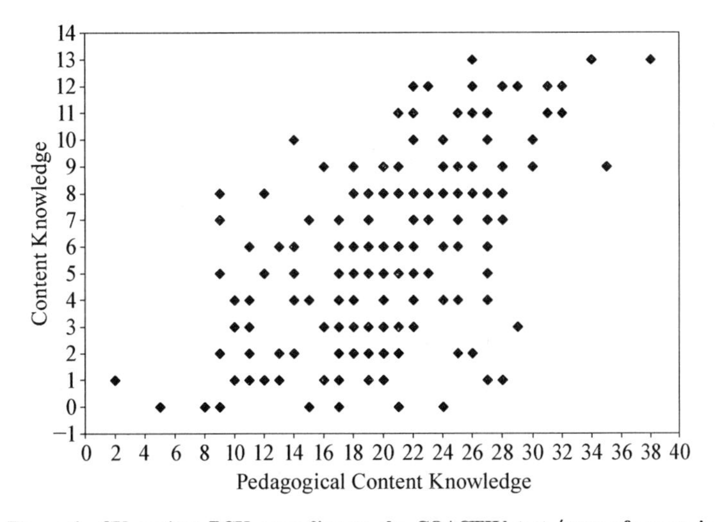


**Figure 6: CK against PCK according to the COACTIV test (sum of scores in each test part; some pixels cover more than one teacher; N=198) (cf. Krauss & al., 2011)**

Two groups are of interest. The upper right corner shows that a very high CK is always connected with a very high PCK. On the other side we find (bottom right) a group of teachers with a sufficiently high PCK but with rather low CK. This is an interesting group, not easy to clarify, so that one has to investigate it further; the upper left corner however seems more obvious to contain the "good" mathematician with less emphasis on educational issues.

## 5. What teachers know and how it affects students' progress

The COACTIV model is differentiated enough to map the influence of teachers' professional knowledge on the learning progress of the students in such a way that one can draw pedagogical consequences from the results. Teachers' professional knowledge is claimed to have an impact on the learning progress of the students on the class level (not on the individual level which is known to be dominated by the prior knowledge of the student). COACTIV discussed several (mediating) models to describe the results (Baumert & al., 2010). The best fitting models include again what was discussed in Chapter 1 of this paper, the quality of the mathematical tasks given in the classroom by the teacher. Quality is measured as the cognitively activating potential of the tasks. Similar as in Chap. 1, a classification system (Jordan & al., 2006) containing features of tasks is the basis. This classification system bounds COACTIV to the views of tasks used in the TIMSS and PISA assessment studies. Very similar features than in PISA (Neubrand, 2004) are contained.

As predictors of how teachers' professional knowledge affects the learning progress of the students from Grade 9 to Grade 10, the final COACTIV model (Models 2 and 6 in Baumert & al., 2010) inserts the cognitive level of the tasks in the class, the curricular level of these tasks, the individual learning support the teacher gives in that class, and the quality of his or her classroom management. The two last predictors were measured by standard questionnaires from general classroom research, however adapted to mathematics, and based on the judgment of teachers or students. The curricular level of the task simply means in how far the teacher also uses tasks from earlier stages of the curriculum.

The cognitive level of the tasks measures three aspects. The cognitively activating potential of a task is as higher as (a) "higher" in the three Types of mathematical Activity (see Chap. 1) the class of the task is, ordered from "technical" to "conceptual"; as (b) more inner-mathematical problems are posed; and as (c) more task with an argumentation activity occur in that classroom.

This is turned out (see Baumert & al., 2010 for details and the corresponding coefficients)

(4) that CK influences PCK,

(5) that CK has not a direct effect, but is mediated by PCK,

(6) that PCK does not affect classroom management (it seems that this due to the knowledge acquired under Shulman's dimension of generic pedagogical knowledge),

(7) that PCK effects significantly the cognitive activation in the class, expressed by the three afore mentioned aspects of cognitively activating tasks,

(8) that cognitive activation indeed significantly affects the learning progress of the students,

(9) that individual learning support and personal care of the teacher indeed—and maybe surprisingly (see Baumert & al., 2010, p 163 for a discussion—is also a function of PCK, however does not affect directly the learning gains of the students.

The following Fig. 7 shows the model and the results in simplified visual form; the figures are correlation coefficients:

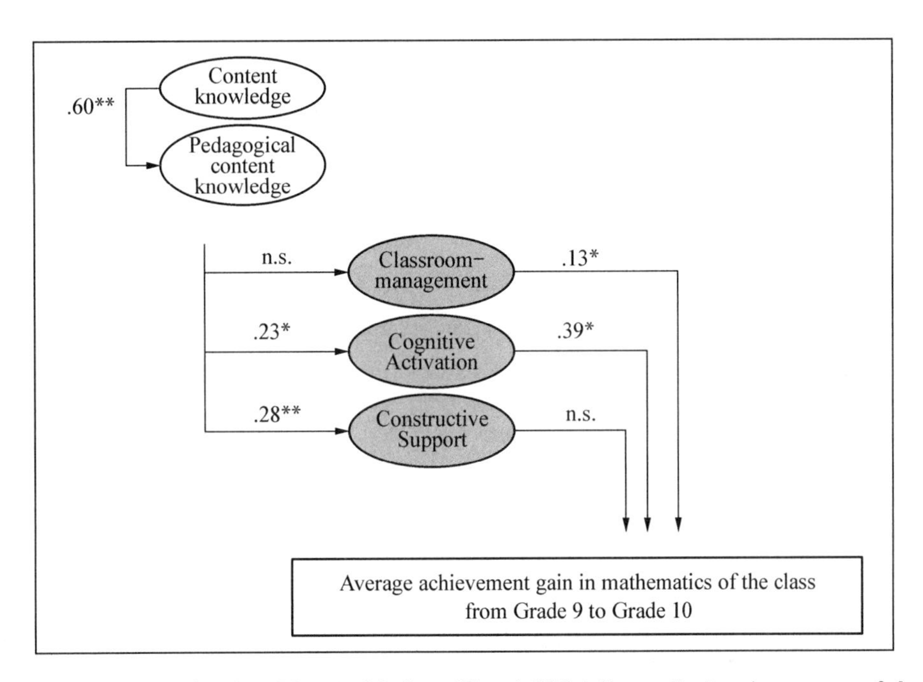


**Figure 7: The COACTIV model to explain how CK and PCK influence the learning progress of the students. (cf. the models described in Baumert & al., 2010, Kunter & al., 2011/2012)**

The new result of COACTIV is the path in the middle of Fig. 7. It shows the content driven path: The more cognitively activating tasks are implemented in the class the more progress is made in that class. This is a result which supports many efforts to revise mathematics instruction towards the goal of cognitive activation. Teachers have thus a means at hand to improve their teaching: a careful and deliberate selection of the tasks they give. And here "careful" has a very decisive meaning: Foster conceptual thinking, pose also inner-mathematical problems, and accustom students to an argumentation attitude.

In this way the role of tasks in mathematics education has changed once more. From tools in assessment tests and tools to research into teachers' professional knowledge, their role is now: Tasks are also tools to reform and develop further the teaching in the classroom, in a way that increases the professionalism of the teachers and is promising to produce learning progress.

**References**

Ball, D., Lubienski, S., & Mewborn, D. (2001). Research on Teaching Mathematics: The Unsolved Problem of Teachers' Mathematical Knowledge. In V. Richardson (Ed.), *Handbook of Research on Teaching* (4th ed., pp.433 - 456). Washington, DC: American Educational Research Association.

Baumert, J., Blum W. & Neubrand, M. (2004). Drawing the Lessons from PISA - 2000: Long Term Research Implications: Gaining a Better Understanding of the Relationship between System Inputs and Learning Outcomes by Assessing Instructional and Learning Processes as Mediating Factors. In D. Lenzen, J. Baumert, R. Watermann & U. Trautwein (Hrsg.), *PISA und die Konsequenzen für die erziehungswissenschaftliche Forschung*. *Zeitschrift für Erziehungswissenschaft*, *Beiheft* 3/2004, 143 - 158.

Baumert, J., Kunter, M., Blum, W., Brunner, M., Voss, T., Jordan, A., Klusmann, U., Krauss, S., Neubrand M. & Tsai, Y. (2010). Teachers' Mathematical Knowledge, Cognitive Activation in the Classroom, and Student Progress. *American Educational Research Journal* 47(1), 133 - 180.

Blum, W., Galbraith, P., Henn, H.-W., & Niss, M. (2007). *Modelling and Applications in Mathematics Education*: *The 14th ICMI study*. New York, Heidelberg, Berlin: Springer.

Bromme, R., Seeger, F., & Steinbring, H. (1990). *Aufgaben als Anforderungen an Lehrer und Schüler* (= IDM-Untersuchungen zum Mathematikunterricht, Bd. 14). Köln: Aulis.

Hiebert, J. (Ed.). (1986). *Conceptual and Procedural Knowledge*: *The Case of Mathematics*. Hillsdale, NJ: Erlbaum.

Jordan, A., Ross, N., Krauss, S., Baumert, J., Blum, W., Neubrand, M., Löwen, K., Brunner M., & Kunter, M. (2006). *Klassifikationsschema für Mathematikaufgaben*: *Dokumentation der Aufgabenklassifikation im COACTIV-Projekt*. (Materialien aus der Bildungsforschung, Nr. 81). Berlin: Max-Planck-Institut für Bildungsforschung.

Kilpatrick, J. (2001). Understanding Mathematical Literacy: The Contribution of Research. *Educational Studies in Mathematics* 47, 101 - 116.

Klieme, E., Neubrand, M. & Lüdtke, O. (2001). Mathematische Grundbildung: Testkonzeption und Ergebnisse. In J. Baumert, E. Klieme, M. Neubrand, M. Prenzel, U. Schiefele, W. Schneider, P. Stanat, K.-J. Tillmann & M. Weiβ (Hrsg.), *PISA* 2000 - *Basiskompetenzen von Schülerinnen und Schülern im internationalen Vergleich* (S. 139 - 190). Opladen: Leske & Budrich.

Krauss, S., Blum, W., Brunner, M., Neubrand, M., Baumert, J., Kunter, M., Besser, M. & Elsner, J. (2011). Konzeptualisierung und Testkonstruktion zum fachbezogenen Professions wissen von Mathematiklehrkräften. In M. Kunter, J. Baumert, W. Blum, U. Klusmann, S. Krauss & M. Neubrand, *Professionelle Kompetenz von Lehrkräften — Ergebnisse des Forschungsprogramms COACTIV* (S. 135 - 162). Münster: Waxmann.

Kunter, M., Baumert, J., Blum, W., Klusmann, U., Krauss, St. & Neubrand, M. (Eds.). (2011).

*Professionelle Kompetenz von Lehrkräften — Ergebnisse des Forschungsprogramms COACTIV*. Münster, New York, München, Berlin: Waxmann (to appear soon in adapted and enlarged form in English: Kunter, M., Baumert, J., Blum, W., Klusmann, U., Krauss, St. & Neubrand, M. (Eds.). (2012). *Cognitive Activation in the Mathematics Classroom and Professional Competence of Teachers: Results from the COACTIV Project in Germany*. New York, Heidelberg, Berlin: Springer).

Kunter, M., Klusmann, U., Dubberke, Th., Baumert, J., Blum, W., Neubrand, M., Brunner, M., Jordan, A., Krauss, St., Löwen, K. & Tsai, Y. (2007). Linking Aspects of Teacher Competence to Their Instruction: Results from the COACTIV Project. In Prenzel, M. (Ed.), *Studies on the Educational Quality of Schools. The Final Report on the DFG Priority Programme* (pp 39 - 59). Münster: Waxmann.

Ma, L. (1999). *Knowing and Teaching Elementary Mathematics: Teachers' understanding of Fundamental Mathematics in China and the United States*. Hillsdale, NJ: Erlbaum.

Neubrand, J. (2002). *Eine Klassifikation mathematischer Aufgaben zur Analyse von Unterrichtssituationen — Selbsttätiges Arbeiten in Schülerarbeitsphasen in den Stunden der TIMSS-Video-Studie*. Hildesheim: Franzbecker.

Neubrand, J. (2006). The TIMSS 1995 and 1999 Video Studies. In F. Leung, K. Graf & F. Lopez-Real (Eds.), *Mathematics Education in Different Cultural Traditions: A Comparative Study of East Asia and the West: The 13th ICMI Study* (pp 291 - 318). Berlin, Heidelberg, New York: Springer.

Neubrand, J. & Neubrand, M. (2003). *Profiles of mathematical achievement in the PISA - 2000 mathematics test and the different structure of achievement in Japan and Germany*. Paper presented at AERA - 2003 -Annual Meeting, Chicago.

Neubrand, J. & Neubrand, M. (2004). Innere Strukturen mathematischer Leistung im PISA - 2000 - Test. In M. Neubrand (Ed.), *Mathematische Kompetenzen von Schülerinnen und Schülern in Deutschland: Vertiefende Analysen im Rahmen von PISA - 2000* (S. 87 - 107). Wiesbaden: VS-Verlag für Sozialwissenschaften.

Neubrand, M. (2004 a). Mathematical Tasks Can Indicate Differences in Teaching and Learning: Selected Cases From the International PISA - 2000 data. In J. Wang & B. Xu (Eds.), *Trends and Challenges in Mathematics Education* (pp 269 - 281). Shanghai: East China Normal University Press.

Neubrand, M. (Ed.). (2004 b). *Mathematische Kompetenzen von Schülerinnen und Schülern in Deutschland: Vertiefende Analysen im Rahmen von PISA - 2000*. Wiesbaden: VS-Verlag für Sozialwissenschaften.

Neubrand, M. (2005). The PISA-study: Challenge and Impetus to Research in Mathematics Education. In H. L. Chick & J. L. Vincent (Eds.), *Proceedings of the 29th Conference of the International Group for the Psychology of Mathematics Education. Melbourne, Australia, July* 10 - 15, 2005. Vol. 1 (ppl/79 - 1/82). Melbourne: University of Melbourne.

Neubrand, M. (2011/12, in press). PISA-Mathematics in Germany: Differentiated Assessment by Enlarging the Conceptual Framework. In M. Prenzel, M. Kobarg, K. Schöps & S. Rönnebeck (Eds.), *Research in the Context of the Programme for International Student Assessment* (in press). New York, Heidelberg: Springer.

Neubrand, M., Biehler, R., Blum, W., Cohors-Fresenborg, E., Flade, L., Knoche, N., Lind, D., Löding, W., Möller, G., & Wynands, A. (Deutsche PISA - 2000 - Expertengruppe Mathematik) (2001). Grundlagen der Ergänzung des internationalen PISA-Mathematik-Tests in der deutschen Zusatzerhebung. *Zentralblatt für Didaktik der Mathematik*, 33 (2), 45 - 59.

OECD-Organisation for Economic Co-operation and Development (1999). *Measuring Student Knowledge and Skills: A New Framework for Assessment*. Paris: OECD.

OECD (2003). *The PISA 2003 Assessment Framework: Mathematics, Reading, Science and Problem Solving Knowledge and Skills*. Paris: OECD.

Shulman, L. (1986). Those Who Understand: Knowledge Growth in Teaching. *Educational Researcher*, 15(2), 4 - 14.

Stein, M. K., Grover, B. W. & Henningsen, M. (1996). Building Student Capacity for Mathematical Thinking and Reasoning: An Analysis of Mathematical Tasks used in Reform Classes. *American Educational Research Journal* 33, 455 - 488.

Ulfig, F. (2011). *Geometrische Denkweisen beim Lösen von PISA-Aufgaben. Eine Verbindung quantitativer und qualitativer Analysen*. Unpublished Doctoral Dissertation. Carl von Ossietzky University Oldenburg (Germany).

# 学生所知，教师所知：理论—工具—结果

Michael Neubrand

【摘要】评估(assessment)——无论采用何种形式——都不得不建立在对不同水平和质量的理论思考基础之上。其中至关重要的是测验内容领域要依据教与学的过程来构建。其次，任务是评估相关内容结构的核心工具。因此，在设计对数学的教育评估时，按照合理的标识和特征对任务进行分类就成为一个息息相关的问题，也是一个巨大的挑战。

本文重点研究PISA(国际学生评估项目的缩写，是以数学素养为目标的国际比较研究，包括在国家层面德国所做的许多调整)和COACTIV(德国教师数学知识和数学教学知识的一个代表性研究)。两者都旨在实现区分性评估(differentiated assessment)，都考虑了评价内容和任务分析的不同方面。区分性(评估)结果使得(我们)能够获取有用的信息，进一步推动课堂教与学的发展。这些信息主要表现为两个方面：评估学生不同类型的知识，这些知识类型直接

指向课堂教学与学习中存在的各种问题；探索教师知识对学生学习进展的影响，表明哪种教学行为是有效的。
【关键字】评国际学生评估项目；课堂评价；理论；工具；结果
【作者简介】Michael Neubrand/德国卡尔冯奥西茨基大学数学教育专业教授

# 教师课堂评价任务的设计与实施情况①

## ——一种理论驱动的分析模式

豆雨松　杨向东

【摘要】课堂评价在推进新课程所倡导的学业成就评价模式中占有极其重要的地位，但长期以来，总结性评价占据了我国学业评价的绝对主导地位，而课堂评价的研究和改进主要依靠一线教师的经验总结。本研究采用理论驱动，以证据为中心、注重整体的资料分析方法，分析了两位数学教师的课堂评价任务设计与实施的状况。结果显示，两位老师在目标制定上往往只注重内容逻辑，忽视认知水平这个维度。对于评价任务的设计，两位老师都没有非常清晰的意识。在评价任务的使用上，学生很少有充分的思考和表达的机会。

【关键词】课堂评价；任务设计；任务实施；数学教师

【作者简介】豆雨松/上海师资培训中心实验基地教师

杨向东/华东师范大学课程与教学研究所副教授

## 一、引言

课堂评价是指围绕学校日常教学活动的各种评价形式的总称。它通常泛指所有收集有关学生学习情况的信息的活动，既包括各种课堂练习、课堂测验以及课后作业，也包括教学情境中师生问答和引导，还包括教师对学生表情、动作、学习状态和个性特征等情况随时随地的观察和判断。[1]在学生学业成就评价体系中，只有课堂评价与学生日常的学习生活紧密相关，与教师和学校的教育活动水乳交融。在这个意义上，课堂评价才是实现新型学业成就评价的核心形式，在推进新课程所倡导的学业成就评价模式中占有极其重要的地位。[2]—[7]

虽然课堂评价在学生学业成就评价体系中占有重要的地位，但长期以来，总结性评价占据了我国学业评价的绝对主导地位，而课堂评价的研究和改进却常常无人问津。[8]当前课堂评价研究的主体是一线教师，不受大学研究工作者的重视，多经验总结，缺少系统的实证研究，导致课堂评价的理论水平和研究质量都偏低。

基于这种情况，本研究抽取了不同学科背景和专长水平的四位一线教师，收集了每位教师一个教学单元的所有教案、课堂实施情况以及课后作业等资料，并通过个别访谈的方法调

① 本文是上海市教育研究2011重点项目“测量学视角下的课堂评价任务设计和实施模式研究”（项目编号A1117）的阶段性研究成果。

查了教师设计和实施相关课堂评价任务的思考和认识，并在此基础上对一线教师的课堂评价任务的设计和实施情况进行了系统的分析和梳理，以试图发现教师课堂评价任务设计和实施中存在的问题及其可能原因。与以往研究不同，本研究的特色：(1)理论驱动：构建了一个系统的理论框架；(2)以证据为中心的、注重整体的资料分析方法。

## 二、课堂评价任务设计和实施的理论框架

杨向东在已有文献的基础上提出了课堂评价任务设计和实施的框架(见表1)。[9]表1清晰地描述了课堂评价的一般过程以及教师和学生在每个过程中的任务。

表1 课堂评价中教师和学生的相关活动

| | 教师的工作 | 学生的参与 |
| --- | --- | --- |
| 目标制定 | 理解课程标准与当前教学内容的关系；<br>明确标准在当前学习中的具体体现；<br>制定当前学习所要达成的目标；<br>用学生理解的语言阐述学习目标。 | 了解和明晰这些学习目标；<br>明白达到目标时所能解答的任务特征；<br>知道该过程需要培养的策略、方法和能力。 |
| 学习过程 | 思考学生已有基础；<br>分析从学生现有水平到学习目标转换的过程和阶段；<br>理解不同水平学生的常见问题和表现特征。 | 了解和明晰自己的学习基础；<br>分析自己的学习特点、习惯和常见问题。 |
| 情境与任务创设 | 创设具体的教学情境、变换关系和呈现顺序；<br>设计评价任务的呈现方式，提问的措词，不同提问间的结构和顺序；<br>设计迁移程度逐步加强的练习、作业以及小测验等。 | 分析教学情境和评价任务，知晓自己理解和不理解的地方；<br>通过提问向教师和同学交流自己的理解和疑惑。 |
| 结果解释与反馈 | 对学生表现的学习程度进行合理评判；<br>分析学生表现的特征、进步和不足；<br>思考学生表现的可能原因；<br>分析和指出学生后继的努力方向。 | 通过自己解答、听取他人回答、班级讨论以及教师讲解，学会评价自己当前的学习状态；<br>学会根据课堂学习目标制定符合自己情况的具体目标。 |
| 决策和措施 | 及时调整提问问题和提问方式；<br>及时调整教学情境和评价任务；<br>及时调整预定教学目标。 | 制定符合自己情况的改进方案；<br>积极与家长、教师交流自己的学习情况和改进情况，并寻求帮助和指导。 |

目标的制定，目前最常用的方式，是以逻辑的方式对预期学习结果进行清晰鉴定。[10]—[15]一般的做法是根据内容和认知两个维度设计双向细目表，并给每个项目一定的权重。

近年来，随着建构主义理论的传播，对学生学习过程的思考越来越受到重视，人们越来越关注学生在达到学习结果的过程中是如何学习的。一种系统的做法是建立认知和学习模型(the model of cognition and learning)(简称学习模型)。[16]学习模型是基于对某一群体在某一内容领域的实证研究，提炼出这一群体在这一领域是如何学习的。由于要求相对较高，在实践使用中受到限制，但这一取向至少可以唤醒教师的意识：学生是如何学习的。

相对于学业目标逻辑鉴定的方法，学习模型提供了教师判断的更加清晰和详细的学业目标。同时，这些单个的子目标是置于整个的学习模型中来认识的。这些特征都使得学习模型

更加具有诊断性，而这是传统的对学业目标的鉴定方法所做不到的。

学业目标的设计是评价任务的设计的蓝图，除此之外，还涉及任务的刺激情境的设置以及对应答的规定，同时还要进行质量分析。[17][18]

在任务的情境设计上，对任务情境的真实复杂性越来越受到关注。[19]任务类型选取上，是为学业目标服务的，其本身并无优劣之分。同时，任务的类型和认知要求并没有存在线性的对应关系，虽然选择题考查大量的识记类的知识具有很大的优势，但是设计得好的选择题同样可以考查复杂的认知要求。同样即使是表现性评价，如果设计不好也可能测低水平的认知。[20][21]对学生应答的评价规则和相应任务的设计必须同时考虑。[22]为了收集到更丰富的信息，越来越强调在制定评价规则时考虑学生的学习过程，最好能建立完整的学习模型。除此之外，在整体的任务设计上，强调任务间的迁移程度不断增加。评价任务初步设计完成后，还需要对评价任务的效度、评价的偏见（assessment bias）进行分析，以保证评价任务的质量。[23]

在评价任务结果和解释上，本文主要研究课堂中的提问，在这里包括任何口头的说法或者手势，只要能引起学生的回应或回答，就被看做是问题。[24]并侧重提问顺序、叫答方式和反馈三个方面。本研究将以该理论框架为指导性框架，设计实证研究的被试选择、资料收集、文本编码和分析。

## 三、研究方法

### （一）被试

在被试的选择上，按照学科和专长两个维度进行抽取，并在校方的推荐下，选取了两位数学教师和两位语文教师，数学教师沈老师是县名师，数学年级组组长，有近 30 年的教龄，数学教师殷老师今年是工作的第五个年头。语文教师范老师是教研组长，有 20 多年教龄，语文教师安老师今年也是工作的第五个年头。

### （二）资料的获取

本研究跟踪每个教师的一个完整的教学单元。同学科的两位教师抽同样的教学单元。资料的类型包括两方面，第一种资料收集教师是怎么做的，包括教案、课堂实施情况、课后作业等，主要采用文本收集，课堂录音和观察的方法。第二种资料收集教师是怎么想的，主要采用访谈的方法收集教师思考和认识。

### （三）资料分析框架

1. 整体框架

依据研究问题，资料地分析分三个层次，这三个相互联系的层次为分析指示了清晰的思路（见图 1）。本文主要呈现课堂内评价任务设计与使用的状况。

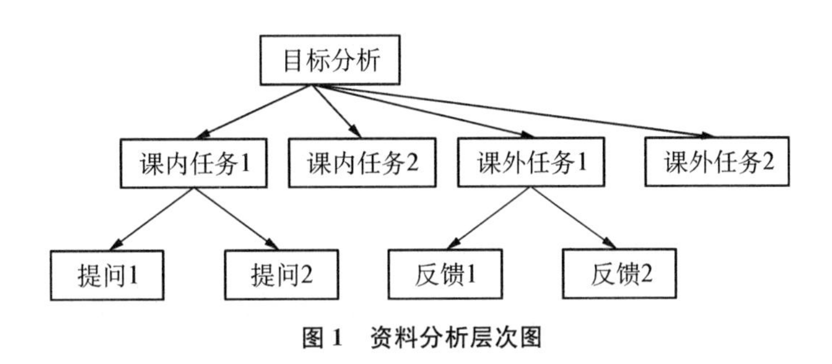


**图1　资料分析层次图**

资料的分析顺序遵循自下而上的原则，对原始资料进行层层提炼。这种分析方式尊重原始资料，避免在没有证据支持或部分证据支持下的过度推断。分析的具体框架见表2。

**表2　资料的分析框架**

| 维度 | 研究问题 | 资料类型 |
| --- | --- | --- |
| 目标设计 | 教师是怎样设计教学目标的？ | 访谈；文本；课堂录音 |
| 任务设计 | 教师怎样设计任务顺序？ | 访谈；文本 |
|  | 教师怎样设计任务情境？ | 访谈；文本 |
|  | 教师怎样设计任务类型？ | 访谈；文本 |
|  | 教师怎样设计评价规则？ | 课堂录音；访谈 |
|  | 教师怎样做质量分析？ | 访谈 |
| 任务使用 | 教师的提问顺序有怎样特点？ | 课堂录音；课堂观察 |
|  | 学生的回答方式及指向有哪些？ | 课堂录音；课堂观察 |
|  | 教师的反馈方式和指向是什么？ | 课堂录音；课堂观察 |

2. 评价任务的分析

评价任务的分析包括任务顺序、目标对应性、任务情境和题型、评价规则等方面。我们需要先鉴定认知水平和情境分类的框架。表3呈现了认知水平的分析框架。

**表3　认知水平的分析框架**

| 认知水平 | 描　述 |  | 示　　例 |
| --- | --- | --- | --- |
| 低认知水平 | 1. 记忆 | 记忆水平指向学生直接从长时记忆中提取信息便能解决的问题。 | 以下各个多面体分别是几面体？ |
|  | 2. 简单领会 | 简单领会涉及信息的简单转换，一般只需要一到两步的认知操作。 | 说出圆锥，球的三视图各是什么图形。 |

<table>
<tr><th>认知水平</th><th colspan="2">描　述</th><th>示　　例</th></tr>
<tr><td>低认知水平</td><td>3. 简单应用</td><td>简单应用指能将学过的知识应用于新的具体情境中，解决一些简单的问题。</td><td>观察如图所示的首饰盒，它是一个怎样的多面体？这个多面体与直四棱柱有什么关系？<br>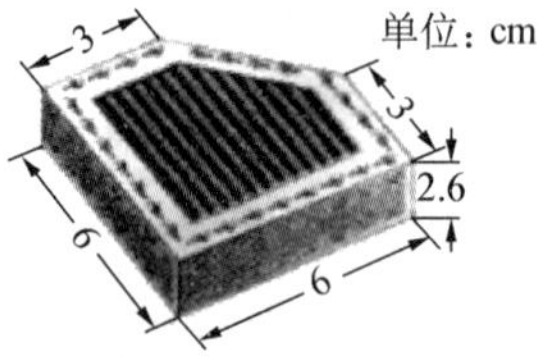<br></td></tr>
<tr><td rowspan="3">高认知水平</td><td>4. 复杂领会</td><td>复杂领会涉及到信息的复杂转换，一般需要两步以上的认知操作。</td><td>由5个相同的小立方块搭成的几何体如图所示，请画出它的三视图。<br>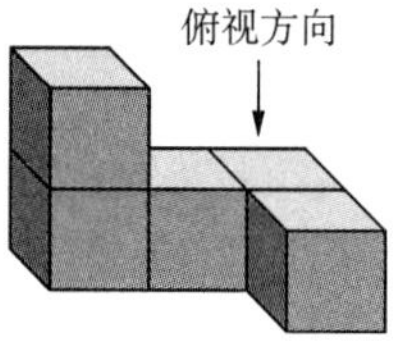<br></td></tr>
<tr><td>5. 推理</td><td>推理在这里取一个比较宽泛的定义，指根据已有的信息进行归纳、比较、推断，得出一个新的结论。</td><td>直棱柱的侧棱数、棱数、顶点数、面数之间有什么关系呢？<br>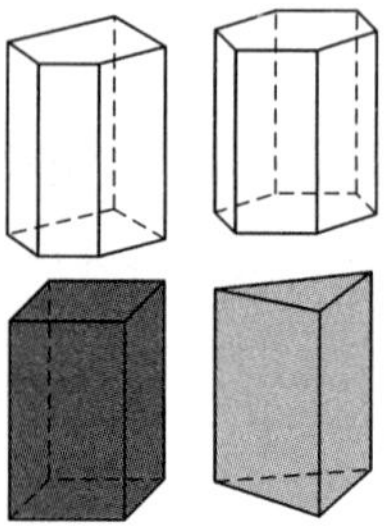<br><table><tr><th></th><th>侧棱数</th><th>棱数（E）</th><th>顶点数（V）</th><th>画数（F）</th></tr><tr><td>直三棱柱</td><td></td><td></td><td></td><td></td></tr><tr><td>直四棱柱</td><td></td><td></td><td></td><td></td></tr><tr><td>直五棱柱</td><td></td><td></td><td></td><td></td></tr><tr><td>直六棱柱</td><td></td><td></td><td></td><td></td></tr><tr><td>…</td><td></td><td></td><td></td><td></td></tr><tr><td>直 $n$ 棱柱</td><td></td><td></td><td></td><td></td></tr></table></td></tr>
<tr><td>6. 综合应用</td><td>综合应用指将学过的知识综合应用于新的情境中，灵活解决一些较复杂的问题，表现为对知识作横向联系，对要解决的问题个组成部分的辨认，分析，并综合应用。</td><td>在一个边长为4 m的正方体的房间里，一只蜘蛛在A处，一只苍蝇在G处，试问：蜘蛛去抓苍蝇需要爬行的最短路程是多少？<br>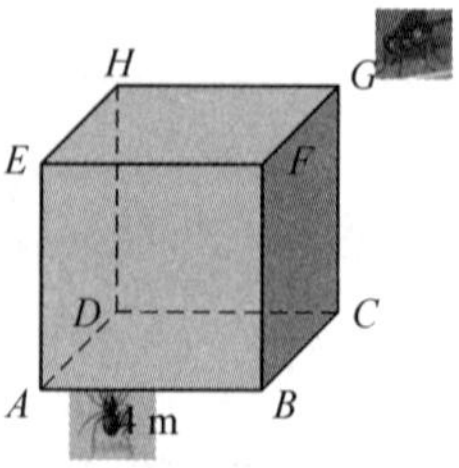<br></td></tr>
</table>

评价任务分析涉及任务情境的分类，表 4 呈现了情境分类的分析框架。

**表 4　情境分类的分析框架**

| 纯数学特征题目 | 结合不吻合学生自己生活的情境 | 结合学生自己生活的情境 |
| --- | --- | --- |
| 下面的图形都是立方体的展开图吗？ 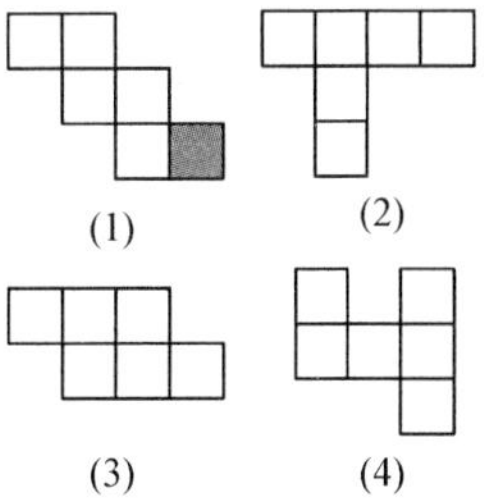<br>(1)　(2)<br>(3)　(4) | 例题　观察如图所示的首饰盒，它是一个怎样的多面体？这个多面体与直四棱柱有什么关系？ 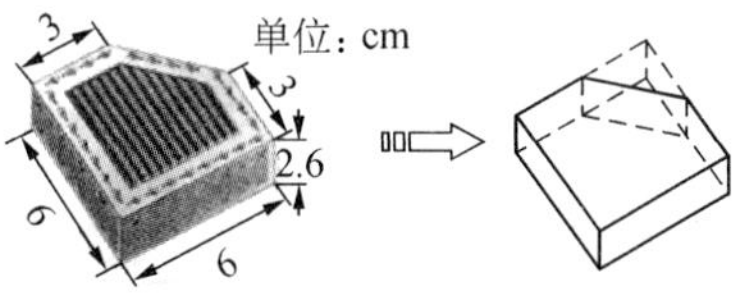<br>单位：cm　3　3　2.6　6　6 | 在一个边长为 4 m 的正方体的房间里，一只蜘蛛在 A 处，一只苍蝇在 G 处，试问：蜘蛛去抓苍蝇需要爬行的最短路程是多少？ 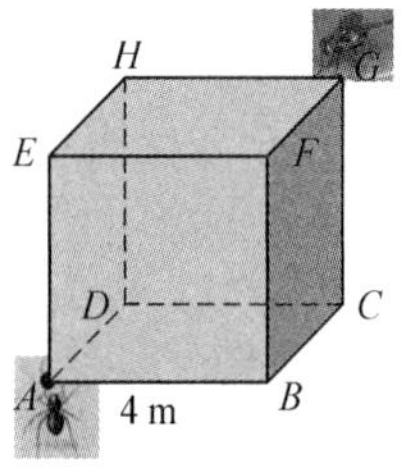<br>H　G　E　F　D　C　A　4 m　B<br>图？已有知识应用的题目 |

3. 提问分析

提问顺序的分析，以每个初始问题的整个处理过程为单位，提取提问顺序的类型。此外，对学生回答和反馈的分析，根据已有的研究文献和对原始材料的提炼，我们制定了相应的分析框架。

**表 5　学生回答的分析框架**

| 课时片段 | 访谈实录(信息编码) | 编码与分析 |
| --- | --- | --- |
| 片段 1 | 问：这堂课的学习目标，你当时是怎么考虑的呢<br>沈：这堂课它主要是认识直棱柱，认识，还是以概念为主啦，是不是，就是从多面体到棱柱，里面的一些，棱柱里面有直棱柱和斜棱柱喽，这些基本概念让他们弄清楚，那么常见的就是三棱、四棱、五棱啊六棱啊，这些比较常见的图形。再一个呢就是，直棱柱它的那个性质，它的几条性质给他们理一理，其实这些呢，他小学里有这个基础了，所以现在无非就是给他整理整理，在原有的基础上再系统一点啦就是。 | 学习目标：<br>(1) 认识直棱柱<br>(2) 理解有关棱柱的基本概念<br>(3) 系统理解直棱柱的性质 |
| 片段 2 | 问：那你觉得，学生学到怎样的程度，你觉得这个目标掌握了呢<br>沈：这个呢就是他能够描述这个图形。再一个呢就是，就比方说这个例题那，就是能够分析。 | 学习目标：<br>(4) 能够分析和描述有关直棱柱的图形 |
| 片段 3 | 问：你设计时用了很多图片。设置这些活动当时是怎样的考虑呢。<br>沈：我们数学当中呢，一些图形是从生活中抽象出来的，反过来又为生活服务啦，这样子，那用生活当中的一些例子，这样更贴近生活的实际，这样呢让学生能更加容易认识这些数学知识。 | 任务设计：<br>(1) 数学知识在生活实际问题中的应用 |

**表 6　教师课堂反馈的分析框架**

| | 课次 | 内容简介 | 教 学 目 标 |
| --- | --- | --- | --- |
| 沈教师 | 1 | 认识直棱柱 | 认识直棱柱的概念，性质；观察能力；立体感；探索规律；空间能力 |
| | 2 | 表面展开图 | 知道 11 种展开图类型；空间想象能力；会画 |

续 表

| | 课次 | 内容简介 | 教学目标 |
|---|---|---|---|
| 殷教师 | 1 | 认识直棱柱 | 知道直棱柱特征(详述各个特征); |
| | 2 | 表面展开图 | 理解这个展开图,它的11种类型,然后是这些展开图的应用,根据这些展开图解决一些几何问题。 |

### (四)资料分析过程

1. 相关信息的分类与编码

按照研究问题寻找对应的原始资料,然后按照分析框架对原始资料进行编码处理。给每个意义单位一个码号,码号的设置注重“本土概念”的提取,在不能提取的情况下,也可以自己设定。例如,访谈资料中显示教师对知识点的提取作为教学的目标,而对知识点的认知水平的关注相对比较模糊,我们可以用“知识点”作为这一类现象的码号。

2. 信息的组织与统计

按照分析框架将相关码号进行归类统计,并按照分析层次图进行组织。

3. 信息的整合和解释

针对分析框架中的每个问题,结合老师所给信息进行描述和解释。

## 四、结果分析

限于篇幅,只分析两位数学老师。

### (一)教学目标的内容及其分析

表7 两位老师其中两堂课的教学目标内容

| 教师 | 课次 | 内容简介 | 目标 |
|---|---|---|---|
| 1 | 1 | 认识直棱柱 | 认识直棱柱的概念,性质;观察能力;立体感;探索规律;空间能力; |
| 1 | 2 | 表面展开图 | 知道11种展开图类型;空间想象能力;会画; |
| 2 | 1 | 认识直棱柱 | 知道直棱柱特征(详述各个特征); |
| 2 | 2 | 表面展开图 | 理解这个展开图,它的11种类型,然后是这些展开图的应用,根据这些展开图解决一些几何问题。 |

分析和评论:两位老师对教学目标的内容维度有非常清晰的把握,能认识到对知识的把握不仅仅是记忆,还有理解,应用,培养空间能力,观察能力等。但相对来说,对内容知识的阐述清晰,对目标的认知维度表述相对含糊,特别在提到一些高认知水平时常常脱离具体内容。

**(二) 教师是怎么设计评价任务的**

1. 评价任务的来源

两位教师基本选择现成材料，很少自编课堂评价任务，这一行为本身，就反映出教师结合自己所教学生实际情况的意识淡漠。

2. 两位老师的评价任务安排情况

我们这里整体呈现沈老师其中的三堂课和殷老师四堂课的评价任务安排。

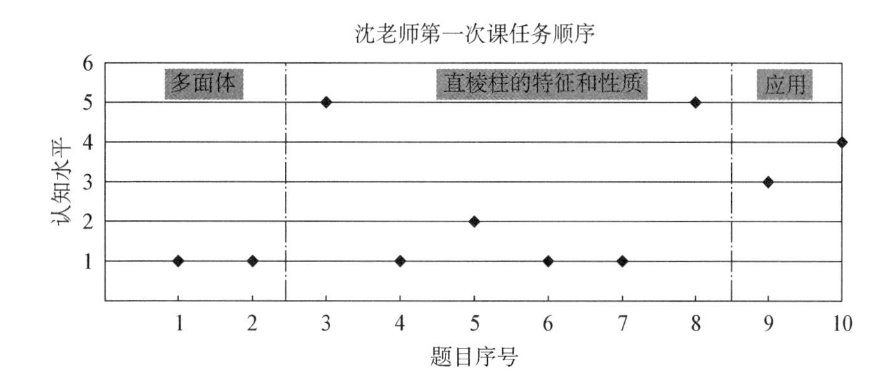


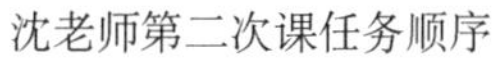


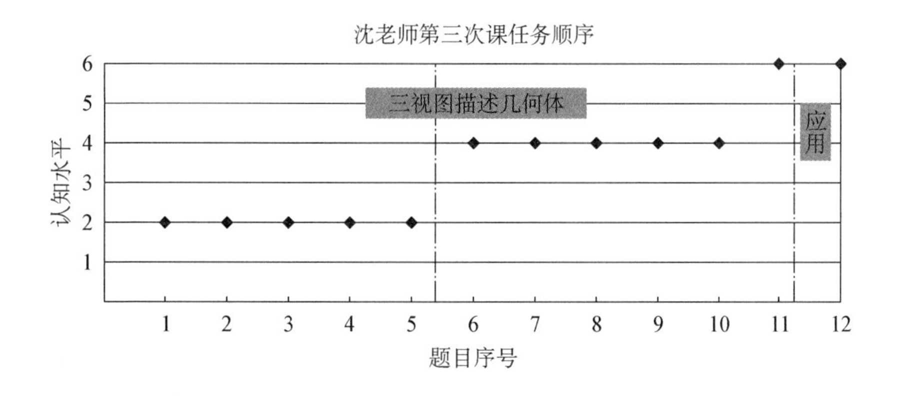

殷老师第一次课任务顺序

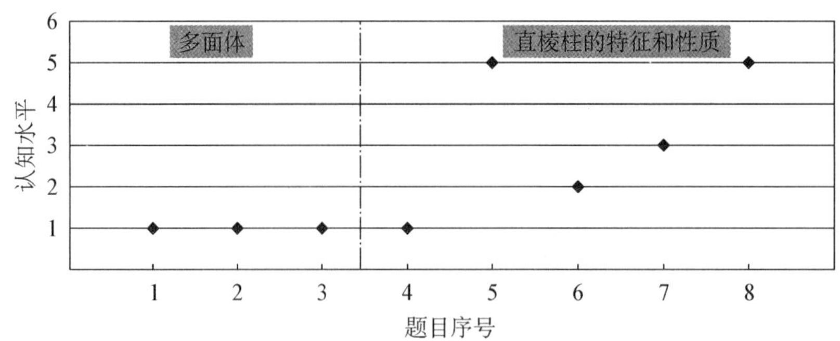


殷老师第二次课任务顺序

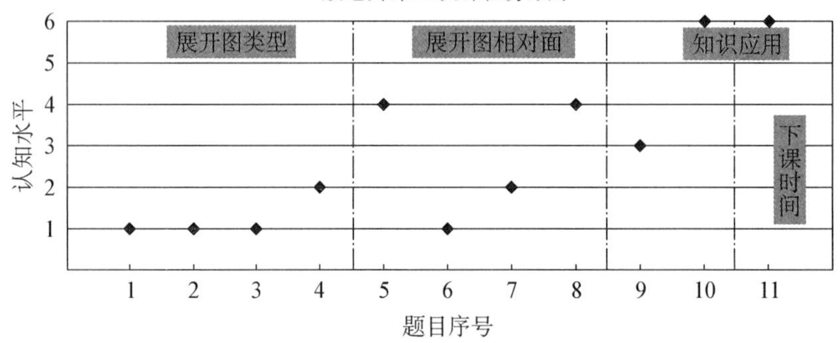


殷老师第三次课任务顺序

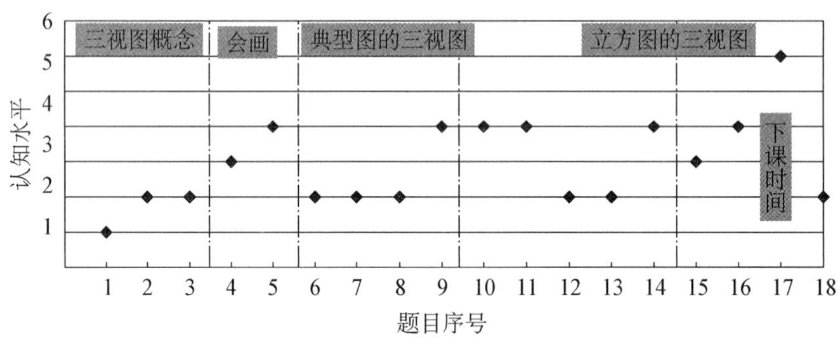


殷老师第四次课任务顺序

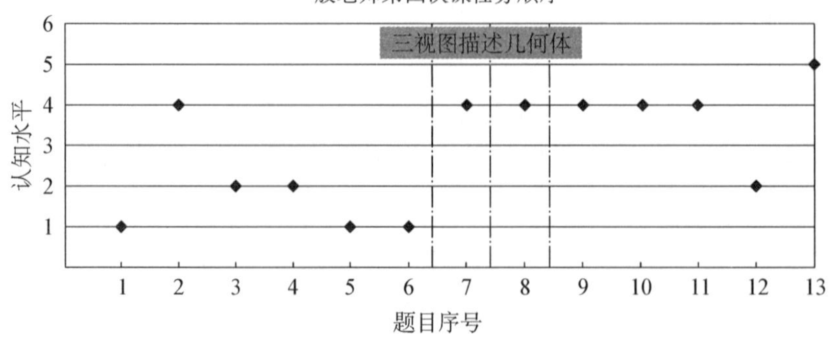

3. 目标的对应性

沈老师在题量上相对少,殷老师在题目容量上明显大大超过沈老师。在任务顺序上,沈老师安排的评价任务在认知水平上有一个逐渐迁移的过程,而殷老师在这方面相对来说显得随意。

沈老师相对清晰地意识到教学目标的对应性。比如下面一段对话是我针对一组题目进行的询问。

豆:这几道题目出的质量怎么样,你当时是怎么一个判断呢?

沈:根据我这个教学目标啦,因为我这个课呢教学目标主要是掌握一些概念啦,掌握一些性质就可以了。然后呢这个还有点探究精神就可以了。

沈老师这种目标对应性的意识,使得沈老师选择的评价任务显得紧凑,一定程度避免了随意增加题量(详见任务顺序的分析)。

而殷老师对教学目标对应性的意识相对模糊。当我询问这些题目具体是怎么选来的,殷老师有一段总结性的表达:"……那我肯定要自己看一下的,自己做一下的,然后筛选一下,肯定跟今天这堂课的内容有关啦。"这也突出表现在任务安排的大容量,且任务顺序显得随意(详见任务顺序的分析)。

4. 任务情境和任务类型

**表 8 两位老师设计的评价任务情境统计表**

| | 纯数学特征 | 结合不吻合学生生活体验的情境 | 结合吻合学生生活体验的情境 |
|---|---|---|---|
| 沈老师 | 25(83%) | 3(10%) | 2(6.7%) |
| 殷老师 | 40(89%) | 3(6.7%) | 2(4.3%) |

从两位老师的任务情境统计表中可以发现,基本上是纯数学特征的题目,分别占了83%和89%。由于教师用的评价任务基本上是现成拿来的,因此在任务情境和学生生活体验的结合上,也是一个值得探讨的问题,两位老师满足吻合学生体验的任务情境分别只占6.7%和4.3%。

事实上,教师常会说到结合学生的生活。例如沈老师说:"我们数学当中呢,一些图形是从生活当中抽象出来的,反过来又为生活服务啦,这样子,那用生活当中的一些例子,这样更贴近生活的实际,这样呢让学生能更加容易认识这些数学知识。"对照任务情境的统计表,可以发现,这种阐述仅仅停留在"宣称理论"的阶段。在我对沈老师的访谈过程中,有一个细节可以充分的体现沈老师对结合学生生活情境的态度。在我的访谈中,我询问了一道题目(见题目)的设计意图。

这是沈老师的反应:"第一个呢联系实际吗,让他看看,实际这个也不大看得出,这个我还是把它去掉。这个很难描述,叫我也描述不好,这个建筑物的外形很难表达。"于是沈老师立马下面图片所示的建筑中，哪些体现了直棱柱的立体形状，哪些不是？

题目

**图 3　题目示例**

把这道题目刷掉了。

在任务类型的考虑上，对一直跟考试打交道的老师来说，似乎是理所当然的事。沈老师说："根据我的经验基本上能够覆盖，就是学生可能碰到的题型。"当我问到题型的设计上是怎么考虑时，殷老师对我的提问似乎感到有点惊讶。下面是殷老师的答复："题型是哇，你这个选择题的话，问题就比较少，这样的话我们可以提很多问题，比方说，3 跟谁对应？'情'跟谁对应，'好'跟谁对应，这样口答就可以了，而且很直接的，不需要做填空题，也不需要做选择题，而且这一个的话，也是要通过计算，比方求相反数，要会写一个相反数，负号跟负号……这样的话其实也可以作为填空题的形式。这个的话它比较有点难度，所以这里用了一个选择题，这样的话，学生只要判断一下就可以了，通过这个给出的图形去判断就可以了，一个一个去判断。"这段话的回答显得有点语无伦次，可以看出殷老师对于题型似乎没有特意的注意过。

5. 评价规则

从两位老师在课堂上的反馈情况看（详见表 11），几乎所有的反馈都是针对答案本身，两位老师的比例分别占了 91.9%和 99.5%，即使是少部分的追问也是针对学生不完整的回答，由此看出两位老师对正确答案预设的强烈程度，使得他们奉行的评价规则只有对错两种情况。

6. 评价任务设计时的其他思考

沈老师在选取题目时，对学生薄弱环节有比较清楚的认识。例如有一道题目是教师在书本原有题目的基础上自己加上去的，他说："这个还是跟原来学的东西有个承上启下的联系，然后呢这个东西，算呢是个薄弱点，平时呢学生算个体积、面积都不会算。所以呢，这样可以加强一些。"

此外，对应试要求的考虑是很重要的部分，例如在询问某一组题目设计的意图时，沈老师解释到："这个巩固练习呢（指第二题，实际上是教师的总结，没有设问）因为立方体、长方体，这个是虽然是最简单，但是也是呢这个使用最广泛，一般的题目都是在这个里面的。"

### (三) 教师是怎么使用评价任务的

1. 两位教师的课堂提问顺序分析

沈老师四堂课总计有37个对话主题，其中初始问题是低认知水平的提问总共有19个，占51%，初始问题是高认知水平的提问总共有18个，占49%。殷老师四堂课总计有67个对话主题，其中初始问题为低认知水平提问总共有48个，占72%。初始问题为高认知水平的提问总共有19个，占28%。殷老师课堂容量相对大很多。

在低认知水平提问中，教师的处理基本都是随问随答的封闭性问题，学生是封闭性的回答。这样的提问更多是为记忆考虑的。而在高认知水平提问中，沈老师主要用讲解提示和提问封闭性问题的方式来减少学生的认知负担。因此，高认知的提问却基本上只有低认知水平的封闭性答案(详见学生回答的分析)。两位老师很少有追问，且多数为强化答案的追问，对学生思考过程不感兴趣。

**表9 两位老师课堂提问顺序特征的归类**

| 提问顺序类型 | 类型描述 | 主题编号统计数 | |
|---|---|---|---|
| | | 沈老师 | 殷老师 |
| 1. 低认知水平平行式提问 | 同一个主题的一系列同一类型的问题，且这同一类型的问题处于低认知水平 | 12 | 34 |
| 2. 单个低认知水平提问 | 教师的整个提问过程只有一个低认知水平的问题 | 4 | 12 |
| 3. 低认知水平提问，教师追问 | 教师的初始问题是低认知水平，教师针对学生答案进行了追问，有时是针对学生的思考过程，有时为强化答案 | 3 | 2 |
| 4. 高认知水平问题，讲解提示＋低水平封闭性提问 | 初始的核心问题是高认知水平的，没有给学生思考时间，教师直接用的策略是：讲解和提一些封闭型的低认知水平问题 | 6 | 11 |
| 5. 高认知水平问题，教师分步引导 | 初始问题属于高认知水平，并给予学生比较充分的思考时间，但没有充分表达机会。教师以讲解和低认知水平提问作为反馈 | 9 | 3 |
| 6. 高认知水平问题，没有分步引导 | 初始问题属于高认知水平，并给予学生比较充分的思考时间，个别学生有较充分的表达 | 2 | 4 |
| 7. 高认知水平提问，有追问 | 教师提出高认知水平的初始问题，伴有不同程度的追问 | 1 | 1 |

2. 两位教师课堂上学生回答的分析

从学生的回答方式看，学生齐答的比率特别的高，沈老师课堂上占了52.6%，殷老师课堂上占了62.1%。再进一步对照齐答的内容，都包括在低认知水平和机械判断和无回答上。其次，学生喊答的比例上，沈老师课堂上占了17.9%，殷老师课堂上占了25.2%，对照喊答的认知水平，仍然主要集中在低认知水平上，这也反映出即使是喊答的学生，其思考的深度是值得疑问的。从学生个答的情况看，高认知水平的回答也只占了很小的比例，大部分仍属于低认知水平的回答。

从认知水平的角度看，两位老师课堂上低认知水平的回答都为79%，而机械判断是否沈老师和殷老师课堂上分别占了11.5%和6.4%。这两项的总和分别为90.5%和85.4%。对照两位老师提问中的初始问题情况看(详见提问顺序部分的分析),学生的高认知水平的回答比例远远低于高认知水平初始问题的比例,绝大部分高认知水平的初始问题都被转化成了低认知水平的问题。

此外,一个有趣的现象是学生的提问,而这里的提问第一次是齐答的形式说“听不懂”,第二次是有个别学生还没听懂,喊答的形式说“听不懂”,这种学生提问自己疑惑的方式是紧跟在教师讲解而听不懂的情境下。

**表10 两位老师四堂课学生回答情况统计表**

| 回答方式 | 回答内容 | | | | | 总计 |
|---|---|---|---|---|---|---|
| | 无回答 | 机械判断是否 | 低认知水平回答 | 高认知水平回答 | 学生提问 | |
| 沈教师 | | | | | | |
| 提问前,先点名 | | | | | | |
| 提问后,学生个答 | 3(4%) | | 51(74%) | 15(22%) | | 69(29%) |
| 提问后,学生齐答 | 3(2.4%) | 22(17.8%) | 98(79%) | | 1(0.8%) | 124(53%) |
| 提问后,学生喊答 | | 5(11%) | 34(82%) | 2(5%) | 1(2%) | 41(18%) |
| 总计 | 6(3%) | 27(12%) | 183(78%) | 17(7%) | 2(0.8%) | 235 |
| 殷教师 | | | | | | |
| 提问前,先点名 | | | | | | |
| 提问后,学生个答 | | | 30(65%) | 16(35%) | | 46(13%) |
| 提问后,学生齐答 | 3(2%) | 21(9%) | 200(89%) | | | 225(62%) |
| 提问后,学生喊答 | | 3(4%) | 56(62%) | 31(34%) | | 91(25%) |
| 总计 | 3(0.8%) | 24(6.7%) | 286(80%) | 47(13%) | | 360 |

从以上的分析可以看出,殷老师的课堂上学生是很少有充分思考和表达的机会的。

3. 两位教师课堂反馈分析

从教师反馈内容上看,两位老师四堂课中针对答案的反馈分别为91.9%和99.5%,针对得出答案的思考过程分别为5.1%和0.5%,沈老师还有3%的反馈是针对学生“自我”的。可以说,绝大部分属于教师用预设的答案在核对学生的回答,而对学生的思考过程没有什么兴趣。

另外一个有趣的现象是:表扬和批评很少见。沈老师的表扬总共出现了1次,批评总共出现了6次,而殷老师没有出现。对照两位老师的提问(详见提问顺序的分析),两位老师通过多种策略转化高认知水平的问题,以减少学生认知障碍,使得学生回答的问题绝大部分是复述式的。在这样的大背景下,即使学生回答对了,也没有特意表扬的必要(沈老师唯一的这次表扬是因为一位学生回答正确了一道高认知水平的题目)。同样,在这样的大背景下,学生很少在课堂上公开犯错的机会,批判当然也不多见。

从教师反馈方式上看,前六种反馈方式占据了所有反馈中的绝大部分的比率。概括的说,教师在反馈方式上基本是对学生回答作出肯定或否定的评判，还经常伴随详细的讲解。即使是追问，大部分类似于“沈：这个我们刚才已经看到过了。生：直三棱柱。沈：什么柱啊？生齐：直三棱柱”这种确认答案式的追问。而针对学生思考过程的追问很少出现，此外，四堂课没有出现教师鼓励学生提出问题的行为。

**表 11　两位老师反馈情况统计表**

| 反馈方式 | 沈教师 | | 殷教师 | |
|---|---|---|---|---|
| | 针对答案 | 针对思考过程 | 针对答案 | 针对思考过程 |
| 对错判断或重复学生答案 | 84(39%) | | 157(43%) | |
| 对错判断＋引申讲解 | 65(30%) | | 75(20%) | |
| 无正面反馈的肯定性默认 | 37(17%) | | 77(21%) | |
| 肯定性默认＋引申讲解 | 7(3%) | | 7(2%) | |
| 忽视学生回答，提供正确答案 | 7(3%) | 2 | 21(6%) | |
| 打断学生，自己代答 | 1(0.5%) | | | |
| 追问 | 13(6%) | 9 | 30(8%) | 2 |
| 总计 1 | 214(92%) | 11(4.7%) | 367(99.5%) | 2(0.5%) |
| 鼓励称赞学生回答 | 1 | | | |
| 消极批评 | 7 | | | |
| 鼓励学生提出问题 | | | | |
| 总计 2 | 222 | 11 | 367 | 2 |

## 五、结论

1. 两位老师在描述教学目标时，注重内容的逻辑，对具体内容的认知水平这个维度没有清晰的意识。

2. 从严格意义上讲，两位老师几乎没有评价任务设计的行为，几乎没有自编的评价任务。但另一方面，教师在选择具体评价任务时也体现着他们的思考，我们这里的评价任务设计是从宽泛的角度讲的。因此，对于评价任务的设计，两位老师都没有非常清晰的意识。概括地讲，根据知识点选取相应的题目，并凭经验对题目的质量作出判断。

3. 在评价任务的使用上，学生很少有充分的思考和表达的机会。体现在提问上，多是低认知水平的提问，即使初始问题是高认知水平的提问，也多转化成了低认知水平的问题。学生回答的内容也几乎都是低认知的封闭性答案。教师的反馈只是在核对答案，反馈的方式也带有封闭性，并不能揭示学生的思考。

参考文献

[1] Guskey, T. R. (2003). How Classroom Assessment Improve Learning. *Educational Leadership*, 60

(5),1-6.

[2][8][19] 杨向东.谈课堂评价的地位与重建[J].全球教育展望,2009(9).

[3] Black, P. & Wiliam, D. (1998). Assessment and Classroom Learning. *Assessment in Education: Principles, Policy & Practice*, 5(1),7-74.

[4] Crooks, T.J. (1988). The Impact of Classroom Evaluation on Students. *Review of Educational Research*, 58(4),438-481.

[5] S tiggins, R. J. (2001). The Unfulfilled Promise of Classroom Assessment. *Educational Measurement, Issues and Practice*,20(3),5-15.

[6] Stiggins, R. J. (2008). *A Call for the Development of Balanced Assessment Systems*. ETS, Portland, OR.97204.

[7] Shepard, L. A. (2000). The Role of Classroom Assessment in Teaching and Learning. *CSE Technical Report* 517. CRESST/University of Colorado at Boulder.

[9] 杨向东.促进学习的课堂评价的设计与使用[J].基础教育课程,2010(6).

[10] [美]拉尔夫.W.泰勒.课程与教学的基本原理[M].施良方,译.北京:人民教育出版社,1994.

[11] B.S.布卢姆,等.教育目标分类学——第一分册 认知领域[M].罗黎辉,等,译.上海:华东师范大学出版社,1986.

[12] Linn R. L. & Gronlund N. E. (2000). *Measurement and Assessment in Teaching* (*8th. ed*). Englewood Cliffs, NJ:Prentice Hall.

[13] Mcmillan. J.H.(2001). *Classroom Assessment: Principles and Practice for Effective Teaching*. NJ: A Pearson Education Company.

[14] Richard J. Stiggins.促进学习的学生参与式课堂评价[M].“促进教师发展与学生成长的评价研究”项目组,译.北京:中国轻工业出版社,2005.

[15] L. W.安德生,等.学习、教学和评估的分类学——布卢姆教育目标分类学修订版(简缩本)[M].皮连生,主译.上海:华东师范大学出版社,2007.

[16][18][20][21] National Research Council. (2001). Knowing what students know: the science and design of educational assessment. Pelligrino, J., Chudowsky, N., & Glaser, R., editors. *Board on testing and assessment*, Washington, DC: National Academy Press.

[17] 杨向东.教育测量在教育评价中的角色[J].全球教育展望,2007.(11).

[22] 波帕姆.促进教学的课堂评价[M].“促进教师发展与学生成长的评价研究”项目组,译.北京:中国轻工业出版社,2003.

[23] [美]加里·D.鲍里奇.有效教学方法[M].易东平,译.南京:江苏教育出版社,2002.

# A Theory-driven Approach to Analyzing the Design and Implementation of Classroom

## Assessment Tasks by Teachers

Yusong Dou Xiangdong Yang

Classroom assessment bears a central role in the achievement assessment systems that are advocated by the new curriculum reform. However, due to the dominance of summative assessment in the current assessment systems, little efforts have been put into the research and improvement of classroom assessment. Consequently, subjective reflections over actual practices become the salient feature for the current studies on classroom assessment, which are mainly conducted by in-service teachers. The current study investigated the practices of designing and implementing classroom assessment tasks of two mathematics teachers, employing a new way of data analytic approach that is theory-driven, evidence-centered and holistic. Results show that, the two teachers focus more on content than on cognitive dimensions when it comes to goal setting for a teaching unit or lesson. No clear metacognitive awareness are found for both teachers in terms of assessment task design. Rarely do students have the opportunities to engage high-order thinking or to express themselves during the process of implementing such assessment tasks in classes by the teachers.

**Keywords**: classroom assessment; task design; task implementation; Mathematics teacher

# 发展教师评价素养：学业评价政策的视角①

郑东辉

【摘要】学业评价政策通过自身的规范性和强制性以及不同层级的执行，影响教师评价素养的养成与发展。从促进教师评价素养发展的视角来考察，现有的学业评价政策存在一些遗漏与不完善之处，一是用于改善课堂评价实践的投入不足，二是过分关注外部评价，义务教育阶段学生统考失范。改善现有的学业评价政策，需要建立和执行权力分享的学业评价政策，合理分配学业评价权力，培育学业评价中介组织，加大对课堂评价的实际投入。

【关键词】评价素养；学业评价；政策

【作者简介】郑东辉/宁波大学教师教育学院副教授，博士

教师评价素养是指教师开展学生学业评价所应具备的专业智能。具有良好评价素养的教师，能够教的更有效，而且能帮助学生轻负高效地学习，提升教和学的品质。然而，据笔者调查发现：中小学教师的评价素养处于较低水平，与所期望的素养水平相差很远。究其原因，一个重要的影响因素是学业评价政策。[1]那么，学业评价政策到底对教师评价素养的发展产生了怎样的影响？学业评价政策如何变动才有助于教师评价素养的提升？就需要我们去探个究竟。

## 一、学业评价政策对教师评价素养的影响

政策，字面上理解就是政治上的策略或谋略。在公共政策的视域里，“政策是国家机关、政党及其他政治团体在特定时期为实现或服务于一定社会政治、经济、文化目标所采取的政治行为或规定的行为准则，它是一系列谋略、法令、措施、办法、方法、条例等的总称”[2]。简而言之，政策是政府或执政党用以规范、引导和协调有关团体和个人行动的准则或指南。如果从政策执行的视角来看，政策又往往被理解为一种由特定政策制定者所产生的而在政策实施过程中又被实施者所阅读的文本(text)。[3]为了考察的方便，我们把政策理解为一种行动准则的文本，不管是法规、指令，还是指示或计划。学业评价政策作为下位概念，可以把它概括为这样一种政策，即党政机关为规范与引导合理的学生学业评价行为所采取的一系列行动，并以法令、条例、措施、办法与意见等形式加以规定。其中学业评价是对学生的学习结果和课堂中的学习

① 本文系浙江省社科规划课题“中小学教师课堂评价知识发展研究——以浙江省为例”(课题编号为10CGJY13YB)的成果，同时得到宁波大学胡岚优秀博士基金资助。

表现进行评价，主要关注学业成就评价。

学业评价政策对学生学业评价的种种规范和期待，表面看来与教师评价素养似乎没有多大关系，政策落实到教师身上要经历许多环节，可能会稀释掉许多内容。实际上，教师作为学生学业评价最为重要的执行者，不可避免地受制于政策，教师所坚守的评价理念以及所表现出来的评价行为很多都源于政策的规定。如果从学业评价政策本身以及政策执行过程两个方面来看，政策对教师评价素养的形成与发展却有着重要的影响，甚至可以说是决定性的影响。

政策本身的规范性、强制性影响教师对学业评价的理解与判断。由于学业评价不仅关系学生的学业成长，而且也与学生的升学相关，具有一定的利害性，教师一般不愿意对此作出自己独到的理解并落实，往往会从众或追随一般性的关于学业评价的集体行动，或者更愿意听从教育行政部门关于学生学业评价的规定，以降低学业评价带来的各种风险。由此看来，学业评价政策对于教师理解学业评价发挥着重要的示范作用，或者说，与其他教育政策相比，学业评价政策对教师的威慑力更强，也更容易影响或主导教师对学业评价的理解。另一方面，通过执行与落实学业评价政策，教师来源于政策的学业评价理解就会被不断强化，进而表现出与政策基本一致的评价行为。当然，前提条件是保证政策的正当性和合理性，并能在不同层级得到有效的执行，促使教师去学习那些适合政策的评价知识与技能，开展评价实践。如果不然，学业评价政策与教师现实行为之间就无法形成一种联系，甚至会断裂，教师更愿意相信与践行所在学校或教师群体形成的评价惯习，进而产生“上有政策、下有对策”的现象。在政策本身的规则和政策执行的引导下，教师会有选择地学习和实践学业评价，生成和发展那些迎合政策的评价素养。概而言之，学业评价政策对于教师评价素养的养成和发展具有重要的导向作用，如果它有利于教师实践合理的学业评价，在一定程度上就会促进素养的发展，反之则不然。

## 二、现有学业评价政策的考量

既然学业评价政策对教师的评价素养有着重要的影响，那么就有必要去分析现行的学业评价政策，考察它给教师的素养发展产生了那些影响，正面或负面，抑或兼而有之。当然，我们不可能也没有必要对所有层级制定的全部学业评价政策进行全方位考察，只要重点分析国家教育部颁发的有关学业评价政策的重要文本，加上调查地方的执行情况以及为执行发布的相关政策，就可以窥其大概面貌。因为从理论上说一个大一统的中央集权制国家，政令出自中央，地方应该与此保持基本一致，而且重要或关键政策具有指导性和权威性，很多与之相关的政策大多是它的补充或解释。下面就以国家教育部颁发的几个重要政策为例进行具体分析。

自 1996 年开始酝酿第八次基础教育课程改革以来，国家教育部专门就学生学业评价发布的政令并不多，集中体现在以下一些文件或法规中。《基础教育课程改革纲要(试行)》(2001)提出：“建立促进学生全面发展的评价体系。评价不仅要关注学生的学业成绩，而且要发现和发展学生多方面的潜能，了解学生发展中的需求，帮助学生认识自我，建立自信。发挥评价的教育功能，促进学生在原有水平上的发展。”“考试命题要依据课程标准，杜绝设置偏题、怪题的现象。教师应对每位学生的考试情况做出具体的分析指导，不得公布学生考试成绩并按考试成绩排列名次。”这主要是从推进课程改革的宏大背景下提出的最高指示，特别强调课程评价中有关学业评价的基本原则。2002年出台的《教育部关于推进中小学评价与考试制度改革的通知》则更具解释和指导意义，明确提出从评价内容、标准、评价方法和改进计划等方面来建立以促进学生发展为目标的评价体系，改革和完善中小学升学考试与招生制度、普通高中会考制度和高校招生制度，并强调“考试是评价的主要方式之一，考试应与其他评价方式相结合，要充分利用考试促进每个学生的进步”。“不得以学生考试成绩作为评价教师的唯一标准。”还特别提到教师评价学生的重要方法，如行为观察、成长记录和评语等。接下来的一些关键政策大多依据该通知来制定，如《教育部关于基础教育课程改革实验区初中毕业考试与普通高中招生制度改革的指导意见》(2005)明确：“学业考试的命题应根据学科课程标准，……学业考试的方式要多样化。”“普通高中招生要坚持综合评价、择优录取的原则。学业考试成绩和综合素质的评价结果应成为普通高中招生的主要依据。”《教育部关于贯彻“义务教育法”进一步规范义务教育办学行为的若干意见》(2006)重申“要严格控制学生在校考试次数，不得公布学生考试成绩，不得按考试成绩对学生进行排名”。

就上述文本所列的条款而言，国家在学业评价方面表达了两个层面的意图。一是要转变评价功能，由过分强调甄别与选拔转向促进学生的发展，并为此建立完善的评价系统；二是规范评价行为，主要是各类考试行为，引导地方教育行政部门、学校、教师按正确的评价理念行事。这些意图是否得到了有效的落实呢？不可否认，全国各地教育行政部门按政策要求积极推进中小学生评价改革工作，如“北京、上海、湖北、湖南、海南、吉林、江苏、山东、广东、广西、安徽等省(自治区、直辖市)和深圳、青岛等地区开始实施新的中小学生评价方案或初中毕业生综合素质评价方案”，[4]应该说，政策的主要精神在一定程度和范围内得到了贯彻，有些省份还专门就初高中学生综合素质评价问题制定了省、市、县三级政策以及相关的评价体系。如果从促进教师评价素养发展的视角来考察，政策及其执行仍有一些遗漏与不完善之处，尚待改进。

第一，用于改善课堂评价实践的投入不足。尽管政策对课堂评价着墨不少，提出了许多改进建议，也期望它发挥促进学生发展的作用，但实际上分配给课堂评价的资源和权力远不如外部评价那样充实，致使课堂评价在现实中遭受冷遇，并没有得到应有的重视。课堂评价是指教师主导的以课堂为中心的学业评价，即教师借助某种评价工具采集、分析和利用学生学习信息，并据此做出判断或改善教学的活动过程。外部评价主要指大规模的考试与其他评价，如高利害的标准化考试(中考、高考)、地区性的统一考试或质量监测，用于测量学生的学业成就状况，教师只是部分参与，甚至只是一个评价结果或信息的用户，主要是理解、解释和运用外部评价结果来支持学生的学习。称其为外部评价，“因为它们是由那些一般并不在教学一线的人强制执行的"[5]。这可以从各级地方教育行政部门对课堂评价十分有限的关注和支持中窥其一斑,教育行政部门针对课堂评价的政策微乎其微,涉及该方面的内容也是片语只言,将焦点集中在外部评价和评价后的问责,往往以外部评价的绩效来评估课堂评价的效果,很少关心课堂里到底发生了什么,也很少为教师提供课堂评价方面的智力和资源支持。这种行为影响了教师对外部评价的看法和课堂评价的实践。如果追问其中的原因,除了政策执行不力外,还有政策自身的问题,国家提出建立促进学生发展的评价体系之后,并没有在政策上建立起完备的涵盖国家、地方、学校、课堂层级的评价系统,没有明确各个层级的评价权力和责任。简而言之,在当下的评价政策设计中,课堂评价有责无权。

第二,过分关注外部评价,义务教育阶段学生统考失范。既然政府十分重视外部评价,外部评价理应得到健康发展,但却出现了两种耐人寻味的怪现象。一是外部评价的行政化,许多评价结果与数据没有得到专业化的解释;二是统考异化,成为教学的指挥棒。可以说,外部评价是有权无责。政府对外部评价赋予过多的权力和资源,却没有规定所要承担的专业责任。

对于第一种现象,有人作过这样的描述:每次高考、会考、初中学业水平考试后,考试机构通常只向考生提供每个科目的考试成绩或等第,对成绩或等第的意义不做任何解释,没有将考试结果与教育评价联系起来。(而且也)没有适时地向考生、学校、甚至地方教育行政部门提供必要的考试结果信息。[6]可见,接受教育行政部门管理的考试机构并没有对评价结果进行专业的解释,事实上这是它们必须担当的责任。这就为教师的评价实践提供了一个反例,缺乏测量学专业知识的教师就更不能很好地对外部考试结果进行解释与利用,进而影响教师对自己日常评价结果的处理态度与方式。

关于第二种现象,在最近的一项全国性义务教育阶段学生统考情况调查中得到充分的反映。这里的统考是指校外教育机构组织的完全统一考试或抽样统一考试、校际联合统一考试和学校自行组织的年级统一考试,不包括中考。调查发现,统考次数过多;统考涉及各个年级,一入学就等于进入"统考学涯";统考组织权集中在教研员身上,教研员被异化为"考官";统考后公布成绩、排名之风盛行等。[7]这都是与国家政策背道而驰的,各级教育行政部门在执行过程中完全走样,不仅没有加强对统考的监控,反而放任统考,还有意无意地剥夺了教师的评价权,这在很大程度上鼓励了教师"以考代教、以考代考"的行为,也严重影响了教师的评价实践。当然这种现象的产生不能完全责备地方教育行政部门,其实政策本身也负有一定的责任,因为在政策上并没有明确统考的责任主体、组织程序、内容与形式等。

根据上述分析,现有学业评价政策及其执行存在的关键问题在于评价权力分配不合理,如外部评价和课堂评价失衡,国家、地方、学校和课堂层级的评价权力和责任不明晰,教师参与外部评价和实施课堂评价的权力得不到保障等,就很难谈及具体的合理的学业评价实践。要知道,教师的评价素养涵盖课堂评价和外部评价两个层面六大方面的内容,其中有效操控课堂评价是最为核心的要素。[8]可见,要切实提高教师的评价素养,政府在评价政策方面仍有许多事要做，如规范外部评价或让渡评价的部分专业权，为教师的评价实践提供专业示范。有学者就提议，“打破评价考试是教育行政部门‘专权’的禁区，可以尝试建立一个不受教育行政部门领导的、非营利性的评价考试‘中介’机构”。[9]但重中之重是建立权力分享的学业评价政策。

## 三、建立和执行权力分享的学业评价政策

要建立权力分享的评价政策，并使其得到有效地执行，关键是平衡外部评价与课堂评价，建立完善平衡的、相互协调的评价系统，这是从上述政策文本与执行情况的分析中得到的启示。那么，如何通过建构学业评价系统来实现权力的分享呢？我们可以借鉴美国的有益经验，为政策的规划提供一些建议。

### （一）美国规制权力分享的学业评价政策经验

美国在学生学业成就评价方面积累了丰富的研究成果与实践经验，但大部分又与外部评价有关，如在州、国家甚至国际层面上开展的基于标准的学业成就评价。在政策层面关注课堂评价、规划平衡的评价系统却也是近几年的事，这与20个世纪80年代末以来课堂评价研究成果的不断涌现与广泛传播有关。克鲁克斯（Crooks，T.J.）、萨德勒（Sadler，R.）、布莱克和威廉（Black，P. & William，D.）以及斯蒂金斯（Stiggins，R.J.）、谢泼德（Shepard，L.A.）等人卓有成效的研究，在一定程度上影响了所在国家或其他国家政策制定者对课堂评价的看法，把课堂评价看作是提升学业标准与学业成就的重要工具，认为它与外部的标准化测验同等重要，也引发政策制定者重新思考课堂评价的政策问题，美国就是其中的一个。

在美国，有一个非赢利的全国性组织：州中小学教育主管联席委员会（The Council of Chief State School Officers，简称CCSSO），提供一种州评价与学生标准合作项目（State Collaborative on Assessment and Student Standards），旨在为开发与实施高标准与有效的评价系统提供领导与服务。[10]该项目组于2001年开发了一个综合评价系统（Comprehensive Assessment Systems），其构成成分包括课堂、学区与州层面的评价，在系统内可以运用多种不同的常模参照的测验、基于标准的评价以及其他类型的评价以实现相互补充的目标。[11]这种评价系统是相互协调的。“相互协调”就是“教育系统中不同层级的评价相互配合构成一个系统，提供比任何单一的评价所能提供的关于学生成就的更为全面的图景”。[12]综合评价系统的目的在于运用不同层级的评价来获取全面的学生学业信息，使这些信息服务于学生的标准达成，确保“不让一个孩子掉队”。该评价系统对不同层级的评价在整个评价系统中所扮演的角色、功能及相互关系作了明确的界定，并重点对评价系统与课堂之间的关系进行解释。[13]在课堂层面，评价通常是由教师开发，以此来决定针对特定的学业标准学生学的怎样，其作用在于监控学生持续的进步并作出持续的调整。在学区层面，评价的结果用于监控学校的进步以帮助学生达成标准，依据评价结果作出学区政策、经费资助、课程以及教师培训等方面的调整。在州层面，评价提供一个基准测量（benchmark measurement），让学校和学区判断自己的课堂

和学区评价是否严格，其作用在于监控州标准的达成、确保学习机会均等、提供改进目标以及进行政策调整。当然，这三个层面的评价不是相互独立的，而是相互联系、互为补充的。由于CCSSO的成员是每个州的教育主管，它的一些专业服务容易进入每个州的教育与政府机构，也能借助独特的地位在全国范围内产生影响，所以由它开发的综合评价系统得到了各方的支持，被多个州认可与采用。

此外，美国缅因州（Maine）的地方评价系统也提供了一个很好的例子。缅因州教育部强调，地方评价系统必须具有以下几个特征：评价总体上与当地采用的四个关键学习结果和三大知识领域的标准相关，并代表这些标准；这些评价在课堂、学校、学区和州等多个层面上实施；评价在多个年级实施，应该是教师开发的课堂层级的评价，学校与地方的评价主要是监控学生实现标准的达成情况；评价应当运用多种方法——传统的与非传统的；评价应提供多种机会来证明与标准相关的知识、理解和技能的发展；评价应有公开的原则，即应当清楚地陈述每一种评价的目的、对象及与系统中其他评价的关系。[14]

虽然我们只提供了美国的个别经验，但从中至少可以悟出两点值得借鉴的地方，一是在一个系统内各个层级的评价相互补充，并保持外部评价与课堂评价的平衡，同时明确各个层级的评价职责与功能，使教师该做什么与不该做什么变得清晰起来。另外，政府进行政策决定时，对于那些专业性工作往往借助中介组织的专业力量，学业评价系统框架就是委托公共的专业机构来研制，然后采用、实施。这样的做法尽管与美国发达的教育中介服务市场有关，却也预示着政府处理专业事务的一种新取向：培育中介组织或加强与中介组织的合作。

### （二）若干建议

基于上述分析，我们尝试为政府建立与执行权力分享的评价政策提供如下建议，建议的目的在于为教师发展评价素养提供政策支持与实践动力。

**建议之一：合理分配学业评价权力**

就目前的教育状况来看，我国基础教育领域学业评价的权力分配处于一种很不平衡的状态中：权力高度集中于地方层面，高考权力集中于省级，中考权力大多集中于地市级，学校与课堂层面尽管非常频繁地实施学业评价，但因为都受制于地方的管制或行政安排，在很大程度上已经成为高考、中考等高利害考试的附庸，国家层面于2007年才建立基础教育质量监测中心，负责全国范围的学生学业水平检测，但也没有强有力的措施规制地方的评价行为。这样一种制度安排，抽离了学校与课堂层面的评价权，弱化了国家的评价管理权，使地方层级的权力过于膨胀，才会出现统考调查中发现的种种不良现象，这对课堂中的教师来说是有害无益的。国家应该对现行的安排进行调整，重新分配不同层级的学业评价权，突出国家对地方的监控；赋予学校实际的评价权，建立学生学业成就评价管理系统，规范各个层级的评价行为，平衡国家、地方、学校、课堂的评价。在条件成熟的情况下，国家还应考虑对教育考试立法，治理考试秩序，约束不合法的教育考试，消解外部评价对学校与课堂评价的干扰与压制，使原本属于教师的课堂评价回归本真。不过，“考试立法应当注意对考试的分类，应能全面涵盖各种考试并规范考试的组织和管理的全过程，界定考试违规行为的种类及其性质，限定对考试违规行为的处罚手段并规范处罚程序及其法律救济程序”[15]。

**建议之二：培育学业评价中介组织**

学业评价不仅需要良好的管理，也需要专业的设计与开发。偏于行政领导的政府机构要独立操纵两项任务是很难的，所以美国将有关学业评价技术性与专业性很强的事务置于政府之外，交由一些非赢利的中介组织来承担，其实就是政府让渡专业的评价权给中介组织或非政府组织，实现评价权力与资源的共享。当前实施教育评价的经济合作发展组织成员国中有75%的国家将这些评价项目交由一个单一的非政府组织负责，由它与政府签约提供评价服务，[16]也正说明了这一点。然而，在我国，专业中介整体发育不良，政府需要采取有效措施，促进评价专业中介的发育。对于学业评价来说，各级政府应积极鼓励与扶持中介组织的建立，为中介组织的准入设定标准，给予中介组织以合法与独立的地位，以项目的方式委托中介组织开展外部评价与课堂评价方面的专业研究，并向其购买专业服务，实施相应层级的评价，为教师的课堂评价提供专业示范。

**建议之三：加大对课堂评价的实际投入**

课堂评价和标准化测验本该给予同等的重视，在学校政策和评价资源分配方面保证其质量，但是很明显，事实上大多数教育政策制定者并不了解这个原则。[17]如果国家与地方政策不重视课堂评价，只提升外部评价的地位，将其作为一个竞争性的教育市场的重要成分，可能是非常有害的。政府应重新认识到，改善与提升学生学业成就的主阵地是课堂，因此，“提升课堂变革的质量并提供支持，应具有最大的优先权”[18]。所以，各级教育行政部门，尤其是地方教育行政部门，应加大对课堂评价的投入，使课堂评价得到与外部评价同等的待遇。一方面在政策上为课堂评价的实践提供保护性支持，明确课堂评价独特的地位与价值，并为改善课堂评价实践提供必需的经费保障；另一方面，加强对课堂评价专项研究的资助，鼓励与引导当地高等院校、教科研院所等各种专业学术机构关注课堂评价，研究课堂评价，发展课堂评价的知识与技术。

参考文献

[1] 郑东辉.中小学教师评价素养状况：来自Z省的报告[J].全球教育展望，2010(2).

[2] 陈振明.政策科学——公共政策分析导论[M].北京：中国人民大学出版社，2003：50.

[3] Yanow, D. (2000). *Conducting Interpretive Policy Analysis*. Newbury Park, CA: Sage.

[4] 沈玉顺.课堂评价[M].北京：北京师范大学出版社，2006：181.

[5] L·W·安德森,等.学习、教学和评估的分类学:布卢姆教育目标分类学修订版[M].皮连生,主译.上海:华东师范大学出版社,2008:207.

[6] 周群,雷新勇.从单纯考试向全面评价发展——考试机构应对新课程改革的必然选择[J].上海教育科研,2008(1):29.

[7] 崔允漷,刘辉,郑东辉.我国义务教育阶段学生统考情况调研报告[J].全球教育展望,2008(3):17—25.

[8] 郑东辉.教师评价素养内容框架探析[J].教育科学研究,2010,(10).

[9] 张敏强,刘晓瑜.中小学课程的改革与评价考试体系的完善[J].教育研究,2003(12):64.

[10] 参见 http://www.ccsso.org/projects/SCASS/

[11][13] Sheinker, J. & Redfield, D.(2003). *Handbook for Professional Development in Assessment Literacy*. Monpelier: Vermont Department of Education, p.7,9-24.

[12] Roeber, E.D.(1997). *Design Coordinated Assessment Systems for IASA Title I*. Paper presented at the Annual Meeting of American Educational Research Association, Chicago IL, p.4.

[14] Maine Comprehensive Assessment System Technical Advisory Committee.(2000). *Measured Measures: Technical Considerations for Developing a Local Assessment System*. Augusta, ME: Maine Department of Education.

[15] 李晓燕.关于教育考试立法的思考[J].湖北招生考试,2008(12):30—34.

[16] Lockheed, M. E.(1996). *Assessment and Management: World Bank Support for Educational Testing*. In Little, A. & Wolf, A. Assessment in Transition. Amsterdam: Elsevier Science Ltd, p.37.

[17] Stiggins, R.J.(2001). *The Unfulfilled Promise of Classroom Assessment*. *Educational Measurement: Issues and Practice*, 20(3),13.

[18] Black, P. & William, D.(1998). *Inside the Black Box: Raising Standards Through Classroom Assessment*. Phi Delta Kappan, 80(2),146.

## Development of Teacher Assessment Literacy: The Perspective of Achievement Assessment Policy

Zheng Donghui

**Abstract**: Affects the development of teacher's assessment literacy through its own standard and enforcement as well as the implementation at different levels. From the perspective of promoting the development of teacher's evaluation literacy, there are some omissions and imperfections in the existing achievement assessment policy. First, the input to the improvement of classroom assessment practices is inadequate. Second, too much attention is paid to the external assessment and at the same time standardized test students received in compulsory education is anomy. To improve the existing achievement assessment policy, we need to establish and implement a power-sharing policy in achievement assessment, allocate the power of achievement assessment reasonably, cultivate intermediary organizations, increase actual input to the classroom assessment.

**Key words**: assessment literacy; achievement assessment; policy

# 专家—熟手—新手教师高中英语阅读课课堂互动比较研究

罗晓杰　王　雪

【摘要】本文以三位高中英语专家、熟手和新手教师为研究对象，采用弗兰德斯互动分析系统，结合师生课堂语言实录和教学录像，从教师话语和课堂沉寂两个维度分析比较了专家、熟手和新手教师在高中英语阅读课上的言语行为以及阅读教学效果，得出以下结论：在问题设计与提问，候答和理答策略的运用上，其合理程度依次为专家教师、熟手教师和新手教师；专家、熟手和新手教师在问题类型及其比例方面均有待进一步优化。作者建议如下：关注问题有效性，培养学生批判性思维；合理运用候答策略，有效利用教学时间；合理运用理答策略，提高课堂互动质量。

【关键词】专家教师；熟手教师；新手教师；问题设计与提问；候答；理答

【作者简介】罗晓杰/温州大学外国语学院教授，硕士生导师

王雪/温州大学外国语学院课程与教学论（英语）专业10级研究生

## 一、引言

“90年代以来，关于教师成长的研究逐渐成为教师心理研究的一个重要课题，其中日益受到重视的是专家型—新手型教师的比较研究”[1]，对于专家—熟手—新手教师的比较研究则相对较少。笔者检索中国期刊网发现，同时关注专家、熟手和新手教师专业发展方面的研究仅有13条记录，主要针对教学动机、教学策略和教师心理特征等，尚未有研究者对处于三个不同专业发展阶段的教师的课堂互动以及具体学科具体课型的课堂互动进行比较研究。因此，本文采用弗兰德斯互动分析系统，对专家、熟手和新手教师在高中英语阅读课上的课堂互动进行比较分析，针对新手教师与专家和熟手教师之间，熟手教师与专家教师之间进行比较，旨在帮助熟手教师和新手教师发现其在课堂互动中存在的问题，并加以改进。

## 二、研究设计

（一）研究对象。笔者依据美国亚利桑那州立大学心理学教授伯林纳（Berliner）关于“新手阶段、进步的新手阶段、胜任阶段、熟练阶段和专家阶段”五个教师专业发展阶段教学行为的描述，在某重点高中遴选三位教师（专家、熟手和新手），将其作为研究对象并对其英语阅读课进行课堂观察。

（二）研究方法及相关概念界定。本文采用弗兰德斯的课堂教学师生言语行为互动分析系统（Flanders Interaction Analysis System，简称FIAS），课堂观察和话语实录分析等研究方

法。课堂教学师生言语行为互动分析系统是由美国教育学家弗兰德斯在20世纪60年代提出来的一种结构性的、定量的课堂行为分析技术,是分析评价课堂教与学行为、进行教育研究的一种较为理想的工具。该系统将课堂师生言语互动行为分为三类十种情况。第一类为教师话语,包括:1.接纳学生情感、2.鼓励称赞学生、3.采纳学生的想法、4.提问、5.讲解、6.下指令和7.批评学生及维护权威;第二类为学生话语,包括8.学生反应——被动驱动和9.学生主动说话;最后一类即为10.沉寂或混乱。在观察课堂教学录像的同时,笔者以5秒钟为一个单位时间,记录下与各类行为相对应的编码,利用弗兰德斯互动分析软体计算出12个变项的百分比,通过对比其中教师话语百分比、学生话语百分比法、沉寂或混乱比率、教师实时发问比率和学生自发比率的数据,得出专家、熟手和新手教师的课堂互动差异,并通过分析师生话语实录来进一步佐证这些差异,从而得出每位教师的问题设计与提问、候答时间和理答行为的区别。

## 三、研究结果与分析

2011年6月,笔者在某高中分别观察了专家、熟手和新手教师的一堂英语阅读课,教材选自人教版普通高中实验教科书Module4, Unit3 A Master of Nonverbal Humor,并用数码摄像机录制整个教学过程。表1就是在观察教学录像时采用弗兰德斯互动分析系统方法计算出的教师话语百分比、学生话语百分比以及沉寂或混乱比率,并在此基础上换算出一节课40分钟(在弗兰德斯互动分析系统中,课堂时间由教师话语时间、学生话语时间和沉寂或混乱时间构成)三位教师的教师话语时间、学生话语时间和沉寂或混乱时间分配情况,如表1所示。

**表1 专家—熟手—新手教师课堂话语量统计**

| | 教师话语 | | 学生话语 | | 沉寂或混乱 | |
|---|---|---|---|---|---|---|
| | % | 分钟 | % | 分钟 | % | 分钟 |
| 常模 | 68% | 27 | 20% | 8 | 12% | 5 |
| 专家教师 | 61.95% | 25 | 19.79% | 8 | 18.26% | 7 |
| 熟手教师 | 63.69% | 25 | 19.09% | 8 | 17.21% | 7 |
| 新手教师 | 47.36% | 19 | 17.96% | 7 | 34.68% | 14 |

弗兰德斯互动分析系统将课堂上教师的话语划分为七类,表2即为专家、熟手和新手教师的七类言语行为所占的时间比例。

**表2 专家—熟手—新手教师言语行为百分比**

| | 接纳学生情感 | 鼓励称赞学生 | 采纳学生的想法 | 提问 | 讲解 | 下指令 | 批评学生及维护权威 |
|---|---|---|---|---|---|---|---|
| 专家教师 | 1.37% | 7.46% | 0.15% | 19.33% | 27.09% | 6.54% | 0.00% |
| 熟手教师 | 0.00% | 2.03% | 7.89% | 12.21% | 28.01% | 13.30% | 0.16% |
| 新手教师 | 0.18% | 5.11% | 5.11% | 15.67% | 11.97% | 8.27% | 1.06% |

“从教师发问，指名回答，直到学生开口说话这段时间，被称为候答。”[2]因此笔者统计了三位教师的课堂上不同问题类型的候答时间，具体差异如表3所示。

**表3 专家—熟手—新手教师问题类型与候答时间统计表**

| 教师问题层级 | 专家教师 | | | 熟手教师 | | | 新手教师 | | |
|---|---|---|---|---|---|---|---|---|---|
| | 问题数量 次/节 | 比例 % | 候答 秒/题 | 问题数量 次/节 | 比例 % | 候答 秒/题 | 问题数量 次/节 | 比例 % | 候答 秒/题 |
| 展示型 | 18 | 67% | 15.56 | 17 | 77% | 15.88 | 18 | 75% | 25.20 |
| 参阅型 | 9 | 33% | 27.56 | 5 | 23% | 24.60 | 6 | 25% | 18.50 |
| 评价型 | 0 | / | / | 0 | / | / | 0 | / | / |
| 合计 | 27 | 100% | / | 22 | 100% | / | 24 | 100% | / |

（注：表格中所指的问题均是与阅读文本相关的问题。）

### （一）教师话语分析

教师话语是指“英语教师在英语课堂内组织和实施课堂教学所采用的教学语言，包括教师讲授用语，组织用语，课堂提问，反馈和意义协商等”[3]。

通过纵向比较表1中“教师话语时间”的数据，我们发现专家教师和熟手教师的教师话语时间基本相同，略低于常模要求；新手教师的课堂话语时间与专家和熟手教师相差6分钟，与常模相差8分钟。纵向比较表2中“讲解”（指“演讲、表达见解、说明事实、导入想法以及非正式的议论或闲谈”[4]）一列的数据，专家教师和熟手教师的讲解时间比率相差无几；新手教师的讲解时间比率比前两者的一半还低。通过分析师生话语实录和课堂观察，发现新手教师的词汇讲解方式有所欠缺。

以下是笔者在三位教师的话语实录中选取的词汇讲解的片段。在新手教师的课堂，以worse off和astonishing为例，教师设计了两个选择题来解释新词。

T：Ok，in this paragraph，what does “worse off” mean?

Ss：Poor.

T：Yeah ... How about “astonishing”?

Ss：Amazing.

T：Yeah，that’s amazing. That’s amazing.

再如，新手教师采用英语释义法来讲解convincing一词——“Make you believe，make somebody believe.”

在熟手教师的课堂，教师则将词汇放到文本语境中来解释，同样的以worse off一词的讲解为例。

T：What does “worse off” mean? Actually，“worse off” comes from the word “badly off”，right，“badly off”. Just now we say ah... Charlie was born in a poor family，so his family was badly off. “badly off” means poor. “worse off”, leaving his family even worse off means leaving his family even poorer.

在专家教师的课堂，教师在完成对第二段的阅读理解后，要求学生当堂运用本段中的七个重点词汇（performers, astonishing, unfortunately, worse off, ordinary, bored, entertaining）来总结概括卓别林孩提时候的艰苦生活。由于此问题难度较高，教师向学生示范如何根据关键词复述语篇片段。其中教师对 worse off 的解释为“the economic situation, very poor, no money, no food”。

T：So “astonishing”, because he could sing and dance when he was very young. “Unfortunately”, very unluckily. And the economic situation, very poor, no money, no food. “Ordinary”：daily tasks, so he could do all kinds of work to make a living, to live and exist. To make bored people entertained. We can draw a picture, to form a picture in mind about Charlie Chaplin. We can conclude that what kind of childhood Charlie Chaplin had. Very hard, very difficult and hardworking. So that we can conclude from these words.

通过分析课堂话语实录和观察教学录像，笔者发现专家教师和熟手教师的理答内容要优于新手教师。“理答有消极和积极之分。消极理答有三种表现形式：一是模糊理答，让人雾里看花；二是重复理答，拖沓了课堂；三是简单理答，肤浅寡淡。积极理答主要分为两大类：语言性理答和非言语理答。语言性理答包含激励性理答（简单表扬和激励鼓励），诊断性理答（对学生的回答给予肯定或否定的回答），发展性理答（主要包括探问、追问、转问、反问）和再组织（对学生的回答进行重新组织、概括）。”[5] 以本篇阅读文章中第二段的重点句子“Not that Charlie's own life was easy.”为例，新手、熟手和专家教师的理答分别如下：

在新手教师的课堂，学生没能理解这句话的含义，保持沉默，因而由教师代答，仅用一句同义句解释句子含义，未结合文本语境来进一步阐释，且忽略了对“Not that”强调句结构的讲解，属于简单理答。

T：Not that Charlie's life was easy. So what does this sentence mean?

S：(silence)

T：What does this sentence mean — Not that Charlie's own life was easy? It means that Charlie's own life was not that easy, was very difficult.

在熟手教师的课堂，教师先单独讲解“Not that”强调句结构，再通过追问一个问题要求学生找出原句，证明卓别林孩提时代的生活很艰难。学生共从文中找出三点信息：“He was born in a poor family”, “His father died”，以及“He spent his childhood looking after his sick mother and his brother”。教师首先肯定了学生回答，即诊断性理答，然后用原文——leaving the family even worse off; looking after his sick mother and his brother，来总结归纳学生答案，即再组织。

T：Ok，yes，sit down please. Yes，you found the sentence. His father died，leaving the family even worse off. Right... So er... From the sentence we know Charlie's life was not easy right. The sentence read by S7 just now. He spent his childhood looking after his sick mother and his brother.（S7 refers to a student）

在专家教师的课堂，学生的回答是"His life was hard"。由于该班学生的平均成绩要低于熟手教师班级学生的平均成绩，专家教师的理答内容更为详细。教师首先肯定学生回答，即诊断性理答，并多次讲解"Not that"强调句型以保证学生能真正理解，然后抽取文中重点信息，用自己的语言重新组织并归纳卓别林孩提时候的生活为何如此艰苦，即再组织。

T：En? Was difficult. Yes，thank you. Charlie's own life was very difficult. Not easy at all. Charlie's own life was not easy at all. So this is a way to，to emphasize，强调. En，"not that"：it is not this way；it is not that. "Not that Charlie's own life was easy." Charlie's life was not easy at all. Because he，because his father died when he was very young，because he was born in very poor family；because he has to make a living when he was very young. Yeah，so sing and dance to make a living.

纵向比较表 3 中"提问"一列的数据，发现专家教师的提问比率最高，熟手教师则是最低，比专家教师相差 7.12%；由表 1 又可知专家和熟手教师的实时发问比率依次为 60.00% 和 22.22%，后者仅为常模 44% 的二分之一。通过统计预设问题和生成问题的数量，结果如下：专家教师的预设问题 12 个，生成问题 15 个，其中深层次追问 8 个；熟手教师的预设问题 16 个，生成问题 6 个，其中深层次追问 3 个。专家教师的预设问题数量少，生成问题和深层次追问却居首；相较之下，熟手教师的预设问题数量比专家教师的要多出 4 个，生成问题数量却减少 9 个，其中深层次追问要少 5 个。除了比较提问数量的差异，笔者还发现三位教师在问题设计上存在如下问题。"英语阅读课上展示型问题、参阅型问题和评价型问题的大致比例为 6∶3∶1"[6]，换算为百分比即为 60%，30% 和 10%。表 4 的数据却显示专家教师的展示型问题多出 7%，参阅型问题多出 3%；熟手教师和新手教师的展示型问题远远高于正常要求的比例，分别多出 17% 和 15%，他们的参阅型问题低于正常百分比，分别降低了 7% 和 5%；三位教师均没有设计评价型问题。

### （二）课堂沉寂时间分析

"课堂沉寂或混乱是指暂时停顿、短时间的安静或混乱，以致观察者无法了解师生之间的沟通。"[7]根据弗兰德斯互动分析系统，非教师话语和非学生话语的时间属于沉寂，并且课堂观察发现三位教师的阅读课并未出现课堂混乱现象，课堂沉寂时间主要用来等候学生的回答。因此，笔者把阅读课上的沉寂划分为暂时停顿、短时间安静和默读（三位教师课上学生默读时间大致相同）。

表 1 的数据表明专家、熟手和新手教师在阅读课上的沉寂时间均高于常模，主要原因是阅读课上默读时间占有一定比例。数据显示，新手教师课堂沉寂比率是专家教师和熟手教师的两倍，比常模要求多出 22.68%。通过横向比较表 1 中的数据，发现新手教师的课堂话语时间少导致课堂沉寂时间过多；课堂观察发现新手教师的候答时间过长导致沉寂时间过多。横向比较表 3 中三位教师展示型问题的平均每题候答时间，专家教师和熟手教师无甚差别，而新手教师的候答时间要多出 10 秒左右；而参阅型问题的平均每题候答时间从专家教师、熟手教师到新手教师呈现递减的顺序，其中专家教师和熟手教师之间差别不是很大，而新手教师的参阅型问题的候答时间最少，比专家教师少 9 秒左右，比熟手教师少 7 秒。纵向比较各个类型问题的候答时间，专家教师给予参阅型问题的候答时间最多，展示型问题最少；新手教师给予参阅型问题的候答时间最少，展示型问题最多；熟手教师介于专家和新手教师之间，在展示型问题的候答时间上与专家教师无甚差别，在参阅型问题上少了 3 秒。

## 四、研究结论与教学建议

采用弗兰德斯的课堂教学师生言语行为互动分析系统，课堂观察和话语实录分析等研究方法，结合对三位高中英语教师阅读课的质性观察，比较教师话语百分比和课堂沉寂百分比两个维度，得出以下几条结论：

在词汇讲解上，新手教师的词汇处理方式就是寻找其近义词和英语释义法，将原本置于文本的词汇脱离出文本，单独解释，而且关注的词汇量有限；熟手教师则是将重点词汇置于语篇中进行解释；专家教师既注重词汇的解释，又注重词汇的运用，并且指导学生运用构词法知识来记忆派生词的词义和词类，实现了词汇学习与篇章理解的有效结合，实现了词汇在语境中的有效应用。

在问题设计和提问上，笔者得出两条结论：其一，在专家教师的阅读课堂上师生互动更富生成性，不是按部就班地围绕预设问题展开阅读教学，而是灵活地生成更多问题，相比之下熟手教师略显得被预设问题所束缚，生成问题的数量有待增加；其二，三位教师的阅读课上展示型、参阅型和评价型问题的比例失衡，展示型问题偏多，参阅型和评价型问题偏少，使得学生的创造性思维和批判性思维不能得到充分发展，学生缺乏质疑能力，故而学生在课堂上没有主动提问和表达观点，学生自发比率为零，语言输出质量不高。

在候答时间上，新手教师尚未掌握候答策略，不能根据问题类型给予恰当的候答时间，甚至出现了层级低的问题候答时间反而要多于层级高的问题，换句话说，无需思考的展示性问题比需要思考的参阅性问题候答时间更长的现象，候答时间总体偏多，从而导致课堂沉寂时间较多。

在理答方面，当学生回答不出来时，新手教师选择代答，理答内容比较简短，只关注句子的表层意思，是简单理答；熟手教师和专家教师虽然都采用再组织理答，但存在些微区别。熟手教师的再组织遗漏学生的一个信息,仍是照搬原文,专家教师的再组织是提取关键信息,加以概括。除了再组织理答,专家教师的生成问题和深层次追问的数量最多,表明教师善用发展性理答,即通过追问等发展学生的批判性思维能力,

鉴于此,为推动教师专业成长,笔者提出以下建议,以期给新手教师和熟手教师的专业成长带来有益启示。

**(一) 关注问题有效性,培养学生批判性思维**

笔者认为教师要关注问题设计的有效性,使不同类型的问题保持一定的比例,满足不同层次的学生的学习需求。专家教师应适当降低展示型问题比例,增加评价型问题的数量;熟手教师和新手教师需要降低展示型问题比例,提高参阅型问题和评价型问题的比例,为学生创造机会独立组织语言表达观点,以改变学生用文章原句来回答问题的现状,培养学生的创造性和批判性思维能力,从而使学生形成主动提问的习惯。

**(二) 合理运用候答策略,有效利用教学时间**

为激发学生给出更详细更好的答案,提高学生的自信心,熟手教师要适当增加参阅性问题的候答时间,给学生足够的时间思考问题。心理学研究也表明,“给提问过程增加 3 秒或更多的候答时间,课堂将出现许多有意义的显著变化:学生会给出更详细更好的答案,拒绝或随意回答的情况就会较少出现;学生在分析和综合水平上的评论就会增加,会作出更多的以证据为基础和更有预见性的回答,提出更多的问题;学生在评论中会显示更强的自信,并且那些被教师认为反应相对迟缓的学生也会提出更多的问题和作出更好的回答”[8]。

新手教师要充分利用课堂教学时间,努力减少课堂沉寂,根据问题类型和学生回答问题的认知深度,合理分配候答时间,提高课堂教学时间的有效利用率。如,减少展示型问题的候答时间,适当增加参阅型问题和评价型问题的候答时间。

**(三) 合理运用理答策略,提高课堂互动质量**

在教师理答行为中,发展性理答和再组织属于较高层次的理答。针对熟手教师和新手教师的发展性理答和再组织的问题,笔者建议,新手教师和熟手教师要有意识地运用高层次的理答策略,采用探问、追问、转问、反问等方式,获取学生更有深度与宽度的回答,促进学生思维的发展。例如,当学生因为不理解问题意思或问题意图时,教师可改变提问角度,把原来的问题分解成多个小问题引导学生回答,此为探问。当探问不能得到教师想要的答案时,可转问其它学生,使问题得到更好的解决。当学生回答正确时,教师还可就正确答案继续进行追问和深问。

教师通过探问和转问引导学生回答,对比较零散,没有连贯性的回答进行重新组织,在学生回答问题后要及时归纳总结,给学生一个更加准确、清晰、完整的答案。因此为使组织完整,

教师要注意倾听学生的回答，抓住每一个有用的信息，用自己的语言加以整理归纳，从而切实提高理答艺术和理答效果。

## 五、结语

阅读课问题设计与提问，候答和理答等是教师课堂互动的主要教学行为，也是衡量教师专业发展水平的一个重要指标。本文从分析高中英语教师阅读课的教师话语和课堂沉寂或混乱两个角度比较专家、熟手和新手教师的语言行为，针对新手教师在问题设计与提问，候答时间和理答行为上所存在的问题，提出以上建议。虽然只是个案研究，但某种程度上也反映出高中英语专家教师的课堂互动行为也有一定的借鉴意义。希望本研究能引起有关教师的思考。

参考文献

[1] 连榕，孟迎芳. 专家——新手型教师研究述评[J]. 福建省社会主义学院学报，2001(4)：66.

[2] 马会梅. 教师教学提问行为研究[J]. 教育探索，2009(5)：89.

[3] 王艳杰. 高中英语课堂中专家型教师与新手教师话语对比研究[D]. 长春：东北师范大学，2009.

[4] 郭慧龙. 教师评鉴、教室观察与 Flanders 互动分析系统简介[J]. 竹县文教(台湾)，2002(25).

[5] 徐红英. 课堂理答及其类型和原则[J]. 小学教学研究(教学版)，2010(3).

[6] 梁美珍. 高中英语文本处理阶段的问题类型及设计方法[J]. 中小学外语教学，2011(4).

[7] 郭慧龙，林建伸. Flanders 互动分析系统辅助软件介绍[J]. 竹县文教(台湾)，2005(27).

[8] 郑友富. 专家型教师与新手教师课堂提问的比较研究[J]. 教育科学研究，2009(11)：60.

# The Comparison of Classroom Interaction among Expert, Proficient and Novice Teacher in Senior High School English Reading Class

Xiaojie Luo　Xue Wang

**Abstract**: Taking expert, proficient and novice English teachers in senior high school as samples, this paper analyses and compares their verbal behaviors and related teaching effects in reading class from two aspects: teacher talk and classroom silence, by adopting Flanders Interaction Analysis System, by observing the video clips and by analyzing the teacher's and students' talk. The main findings are as followed: The extend of reasonability to which the three teachers design and ask questions, use strategies of rational response and waiting response decreases successively from expert teacher, proficient teacher to novice teacher; their ratio of question types need be improved. To solve these problems, the authors offer following suggestions: All the three teachers should design some evaluation questions to develop their students' critical thinking; novice teachers should develop their teaching strategies of waiting response to students' answers for effective teaching; both novice and proficient teacher should develop their rational response to improve the quality of classroom interaction.

**Keywords**: expert teacher; proficient teacher; novice teacher; question designing and asking; waiting response; rational response

# 高中英语词汇课专家和新手教师的课堂互动对比研究

韩晓敏　徐永军

【摘要】词汇教学是中学英语教学的重要组成部分，词汇教学的有效性一直是英语教师和教育教学研究者的关注焦点。本文作者对一名高中英语专家教师和一名新手教师的词汇课进行实录，使用弗兰德斯互动分析系统对其课堂互动行为进行对比分析，并结合质的课堂观察对两者的课堂互动行为差异进行解释，以揭示专家教师在提高词汇教学的有效性所采用的教学策略，为新手教师实施词汇教学提供参考。

【关键词】弗兰德斯互动分析系统；专家教师；新手教师；课堂观察；词汇教学

【作者简介】韩晓敏/浙江温州大学外国语学院课程与教学论(英语)专业10级研究生

徐永军/浙江宁波教育学院外语与经贸学院教师

## 一、引言

英国语言学家威尔金斯曾经说过："没有语言，人们表达的事物寥寥无几，而没有词汇，人们则无法表达任何事物。"[1]词汇学习的重要性是不言而喻的。然而，"由于词汇具有数量大、没有系统的规律、难以控制等特点，使词汇教学往往成为英语教师所面临的一个难题"[2]。在我国，英语词汇教学也一直是中学英语教学难以突破的瓶颈。只有解决了词汇问题，才能有效地提高学生的英语学习效率及综合语言运用能力。传统的词汇教学研究多关注教师的词汇教学策略及学生的词汇学习策略，鲜有研究关注教师在词汇教学中的课堂互动行为。因此，本研究采用弗兰德斯互动分析系统对高中专家型英语教师及新手型英语教师的词汇课课堂互动行为进行对比研究，以揭示专家教师在提高词汇教学的有效性所采用的教学策略，旨在为新手教师实施词汇教学提供参考。

## 二、研究方法

### (一) 观察对象与内容

观察对象为：某市高中英语专家教师和新手教师各一名。前者为中学高级教师，市英语教学名师，教龄25年，教学经验丰富，对英语词汇教学有独到见解。后者是一名刚参加工作的新手教师，英语课堂教学经验较欠缺。课堂观察内容为人教版高中英语必修二第一单元Cultural Relics的词汇课教学。

### （二）观察方法

本研究主要采用课堂观察的方法对上述两位教师在英语词汇课上的课堂互动行为进行实录，按照弗兰德斯所提出的课堂教学中师生语言互动情况的分类方法（表1），对所观察到的师生课堂互动行为进行编码，并借助弗兰德斯互动分析系统[①]对上述编码进行阐释。弗兰德斯将课堂教学行为的记录时间间隔设定为3秒钟，但是3秒的记录时间间隔过短，很难判断诸多行为类型，而且工作量大，记录过程中也容易产生偏差，因此，本文将采用国内学者的惯用方法，将观察时间间隔设定为每5秒一个单位，也就是说，观察员要把在5秒钟之内发生的多个类别的行为记录下来。

**表1　弗兰德斯互动分析分类表（Flanders，1970）**

| 编码 | 教师话语 | | | | | | | 学生话语 | | 沉默或混乱 |
|---|---|---|---|---|---|---|---|---|---|---|
| | 1 | 2 | 3 | 4 | 5 | 6 | 7 | 8 | 9 | 10 |
| 内容 | 表达情感 | 鼓励表扬 | 采纳意见 | 提问 | 讲授 | 指令 | 批评 | 学生反应 | 学生主动说话 | 无有效语言 |

### （三）观察工具

摄像机、课堂行为观察量表、课堂行为记录单。

### （四）研究过程及方案

首先，笔者与另外两位教师组成一个课堂观察小组，利用观察量表和记录单，从学生和教师两个维度对专家教师和新手教师的词汇课分别进行课堂观察，并用摄像机进行现场录像，以便课堂观察者更准确地记录、分析两位教师的课堂互动行为。第二步，按照弗兰德斯对师生语言互动情况的分类方法，分别对两节词汇课的课堂互动行为进行编码，并记录。第三步，将编码输入弗兰德斯互动分析系统软件，可以得出变项分析结果（见表2）。第四步，对观察量表和记录单进行数据统计（见表3）。第五步，数据解析。

**表2　专家教师和新手教师变项分析对比**

| | 弗兰德斯互动分析系统变项 | | |
|---|---|---|---|
| | 缩写 | 专家教师分析结果 | 新手教师分析结果 |
| 教师话语百分比 | TT | 71.22 | 57.87 |
| 学生话语百分比 | PT | 22.70 | 15.34 |
| 教师间接影响比率 | I/D ratio | 51.92 | 34.21 |

① 弗兰德斯互动分析系统（Flanders interaction analysis）是美国明尼苏达大学的学者弗兰德斯在20世纪60年代提出的一种课堂行为分析技术。

续 表

| | 弗兰德斯互动分析系统变项 | | |
|---|---|---|---|
| | 缩写 | 专家教师分析结果 | 新手教师分析结果 |
| 教师直接影响比率 | I/D ratio | 34.89 | 56.89 |
| 安静或混乱百分比 | SC | 6.09 | 22.79 |
| 教师发问比率 | TQR | 24.01 | 23.70 |
| 教师实时发问比率 | TQR89 | 41.18 | 23.68 |
| 学生稳定状态区比率 | PSSR | 44.93 | 17.80 |

**表 3　课堂观察量表、记录单统计结果**

| | 问题层次 | | | |
|---|---|---|---|---|
| | 问题数量 | 不假思索的问题 | 简单思维的问题 | 高级思维的问题 |
| 专家教师 | 14 | 1 | 11 | 2 |
| 新手教师 | 18 | 11 | 7 | 0 |

## 三、研究结果及对比分析

### （一）教师话语比率及学生话语比率

教师话语比率是指教师话语时间占全部教学时间的比例，学生话语是指学生话语时间占全部教学时间的比例。通过表 1 可知，专家教师的话语比率(71.22%)明显高于新手教师的话语比率(57.87%)，但是学生在专家教师的词汇课堂的话语比率(22.70%)也相对高于在新手教师的词汇课堂的话语比率(15.34%)。笔者通过课堂实录发现：专家教师在进行词汇教学时，常常会使用相应的教学语言衔接教学步骤，为学生创设更多的机会参与到课堂互动中，启发学生思维，让学生思考新词汇的含义及用法，并结合学生的实际生活体验，积极创设真实的情境，帮助学生运用、内化所学新词汇。如讲解 worth 和 be worthwhile 的用法时，专家教师就分别举了“雁荡山值得一游”和“这本书值得一看”这两个意思相同但结构不同的例句，突出了两个单词的对比，加深了学生对这两个单词的理解。而新手教师在进行词汇教学时，往往会为学生直接呈现词汇的含义及用法，没有启发学生去思考新单词的含义及用法，也没有为学生提供有针对性的词汇讲解，只是要求学生死记硬背新词汇的含义及用法。例如，在讲解新词汇的含义及用法时，新手教师的课堂话语为：Can that expression be replaced by this one? You must remember that it can't be replaced. 另一方面，专家教师能够准确地判断词汇教学的重点及难点，并有意识地分散词汇的重难点，由词到句，由句到语篇，使教学明显有梯度。如，专家教师先一个一个讲解语言点，然后要求学生进行替换性质的语篇填空。另外，专家教师的词汇讲解也比新手教师更加深入，更加透彻，从而提高了词汇教学的有效性。而新手教师在讲解词汇的重难点时，往往在学生尚未掌握新知识前，就过早地进行词汇的辨析或拓展词汇的相关知识,以致词汇教学重点不突出。如新手教师在讲解 have something done 这一语言结构时,就过早拓展与之相关的语言知识(have somebody do = get somebody to do, have somebody / something doing),从而使学生陷入迷惑中,使课堂陷入沉静状态。

**(二) 间接影响与直接影响的比率**

教师课堂话语对学生的影响可以分为间接影响和直接影响,间接影响与直接影响的比率可以反映一个教师的教学风格及倾向。如果比值大于 1,则表明该教师倾向于对学生施加间接影响,反之亦然。在笔者所观察的两节词汇课堂教学中,专家教师侧重对学生施加间接影响(1.49),而新手教师侧重对学生施加直接影响(0.6)。如:在两节词汇课中,专家教师注重启发学生思维,让学生自己去发现、探索新词汇的含义及用法。专家教师会要求学生根据上下文猜测词汇的含义,总结词汇的用法;而新手教师直接为学生呈现词汇的含义及用法,并要求学生机械地记忆所学词汇知识。因此,在进行词汇教学时,如何增加对学生的间接影响,提高教学的启发性,引导学生探究是新手教师面临的一个难题。

**(三) 教师发问比率与教师实时发问比率**

教师发问比率是指教师发问时间占教师实施教学时间的比率。数值越高,表明教师越擅长利用发问来组织课堂教学,常模约为 26%。在这方面,专家教师(24.01%)与新手教师(23.70%)都略低于常模比值。虽然专家教师与新手教师在发问比率方面的数值相接近,但两者之间仍然存在一些差异,特别是在问题的设置方面。如表 3 所示,虽然专家教师所提问题的总数(14 个)略少于新手教师所提问题的总数(18 个),但专家教师提出的深层问题的数量(2 个)高于新手教师(0 个),这说明专家教师倾向于进行深层问题的发问,并注重问题的追问,创造机会,提高学生的词汇运用能力。如在为学生创设词汇应用情境时,专家教师提问的问题是:Do you know, what cultural relics in our city? Have you ever heard about that? Why do you think that they are cultural relics? 而新手教师更倾向于表层问题的发问,新手教师所设计的大部分问题的答案都是“Yes\No”。这样的教学方式不能有效地将词汇学习与词汇运用结合在一起,降低了词汇教学的有效性。

教师实时发问表示当学生停止说话,教师立即使用发问的方式以响应学生的话语。教师实时发问比率是指教师实时发问的时间占教师用于教学直接相关的话语响应学生话语时间的比率,常模约为 44%。通过表 2 可知,专家教师(41.18%)比新手教师(23.68%)更擅长于采用实时追问的方式以进行新一轮的师生互动,例如,在讲解词组 cultural relics 时,专家教师用下列话语启发学生思维,帮助学生探究这个词组的含义:

T: what is a cultural relic?

T: Is it a person?

Ss: No.

T：Yes. Relics can not be a person. Is it a cup?

Ss：Maybe.

T：Yes，It may be，if it is very old. So what is a relic?

S1：Something that is very old.

S2：It may be valuable.

S3：It may be rare.

T：Yes，very good! It has to be something that is very old，rare，and valuable.

从上例可以看出，专家型教师善于实时发问以便维持师生之间的交流，启发学生去发现、探索新词汇的含义及用法。

**(四)学生稳定状态区比率与课堂安静\混乱比率**

学生稳定状态区比率指学生说话持续达5秒以上的话语时间占学生话语时间的比率。数据越高，表示学生的言谈风格越稳定，常模约在35%或40%。在专家教师的词汇课堂上，学生的思维稳定状态比率达到44.93%，远远高于学生在新手教师词汇课堂上的思维稳定状态比率(17.80%)，这说明在专家教师的词汇课堂教学中，学生的学习主体地位得到了充分的尊重，他们可以有机会表达他们对新词汇的理解，与教师、同学进行平等的沟通与交流。而新手教师在此方面比较欠缺，没有充分发挥学生学习英语词汇的主体能动性，从而降低了词汇教学的有效性。

课堂安静\混乱是指暂时停顿、短时间的安静或混乱，以致观察者无法了解师生之间的沟通。课堂安静\混乱比率指课堂安静\混乱时间占课堂教学时间的比率，常模参照约为11%或12%，比率越高，则表明课堂互动行为的数量越少，质量越差。专家教师的课堂安静\混乱比例是5.09%，而新手教师的课堂安静\混乱比例高达22.79%，这表明：专家教师的课堂控制能力较好，能够充分利用有限的课堂教学时间，实施词汇教学。即使专家教师偶尔会出现一些小的教学疏漏，他也能够迅速做出调整，巧妙的处理；而新手教师的课堂控制能力较薄弱，不能灵活处理课堂教学中所出现的一些小的教学疏漏，从而使课堂陷入安静或混乱状态的时间增多，降低了词汇课堂教学的效率。如：新手教师在导入新词举例说明时，临时举例说明会出现口误或例句不够恰当的现象，从而使课堂教学陷入安静或混乱状态，降低了词汇教学的有效性。

## 四、结论

通过使用弗兰德斯互动分析系统对专家教师和新手教师在高中英语词汇课堂教学中的师生互动行为进行对比发现，专家教师在词汇呈现、词汇讲解、词汇应用情境的创设、课堂教学时间的有效利用等方面都优于新手教师，其词汇教学的有效性也远远高于新手教师。接下来，笔者将参照专家教师所采用的词汇教学方式，为新手教师实施词汇教学提供下列建议：

1. 新手教师在进行词汇教学设计时，要设计相应的教学环节或教学语言以衔接教学活动，提高教学活动之间的连贯性，避免教学时间的浪费。同时，每个教学活动都要尽量为学生的词汇学习创设真实的、有意义的情境，以便帮助学生理解、运用、内化所学新词汇。

2. 新手教师应为学生创设更多的机会去探究、发现新词汇的含义及用法，并为学生讲解词汇学习策略，提高学生的自主学习能力。此外，新手教师在进行词汇的举例讲解时，应联系学生的实际生活体验，列举相应的例子，从而更好地帮助学生理解词汇的含义及用法，调动学生学习英语的积极性。

3. 新手教师在备课时，应该对教材的内容及学生的学情进行细致的分析，以便预测词汇教学的重难点，设计相应的教学活动，帮助学生理解、掌握这些重点知识。对词汇难点进行分散教学，以便减少学生的认知负担。

4. 新手教师在设计问题时，应合理安排表层问题及深层问题的比例，并设计一些额外的备选问题，以便根据学生的实际情况，及时调整，从而提高课堂提问的效率。

5. 新手教师在进行词汇教学时，应该增加学生的话语比率，为学生提供丰富的机会去表达他们对新词汇的理解，并鼓励学生在课堂交际活动中尽可能多地使用所学新词汇，以便充分发挥学生在词汇学习中的主观能动性。

“课堂提问是词汇有效教学的核心。”[3]新手教师应该加强英语教学理论的学习，特别是词汇教学理论的学习，不断更新自己的词汇教学理念，改进自己的词汇教学方法，积极开展反思性教学及教师行动研究，才能不断提高词汇教学的有效性。

参考文献

[1] 于国强.英语学习策略阐述[J].教学与管理，2007(6)：104—105.

[2] 马文颖.英语词汇教学初探[J].长春大学学报，1999(10)：40—41.

[3] 潘笑洁.中学英语的词汇教学[J].湖州师范学院学报，2001(5)：228—229.

[4] N. A. Flanders. (1970). Analyzing Teaching Behavio. *Reading*, MA: Addison-Wesley, 100 - 107.

## The Comparative Study of Expert Teachers and Novice Teachers' Classroom Interaction in High School English Vocabulary Lesson

Han Xiao-min　XU Yong-jun　Luo Xiao-jie

**Abstract**: As an essential part of the high school teaching, vocabulary is inevitably a headache of English teachers. How to make full use of limited class time and to improve the effectiveness of vocabulary teaching has become the hotspot of English teaching researchers. In this paper，the classroom observation methods will be adopted to live record the vocabulary lessons separately given by an expert teacher and a novice one. After that，the authors will make a comparative analysis of the two English teachers' classroom interaction behaviors under the instruction of Flanders interaction system，find differences，reveal the expert teacher's strategy on the effectiveness of vocabulary teaching，and eventually provide reference to the novice teacher's implementation of vocabulary teaching.

**Key Words**：Flanders Interaction System；expert teachers；novice teachers；classroom observation；vocabulary teaching